ARBA In-depth:
Economics and Business

ARBA In-depth Series:

Children's and Young Adult Titles

Economics and Business

Health and Medicine

Philosophy and Religion

ARBA In-depth:
Economics and Business

Dr. Martin Dillon, EDITOR IN CHIEF

Shannon Graff Hysell, ASSOCIATE EDITOR

LIBRARIES
UNLIMITED
A Member of the Greenwood Publishing Group

Westport, Connecticut • London

Library of Congress Cataloging-in-Publication Data

ARBA in-depth. Economics and Business /edited by Martin Dillon and Shannon Graff Hysell.
 p. cm. —(ARBA in-depth)
 "Consists of reviews chosen from the past six volumes of 'American reference books
 annual' (ARBA)—years 1997-2003 ... reviews of reference books, CD-ROMs, and
 Websites ... that are candidates for academic and public business collections as well as
 corporate business libraries"—P. .
 Includes index.
 ISBN 1–59158–121–4 (alk. paper)
 1. Economics—Reference books—Bibliography. 2. Business—Reference
books—Bibliography. 3. Economics—Book reviews. 4. Business—Book reviews. 5.
Economics—Electronic information resources—Reviews. 6. Business—Electronic
information resources—Reviews. I. Title: Economics and business. II. Dillon, Martin,
1938- III. Graff Hysell, Shannon. IV. American reference books annual. V. Series.
Z7164.E2A72 2004
[HB71]
016.33—dc22   2003060526

British Library Cataloguing in Publication Data is available.

Library of Congress Catalog Card Number: 2003060526
ISBN: 1–59158–121–4

First published in 2004

Libraries Unlimited, 88 Post Road West, Westport, CT 06881
A Member of the Greenwood Publishing Group, Inc.
www.lu.com

Printed in the United States of America

The paper used in this book complies with the
Permanent Paper Standard issued by the National
Information Standards Organization (Z39.48–1984).

10   9   8   7   6   5   4   3   2   1

Contents

Introduction

This first edition of *ARBA In-depth: Economics and Business* is designed to assist academic, public, and corporate libraries in the systematic selection of suitable reference materials for their collections. As with all publications in this series, its purpose is to aid in the evaluation process by presenting critical and evaluative reviews in all areas of economics and business. The increase in the publication of reference resources in the United States and Canada, in combination with the decrease in library budgets, makes this guide an invaluable tool.

ARBA In-depth: Economics and Business consists of reviews chosen from the past seven volumes of *American Reference Books Annual* (ARBA)—years 1997-2003. This work provides reviews of reference books, CD-ROMs, and Websites published in the United States and Canada, along with English-language titles from other countries. ARBA has reviewed more than 55,000 titles since its inception in 1970. Because it provides comprehensive coverage of reference resources in all subject areas, not just selected or recommended titles, many titles in ARBA are of interest only to large academic and public libraries. Thus, *ARBA In-depth: Economics and Business* has been developed as an abridged version of ARBA with selected reviews of resources that are candidates for academic and public business collections as well as corporate business libraries. Titles reviewed in *ARBA In-depth: Economics and Business* include dictionaries, encyclopedias, indexes, directories, bibliographies, guides, and other types of ready-reference tools.

This volume provides 531 unabridged reviews selected from ARBA 1997 through ARBA 2003. More than 100 subject specialists throughout the United States and Canada have contributed these reviews. Reviewers are asked to examine the resources and provide well-documented critical comments, both positive and negative. Coverage usually includes the usefulness of a given work; organization, execution, and pertinence of contents; prose style; format; availability of supplementary materials (e.g., indexes, appendixes); and similarity to other works and previous editions. All reviews provide complete ordering and bibliographic information, including title, publisher, price, and ISBN. References to all reviews published in periodicals during the year of coverage are appended to the reviews (see page xiii for journals cited). All reviews are signed and the title and affiliation of all reviewers at the time the review was published can be found on page ix. Comprehensive author/title and subject indexes can be found at the end of the volume.

The present volume contains 16 chapters that follow the organization of ARBA. Chapter 1, "General Works," is subdivided by form: bibliography, biography, dictionaries and encyclopedias, handbooks and yearbooks, and so on. The remaining chapters are arranged alphabetically by subject (e.g., finance and banking, international business, marketing and trade) and then by reference type (e.g., dictionaries and encyclopedias, indexes).

ARBA and its companion volume *Recommended Reference Books for Small and Medium-sized Libraries and Media Centers* have been favorably reviewed in such journals as *Library Journal*, *Booklist*, and *Journal of Academic Librarianship*. The editors continue to strive to make the companion volumes in this series valuable acquisition tools for academic, public, and special libraries.

On behalf of our readers and Libraries Unlimited, I would like to express my gratitude to the contributors whose reviews appear in this volume. ARBA and its companion volumes would not be possible without their dedication and continued involvement. I would also like to thank the staff members of Libraries Unlimited who have been instrumental in the preparation of this work, and particularly Associate Editor Shannon Hysell for her contribution to this volume.

Martin Dillon, Editor in Chief

Contributors

Gordon J. Aamot, Head, Foster Business Library, Univ. of Washington, Seattle.

Laural L. Adams, Reference Librarian—Business, Univ. Library, New Mexico State Univ., Las Cruces.

Mark A. Allan, Reference Librarian, New Mexico State Univ., Las Cruces.

Donald Altschiller, Reference Librarian, Boston Univ.

Susan B. Ardis, Acting Head of Science Libraries Div., Univ. of Texas, Austin.

Susan C. Awe, Asst. Director, Univ. of New Mexico, Albuquerque.

Susan D. Baird-Joshi, Database Programmer/Analyst, Rho, Redmond, Wash.

Craig W. Beard, Reference Librarian, Mervyn H. Sterne Library, Univ. of Alabama, Birmingham.

Sandra E. Belanger, Reference Librarian, San Jose State Univ. Library, Calif.

Laura J. Bender, Science Librarian, Univ. of Arizona, Tucson.

David Bickford, Information Specialist, Univ. of Phoenix, Ariz.

Adrienne Antink Bien, Medical Group Management Association, Lakewood, Colo.

Ron Blazek, Professor, School of Library Science, Florida State Univ., Tallahassee.

Bobray Bordelon, Social Science Reference Center, Firestone Library, Princeton Univ. Libraries, N.J.

Georgia Briscoe, Assoc. Director and Head of Technical Services, Law Library, Univ. of Colorado, Boulder.

Barbara E. Brown, (formerly) Head, General Cataloguing Section, Library of Parliament, Ottawa, Ont.

Sue Brown, Reference Librarian, Louisiana State Univ., Shreveport.

Patrick J. Brunet, Library Manager, Western Wisconsin Technical College, La Crosse.

Robert H. Burger, Assoc. Univ. Librarian for Services, Univ. of Illinois, Urbana-Champaign.

Joanna M. Burkhardt, Head Librarian, College of Continuing Education Library, Univ. of Rhode Island, Providence.

John Lewis Campbell, Asst. Head of Reference Department, Univ. of Georgia Libraries, Athens.

Dene L. Clark, (retired) Reference Librarian, Auraria Library, Denver, Colo.

Juleigh Muirhead Clark, Public Services Librarian, John D. Rockefeller, Jr. Library, Colonial Williamsburg Foundation, Williamsburg, Va.

Paul F. Clark, Assoc. Professor, Pennsylvania State Univ., University Park.

Barbara E. Clotfelter, Head, Business Dept., Birmingham Public Library, Ala.

Holly Dunn Coats, Asst. Librarian, Florida Atlantic Univ., Jupiter.

Gary R. Cocozzoli, Director of the Library, Lawrence Technological Univ., Southfield, Mich.

Barbara Conroy, Career Connections, Santa Fe, N.Mex.

Kay O. Cornelius, (formerly) Teacher and Magnet School Lead Teacher, Huntsville City Schools, Ala.

Elizabeth D'Antonio-Gan, Instructor/Reference Librarian, Auraria Library, Denver, Colo.

Erin C. Daix, Reference Librarian, Univ. of Delaware Library, Newark.

Gail de Vos, Adjunct Assoc. Professor, School of Library and Information Studies, Univ. of Alberta, Edmonton.

Barbara Delzell, Vancouver, Wash.

Elie M. Dick, President, Mintra, Inc., Woodbury, Minn.

G. Kim Dority, G. K. Dority & Associates, Colo.

Jean Engler, Reference Librarian, Koelbel Public Library, Englewood, Colo.

Edward Erazo, Head of Reference, Florida Atlantic Univ., Boca Raton.

Elaine Ezell, Library Media Specialist, Bowling Green Jr. High School, Ohio.

Judith J. Field, Senior Lecturer, Program for Library and Information Science, Wayne State Univ., Detroit.

Joan B. Fiscella, Bibliographer for Professional Studies, Library, Univ. of Illinois, Chicago.

Lynne M. Fox, Information Services and Outreach Librarian, Denison Library, Univ. of Colorado Health Sciences Center, Denver.

Thomas K. Fry, Assoc. Director, Public Services, Penrose Library, Univ. of Denver, Colo.

Pamela J. Getchell, (formerly) Staff, Libraries Unlimited.

Gerald L. Gill, Assoc. Professor/Business Reference Librarian, James Madison Univ., Harrisburg, Va.

Barbara B. Goldstein, Media Specialist, Magothy River Middle School, Arnold, Md.

Stephen W. Green, Coordinator, Reference and Instruction Services, Auraria Library, Denver, Colo.

Leonard Grundt, Professor, A. Holly Patterson Library, Nassau Community College, Garden City, N.Y.

Kwabena Gyimah-Brempong, Professor of Economics, College of Business Administration, Univ. of South Florida, Tampa.

Susan B. Hagloch, Director, Tuscarawas County Public Library, New Philadelphia, Ohio.

Karen D. Harvey, Assoc. Dean for Academic Affairs, Univ. College, Univ. of Denver, Colo.

Lucy Heckman, Reference Librarian (Business-Economics), St. John's Univ. Library, Jamaica, N.Y.

Mark Y. Herring, Dean of Library Services, Winthrop Univ., Dacus Library, Rock Hill, S.C.

Christopher J. Hoeppner, Reference Instruction Librarian, DePaul Univ., Chicago.

Sara Anne Hook, Assoc. Dean of the Faculties, Indiana Univ., Purdue Univ., Indianapolis.

Marilynn Green Hopman, Librarian, NASA Johnson Space Center, Scientific and Technical Information Center, Houston, Tex.

Renee B. Horowitz, Professor, Dept. of Technology, College of Engineering, Arizona State Univ., Tempe.

Shannon Graff Hysell, Staff, Libraries Unlimited.

Ludmila N. Ilyina, (retired) Professor, Natural Resources Institute, Winnipeg, Man.

Scott Johnston, Reference Librarian and Asst. Professor, CUNY Graduate Center, New York.

Florence W. Jones, Librarian, Auraria Campus Library, Denver, Colo.

Sue Kamm, Head, Audio-Visual and Stack Maintenance Divisions, Inglewood Public Library, Calif.

Thomas A. Karel, Assoc. Director for Public Services, Shadek-Fackenthal Library, Franklin and Marshall College, Lancaster, Pa.

Sung Ok Kim, Senior Asst. Librarian/Social Sciences Cataloging Librarian, Cornell Univ., Ithaca, N.Y.

Christine E. King, Education Librarian, Purdue Univ., West Lafayette, Ind.

Bruce Kingma, Assoc. Professor, School of Information Studies, Syracuse Univ., N.Y.

Diane Kovacs, Internet Consultant/Library School Faculty, Kent State Univ., Ohio.

Carol Krismann, Head, William M. White Business Library, Univ. of Colorado, Boulder.

Marlene M. Kuhl, Library Manager, Baltimore County Public Library, Reisterstown Branch, Md.

Edward Kurdyla, (formerly) Staff, Libraries Unlimited.

Robert V. Labaree, Reference/Public Services Librarian, Von KleinSmid Library, Univ. of Southern California, Los Angeles.

Larry Lobel, Virtuoso Keyboard Services, Petaluma, Calif.

S. D. Markman, Professor Emeritus, Art Dept., Duke Univ., Durham, N.C.

Glenn Masuchika, Senior Information Specialist, Rockwell Collins Information, Iowa City, Iowa.

Judith A. Matthews, Physics-Astronomy/Science Reference Librarian, Main Library, Michigan State Univ., East Lansing.

John Maxymuk, Reference Librarian, Paul Robeson Library, Rutgers Univ., Camden, N.J.

George Louis Mayer, (formerly) Senior Principal Librarian, New York Public Library and Part-Time Librarian, Adelphi, Manhattan Center and Brooklyn College.

Dana McDougald, Lead Media Specialist, Learning Resources Center, Cedar Shoals High School, Athens, Ga.

Peter Zachary McKay, Business Librarian, Univ. of Florida Libraries, Gainesville.

George A. Meyers, Chairman, National Labor Commission, Baltimore, Md.

Elizabeth M. Mezick, CPA/Asst. Professor, Long Island Univ., Brookville, N.Y.

Bogdan Mieczkowski, Cocoa Beach, Fla.

Elizabeth B. Miller, Instructor, College of Library and Information Science, Univ. of South Carolina, Columbia.

Richard A. Miller, Professor of Economics, Wesleyan Univ., Middletown, Conn.

Carol L. Mitchell, Southeast Asian Bibliographic Services Librarian, General Library System, Univ. of Wisconsin, Madison.

Gerald D. Moran, Director, McCartney Library, Geneva College, Beaver Falls, Pa.

Kerie L. Nickel, Librarian, St. Mary's College of Maryland, St. Mary's City.

O. Gene Norman, Head, Reference Dept., Indiana State Univ. Libraries, Terre Haute.

David G. Nowak, Asst. Professor and Reference Librarian, Mississippi State Univ. Libraries, Mississippi State.

Herbert W. Ockerman, Professor, Ohio State Univ., Columbus.

Ray Olszewski, Independent Consultant, Palo Alto, Calif.

Gari-Anne Patzwald, Freelance Editor and Indexer, Lexington, Ky.

Randall Rafferty, Reference Librarian, Mississippi State Univ. Library, Mississippi State.

Jo Anne H. Ricca, (formerly) Staff, Libraries Unlimited.

Robert B. Marks Ridinger, Head, Electronic Information Resources Management Dept., Univ. Libraries, Northern Illinois Univ., De Kalb.

Cari Ringelheim, (formerly) Staff, Libraries Unlimited.

Ilene F. Rockman, Assoc. Dean of Library Services, California Polytechnic State Univ., San Luis Obispo.

JoAnn V. Rogers, Professor, College of Library and Information Science, Univ. of Kentucky, Lexington.

Michele Russo, Acting Director, Franklin D. Schurz Library, Indiana Univ., South Bend.

Edmund F. SantaVicca, Librarian, Phoenix College, Ariz.

Deborah K. Scott, Asst. Librarian, Employer's Reinsurance Corp., Overland Park, Kans.

Ralph Lee Scott, Assoc. Professor, East Carolina Univ. Library, Greenville, N.C.

Karen Selden, Catalog Librarian, Univ. of Colorado Law Library, Boulder.

Deborah Sharp, Head Librarian, Lexmark Information Center, Univ. of Kentucky, Lexington.

Robert M. Slade, Independent Consultant, North Vancouver, B.C.

Kay M. Stebbins, Coordinator Librarian, Louisiana State Univ., Shreveport.

William C. Struning, Professor, Seton Hall Univ., South Orange, N.J.

Bruce Stuart, Professor and Parke-Davis Chair, Univ. of Maryland, Baltimore.

Timothy E. Sullivan, Asst. Professor of Economics, Towson State Univ., Md.

Richard H. Swain, Reference Librarian, West Chester Univ., Pa.

Nigel Tappin, (formerly) General Librarian, North York Public Library, Ont.

Martha Tarlton, Head, Reference and Information Services, Univ. of North Texas Libraries, Denton.

Marit S. Taylor, Reference Librarian, Auraria Libraries, Univ. of Colorado, Denver.

Paul H. Thomas, Head, Cataloging Dept., Hoover Institution Library, Stanford Univ., Calif.

Linda D. Tietjen, Senior Instructor, Instruction and Reference Services, Auraria Library, Denver, Colo.

Dean Tudor, Professor, School of Journalism, Ryerson Polytechnical Institute, Toronto, Ont.

Elias H. Tuma, Professor of Economics, Univ. of California, Davis.

Nancy L. Van Atta, Dayton, Ohio.

Debra S. Van Tassel, Reference Librarian, Univ. of Colorado, Boulder.

J. E. Weaver, Dept. of Economics, Drake Univ., Des Moines, Iowa.

Robert L. Wick, Asst. Professor and Fine Arts Bibliographer, Auraria Library, Univ. of Colorado, Denver.

Frank L. Wilson, Professor and Head, Dept. of Political Science, Purdue Univ., West Lafayette, Ind.

Bohdan S. Wynar, (formerly) Staff, Libraries Unlimited.

Hope Yelich, Reference Librarian, Earl Gregg Swem Library, College of William and Mary, Williamsburg, Va.

Arthur P. Young, Director, Northern Illinois Libraries, Northern Illinois Univ., De Kalb.

Anita Zutis, Adjunct Librarian, Queensborough Community College, Bayside, N.Y.

Journals Cited

FORM OF CITATION	JOURNAL TITLE
AG	*Against the Grain*
ARBA	*American Reference Books Annual*
BL	*Booklist*
BR	*Book Report*
C&RL	*College and Research Libraries*
C&RL News	*College and Research Libraries News*
Choice	*Choice*
EL	*Emergency Librarian*
JAL	*Journal of Academic Librarianship*
LJ	*Library Journal*
RUSQ	*Reference & User Services Quarterly*
RBB	*Reference Books Bulletin*
SLJ	*School Library Journal*
SLMQ	*School Library Media Quarterly*
VOYA	*Voice of Youth Advocates*

1   General Works

ATLASES

1.   Charlesworth, Andrew, and others. **An Atlas of Industrial Protest in Britain, 1750-1990.**
New York, St. Martin's Press, 1996. 225p. maps. $55.00. ISBN 0-312-15889-0.

This interdisciplinary scholarly work is on the cusp between geography, industrial relations, and social history. It is largely text, but extensive cartographic illustrations justify the atlas label. The work belongs in research collections on economic, social, and industrial history covering Great Britain.

The atlas is divided into four chronological parts covering the periods 1750-1850, 1850-1900, 1900-1939, and 1940-1990, respectively. Each section contains an introductory review essay on industrial unrest in the period covered. Then (with the exception of the first section, for which sources are inadequate) there is a geographic and statistical essay. Case studies on particular disputes follow. The 25 case studies cover such topics as the Luddite disturbances, the general strikes of 1842 and 1926, the coal lockout of 1893, the Winter of Discontent of 1979, the coal miners' strike of 1984-1985, and many more. Each chapter has a brief note on sources and suggestions for further reading.

There is a detailed table of contents, but no index. The contributors are history, geography, and social science academics associated with a variety of British institutions, including the universities of London, Birmingham, and Edinburgh. The cartography was done by the geography department cartographer at Queen Mary and Westfield College, London University. This is an impressive scholarly effort that deserves a place in research collections covering the relevant disciplines. It should also be considered for larger general collections where scope and client demand warrant. —**Nigel Tappin**

BIBLIOGRAPHY

2.   **Bibliographic Guide to Business and Economics 1998.** New York, G. K. Hall/Macmillan Library Reference, 1999. 3v. $795.00/set. ISBN 0-7838-0192-0. ISSN 0360-2702.

This bibliographic guide is a compilation of recent publications cataloged by the Research Libraries of the New York Public Library. The selection of titles is based on titles cataloged with Library of Congress Classification HA-HJ. Therefore, the *Bibliographic Guide to Business and Economics 1998* is comprehensive and includes the latest publications in the areas of business administration, economic theory, public finance, labor, insurance, transportation, communication, demographics, and statistics.

The arrangement is alphabetic by main entry (e.g., personal author, corporate body, name of conference). The scope is international and the guide is presented in a 3-volume set. It is easy to use, with *see* and *see also* references throughout the bibliography. This volume is recommended to large academic libraries and special business libraries to use as a collection development guide for business and economic collections.—**Kay M. Stebbins**

3.   Burden, Paul R., comp. **Knowledge Management: The Bibliography.** Medford, N.J., Information Today, 2000. 181p. index. $18.00 (ASIS members); $22.50 (nonmembers). ISBN 1-57387-101-X.

Every few years a new concept inundates businesses like a tsunami, and within the past few years "knowledge management" (KM) has become the new concept that promises to improve the competitiveness of businesses. This new concept, simply stated, is the organization, analysis, storage, retrieval, and dissemination of information to those in any organization that can improve its efficiency, value, and worth. With this system in place, businesses can react faster to market conditions, managers can make better decisions, and the fiscal health is strengthened. Courses in KM are rapidly appearing as offerings in business schools, and this book began as an adjunct to the syllabi and textbooks for KM courses at Dominican University in Illinois. The book is divided into four categories: books, articles, Web pages, and videos. The article category is further divided into 16 KM topics: KM background, intellectual capital, learning organizations, knowledge cultures, knowledge mapping, organizational aspects, information professionals, general issues, information technology, intranets, application packages, initiatives, training, e-commerce, chapters found in conference proceedings, and competitive intelligence. There are 3,606 total citations.

The expansiveness and comprehensiveness of this bibliography are due to the methodology used by its compiler. Utilizing the terms "intellectual capital" and "knowledge management" as keywords, they searched numerous bibliographies, indexes, databases, listings in commercial book-selling Websites, and derived this list. This methodology does have its drawbacks. It includes materials that are both fully involved and tangentially involved with KM, not differentiating one from the other, and it further excludes those articles that pertain to KM but are not identified with those two search terms. None of the citations are annotated. There is also a feeling that this bibliography has remained a supplementary resource rather than evolving into a bibliography of the primary sources used in business school classes. Yet these are minor complaints, and this book, one of the first bibliographies devoted to KM, should be in the library of any business school library or business information library.—**Glenn Masuchika**

4.   **Business A to Z Source Finder: A Locator Guide to Sources....** Elizabeth Louise Vandivier and Kathleen Brown, eds. Annapolis, Md., Beacon Bay Press, 1996. 590p. $85.00pa. ISBN 0-9649579-0-6.

Similar in arrangement and purpose to the *Encyclopedia of Business Information Sources* (16th ed.; see entry 6) but covering less than half as many subjects, this locator guide appears to be directed toward the novice researcher. Each subject entry begins with a definition of the topic followed by Library of Congress (LC) subject headings, LC and Dewey call numbers, and citations to published introductions to the topic. The 500 topics, along with cross-references, are listed in a table of contents. The 2d section of the guide is devoted to listing such sources as handbooks, dictionaries, directories, bibliographies, abstracts and indexes, databases, CD-ROMs, journals and newsletters, selected books, and associations and research centers.

The editors used online catalogs, publishers' catalogs, bibliographies, and other standard sources to compile this source. One wishes they had been more selective rather than inclusive. A list of 5 recommended titles is more useful than 16 recent titles on the subject. Locator guides provide a starting point, are a great time-saver, and are well used in business collections. This is a good addition for libraries needing this type of source and unable to afford the *Encyclopedia of Business Information Sources*. [R: Choice, July/Aug 96, pp. 1768-1770; RBB, June 96, p. 1764]—**Barbara E. Clotfelter**

5.   Crainer, Stuart. **The Ultimate Business Library: 50 Books That Shaped Management Thinking.** New York, AMACOM, 1997. 323p. index. $24.95. ISBN 0-8144-0395-6.

   Stuart Crainer's *The Ultimate Business Library: 50 Books That Shaped Management Thinking* provides a summary of the 50 greatest books on management. The selection is based on opinions from experts in both the United States and the United Kingdom. Selections span the centuries and range from *The Art of War* by Sun Tzu (500 B.C.) to Gary Hamel and C. K. Prahalad's *Competing for the Future* (1994). Other authors represented include Abraham Maslow, Peter F. Drucker, Rosabeth Moss Kanter, Dale Carnegie, Niccolo Machiavelli, Henry Ford, Adam Smith, and Max Weber. Each entry provides biographical information about the author, a description of the work, and a discussion of its contribution to management. Additionally, Gary Hamel, a noted author in management, wrote the foreword and a brief commentary on each book. Hamel groups the books within specific issues in management, including leadership, customers, competition, efficiency, and strategy, which enables readers to focus in on their specific areas of interest. The appendix contains a list and brief description of 50 additional titles that had been considered for the list of greatest books. A bibliography for further reading is also provided.

   This important work is primarily recommended to academic library collections. Business librarians or collection development librarians will want to use this book to build or enhance management holdings. Business faculty should consider this book in preparing assignments.—**Lucy Heckman**

6.   **Encyclopedia of Business Information Sources: A Bibliographic Guide to More Than 34,000 Citations Covering over 1,100 Subjects of Interest to Business.** 16th ed. James Woy, ed. Farmington Hills, Mich., Gale, 2002. 1177p. $355.00. ISBN 0-7876-3494-8. ISSN 0071-0210.

   In its 16th edition, the *Encyclopedia of Business Information Sources* is intended to be a convenient and accessible volume for business managers and information professionals to use to locate key sources for a variety of topics. It includes references to more than 34,000 citations grouped into over 1,100 specific topics. The wealth of topics covered by the volume makes it an interesting publication. Many specific types of industries are covered, including the cheese industry, the musical instrument industry, and the greeting card industry, along with professional groups, geographic regions, government and regulatory agencies, and current issues. According to the publisher, this edition of the volume has been extensively updated.

   A typical entry in the *Encyclopedia* begins with cross-references to other subject entries in the volume. Sources for an entry are then divided into broad categories of types of works, with general works listed first, followed by almanacs and yearbooks, directories, financial ratios, handbooks and manuals, Internet databases, online databases, periodicals and newsletters, statistics sources, trade and professional associations, and other sources. Other categories in entries cover abstracts and indexes, bibliographies, CD-ROM databases, encyclopedias and dictionaries, price sources, research centers, and institutes. The titles and names of individual sources, such as publications or organizations, are then listed under each category in alphabetic order. The information included with these source listings can include contact information, prices, frequency of publication, and a brief annotation. Entries are easy to use and there is also a helpful user's guide at the front of the volume, along with an outline of the contents that alphabetically lists the topics with page numbers.

   The final 266 pages of the *Encyclopedia of Business Information Sources* provide an alphabetic listing of the sources cited in the volume. Sources are listed by publication or organization name, with contact information (including e-mail and Website addresses), price, updates, and a brief annotation. This section may be useful for collection development librarians selecting materials for public, academic, and special libraries that cover business, government, financial, and environmental issues. The *Encyclopedia of Business Information Sources* would be a good addition to reference collections in public, academic, and a wide variety of special libraries. It is comprehensive, well organized, attractively produced, and easy to use.—**Sara Anne Hook**

7. **Harvard Business School Core Collection, 1998: An Author, Title, and Subject Guide.** Sue Marsh, ed. Boston, Harvard Business School Press, 1998. 430p. index. $65.00pa. ISBN 0-87584-774-9.

This work is a bibliographically annotated catalog of essential business-oriented textbooks, handbooks, biographies, company histories, and other pertinent publications collected within the Baker Library at the Harvard Business School. As defined, this collection of roughly 3,500 business books is intended to provide students, faculty, and other interested users with a manageable index of relevant materials that is revised and updated annually. These materials, representing a diverse array of business topics, are listed alphabetically by subject and indexed by title and author. This handy and useful reference work also includes a list of notable business books that have won awards or been named to various best books lists.

Since its inception in 1969, items have been added or removed from the collection to keep the series current and practical. Some 50 items within the core collection are designated as "core classics" and as such provide a meaningful overview of the development and evolution of the business curriculum, at least over the past few decades. Because the materials included within the collection reflect both the teaching and research interests of the faculty at the Harvard Business School, business educators and researchers in other business programs can essentially use this list to more efficiently identify topical materials. Conveniently, this reference work also includes the names and addresses of applicable publishers in an appendix.—**Timothy E. Sullivan**

8. **International Bibliography of Business History.** Francis Goodall, Terry Gourvish, and Steven Tolliday, eds. New York, Routledge, 1997. 668p. index. $125.00. ISBN 0-415-08641-8.

This is an excellent reference in terms of coverage, diversity of scholarly viewpoints in the selection, relevance, and quality of annotation. Although only three people are listed as editors, a large number of people from around the world participated in selecting the 4,421 entries, which cover general sources, primary and extractive industries, traditional and heavy industries, light manufacturing industries, trade and distribution, banking and finance, utilities, transport and other services, strategy and structure (approaches to business history), and entrepreneurship and management. The entries are listed alphabetically by author in each category. These categories are treated differentially in terms of space allocation and the number of entries from different parts of the world. For example, general sources fill 22 pages, whereas utilities and transport occupy 100 pages. Light manufacturing sources are classified as from the United Kingdom, the United States, and the rest of the world. In contrast, banking and finance entries are classified as from 15 countries and several regions. This differentiation may be only, in part, a function of the limited number of studies of business in the various countries and regions. The index of authors and industries is fairly comprehensive.

Another attractive feature of this volume is that it complements existing business references by filling gaps evident in those references. This reference should be of great use to business students and historians. It would have been of even greater use had it included theories of business or history of thought in business as a separate category. Although references to theory and thought are partially covered under entrepreneurship and management, a separate section would have been a major contribution, especially to academicians and graduate students of business, economics, and history.—**Elias H. Tuma**

9.   **International Business and Trade Directories: A Worldwide Directory of Directories.** 2d ed. Richard Gottlieb, ed. Lakeville, Conn., Grey House Publishing, 1998. 1151p. index. $200.00; $185.00pa. ISBN 1-891482-07-6; 0-939300-44-3pa.

As the "global economy" changes from a buzzword to an essential, the emphasis on foreign trade will continue to increase. First published in 1995, this 2d edition of a useful directory has nearly 4,000 new entries and 4,952 updates to existing entries. Within 81 industry groups such as biotechnology, jewelry, toys, video, and water supply, entries are arranged alphabetically. Each industry chapter is broken down into 10 regions of the world, which are again broken down by specific country.

Each entry includes content descriptions with number of pages, prices and ISBN, publisher's name and address, homepage and e-mail addresses, editorial staff information, and telephone and fax numbers. The content descriptions vary from a line or two of general descriptors (e.g., wholesale distributors, importers, manufacturers, liquidators), to six or seven lines with facts and figures. "The Directory of Apparel Specialty Stores" entry states that it "profiles more than 3,400 men's and boys' wear . . . in over 39,000 stores" (p. 824) and continues to state that it lists 13,235 individual personnel of these firms.

Three useful indexes complete the volume: an entry index, a geographic index, and a publisher index. The geographic index is particularly helpful because it is sometimes difficult to find a directory for a specific country and a specific industry. Libraries with an international business focus, especially in the marketing area, will want to purchase this volume.—**Susan C. Awe**

10.   King, J. E. **Post Keynesian Economics: An Annotated Bibliography.** Brookfield, Vt., Edward Elgar/Ashgate Publishing, 1995. 1v. (unpaged). index. $215.95. ISBN 1-85278-801-1.

The publication of John Maynard Keynes's classic work, *The General Theory of Employment, Interest and Money*, in 1936 (Harcourt, Brace) transformed modern economic theory and ultimately helped to reshape public policies. The book also spawned an enormous volume of literature, both pro and con. Indeed, the influence of this work has been so significant that a distinct, albeit diverse, school of economic thought has emerged and been labeled as "Post Keynesian Economics." Despite the inherent ambiguity in succinctly defining this school, economists associated with it have attempted to interpret the issues raised by the work of Keynes and to provide coherent and alternative views to neoclassical economic analysis.

This ample and informative reference work is a comprehensive view of that literature, and its 3,293 annotated entries are reasonably arranged, chronologically, by author and into 18 subject headings. Entries are organized into such subject headings as general studies; methodologies; collections and biographical studies; various interpretations of Keynes's work as well as empirical studies and the more traditional disciplinary topics of macroeconomic and microeconomic theory; labor; monetary theory; distribution and capital theory; development; growth and cycles; and international economics. The work outlines the contributions of a diverse array of scholars, including those who were contemporaries of Keynes along with the disciples and detractors of Keynesian analysis. It is a useful and thorough reference work that will increase awareness of the breadth of scholarly work carried out by various economists from the 1930s to the 1990s. [R: Choice, May 96, p. 1452]—**Timothy E. Sullivan**

11.   **The Search for Economics as a Science: An Annotated Bibliography.** Lynn Turgeon, ed. Pasadena, Calif., Salem Press and Lanham, Md., Scarecrow, 1996. 428p. index. (Magill Bibliographies). $55.00. ISBN 0-8108-3120-1.

Designed as a starting point for high school or college students researching economic topics, this selective bibliography includes approximately 2,000 English-language publications—monographs, book chapters, serials, and journal articles—that represent, according to the editor, "a collection of the best in worldwide economic thinking of the past three centuries." Turgeon, who taught economics at Hofstra University for 35 years, has divided this work into 5 chapters comprising 14 sections, each section corresponding to a course frequently offered by economics and business departments at U.S. colleges and universities. Courses not covered include accounting, consumer finance, economic geography, and marketing.

The majority of bibliographic entries are for textbooks rather than primary sources or reference titles. Only one or two books published within the past five years are listed. Some publications are placed in more than one section, but when they are, different editions are frequently cited. There are no cross-references linking identical titles found in separate sections. Turgeon's annotations, which vary in length from 10 to 125 words each, lack consistency. Many are critical as well as descriptive, but many are only one or the other. Also, the author and subject indexes supplied in this volume are inadequate. Given its shortcomings, *The Search for Economics as a Science* is not recommended as a guide to the literature.—**Leonard Grundt**

BIO-BIBLIOGRAPHY

12. Cicarelli, James, and Julianne Cicarelli. **Joan Robinson: A Bio-bibliography.** Westport, Conn., Greenwood Press, 1996. 179p. index. (Bio-bibliographies in Economics, no.2). $69.50. ISBN 0-313-25844-9.

In 1975, everyone expected noted post-Keynesian economist Joan Robinson to win the Nobel prize in economics. Robinson, who is viewed by many as the greatest female economist, was denied the prize and never won it. This biographical bibliography serves as a concise source for biographical information and provides an annotated, chronological bibliography of Robinson's works as well as a selected, annotated bibliography of works about her. The most useful feature is the chronological section highlighting major works about Robinson and her writings.

Electronic bibliographic tools make it easy to compile bibliographies. This work's strength is its carefully researched selectivity and conciseness. The biographical sketch is very brief. For more detail on Robinson's life and her influence on economic thought, one should consult such works as *The Joan Robinson Legacy* (M. E. Sharpe, 1991); *Joan Robinson and Modern Economic Theory* (New York University Press, 1989); or *The Economics of Joan Robinson* (Routledge, 1996). The index is poor and inconsistently references Robinson's works. The bio-bibliography is recommended for economic research collections only.—**Bobray Bordelon**

BIOGRAPHY

13. **A Biographical Dictionary of Dissenting Economists.** 2d ed. Philip Arestis and Malcolm Sawyer, eds. Northhampton, Mass., Edward Elgar, 2000. 722p. $225.00. ISBN 1-85898-560-9.

This is a practical and interesting guide to the origins, philosophies, and writings of some 100 economists and social scientists. Any collection of diverse opinions on such complex and unfinished issues as discussed throughout this work will be in itself incomplete, but the choice of economists in this reference work laudably represents a variety of ideological and political opinions as well as a variety of geographic locations. Economists featured in this concise survey are essentially twentieth-century writers and many are still active participants in the development and debate over economic issues. They have influenced generations of students, social scientists, and policy makers and should continue to influence future generations. Many of the economists featured in this work will be familiar to a number of readers; others may be less familiar but deserve to be more widely recognized for their contributions. This book not only provides insight into how and why these economists adopted and developed their own perspectives on economics, but it also reveals how alternative theories can be used to examine similar events and circumstances.

Considering that the dominant paradigm of economics, namely neoclassical economics, so often overshadows most popular discussions of economics, this reference work will be a valuable guide to the diversity and richness of opinion that can make economics more relevant and appealing. Proceeding from the reasonable, although not always recognizable, premise that economics is not a neutral science, this reference work considers not only some of the social and political origins of the writers but also some of the effects of economic analysis. Moreover, since many of the entries are autobiographical, readers of this work should come away with an appreciation of the lives and times of some interesting social and political theorists. As a reference work, it offers a useful guide to the potential diversity of modern economic thought; it not only provides useful information, it is also entertaining to read.—**Timothy E. Sullivan**

14. **Biographical Dictionary of European Labor Leaders.** A. Thomas Lane, ed. Westport, Conn., Greenwood Press, 1995. 2v. index. $225.00/set. ISBN 0-313-26456-2.

This 2-volume set contains more than 1,400 biographical listings of individuals connected with the labor movement in Europe from the beginnings of industrial capitalism in the nineteenth century to the present. All European countries are included. The editor has defined *labor* in broad terms and has listed individuals not only from the traditional areas, such as trade unions and labor ministers, but also from such areas as political parties, cooperatives, and what he refers to as "anarchosyndicalist" groups (introduction). Individuals from state-controlled bodies that lack any democratic procedures (e.g., the former Soviet Union and its satellites) are not discussed.

Each entry provides the name of the individual, birth and death dates, and a brief biography generally ranging between 150 and 300 words. In addition, at the end of each biography there are references to other sources where biographical information may be obtained. Also, extensive cross-references between labor leaders of different geographic areas and different intellectual viewpoints provide important links. The editor provides a number of useful appendixes, including a list of labor leaders by state or national/ethnic group, a selective bibliography, a detailed index, and a list of editors and contributors to the work.

Biographical Dictionary of European Labor Leaders is a much-needed current source of information concerning European labor leaders in general and also information on many individuals who are not generally considered in other sources on labor leaders. The dictionary is recommended for all college and university and larger public libraries. Also, it may be useful for government agencies dealing with Europeans involved in labor. [R: Choice, May 96, p. 1445]—**Robert L. Wick**

15. **Business Leaders for Students.** Sheila M. Dow, ed. Farmington Hills, Mich., Gale, 1999. 914p. illus. index. $95.00. ISBN 0-7876-2935-9. ISSN 1520-9296.

The purpose of this new book in Gale's popular line of business products for students is "to provide readers with a comprehensive resource of business biographies, giving them easy access to information on past and resent business leaders." This goal is met with 248 alphabetically arranged, engaging entries of historical and popular business leaders. It is, of course, impossible to be comprehensive in one volume. The advisory board of five teachers and librarians of young adults from diverse geographic locations did an excellent job of selecting the leaders for inclusion. The first entry is illustrative of the selections—Scott Adams, creator of the *Dilbert* comic strip.

Historical figures such as Alexander Graham Bell, Benjamin Franklin, and Samuel Morse balance modern business leaders like Bill Gates, Charles Schwab, and Ted Turner. Many different areas of business are included, from food processing (e.g., Colonel Sanders, Oscar Mayer, Will Kellogg) to cosmetics (e.g., Mary Kay, Estée Lauder) to entertainment (e.g., Jane Fonda, George Lucas, Michael Jordan). Minority leaders are well represented with businesspeople such as Wally Amos, Akio Morita, and Barbara Proctor.

The entries are 3 to 4 pages in length, usually with a black-and-white photograph. Each begins with a one-paragraph overview, including the leader's major contributions to business, industry, and society. Next comes a summary of their personal life, with family history, vital statistics, education, affiliations, and awards, among other items. The section on career details focuses on career highlights and often reports their management style, business philosophy, or development of a product. The final sections are titled "Social and Economic Impact," which contains more in-depth analysis, and "Sources of Information," which lists mailing addresses and Websites. A basic bibliography provides suggested readings in monographs, periodicals, and databases. The separately boxed chronology features an easy-to-read list of major dates in the leader's life.

A master index provides easy access to business leaders, companies, and industries. This book is fun to peruse and stop off at any stimulating name. Its value as a basic reference tool for students seeking quick data on business leaders is great. This one volume will be much easier to use than the traditional biographical research tools and it is suited for high school and undergraduate students as well as public library patrons. [R: BR, Sept/Oct 99, p. 65; SLJ, Aug 99, p. 182]—**Georgia Briscoe**

16.   **Corporate Yellow Book: Who's Who at the Leading U.S. Companies.** Spring 2000 ed. New York, Leadership Directories, 2000. 1384p. illus. index. $325.00pa. (first subscription). $228.00pa. (w/additional subscriptions). ISSN 1058-2908.

Corporate Yellow Book is a directory updated quarterly and is also available online by subscription. It profiles 1,000 companies whose revenues exceed $500 million annually but includes some technology companies below the threshold. It is unclear exactly how companies are chosen for inclusion.

Each entry lists the company name, ticker symbol, corporate headquarters address, telephone and fax numbers, Web address, number of employees and revenue, and a brief description of what the company does or makes. Lists of people follow, such as officers and their assistants, administrative staff in "critical" departments, the board of directors, the auditor, and outside counsel. Information is verified by the publisher's staff. Indexes are by company, geography, industry, and individual names.

This book provides more detailed information on key staff than one would get on corporate Internet sites but it is worth its price only if one's patrons need to know the names and telephone numbers of various vice presidents in large companies.—**Holly Dunn Coats**

17.   Hamilton, Neil A. **American Business Leaders: From Colonial Times to the Present.** Santa Barbara, Calif., ABC-CLIO, 1999. 2v. illus. index. $150.00/set. ISBN 1-57607-002-6.

This practical and informative reference work is a collection of concise encyclopedic entries for 413 influential American business leaders. Beginning in the colonial era and continuing to the end of the twentieth century, this work chronicles the lives and times of a good number of the influential men and women of U.S. business history. Despite the fact that many of these men and women helped shape and determine the path of business development, not all of them are commonly recognized for their achievements and contributions. Consequently, this book provides an accessible, valuable, and even enjoyable guide to a number of historic business figures. It is the sort of reference book that can be a joy to read and browse through. It is a reference work that will also appeal to a wide range of users. More advanced researchers will find it a useful guide for checking facts and dates, whereas more novice users will benefit from reading and browsing through its concise and candid articles. A lot of interesting details and comparative facts are provided for both the renowned and relatively obscure business leaders who are outlined in this work. In addition, each entry has a useful, although too often brief, bibliography of practical works where interested users can turn for more information.

Examining the helpful indexes of the entries reveals that the largest number of business leaders outlined in the pages of these volumes are manufacturers, merchants, financiers, and publishers. But there are also entries for various business executives, industrialists, and developers. Because the entries in this reference work are arranged alphabetically, it reads like an encyclopedia of American business history. However, because each of the individuals outlined in these two volumes obviously lived and operated in a historic context, reading through and comparing various entries can provide a relative understanding of various social, economic, and political conditions. [R: LJ, 1 Sept 99, p. 178]—**Timothy E. Sullivan**

18. **Nonprofit Sector Yellow Book: Who's Who in the Management of the Leading Foundations, Universities, Museums, and Other Nonprofit Organizations. Summer 2001, Volume 3, Number 2.** Thomas O'Hagan and Anton Borst, eds. New York, Leadership Directories, 2001. 1331p. illus. index. $255.00pa. (first subscription); $179.00pa. (renewal subscription). ISSN 1520-9148.

Published semiannually, the *Nonprofit Sector Yellow Book* provides information on some 1,400 U.S. nonprofit organizations. Listed here are foundations, colleges and universities, museums, performing arts groups, medical institutions, library systems, preparatory schools, and charitable service organizations. The opening introduction, "The Nonprofit Sector News," outlines the criteria for selection of nonprofits featured here. Also listed in the introduction are new listings and any name changes since the last volume.

The entries are arranged into sections by nonprofit type (e.g., foundation, museum). The nonprofits are listed alphabetically by name within each section. Each entry includes the nonprofits contact information (e.g., address, telephone and fax numbers, Web address); a brief mission statement; total net assets; year founded; type of organization; biographical information on the president of chief executive (sometimes with a photograph); and names, educational information, and telephone numbers of officers and managers and persons on the board of trustees. Geographical, name, and organization indexes at the back of the volume will aid users in finding the information they need quickly.

This is a worthwhile directory for those needing this specific type of information. It is also available by annual subscription through *The Leadership Library on the Internet* at http://www.leadershipdirectories.com, where updates are made available daily.—**Shannon Graff Hysell**

19. **Tycoons and Entrepreneurs.** Judy Culligan, ed. New York, Macmillan Library Reference/Simon & Schuster Macmillan, 1998. 349p. illus. index. (Macmillan Profiles, v.2). $75.00. ISBN 0-02-864982-6.

This volume comprises some 120 profiles of tycoons and entrepreneurs from the eighteenth century to the present. Some of the articles were adapted from the publisher's other reference titles, whereas others were commissioned specifically for this volume. The profiles are brief (one to three pages) and written in an engaging style. Their subjects represent a broad range of business and cultural backgrounds. The volume concludes with an index, a 10-page glossary of business terms, and a 20-page list of references to additional readings on many of the figures profiled.

The work's preface indicates that a team of high school teachers and librarians was consulted during the book's preparation. This volume would be a good addition to a reference collection serving young adults. Undergraduates might find this a useful quick reference or starting point for research but would likely need to consult additional sources for more in-depth information.
—Christopher J. Hoeppner

20.   **Who's Who in Asian Banking & Finance 1998-1999 International Edition.** John L. Pellam, ed. Laguna Beach, Calif., Barons Who's Who, 1997. 304p. illus. $210.00. ISBN 1-882292-12-X. ISSN 1059-5392.

This volume is a current compilation of personal and professional biographical information on 1,851 individuals of influence throughout Hong Kong, Indonesia, Japan, Malaysia, the People's Republic of China, the Philippines, the Republic of Korea (South Korea), Singapore, Taiwan (Republic of China), Thailand, and Vietnam. Selection of entries was made from the fields of banking, finance, economics, venture capital, and investment: a few of the regions' investors and prominent business leaders are also included. Individuals managing banking and investment firms and financial executives have been chosen primarily on their value as business contacts. Special attention has been paid to executives of firms with stock exchange prominence and those involved in economics and governmental economic policy.

The book is set up with a biography section and a company profile section. The main biography section provides information about the person's professional endeavors: past and present job functions; employer; education; professional memberships; honors and awards; and contact address, telephone number, and fax number. The company profiles list 1,552 banks and financial institutions within the Pacific Rim region. Each listing gives contact data, addresses, telephone and fax numbers, and key employees. Both the biographical and company sections are in alphabetic order. This book is recommended for large public and university libraries with business collections. Special business libraries for banks and financial institutions and businesses who have trade and banking interests in the Pacific Rim countries would find this volume an essential directory for current information on their business contacts.**—Kay M. Stebbins**

21.   **Who's Who in Canadian Business 2001.** 21st ed. Toronto, University of Toronto Press, 2000. 1034p. $179.95. ISBN 0-920966-60-8. ISSN 0227-3411.

The 21st edition of *Who's Who in Canadian Business* is an attractive single volume that is intended to be a comprehensive and independent reference source for the business community. According to the introduction, there have been thousands of additions and changes to the biographies included in the 21st edition and more than 800 new profiles of Canadian business leaders have been added.

Entries in the work can range from minimal information of an individual's title, company, address, telephone number, birth, and marital status to much longer offerings that include education, directorships, honorary degrees, patents, publications, licenses, community and professional board service, hobbies and personal interests, professional affiliations, and Website addresses. Many of the entries provide substantial information on an individual that would be useful not only for making business connections, but also for fundraising and community board recruitment efforts. Entries are arranged into two columns, with names and degrees in bold, and the entries are in a standard format, making the volume very easy to use.

A report called "Profit 100," which is a listing of Canada's fastest growing companies is included. This report includes revenue, growth, profit, number of employees, percentage of exports, sources of financing, and a brief description of the company. A similar report, "The Next 100," provides additional listings. The volume also includes an institutional index that list companies, universities, professional organizations, and nonprofit agencies.

Who's Who in Canadian Business would be useful for any public, academic, or special library whose patrons have an interest in finding information on the leaders of established and up-and-coming companies in Canada. It is attractively produced and provides a wealth of information at a reasonable cost.—**Sara Anne Hook**

22. **Who's Who in Finance and Industry, 1996-1997.** 29th ed. New Providence, N.J., Marquis Who's Who/Reed Reference Publishing, 1995. 941p. index. $259.95. ISBN 0-8379-0330-0.

Although the entry elements and format remain the same, this biographical directory has changed since its 27th edition (see ARBA 93, entry 179). The number of biographies has shrunk from 25,400 to 21,000. Foreign coverage has significantly expanded, now constituting about one-sixth of the entries (reviewer's estimate). A "Professional Area Index," new to this edition, greatly enhances access. Biographees are categorized according to broad areas (e.g., finance, government, industry, law) that are in some cases subdivided (e.g., industry into manufacturing, service, trade, and so on); then they are divided geographically, ultimately at the city level. This arrangement usually produces a manageable number of entries under each city.

Admission to the directory is based upon the biographee's "reference value" as reflected by a position held or a significant achievement. This criterion encompasses principal officers of major corporations, high-level federal government officials, important labor leaders, significant scholars, and winners of major awards. To measure the directory's inclusion of principal officers of major corporations, this reviewer conducted a test using the *Forbes* annual rankings of the 500 largest publicly held companies by assets, sales, net income, and market value. To include truly major companies, only those present on the rankings every year, 1992-1995, were chosen. To allow sufficient time for their CEOs to become noteworthy, the CEO's tenure had to span the same four years. Of the 432 CEOs, 354, or roughly 80 percent, were in the directory. CEOs of Dow Jones, Oracle Systems, Pfizer, Rockwell International, and Tele-Communications Inc. were among those missing.

An informal test was conducted for significant people not on the *Forbes* lists but often mentioned in the business press. The success rate was fairly high. Among those missing, however, were John Bogle (chairman of Vanguard), Felix Rohatyn (investment banker), Arthur Levitt (chairman of the Securities and Exchange Commission), James Wolfensohn (president of the World Bank), and Thomas Monaghan (chairman of Domino's Pizza). Although the directory passed both of these tests with high scores, *Marquis Who's Who* should mount a more concerted effort to improve its coverage.

Entries in this directory are also available electronically as part of *Marquis Who's Who on the Web* (see ARBA 2003, entry 18), the *Marquis Who's Who* file on DIALOG, and the PEOPLE Library/EXECDR File on LEXIS/NEXIS. This directory remains an essential purchase for business reference collections.—**John Lewis Campbell**

23. **Who's Who in the Management Sciences.** Cary L. Cooper, ed. Northhampton, Mass., Edward Elgar, 2000. 484p. $240.00. ISBN 1-84064-237-8.

The editor has defined "management sciences" very broadly for the purposes of this volume. Rather than focus on just management science (an important, but relatively narrow, subdiscipline of management), Cooper has created an extensive biographical directory of top management academics. Categories include "Business Policy and Strategy," "Human Resources," "International Management," "Organizational Behavior," "Organizational and Management Theory," and "Operations Management." This broader scope has resulted in an important contribution to business reference literature.

The more than 330 entries are informative and run from half a page to 2 pages in length. Entries are organized into standard categories, including "Employment History," "Degrees Received," "Offices Held," "Editorial Duties," "Prizes and Honours," "Consultancy Work,"

"Principal Fields of Interest," "Chief Publications," and "Principal Contributions." Management scholars were selected for inclusion in the volume based on nominations by academic peers. Although there is some international coverage, most of the scholars included are British and American.

This volume is relatively expensive, but it is well done and fills an important gap. It is recommended for large reference collections supporting academic business programs. [R: Choice, Feb 01, p. 1067]—**Gordon J. Aamot**

CHRONOLOGY

24.   **Landmarks in Modern American Business.** Hackensack, N.J., Salem Press, 2000. 3v. illus. index. (Magill's Choice). $175.00/set. ISBN 0-89356-135-5.

This three-volume collection is mainly a reduced edition of the five-volume *Great Events from History II: Business and Commerce Series* (see ARBA 95, entry 209). The new collection deals only with events in the United States that the editors consider as major turning points or landmarks in business between the years 1897 and 2000. Each entry identifies the category (e.g., finance) and the locale of the event and includes a summary, an assessed impact, a bibliography, and cross-references. The last volume includes a chronology, category and subject indexes, and a listing of the principal personages.

For a number of reasons it is not clear who will use the collection. First, the entries deal mostly with the environment of business, or rules and regulations relating to business. Second, several major business landmarks are left out, including the tractor and bio-chemical revolutions in agriculture, the trucking industry, high-rise construction (such as the Empire State Building), the spread of shopping malls, the dollar-down-dollar-a-week system, and cellular phones. Third, it is misleading to declare a court ruling to break up Microsoft a landmark while the case is still in litigation. It is equally misleading to regard the threat of the Y2K crisis a landmark since the crisis never materialized. Fourth, not all assessments of the impact are defensible. For example, it is incorrect to regard a court approval of a consensus agreement to solve a specific problem of discrimination, such as approving a quota system. That action did not set a precedent or make a law. More careful editing could have avoided these and other problems.—**Elias H. Tuma**

25.   **Notable Corporate Chronologies.** 2d ed. Kimberly N. Hunt and AnnaMarie L. Sheldon, eds. Farmington Hills, Mich., Gale, 1999. 2v. index. $390.00/set. ISBN 0-8103-9500-2. ISSN 1078-3865.

This work is an expanded, updated, and effective reference book that outlines the business histories and timelines of more than 1,500 prominent corporations. It is a valuable and compelling reference work that provides a concise profile of the historic milestones and events that have shaped the activities and performances of corporations operating in the United States and worldwide. Each of these alphabetically arranged timelines concisely outlines 30 or more significant events in the histories of industrial, commercial, and financial firms. The types of events included within these timelines have been broadly defined so that a variety of users will find useful, meaningful, and even entertaining information within them. These events include the founding and any subsequent reorganization of the firm, the introduction of new products and product lines, mergers and acquisitions, stock offerings, key financial events, the tenure of its leading managers, and even a few notable scandals within the firms. The easy-to-use and engaging chronologies provide a context and appreciation of the growth and evolution of many of the world's leading corporations. Moreover, by evaluating and contrasting comparative individual histories, this reference work also provides a more comprehensive understanding of business organization and commercial activity.

The events outlined within individual corporation timelines are concise and informative. Each entry provides not only contact information for each firm but a short list of further readings to assist in additional research. This detailed reference work includes four useful indexes: an indexed chronology that highlights 400 years of business activity, an anniversary index that lists significant forthcoming anniversaries for these corporations to the year 2021, a geographic index that identifies the corporate headquarters for these firms, and a master index that is particularly useful because many of these firms have reorganized and changed names over time. This is a useful and engaging reference work that will appeal to novice and experienced researchers alike.—**Timothy E. Sullivan**

DICTIONARIES AND ENCYCLOPEDIAS

26. **Barron's Business Thesaurus.** By Mary A. De Vries. Hauppauge, N.Y., Barron's Educational Series, 1996. 365p. $12.95pa. ISBN 0-8120-9327-5.

The focus of this work is to provide businesspeople with a thesaurus that meets their needs and is suitable for desktop or travel. De Vries, an author of secretarial handbooks and business communication books, has drawn the thesaurus terms from a wide variety of sources, including reports, business correspondence, news releases, periodicals, associations, and the like. Only words with five or more business-related synonyms are listed. The thesaurus contains more than 3,000 entries and 73,000 synonyms arranged in alphabetic order. The synonyms under each entry are also alphabetized.

Although entitled a "business thesaurus," the majority of the entries are in fact nonbusiness-related terms, such as *noteworthy*, *notice*, *notify*, *notion*, and *novelty*. It would be more accurate to say that this is a compact thesaurus with a business focus. Some synonyms are really more descriptive statements, such as the term *profits*, which has as one of its synonyms the phrase "income less expenses." This may be helpful as a dictionary definition but not as a thesaurus term, nor is it likely to be used as a synonym. There are also some notable absences, such as the synonyms "receivership" and "Chapter 11" under the term *bankruptcy*, or "bullish" under the term *enthusiasm*. Other major terms missing include *buyout*, *blue collar*, *mentor*, *reorganization/restructuring*, *outsource*, *proprietary*, and *shakeout*. Although the alphabetic organization of synonyms under each term is a common practice in dictionary thesauruses, it would be more helpful to place the synonyms in order of conceptual closeness to the original term.

While this thesaurus may be useful as a quick reference to businesspeople on the road, they would be better served by an up-to-date, full-length thesaurus or synonym finder. This title is not recommended for libraries.—**Gerald L. Gill**

27. Black, John. **A Dictionary of Economics.** New York, Oxford University Press, 1997. 507p. (Oxford Paperback Reference). $12.95pa. ISBN 0-19-280018-3.

A Dictionary of Economics is a compilation of technical terms used in economics, along with terms from the related disciplines of statistics, finance, and general business. Written for British readers, its intended audiences are good students of economics in undergraduate courses and lay readers of such journals as *The Economist*. The high quality of the book makes it a useful reference for U.S. readers, although the pervasive Britishness of the writing imposes some limits on its usefulness outside the United Kingdom.

The core material—definitions of the technical terms used in economic writing—is first class throughout. The range of terms defined is broad, and the definitions are models of good writing: clear, accurate, and concise. Aside from the minor need to adjust to British English spellings (e.g., labour), the U.S. reader will have no trouble here. The treatment of statistical and econometric terminology is equally effective.

The less central material in the book is more severely limited by its British focus. Readers familiar with usage differences will not be slowed down by references to "flats" and "holidays," but some students may find these differences distracting. More serious is an apparent bias toward British usages in business jargon. For example, the term "white knight" is listed, but not "greenmail" or "poison pill." The dictionary lists "pay controls" and "death duties," but not "wage controls" or "estate taxes." "Golden handshake" is defined, but not "golden parachute."

Coverage of U.S. government activities is hit or miss. The generic discussion of social security benefits uses only U.K. examples, and there is no entry for FICA. The Bureau of Economic Analysis gets an entry, but not the Bureau of Labor Statistics. Also the U.S. business censuses, such as the Census of Manufactures and the Census of Retailing, are not listed.

Although somewhat selective, the dictionary does an adequate job of covering tertiary material. It touches on major environmental issues, for example. Even with its real limitations for U.S. audiences, the dictionary provides a useful supplement for U.S. students of economics and business, due mainly to its excellent treatment of the technical language of economics and econometrics.—**Ray Olszewski**

28.   Collin, P. H. **Dictionary of Business.** 2d ed. Middlesex, Great Britain, Peter Collin, 1994; repr., Chicago, Fitzroy Dearborn, 1998. 331p. $45.00. ISBN 1-57958-077-7.

There must be an enormous demand for business dictionaries, judging by the quantity of them published annually. Of course, coverage is not always equivalent, with some focusing on specific areas such as high finance and stock markets, others with an emphasis on economic terminology or management and marketing. Originally a British publication, this entry into the field is targeted toward the general user and intends to provide broad, basic coverage in its 4,500 entries. Definitions are intentionally simple—all but 470 words used in the definitions are themselves defined in the dictionary. Both British and U.S. spelling and vocabulary are included, but the pronunciation guide, which uses International Phonetic Association symbols, favors British form. Illustrative quotations from worldwide newspapers and magazines, translated into simpler language when necessary, are an unusual and useful feature in a dictionary of this type. Supplements offer help with numbers, telephoning, business letters, financial documents, and world currencies. Although inclusion of specialized or technical terminology is limited, this dictionary seems to be comprehensive enough for the average user, with an easy-to-use and attractive design.—**Larry Lobel**

29.   **Elsevier's Dictionary of Financial and Economic Terms: Spanish-English and English-Spanish.** Martha Uriona and Jose Daniel Kwacz, comps. New York, Elsevier Science, 1996. 311p. $172.00. ISBN 0-444-82256-9.

This bilingual dictionary is composed of "the most common terms and phrases used in the economic, financial and business world of today." The book is divided into four parts. The first part presents English translations of Spanish entries, followed by concise definitions in English. The second part features Spanish translations of English entries, followed by Spanish explanations. The authors have been careful in both sections to define terms and phrases plainly so that users from one field can understand definitions that fall within the scope of another. The third and fourth parts give additional word-to-word translations, but no definitions. While these are less ambiguous words and translate more clearly, it is not evident why the latter half has been separated from the former. This organization may not be obvious to users who may look up a word or phrase in the definition section but overlook the word-to-word section. A feature that would have been helpful is the inclusion of genders for Spanish words that are not clearly masculine or feminine. This slim, expensive book's strengths are its succinct and simple approach and its sturdy construction. It is especially recommended for corporate libraries, international businesses, and interpreters. —**Laural L. Adams**

30.   **Elsevier's Economics Dictionary in English, French, Spanish, Italian, Portuguese, and German.** J. L. De Lucca, comp. New York, Elsevier Science, 2001. 967p. $234.00. ISBN 0-444-82448-0.

In the era of globally integrated markets, regional economic unions, transnational corporations, and a trend to adopt common international terminology, *Elsevier's Economics Dictionary* fulfills an important role. Its backbone is British English, translated into French, Spanish, Italian, Portuguese, and German, but the terms used in the various parts of the English-speaking world are included, as well as those from other countries. Each term is classified as belonging to a particular part of economics, such as micro/macro, financial, international, business, or mathematical, all of which are listed in the prefatory material, which includes also geographical labels, abbreviations, and style labels. The gender of nouns is provided, and synonyms are given where available. A novel feature of the *Dictionary* is its inclusion of colloquialisms, jargon terms, and neologism, as well as idioms (e.g., *sawbuck*). The five non-English languages have separate alphabetically arranged sections with references to the main part ("Basic Table") , thus rendering the use of this work more versatile. A separate list of more than 2,500 acronyms and abbreviations in the languages covered is found at the end of the *Dictionary*. A minor drawback of this volume is the lack of a contents page that would provide the user with the means of faster orientation in what is available in it. The usefulness of this volume is not limited to translators. It would be desirable in any office engaged in international business, in academic libraries, and in international bodies. The *Dictionary* is timely, comprehensive, and practical. It should provide good service.—**Bogdan Mieczkowski**

31.   **Encyclopedia of African American Business History.** Juliet E. K. Walker, ed. Westport, Conn., Greenwood Press, 1999. 721p. index. $115.00. ISBN 0-313-29549-2.

Containing essays by more than 100 contributors, this encyclopedia covers a wide variety of topics from the seventeenth century through the 1990s on black business history, biographies of notable business people, and surveys of black participation in selected industries. Each entry includes a selected bibliography. An introductory chapter provides an overview of the topic followed by more than 200 alphabetically arranged entries, ranging from one to several pages. The work concludes with a chronology of black business history, a select bibliography, and an index. A fine ready-reference source, this work culls a vast amount of material covering an eclectic range of subjects, including insurance companies, black slave owners, sports enterprises and entrepreneurs, women business enterprises, and biographies of publisher John H. Johnson and black business scholar Joseph A. Pierce. The selected bibliography at the end of each entry provides invaluable citations for students and scholars looking to pursue further research.

This work, however, is not without its flaws. The entry on the "Nation of Islam Enterprises," for example, contains erroneous material and also omits significant information (i.e., the history of the sect—Farrakhan's death threats against Malcolm X are omitted as are the use of federal money to subsidize questionable housing project security and the unconscionable marketing of quack AIDS drugs at drastically inflated prices). Nevertheless, this unique work is generally an outstanding reference source on the various aspects of the history of African American business.—**Donald Altschiller**

32.   **Encyclopedia of Business.** 2d ed. Jane A. Malonis, ed. Farmington Hills, Mich., Gale, 2000. 2v. index. $405.00/set. ISBN 0-7876-2438-1.

The new edition of Gale's *Encyclopedia of Business* will provide researchers, business professionals, and all patrons interested in business topics a place to begin learning about a huge array of topics. The encyclopedia contains more than 700 signed articles ranging from over 6 pages to a couple of paragraphs and contains charts, graphs, formulas, and tables covering major business concepts and disciplines of national and international interest. Math formulas illustrate financial and economic concepts and models. Topics like business ethics, the Euro, electronic commerce, valuation, financial ratios, International Monetary Fund, doing business in Korea, the North American Free Trade Agreement, and family leave, are included in the alphabetically arranged, two-volume set. Some articles or essays from the previous edition have been substantially updated and expanded.

Within the essays, bold terms lead readers to related entries, as do *see also* notations at the end of the essays. The section of further reading provided at the end of most entries varies from 4 to 10 items and includes books, periodical articles, and Websites. *See title* references lead users to essays that may be recognized by more than one commonly used term. The hugely enhanced, tiered index simplifies accessibility by listing unusual terms, company names, institutions, organizations and associations, key government agencies, legislation, court cases, individuals, groundbreaking literature, and significant studies. Besides a long list of contributors, an advisory panel of recognized experts provided assistance and guidance in the preparation of these volumes. Students, scholars, and business people can use this treasure of current business information.—**Susan C. Awe**

33.   **An Encyclopedia of Keynesian Economics.** Thomas Cate, Geoff Harcourt, and David C. Colander, eds. Northhampton, Mass., Edward Elgar, 1997. 638p. $235.00. ISBN 1-85898-145-X.

John Maynard Keynes merits a voluminous treatment, and so do the many writers who contributed to Keynesian economics. Some 110 of them are included in this encyclopedia, with approximately 140 contributors who each give a synoptic account of the creators of Keynesianism or of its key concepts, such as the liquidity trap, incomes policies, the relative income hypothesis, or the IS/LM model; of institutions, such as the Keynes proposal for an International Clearing Union; and schools of thought, such as the Lausanne School, which provided some antecedents of Keynesianism. Each entry contains references to related subjects or persons, and each has a useful—and sometimes, as in the case of William Baumol, extensive—bibliography. Important contributors, at the present time rarely mentioned (as in the case of Ragnar Frisch), are preserved here for interested scholars. Some of the items in this reference source summarize the overall influence of Keynes, as on national income accounting, or on the question of "what remains of Keynes?" Other items provide a view of alternative schools of economic thought, such as the classical, the monetarist, and the new classical, thus deepening the intellectual content of this encyclopedia. This reviewer found using this source exhilarating and endowed with additional interest in view of the 1997 discussion on the inclusion or non-inclusion of Keynesian economics in introductory economics textbooks. The editors should be applauded for helping to preserve a part of intellectual heritage.—**Bogdan Mieczkowski**

34.   **Encyclopedia of Political Economy.** Phillip Anthony O'Hara, ed. New York, Routledge, 1999. 2v. $265.00/set. ISBN 0-415-15426-X.

Political economy has emerged as the cutting edge of research in several disciplines, including economics, political science, and sociology. The multiple disciplinary interest in this topic suggests correctly that political economy is open to many different approaches, paradigms, and methodologies. Marxists and neo-liberal scholars claim political economy as "their" field. This encyclopedia attempts to identify and explain key concepts, terminologies, theories, and contributors in the broad field of political economy. The editors and article authors represent a wide range of preferences in their approach to political economy. As a result, the encyclopedia represents well

the diversity of ideological and paradigmatic approaches to political economy. The editors, associate editors, and most contributors are economists by training and background. As a result, the economic dimension for political economy is emphasized. Key concepts and issues in political
science and sociology are ignored or given short treatment. For example, corporatism, economic
planning, industrial policy, and trade unions are not given separate entries, although some information on these important areas of political economy can sometimes be gleaned by use of the index. However, the editor should be commended for his inclusion of the new and rapidly growing
feminist political economy in its different dimensions. This set is recommended for college and research university libraries. [R: LJ, 1 Feb 99, p. 76]—**Frank L. Wilson**

35.   **English-Russian Economics Glossary.** By the Languages Service, Terminology and Technical Documentation Section. New York, United Nations, 1996. 344p. $80.00pa. ISBN
92-1-000055-2. S/N GV.R/E.96.0.12.
      This glossary contains some 2,200 entries, an English index that makes it reversible into
an English-Russian dictionary of economic terms, a list of national currencies in the former Soviet
republics, and a bibliography. While potentially useful to foreign direct investors in Russia and
possibly in some of the other former Soviet republics, the glossary is intended primarily as a help
for translators of current texts on the Russian economy, with its new relevant terminology in banking, the securities markets, business law, and accounting. Old terms that are still relevant and in
use are included also. Some of the terms in the glossary carry additional references to the bibliography for further explanation, something that only the most dedicated translators would be likely
to seek. Some concepts, such as that of "the income elasticity of supply," have a doubtful significance as only the concept of the income elasticity of demand makes economic sense. The market
for this volume seems severely limited.—**Bogdan Mieczkowski**

36.   Foldvary, Fred E. **Dictionary of Free-Market Economics.** Northhampton, Mass., Edward
Elgar, 1998. 307p. $85.00. ISBN 1-85898-432-7.
      This is the first dictionary of free market terms. It includes entries on the theory of market
economy, empirical studies of economic freedom, and informative biographies of free-market
economists. The dictionary provides definitions of terms that other economic dictionaries omit,
such as "intervention," "regulation," and "public goods." It also includes topic terms used in law,
finance, and classical liberal philosophy as well as basic terms used in economics. Well-known
economists' biographies, such as Keynes and Friedman as well as obscure ones such as Gerard
Debren, a Nobel Prize winner for economics, are also included.
      The dictionary is sorted alphabetically with extensive cross-referencing. A solid bibliogra-
phy of source materials is also provided. This book is valuable to the student of economics and to
the professor as well. Librarians will love it too for the short concise definitions. [R: Choice, June
99, p. 1764]—**Kay M. Stebbins**

37.   Folsom, W. Davis. **Understanding American Business Jargon: A Dictionary.** Westport,
Conn., Greenwood Press, 1997. 235p. $65.00. ISBN 0-313-29991-9.
      Folsom's dictionary is designed to be a practical reference tool for students, managers, and
international businesspeople trying to understand the patois of U.S. business. The entries are arranged alphabetically, in an unconventional letter-by-letter scheme, in order to accommodate the
large number of multiword phrases that occur in business jargon. An added, welcome feature is the
frequent inclusion of quotations from business periodicals and newspapers, where the term is used
in context. The author has also supplied a list of acronyms often used in the business environment.
      Folsom's work is useful for the intended audience, especially foreigners. Unfortunately, he
does not explain the criteria for including terms in his dictionary. A bibliography of similar

dictionaries is provided, and the user will infer that this, as well as the sources used for quotations of the words used in context, constitute the base from which his terms were culled. In spite of this lexicographical lapse, and some minor typographic errors in some terms (e.g., "bib leagues" for *big leagues* and "xeriod" for *xeroid*), students of U.S. business should value this dictionary highly.—**Robert H. Burger**

38.   **Gale Encyclopedia of U.S. Economic History.** Thomas Carson and Mary Bonk, eds. Farmington Hills, Mich., Gale, 2000. 2v. illus. maps. index. $195.00/set. ISBN 0-7876-3888-9.

The *Gale Encyclopedia of U.S. Economic History* is a beautifully produced and carefully researched two-volume set that would be appropriate for high school and public libraries as well as for academic libraries that serve an undergraduate population. Intended for juniors and seniors in high school and first-and second-year college students, the encyclopedia provides comprehensive coverage of U.S. economic history from the Paleolithic Age to the present, although the emphasis is on the nineteenth and twentieth centuries. Articles for the encyclopedia were selected by a nine-member editorial board of university and high school teachers and librarians. In addition, Charles K. Hyde, professor of history at Wayne State University, was responsible for reviewing all articles to ensure content of the highest quality.

Articles for the *Gale Encyclopedia of U.S. Economic History* have been crafted with specific purposes in mind and can be characterized as era overviews, issues in economic history, geographical profiles, key events and movements, geographies, historic business and industry profiles, and economic concepts and terms. Articles range from a paragraph or two to several pages. Most articles include suggestions for further reading and there are many cross-references to other articles. For example, the article on Harley-Davidson, Inc., is nearly 3 pages in length, includes an illustration of a 1927 motorcycle typical of Harley-Davidson products, and has 7 citations for additional reading. The article on Indiana is just under two pages of text but includes a full-page map showing major cities, points of interest, and highway routes. An article on George Washington Carver, complete with photograph and suggested readings, covers not only his inventions, but also his work with the Tuskegee Institute and his many honors and awards. Articles are easy to read and offer a good balance between fact and analysis.

There are several additional features of the *Gale Encyclopedia of U.S. Economic History* that make it a particularly good reference source. It has an index of more than 100 pages, so students should be able to find information without difficulty. In addition, a detailed 33-page chronology covering approximately 50,000 years provides a quick way to verify dates and will help students to place an event within its historical context. There is also a list of "contents by era" divided into 10 eras. A research scholar has prepared an overview for each of these eras. In the front of the set these "eras" and their corresponding articles are listed. The encyclopedia has more than 200 finely reproduced photographs and illustrations that make it a treat to look at. There are detailed maps for states and regions, which should be particularly useful to students.

The *Gale Encyclopedia of U.S. Economic History* is attractively produced with clear, easy-to-read type and an engaging cover design and is reasonably priced. It will be an excellent addition to the reference collections of high school, public, and academic libraries. [R: Choice, Sept 2000, p. 104; BR, Sept/Oct 2000, p. 79]—**Sara Anne Hook**

39.   **Knowledge Exchange Business Encyclopedia.** Lorraine Spurge, ed. Santa Monica, Calif., Knowledge Exchange, 1997. 747p. illus. index. $45.00. ISBN 1-888232-05-6.

As business becomes increasingly complex, new concepts and techniques evolve to enable further expansion of knowledge and to promote communication. Consequently, the already large number of business terms constantly increases, making it difficult to keep abreast. *Knowledge Exchange Business Encyclopedia* provides an accessible, concise, and comprehensive source of current business knowledge. It serves the business student just learning business terminology and technology, as well as the seasoned manager who wants to keep informed. Although designed as a reference volume, colorful illustrations, sidebars highlighting important points, numerous examples, and a precise yet relaxed style of presentation invite casual reading as well.

Profiles of business leaders, key industries, and selected growth companies furnish useful and interesting insights into U.S. business. An index of entries by discipline, a general index, and the use of cross-references enable readers to easily locate terms of specific interest. Data tables summarizing the U.S. economy add to the broad spectrum of useful knowledge condensed into this single volume. The book is attractive as well as authoritative and offers excellent value. In future editions, the editor may wish to consider including one or two suggestions for further reading with respect to complex topics for which it would be impractical to include extensive details.—**William C. Struning**

40.   Krouglov, Alexander, Katya Kurylko, and Dmytro Kostenko. **English-Ukrainian Dictionary of Business.** Jefferson, N.C., McFarland, 1997. 119p. $28.50. ISBN 0-7864-0301-2.

This Ukrainian dictionary contains current English terminology used in business sectors. Approximately 1,700 entries consist of the required form of a word, various translations, interpretations, and useful phrases. The dictionary is compiled alphabetically; English word combinations are provided in alphabetic order under the corresponding keyword, regardless of whether or not the keyword appears first in the phrase. Within each entry, the word combinations are listed alphabetically according to the English word beginning the phrase.

There are 2 so-called sections in the dictionary: The English section includes about 15 percent of the dictionary's mass, and the Ukrainian section contains 85 percent. The words in the English section have their grammatical categories indicated. If a word is used only in the singular or plural, this too is indicated in parentheses. Where English terms yield more than one equivalent in Ukrainian, the Ukrainian words are listed according to the following convention: synonyms are separated by commas, whereas words of similar meaning are separated by a semicolon. Different meanings of the same term are enumerated. All nouns in the Ukrainian section, other than those appearing in oblique cases, have their definitions followed by their gender, and if the noun is used in the plural, a plural marker is used. Words having more than one syllable have their stress indicated. There is also a list of abbreviations at the end of the dictionary. The user is advised that English does not have a single norm for fixing the forms of abbreviations or acronyms.

Although designed for Ukrainian businesspeople, the dictionary's value extends mostly to professional interpreters and trade consultants who do not know updated Ukrainian well enough to read this book. In today's Ukraine, readers prefer to use English words, such as *display* and *printer*, *standard* and *progress*, *dispute* and *discussion*.—**Ludmila N. Ilyina**

41.   **The MIT Encyclopedia of the Japanese Economy.** 2d ed. By Robert C. Hsu. Cambridge, Mass., MIT Press, 1999. 523p. index. $60.00. ISBN 0-262-08280-2.

This book explains the structure of the Japanese economy and how it works. It contains 180 essays and 145 short definitions, which are listed alphabetically. The essays discuss the important issues for each topic, provide statistics, and give addresses of relevant companies or government bodies as well as references for additional reading. There is a detailed index referencing the Japanese and English terms for each concept.

The author has gone beyond the expected discourse to show how Japan's unique social and cultural heritage affects its economic functioning. For example, the author points out that mergers are less common in Japan than in the United States because of the strong community feeling among Japanese workers. The idea of a CEO selling a company for financial gain is seen as a betrayal of one's employees. Also, the interlocking relationships with suppliers and distributors, which are so common in Japan, lessen the push for integration.—**Adrienne Antink Bien**

42.   **The New Palgrave Dictionary of Economics and the Law.** Peter Newman, ed. New York, Stockton Press, 1998. 3v. index. $550.00/set. ISBN 1-56159-215-3.

The field of law and economics, although rooted in the contributions of David Hume and Adam Smith and subsequently of Jeremy Bentham and Friedrich Hayek, experienced its main stimulus from the writings of Ronald Coase, and began with what the editor of these volumes regards as a "meteoric rise" in the 1970s and 1980s. The field has developed interconnections, one of which is demonstrated in the companion *New Palgrave Dictionary of Money and Finance* (see ARBA 93, entry 242), while several indicate the practical applications in the transforming post-Communist economies and in the less developed countries. The new field takes account of conventions, customs, and norms in the mix of formal and intellectual problems and solutions.

In the 3 volumes under review the "List of Entries" includes cross-references. A "Subject Classification," which is divided into 7 main categories of society, economy, policy, law in general, common law systems, regulation, and biographies, is subdivided into subheadings, and those are in turn (in a separate listing) helpfully divided into the subjects of the essays found in the 3 volumes under review. This reviewer missed the inclusion of "Subject Classification" in the "List of Entries," which might have helped a general user of the dictionary in finding areas of interest. Classifications are found at the end of each essay, together with cross-references and exhaustive bibliographies. Volume 3 also contains a list of relevant "Statutes, Treaties, and Directives" (many of them emanating from the European Community Council), and a 10-page, double-column list of "Cases." In addition to their usefulness as a focused reference source, these volumes could be used as a textbook, or as a source of individual readings in a course on law and economics, crafted according to the interests or needs of the instructor. About 300 contributors to these volumes hail from many countries, most from the United States, Canada, the United Kingdom, Italy, Germany, Holland, Greece, and international organizations. Their essays are uniformly excellent, informative, and helpful for deeper research. [R: BL, 1 Oct 98, pp. 364-365; LJ, Dec 98, pp. 92, 94; RUSQ, Spring 99, pp. 310-311]—**Bogdan Mieczkowski**

43.   **Routledge German Dictionary of Business, Commerce and Finance: German-English/English-German. Worterbuch fur Wirtschaft, Handel, und Finanzen Englisch.** New York, Routledge, 1997. 961p. $125.00. ISBN 0-415-09391-0.

This impressive dictionary is truly a team product that economically comprises maximum information on its double-column pages. Sections on features, the use of the source, and abbreviations allow the user to make the most of this compendium, while the appendix includes business correspondence (including a handy job application for the translator who uses this dictionary); job titles; a list of stock exchanges in North America, the United Kingdom, and France; financial and economic indexes; basic translation information on countries; and a table on cardinal and ordinal numbers. The latter is a source of a minor criticism because periods and commas that have opposite meanings on the continent and in the United States are not shown, and so 1,000 could be translated as meaning 1.000.

The two main parts of the dictionary are compendious and well done, including examples of the use of words. They show some difficulties in translation as well. For instance, *venture capital* has no strict equivalent in German, and is rendered by several descriptive translations, whereas *Fertigkeit* is translated as *person skill* instead of *personal skill(s)*. Among the useful and interesting features this reviewer found was the distinction between English and American terms (there are also distinctions between Swiss and Austrian German), and information about the obsoleteness of some terms. Thus, this dictionary allows the user to keep up with changing language norms. Cross-references expand the choices available to translators. Translations are conveniently divided into the areas to which they pertain, such as accounting, banking, finance, or law. Grammar is stressed, while grammatical codes allow the translator to avoid some potential pitfalls, as do indications of formal, informal, and jargon uses. The value of this extensive dictionary increases with the inevitable expansion of commercial relations within the European Union and between Germany and the English-speaking world.—**Bogdan Mieczkowski**

44. **Routledge Spanish Dictionary of Business, Commerce, and Finance. Diccionario Ingles de Negocios, Comercio y Finanzas.** By Emilio G. Muniz Castro. New York, Routledge, 1998. 822p. $99.00. ISBN 0-415-09393-7.

This general business and commerce dictionary covers a broad range of terminology from the main fields of business. The editorial team consisted of leading subject experts who verified the accuracy, currency, and translation of the terms. The work attempts to include essential vocabulary; only terms that can be applied in a business context are included. (This is how it differs from a general English-Spanish dictionary.) Terms are also included from both North American and British English; and on the Spanish side, they are included from both Latin America and Spain. Interestingly enough, the English part of the dictionary is more than 10 percent bigger than the Spanish part. English compound terms are especially well represented in this work, as are idiomatic expressions in both languages (e.g., *golden handshake* and *golden parachute* were listed in one entry). Additionally, entries contain one or more subject headings for terms by usage. As with most dictionaries, the parts of speech are provided in the entries, as is gender for the Spanish-language nouns. There is a special section for abbreviations used in the entries for parts of speech as well as geographic codes and level codes. Multiple indexes, letter and resume samples, glossaries of job titles, and other useful information make this dictionary an exceptional single-volume reference. The two-column format is generously spaced; headings and subheadings in the entries are set in bold typeface that is easy on the eyes. This fine reference work is highly recommended.—**Edward Erazo**

45. Shim, Jae K., and Joel G. Siegel. **Dictionary of Economics.** New York, John Wiley, 1995. 373p. (Business Dictionary Series). $39.95. ISBN 0-471-01317-X.

Economists looking for detailed essays on classic economic terms know to consult *The New Palgrave: A Dictionary of Economics* (see ARBA 88, entry 165). Most economic dictionaries assume the user has some basic knowledge of economic terms. Shim and Siegel's new entry in John Wiley's Business Dictionary Series provides relatively jargon-free, short definitions of more than 2,200 economic terms. Slang and newer concepts, such as Clintonomics, are included. Cross-references guide the user through terminology and linkages in terms. Graphs, charts, formulas, and tables help illustrate the principles. The appendix consists of tables that give values for such items as future value, chi square, and Durbin-Watson. Unfortunately, the work fails to define Durbin-Watson and fails to meet its primary purpose of defining any term that may not be readily understood. That flaw aside, the work is useful for general reference, business, and economic collections.—**Bobray Bordelon**

46. Urrutia, Manuel R. **Dictionary of Business, English-Spanish, Spanish-English: Accounting, Management, Finance, Economics, and Marketing.** repr. ed. Balderas, Mexico, Editorial Limusa; distr., Cincinnati, Ohio, AIMS International Books, 1998. 394p. $59.95pa. ISBN 968-18-5482-9.

This paperbound work is the first reprint of the 1995 edition of the same title. Its stated purpose is to provide a bilingual dictionary that pulls together "the terms of most common usage, both in English and in Spanish" from five separate fields of the business world into one convenient volume for business professionals and their support staff. In the preface, the author notes the inclusion of idioms and idiomatic expressions, a feature based on his own work as an editor. Libraries lacking the previous edition should consider adding this relatively inexpensive volume to their business and foreign-language reference holdings.—**Robert B. Marks Ridinger**

47. **Wiley's English-Spanish, Spanish-English Business Dictionary.** By Steven M. Kaplan. New York, John Wiley, 1996. 580p. $19.95pa. ISBN 0-471-12665-9.

Obtaining accurate terminology in the rapidly changing field of international business has always presented librarians with a challenge, beginning with the appearance of I. de Veitelle's *Mercantile Dictionary* in 1864. Since the late 1980s, both British and American publishers have produced reference works addressing the needs of companies and individuals dealing with the expanding markets of the Hispanic world. The present original volume is based on American English and offers extensive coverage of more than 40,000 words and phrases from the fields of accounting, advertising, commerce, economics, finance, trade, taxation, securities, banking, real estate, management, and insurance. Acronyms and abbreviations are not included. A particularly useful feature for speakers of either language is the arrangement of entries by phrasal groups based on a common first term. The author has compiled three other similar bilingual dictionaries in electrical and computer engineering, psychology and psychiatry, and law. An inexpensive price makes this an essential addition to all reference collections, although public libraries and university collections supporting degree programs in all business fields will find it most useful.—**Robert B. Marks Ridinger**

DIRECTORIES

48. **American Big Businesses Directory, 1999.** Omaha, Nebr., InfoUSA, 1998. 3v. $595.00/set. ISBN 1-56105-997-8. ISSN 1061-2173.

American Big Businesses Directory, 1999 provides a comprehensive compilation of some 193,000 businesses in the United States. The term "big businesses" is used in a broad sense to include any organization with 100 employees that purchases supplies, services, materials, or products. For example, government entities and educational institutions are included. Two of the three volumes included in the set list businesses alphabetically. Each entry provides address, telephone and fax numbers, lines of business by SIC code, parent or branch relationships, employee size category, annual sales volume category, credit rating based on estimated ability to pay, and key executives. The 3d volume contains a list of businesses by U.S. city, a list of businesses by SIC code, and an alphabetic list of executives. Compilation of the directory required exhaustive examination of telephone directories, annual reports, SEC reports, government data, and postal information. Data collected were verified by telephone calls to listed businesses.

The directory would be useful to a wide range of practitioners, teachers, and students—particularly those who would like to market a product or service, or those who are engaged in market research or planning. The directory is also available in CD-ROM format (see entry 49), which will enable sorting by characteristics of interest to the user. The publisher can provide additional services, such as prospect lists and mailing labels. The directory offers essential information on large U.S. organizations in a single, authoritative source. Perhaps the publisher will consider including e-mail addresses in the next edition.—**William C. Struning**

49. **The American Big Businesses Disc.** 2d ed. [CD-ROM]. Omaha, Nebr., InfoUSA, 1999. Minimum system requirements: IBM or compatible PC. Double-speed CD-ROM drive. Windows 3.1 or higher. 8MB RAM. 15MB hard disk space. $595.00.

The American Big Businesses Disc is a searchable CD-ROM directory of 193,000 public and private businesses and other organizations in the United States and their 703,000 executives compiled from yellow page telephone directories and public company filings. The directory claims to include all U.S. businesses with more than 100 employees. Each record contains company name and complete address including, zip code, telephone and fax numbers, type of business (both yellow page heading and expanded SIC code), multiple executive names and titles, number of employees, estimated sales volume, headquarters/branch identifiers, stock exchange and ticker symbol for public companies, and a credit rating code. Company Websites are not part of the record. The database may be searched by any of the foregoing criteria as well as by city, state, zip code, county, metro area, area code, telephone prefix, or the entire United States.

There are some anomalous search results that users would not ordinarily associate with "big business." When searching by city, for example, the results include sheriffs' departments, county commissioners, local schools, hospitals, nonprofit agencies, and other entities. Because these organizations are often large employers and significant purchasers there is some justification for including them. It appears that branch relationships for public companies are accurate. For nonprofit organizations and private companies relationships are not always specified.

The layout of the search screens is simple and clear, with tabs across the top for each main search category: company, type of business, geography, business size, and special. Along the right-hand side are additional search criteria for each category. For example, companies may be searched by name, contact person, telephone number, or ticker symbol. The help contents is straightforward, answering basic questions on the scope of the database, searching, displaying and exporting records, and contacting technical support.

The software for the library edition permits downloading up to 75 records at a time into a spreadsheet format. However, users can only pick the first 75 records the first time they download a set. Afterwards each record must be tagged individually and then downloaded in sets of up to 75 records into a separate file. The obvious intent of these limitations is to discourage users from downloading the database. The procedure makes it very cumbersome to create files of companies larger than 75 records. *The American Big Businesses Disc* is reasonably priced in comparison with other business directories available on CD-ROM.—**Peter Zachary McKay**

50. **American Business Locations Directory.** Valerie J. Webster and Lia M. Watson, eds. Farmington Hills, Mich., Gale, 1996. 5v. index. $575.00/set. ISBN 0-8103-8368-3. (Volumes also available individually: $150.00/v. for volumes 1-4 or $50.00/v. with purchase of v.5 [$375.00].).

The U.S. facilities (e.g., plants, offices, centers, divisions) for companies ranked within the Fortune Industrial 500 and Service 500 are identified in this directory. Intended for jobseekers, students, and sales and marketing professionals, the snapshot view of corporate holdings is arranged geographically by state and city. Entries, with as many as eight categories of information, clarify parent and location type, financial performance, and fortune ranking (for parent only); however, the number of employees is rarely noted, and the list of officers neglects position titles. Each volume has two indexes, one by Standard Industrial Classification (SIC) code and one by company name. Additional access is available through the alphabetic parent company index in volume 5.

This is potentially a useful reference tool. Its failure to meet all this reviewer's expectations results from the nature of corporate holdings, mergers, and franchises rather than volume structure or contents. An "unreal" picture of communities emerges, one in which banking dominates entries for smaller cities, and the subsidiary versus franchise option results in numerous Pizza Huts and few McDonalds in large urban areas. The publishers should consider enlarging the parent database for a more representative picture and employing the newer technologies for a format that permits downloading. Despite these limitations, a timely reference query demonstrated the directory's value as an acquisition for library business collections. [R: Choice, July/Aug 96, p. 1767; LJ, Jan 96, p. 86; RBB, Jan 96, p. 876]—**Sandra E. Belanger**

51.   **America's Corporate Families 1995.** Bethlehem, Pa., Dun & Bradstreet, 1995. 3v. index. $495.00; $475.00 (libraries). ISBN 1-56203-393-X. ISSN 0890-6645.

The first two volumes of Dun & Bradstreet's *America's Corporate Families* provide information on approximately 11,000 U.S. parent companies and their 76,000 subsidiaries, branches, and divisions. Volume 1 is alphabetically arranged by parent company and supplies standard directory information, the Dun's number, annual sales figures, a narrative line of business descriptions, the net worth, the number of sites, and up to 6 Standard Industrial Classification (SIC) codes. Under each parent company one also finds the directory listing for its branches, divisions, and subsidiaries with more limited directory information. Volume 2 provides an alphabetic index to all companies; a geographic index by state, then by city; and a third index grouping companies by SIC code. Criteria used for inclusion in this set are that the parent company must have at least 2 business locations, $25 million-plus in sales, and a tangible net worth of more than $500,000. The 3d volume of the set includes information on U.S. companies and their foreign subsidiaries, information on foreign parent companies with U.S. subsidiaries, and the same types of indexes as found in volume 2.

Dun & Bradstreet's policy is to lease these volumes to libraries, which is not an inexpensive undertaking. Because Dun & Bradstreet has a family of publications, much of the information listed here can be found in other publications, such as the *Million Dollar Directory* (see ARBA 87, entry 176). This same information can also be found in National Register Publishing's *Directory of Corporate Affiliations* (see entry 59), which has as an added feature an arrangement of companies by whether they are publicly or privately held. The criteria for inclusion in this set require that the parent company have a sales volume of $10 million, thus encompassing more companies. This set is also available on CD-ROM.

There is a great deal of overlap between the National Register Publishing set and the set under review. If a library is already subscribing to other Dun & Bradstreet publications, it may decide to acquire this title. As both sets are expensive, carefully reviewing the options before selecting one over the other is important. For the occasional question concerning subsidiaries, libraries can consider using one of the online databases in this subject area.—**Judith J. Field**

52.   **Business: Name & Business Type Index.** [CD-ROM]. Carter Lake, Iowa, PhoneDisc, 1996. Minimum system requirements (Windows version): IBM or compatible 386XT. CD-ROM drive. DOS 3.1. Windows 3.1x. 4MB RAM. 1MB hard disk space. Minimum system requirements (Macintosh version): Macintosh Plus/Classic. CD-ROM drive. System 6.04. 1MB RAM. $39.95.

Included in one CD-ROM are the names, addresses, telephone numbers, Web addresses, Metropolitan Statistical Areas (MSA), and Standard Industrial Classification (SIC) codes for U.S. businesses. The documentation did not say how many businesses the product included, but a quick search showed that more than 983,000 businesses started with "A." Indexes by name and SIC provide quick access, and a count button tells how many records were in the list. Two clicks of the mouse lead to 54,082 travel agencies.

Advanced search features allow the user to locate information using alternative spellings of last names; alternate first names, such as "Bob" for "Robert"; and first initial matches. The search can be done for anywhere in the city, state, or country. A user can further refine a search by specifying criteria for address, telephone, MSA, part of a name, and the radius from a geographic center. The user can store a geographic center location in the program by its 5-digit zip code, its latitude and longitude using a reference point from the NAD-1927 datum, or a reference point from a global positioning system (GPS) receiver. According to the documentation, a GPS receiver plugged into the computer will show and update the user's current location in real time on the screen. Travelers with laptops and CD-ROM drives can use this feature to direct themselves to their appointments. The help system also discusses several GPS manufacturers and describes GPS status messages.

There are several features that make this product valuable. Installation on the hard drive is optional, and the program runs fast from a CD-ROM drive. There are customization options for screen presentation and several options for directly dialing the phone number from the computer. Finally, printing address labels, including postal barcodes, is simple.

The major problem of the program is that the content is static. The only option for updating records is to buy an upgrade or export the information into another application and update it manually. The information's benefit is problematic, especially if the user lives in an area like Seattle, Washington, where one area code has recently split into three.—**Susan D. Baird-Joshi**

53. **Business and Economic Research Directory.** London, Europa; distr. Farmington Hills, Mich., Gale, 1996. 624p. index. $225.00. ISBN 1-85743-024-7.

This title provides the reader with an alphabetical list by country to leading business and finance research institutes. The compilers have included descriptions of approximately 2,000 research institutes located in 150 countries. There has been a serious attempt to provide complete addresses and the name of a contact person, a brief description of the institute's major research interest including founding date, and a list of its publications. The leading economic world powers are well represented, but some of the lesser economic powers have only one or two institutes listed. Part 2 is an alphabetic list of nearly 1,500 journals and periodicals that were included in the 1st section as part of the research institute description. Addresses and, in some instances, e-mail or World Wide Web addresses, a brief description of the scope of the journal, and the language in which it is published are included for each title. The index provides access by the names of research institutes. This book would be of primary interest to academic research institutions and to nonaffiliated research institutes that have personnel needing to identify research partners. —**Judith J. Field**

54. **Business Organizations, Agencies, and Publications Directory.** 14th ed. Grant Eldridge and Ken Karges, eds. Farmington Hills, Mich., Gale, 2002. 2140p. index. $460.00. ISBN 0-7876-5920-7. ISSN 0888-1413.

Business Organizations, Agencies, and Publications Directory (BOAPD) is a directory to business information sources, covering areas that include advertising, banking and finance, management, franchising, government regulation, small business and entrepreneurship, investment securities, and business education. The resources listed are arranged within five groupings: "U.S. and International Organizations," "Government Agencies and Programs," "Facilities and Services," "Research and Educational Facilities," and "Publications and Information Services." These groupings are further subdivided into 32 sections, among which are "U.S. Trade Business and Commercial Associations," "International Trade, Business, and Commercial Associations," "Commodity and Stock Exchanges," "U.S. State and Local Chambers of Commerce," "Federal Government Agencies," "Franchise Companies," "Visitor and Convention Bureaus," "Business Libraries and Information Centers," "Periodicals," and "Computer-Readable Databases." For each entry the following is provided: name, address, telephone and fax numbers, and e-mail address; officers; date of founding (where applicable); description; number of members (where applicable); and Website (if available). Each entry is provided with an entry number through which each item is indexed by name and keyword. Information for this directory was obtained from other Gale directories, government sources, and Websites of organizations covered in BOAPD. This directory provides a one-stop guide to locating data and information from various sources. Those using BOAPD can find answers to questions such as: What business libraries are available in

Albany, New York? Where is the Canadian Embassy? What are the trade associations for security systems and services?

This source provides additional data for the researcher on a specific industry, company, or product. Since some of the information will become outdated, this should be a frequently updated source. It is recommended for academic libraries and larger public library collections.—**Lucy Heckman**

55.   **Company Profiles for Students.** Donna Craft, ed. Farmington Hills, Mich., Gale, 1999. 2v. illus. index. $150.00/set. ISBN 0-7876-2936-7. ISSN 1520-2938.

With stock projects proliferating in high schools, students and teachers will be attracted to this multifunction resource. For 270 companies, each profiled on 5 to 7 pages, the editor provides company history and chronology, expenditures, analysts' opinions, current trends, employment, and a brief bibliography. General features of the set include a chronology of key business events; industry profiles, including overview, historical sketch, significant events, global presence, and key competitors in the field; and an annotated directory of business-related Websites. One senses a full range of types of companies, with the emphasis on popular service industries. Some major product names are listed in the index; for example, Kenmore and Craftsman lead to the Sears entry. *Hoover's Handbook of American Business* (see entry 94), the standard bearer that more briefly profiles 750 companies, tends to have straight lists in the general features whereas this resource provides context. As there are about 11,000 publicly owned companies, the editor's challenge was to choose a manageable amount of information to squeeze into 1,600 pages. On the plus side, Craft includes several foreign automobile companies and a few others, which *Hoover's* does not. Updating is already a problem, however. Despite its 1999 copyright date, months-old mergers such as Daimler/Chrysler and MCI/WorldCom are not noted. Teachers may want to ask students to read Craft, then supplement with online sources such as the Electric Library and the individual companies. [R: Choice, Nov 99, p. 514; SLJ, Aug 99, pp. 181-182]—**Bobray Bordelon**

56.   **Consultants & Consulting Organizations Directory.** 24th ed. Julie A. Mitchell, ed. Farmington Hills, Mich., Gale, 2002. 2v. index. $810.00/set. ISBN 0-7876-5278-4. ISSN 0192-091X.

The *Consultants & Consulting Organizations Directory* provides facile access to nearly 26,000 individuals and firms that are engaged in consulting activities for business, industry, and government, and that operate in the United States and Canada. The *Directory* is in its 24th edition, thus every effort has been made to provide up-to-date information. The major portion of the 2-volume set is composed of entries grouped into 14 subject areas, encompassing fields that include business, industry, science, technology, environment, agriculture, social services, and human welfare. Each entry contains, wherever feasible, firm or individual name, contact information (e.g., address, toll-free and standard telephone numbers, fax number), names of executive officers, areas of consulting expertise, SICs, special services available, geographic areas served, recent publications and videos produced, seminars and other presentations given by organization members, and branch office locations. When available, annual revenues are reported. Each entry is numbered sequentially to facilitate referencing via three indexes: geographic, consulting activities, and alphabetical. The *Directory* is also available in electronic formats—disk, CD-ROM, and tape. Data included in the *Directory* were gathered from questionnaires completed and returned by consultants who responded by mail, telephone, fax, and Internet. The entries and indexes are preceded by a table of contents, highlights, an introduction, and a user's guide. The resulting reference volume offers a convenient, accessible, authoritative, and comprehensive guide to consultants of all types in the United States and Canada.—**William C. Struning**

57. **Corporate Affiliations PLUS. Spring/Summer 1995.** [CD-ROM]. New Providence, N.J., R. R. Bowker/Reed Reference Electronic Publishing, 1995. Minimum system requirements: IBM or full MS-DOS compatible 286. ISO 9660-compatible CD-ROM drive with MS-DOS Extensions-compatible device driver and MS-DOS CD-ROM Extensions. MS-DOS or PC-DOS 3.1 (5.0 recommended). Hard disk. 535K conventional memory. Monochrome or color display. $1,995.00/yr. ISBN 0-8352-3333-2.

Although this corporate database compares favorably with other business resources as far as coverage of basic business information, it is weak in the financial information it contains, especially compared to Compact Disclosure. A complete citation contains basic contact information, parent affiliation and the percentage owned by the parent, basic financial figures, Standard Industrial Classification codes, a 10-to 50-word explanation of the company's main work, trade names, officers, board of directors, matching gift and corporate giving amounts, legal and accounting firms, registrar and transfer agent, state of incorporation, number of employees, and the year founded. One address that future editions should record is the business' World Wide Web address.

Installation was quick. While the trouble-seeking techniques in the user's guide were inadequate and inaccurate, a technical support person diagnosed the problem and provided a solution immediately. As any reference librarian knows, users need a simple, intuitive interface they can master quickly. Moreover, they need efficient user guides for reference. The database satisfies the interface requirement. Arrow keys provide access to the intuitive menus, while the Escape key performs logical functions, such as canceling file output or taking the user back to the previous screen. System designers chose text colors for the screen well; commands are in green, white, blue, and yellow on a black background, while error messages appear in red text. The blue Help screens with white messages are a nice contrast.

The publisher could provide better user guides. The bulky three-ring binder has complete instructions, but novices will not refer to large manuals when they need help. Two things would improve the database's usability for the untrained person. First, a Function and Control key template for the keyboard could tell people at a glance what to do. Second, a "cheat sheet," preferably laminated and two-sided, could explain 80 percent of the functions people use—browse, search, print, and save to disk. Because searching is one of the easiest and most intuitive tasks to do in this program, a few examples showing truncation, Boolean search logic, and skillful use of the 19 indexes would be sufficient. This database would be appropriate for high school and community college libraries.—**Susan D. Baird-Joshi**

58. **The Corporate Directory of U.S. Public Companies 2001.** San Mateo, Calif., Walker's Research, 2001. 2726p. index. $360.00. ISBN 1-879346-42-7.

The Corporate Directory of U.S. Public Companies 2001, published by Walker's Research, provides information on more than 10,000 publicly held U.S. corporations. It also covers foreign companies that offer American Depository Receipts (ADRs). This volume has been published annually for several years and is one of many directories on U.S. companies that are available from a variety of publishers. However, given the demand for company information from the business, academic, and investor segments of the population, it is worth considering for purchase, especially since *The Corporate Directory of U.S. Public Companies 2001* may include businesses not covered in other corporate directory sources.

Yellow Corporation offers a typical entry in *The Corporate Directory of U.S. Public Companies 2001*. The entry provides Yellow's previous company name, mailing address, telephone number, and the URL for its Website. Under "General Information," the entry lists Yellow's state of incorporation, number of employees, auditor, stock agent, DUNS number, the price of Yellow's stock on a particular date, stock exchange and ticker symbol, the number of outstanding shares, officers' and directors' shares, and the total number of shareholders. Some entries also include the name of the individual or firm that handles the company's legal matters. There is a brief description of the company in the "Business" section of the entry, and primary and additional SIC codes are provided. If Yellow had any subsidiaries, these would be listed, along with their location. There are separate listings for Yellow's officers and directors, with name, age, and title given. In some cases, the salary is also noted. The "Owners" section lists several companies with major ownership interests. The "Financial Data" section offers a brief snapshot of Yellow's fiscal health, with several years of sales and net income figures, along with accounting data, such as current assets and liabilities and its P/E and debt/equity rations. Entries may cover up to five years of financial history and may also include earnings per share information. Entries in *The Corporate Directory of U.S. Public Companies 2001* are concise but are well organized and presented in a way that makes the information easy to locate.

In addition to the individual company entries, *The Corporate Directory of U.S. Public Companies 2001* has a company index that also lists acquisitions made since the previous volume. There is also an officer's and director's index, an owner's index, an SIC code index, a subsidiary/parent index, a geographic index (broken down by state and then by zip code), a stock exchange/ticker symbol index, and a Fortune 1000 index. The volume includes several pages of introductory information, including a helpful summary of how entries are organized and a brief description of what is contained in each section of an entry.

The Corporate Directory of U.S. Public Companies 2001 will be a good addition to the business reference collections of public, academic, and corporate libraries, especially libraries that serve business leaders and investors. It is attractive, easy to use, and presents a concise picture of the financial and management structure for a broad range of U.S. public and foreign ADR-listed companies.—**Sara Anne Hook**

59.   **Directory of Corporate Affiliations 1998: Master Index.** Christine Kerwin and others, eds. New Providence, N.J., National Register/Reed Elsevier, 1998. 5v. $1,029.95. ISBN 0-87217-217-1.

The *Directory of Corporate Affiliations*, published since 1967, provides business researchers with an invaluable source of basic corporate hierarchy and reportage information for almost 15,000 U.S. and non-U.S. parent companies as well as more than 100,000 subsidiary companies. It is a multifaceted reference tool that can be used to determine either "who owns whom" or to identify a particular companies' affiliates, subsidiaries, divisions, or joint ventures.

Two of the set's five volumes provide a variety of useful indexing. One may search by company name, Standard Industrial Code, or geographical terms. There are also indexes for brand names and personnel. The three other volumes are organized into U.S. public companies, U.S. private companies, and international public and private companies. Companies are arranged in each volume alphabetically. One of the strengths of the set is that each company entry pulls together all its U.S. and non-U.S. subsidiaries into one list.

The criteria for inclusion are described in the front matter as being flexible. Domestic companies need to have revenues greater than $10 million, "substantial" assets or net worth, or more than 300 employees. Foreign companies must have revenues of more than $50 million. Typical directory information one might expect to find includes company address, fax number, e-mail address, ticker symbol and stock exchange, basic financial data, number of employees, description of business, key personnel, board of directors, legal firm, and auditor. The corporate "family tree" information varies with the complexity of the company, but can include listings of affiliates, divisions, joint ventures, and subsidiaries. The entry also indicates the reporting relationships with the company.

Although U.S. public and private companies receive the greatest coverage, more than 2,424 parent companies are non-U.S. in origin. Of the more than 100,000 subsidiaries listed in the volumes, some 54,000 are located outside the United States and, of this latter number, nearly 40,000 are foreign-owned.

Although this is an important reference source, it should be noted here that the print format of the *Directory of Corporate Affiliations* poses some problems for business reference librarians. The set consists of five oversized paperback volumes, each nearly 2,000 pages in length. Users must move back and forth between the indexes and the "Public," "Private," or "International" volumes to view company data. This is possible but awkward if one is researching a long list of companies. The product is also available as a CD-ROM as well as through online service providers like LEXIS-NEXIS and Dialog. Although neither electronic format was examined for this review, readers may wish to consider investigating an electronic alternative. Also, if the set is expected to get heavy use, the volumes should be bound. This adds to the set's considerable cost. The value provided by the *Directory of Corporate Affiliations*, however, far exceeds its cost and awkwardness. This is an essential tool and is recommended for any serious business reference collection.
—**Gordon J. Aamot**

60.   **The EPM Licensing Letter Sourcebook.** 1997 ed. Martin Brochstein, ed. New York, EPM Communications, 1996. 653p. index. $295.00pa. ISBN 1-885747-06-3.

This directory provides a comprehensive source for locating information on licensing a particular property, including Larry Bird, Betty Boop, Elvis Presley, Garfield, and Purdue University. The book is arranged into six sections: licensers, licensing agents, licensees, service providers, trade associations, and cross-reference indexes. In section 1, licensers, or property owners, are divided into 13 categories, ranging from apparel and accessories to toys and games. In section 3, licensees, or manufactures, are subdivided into 17 categories, including accessories, apparel, electronics, food and beverage, and video games and software. Information provided about each licenser, licensee, and consultant includes name of company or institution, name of a major officer, address, and telephone and fax numbers. The 5 indexes in section 6 allow quick access by company name, individual name, property for licensers and agents, property for licensees, and products manufactured.

The only similar publication identified is *The International Licensing Directory* (see ARBA 88, entry 309), which is a British publication that covers 63 countries. *The EPM Licensing Letter Sourcebook* is a larger work that appears to be limited to the United States. Although it is expensive, it will be particularly helpful for licensing professionals and for business, large public, and academic libraries with a need for licensing information.—**O. Gene Norman**

61.   **FaxUSA 2001: A Directory of Facsimile Numbers for Businesses and Organizations Nationwide.** 8th ed. Jennifer C. Perkins, ed. Detroit, Omnigraphics, 2001. 1899p. $145.00pa. ISBN 0-7808-0424-4. ISSN 1075-7112.

FaxUSA, now in its 8th edition, continues to grow with each volume. This resource now provides facsimile and directory information for 124,000 companies and organizations as compared to 117,500 in the 7th edition (see ARBA 2001, entry 117). Information is provided for companies, including financial institutions, service industries, media, manufacturing industries, construction contractors, and transportation and utility companies, as well as organizations, such as government agencies, associations, foundations, colleges and universities, and libraries and research centers. The focus is on larger companies and organizations, although some "up-and-coming" companies are included.

The arrangement remains the same as the last edition: an alphabetic section and a geographic section. Entries provide the company's or organization's name, address, telephone number, and fax number. A classification number is also provided, which corresponds to a list at the beginning of the volume indicating to users what type of industry the company or organization is active in. A list of abbreviations and information on area codes is provides as well.

This is a useful ready-reference volume to have on hand. Much of the same information can be found, however, in Omnigraphics' companion volume, *Headquarters USA* (see entry 63).
—**Shannon Graff Hysell**

62.   **Financial Yellow Book: Who's Who at the Leading U.S. Financial Institutions.** Winter 2000 ed. New York, Leadership Directories, 1999. 929p. index. $245.00pa. (first subscription); $172.00pa. (w/additional subscriptions). ISSN 1058-2878.

This semiannual publication is a directory of 811 public and private financial companies in the United States. In addition to its availability in print format, the *Yellow Book* is accessible over the Internet through an annual subscription to *The Leadership Library on the Internet.*

The first section provides a list of companies appearing for the first time in the *Yellow Week,* completed mergers since the last edition, pending mergers, company name changes, chief executive officer changes, and the main companies in which major companies are located. The work is divided into three sections for financial institutions, government financial institutions, and accounting firms. Companies are arranged alphabetically within each section.

Each company listing contains its name; ticker symbol (when applicable); address; telephone number; e-mail and Internet addresses; fax number; a brief description of company services; brief biographical information about the chief officer; a list of key executives and administrative staff; major subsidiaries, divisions, and affiliates; and a list of the members of the board of directors. In many entries, a photograph of the chief officer is provided.

The directory has an industry, a geographical, a name (of all individuals), and an organization index. It is recommended for larger academic library business collections and to research libraries. The value of the work is that it brings together and lists, in one directory, both public and private institutions representing accounting firms, banks, insurance companies, and government agencies.—**Lucy Heckman**

63.   **Headquarters USA 2001: A Directory of Contact Information for Headquarters and Other Central Offices of Major Businesses & Organizations Nationwide.** 23d ed. Jennifer C. Perkins, ed. Detroit, Omnigraphics, 2001. 2v. index. $175.00/set. ISBN 0-7808-0341-8.

Headquarters USA is the expanded and updated new edition of the ready-reference work formerly known as the *Business Phone Book USA* (22d ed.; see ARBA 2001, entry 116). As explained by the publisher, the new name change reflects the expanded scope of the work—35 percent of the volume consists of organizations, agencies, or institutions and, along with telephone numbers, the work provides fax and toll-free numbers, addresses, and e-mail and Website addresses.

This ready-reference set is organized into two volumes. The first lists the 131,000 businesses and organizations in alphabetic order and the second lists them by subject category. This new edition provides 95 new categories, which aids in the efficiency of the volumes. These new subject categories reflect new industries, such as online reservation services and Website design services. Along with the 131,000 listings, this book provides 22,000 contact telephone numbers in 50 of the largest U.S. cities. These numbers include those of convention and visitor bureaus, travel sources, area hospitals, and local attractions. This information will be especially valuable for the business or frequent traveler. Other useful information provided here includes a map indicating U.S. time zones, telephone area codes by state, stock symbols, and a list of conglomerates with their subsidiaries.

This reference source will answer a lot of questions at a busy reference desk. It would also be an ideal resource to be put in online form, but as a print resource it is both functional and useful. This work is recommended for both public and academic libraries.—**Shannon Graff Hysell**

64. **Hoover's Billion Dollar Directory: The Complete Guide to U.S. Companies.** Austin, Tex., Hoover's, 1997. 1200p. index. $149.95. ISBN 1-57311-019-1.

Hoover's is known for producing attractive, easy-to-use business directories featuring concise company profiles. *Hoover's Billion Dollar Directory* focuses on publicly traded U.S. companies. Each entry includes address, telephone, and fax number; CEO; CFO; fiscal year-end; ticker symbol; and Website address, if available. Five years of financial data are given, followed by a summary describing the company's business. Three indexes provide access to the companies by industry, headquarters location, and ticker symbol. A company rankings section lists the top 500 companies by sales, market value, and 3-year sales growth. Although this directory is fairly straightforward, there are a few caveats. *Hoover's Billion Dollar Directory* excludes companies traded on the U.S. stock exchanges but headquartered in other countries, such as Glaxo Wellcome or British Airways. Also, the directory assumes the parent company name is known, and no subsidiaries are listed. A separate index of companies with *see* references would be helpful to aid in locating entries in the directory. Libraries owning Standard & Poor's *Stock Reports* will not find this to be a necessary purchase. However, students and job-seekers researching companies will like finding directory information, company background history, and financial data all in one volume.—**Barbara E. Clotfelter**

65. **Hoover's MasterList of Major U.S. Companies 2002: The Facts You Need on More Than 5,200 Leading Public and Private Enterprises.** 8th ed. Austin, Tex., Hoover's, 2001. 987p. index. $134.95. ISBN 1-57311-070-1.

As with its other directories, Hoover's presents this material in an attractive format with alphabetically arranged entries printed in bold, easy-to-read fonts. This 8th edition of *Hoover's MasterList of Major U.S. Companies* packs a lot of information into 1 volume, listing over 5,000 companies and organizations in the United States. Public companies with sales over $125 million are included in the directory. Entries are brief due to the large number of listings in one volume. Each entry includes a summary of the company's products and operations, the mailing and Web address of the firm, the top three executives (CEO, CFO, and human resources contact), an indication if the company is publicly traded or privately held, and a selection of recent company financials. The financial information, when available, includes sales, net income, market value, and number of employees for the previous five years, and also indicates the percentage change from the previous year for each category.

Valuable features include company rankings lists arranging the top 500 U.S. companies by sales, employees, 5-year sales growth, and market value. Useful indexes include the "Index by Industry," which allows one to browse for companies by major and specific industry grouping, and the "Index by Headquarters," which lists by state and city the corporate headquarters of each of the companies included in the directory. Another less useful listing, "Index by Stock Exchange Symbol," shows the stock exchange and lists the page number of the entry for each of the public companies listed in the directory. Unlike the *Dun & Bradstreet Million Dollar Directory* (Dun & Bradstreet Information Services) and other business directories, the Hoover publications do not list industrial classification codes such as the SIC code or the newer North American Industrial Classification System code (NAICS). The *MasterList* does provide an index by industry, however, if one wanted to search for companies based upon this criteria.

A unique quality of this publication, the directory lists many private companies and nonpublic entities, such as foundations, sports teams and leagues, universities, not-for-profits, and major government-owned entities such as the United States Postal Service. This inclusion of many organizations that would not normally be listed in a business directory provides a scope of content rarely seen in similar publications. This guide is recommended for all libraries, especially those with small business reference collections in need of a current directory.—**Glenn McGuigan**

66.   Levine, Jeffrey P. **Pittsburgh Business Directory.** Pittsburgh, Pa., Pittsburgh Business Times, 1997. 1041p. index. $49.95. ISBN 0-9650280-1-1. ISSN 1093-457X.

This 2d edition, published by the Pittsburgh Business Times, covers companies located in the greater Pittsburgh area. Businesses must have 35 or more employees to be included. A total of 1,312 companies are listed. Those 1,239 entries for private companies, subsidiaries, or nonprofits provide basic directory information and run about one-half page in length. Entries for the 73 public companies located in the Pittsburgh area contain more informative two-page entries. Of special interest are the 73 executive biographies for selected officers of public companies. Companies are listed alphabetically and the author has provided several useful indexes—county, zip code, officer, executive biography, and SIC code. According to the front matter, the author has also written similar works for other cities, including Boston, Kansas City, New York City, and Chicago.

This is a well-organized and reasonably priced directory that will be of great interest to those business collections in and around Pittsburgh. Business librarians in other parts of the country, however, will find it a less compelling purchase.—**Gordon J. Aamot**

67.   **National Consumer Phone Book USA 1998.** Detroit, Omnigraphics, 1997. 1103p. $60.00pa. ISBN 0-7808-0277-2.

This directory claims nearly 55,000 listings for associations, businesses, manufacturers, government agencies, educational institutions, and other entities that provide information and services for consumers. Additionally, it includes people who are prominent in the news as well as the print and broadcast media themselves. Most listings appear once in an alphabetic section (white pages) and at least once in a classified section (yellow pages). Each occurrence of a listing contains the name of the company, organization, or individual, along with the mailing address, main telephone number, fax number, toll-free number, e-mail address, and World Wide Web address. In the white pages, the last item in each listing is a number that corresponds to a classified heading in the yellow pages. This is useful for identifying competitors. Though a listing may occur under more than one heading, the number accompanying it in the white pages refers to the organization's or person's principal activity. Unfortunately, there is no easy way to determine under which other headings a listing may appear.

Compiling a directory is a major undertaking, not only in gathering and editing the material, but also in deciding what to include. One does not expect perfection (at least, not in the 1st edition), but accuracy and attention to detail are part of what makes such a reference tool useful. On these two points the editors have done a reasonably good job. A random check of a few dozen telephone numbers produced 100 percent accurate hits. (There was no answer at one number, but that does not prove that it is inaccurate.) Cross-checking addresses resulted in only a slightly lower percentage. However, a local athletic shoe store was listed as being in Telham, Alabama, rather than Pelham, Alabama. Jerry Springer is listed in the white pages but does not appear under "Television Talk and Interview Programs" in the yellow pages (though he is listed under "People," which some users may question). Other than "U.S. companies, organizations, agencies, and institutions that serve consumers," there are no stated criteria for inclusion. Thus, we are left to guess why Stephen King, Chris Isaak, Pat Buchanan, H. W. Wilson, and Krystal are listed but Garrison Keillor, Garth Brooks, James Carville, EBSCO, and Morrison's are not.

The editors have packed between the covers of this directory a lot of helpful information that would have to be sought in numerous other reference books. It will be particularly useful in libraries whose budgets do not allow the purchase of all those other titles. This work is recommended with hope that it will continue to improve.—**Craig W. Beard**

68. **National Directory of Corporate Public Affairs, 2001.** 19th ed. Valerie S. Sheridan, G. Keith Finan, Natacha Leonard, and Diane R. Murphy, eds. Washington, D.C., Columbia Books, 2001. 947p. index. $129.00pa. ISBN 1-880873-43-5.

The 2001 edition of the *National Directory of Corporate Public Affairs* is a comprehensive and intriguing volume that contains a wealth of information about the role of corporations in the public affairs arena. In its 19th edition, this volume is intended to provide a full profile of the corporate public affairs profession in the United States, including the identification of key people and principal corporate offices. It has been compiled through review of public sources of information on public and governmental activities, along with annual questionnaires and telephone interviews.

The *National Directory of Corporate Public Affairs* is divided into two main sections. The first section is a listing of nearly 1,600 companies, arranged in alphabetic order, which have been identified as having active public or governmental affairs programs. Although many of the entries are for major national and international corporations, smaller companies are also included, although the amount of information provided on these companies may be minimal. The second section is an alphabetic listing of 12,000 corporate employees who are working in the public affairs arena, including those with roles in the political and philanthropic sectors. However, a memo attached to the volume indicates that about 1,700 corporations and 14,000 people are included in the directory. There is a one-page description of the organization and use of the volume, as well as an essay by the President of the Public Affairs Council on the backlash against large corporations by the public at large as well as suggestions for coping with this backlash. The volume also has a geographic index and an industry index. Additional materials include a description of the Public Affairs Council and its services and programs as well as a directory of Public Affairs Council members.

There is a large variation of information that is included for each company. Entries also indicate by a symbol whether the company is a member of the Public Affairs Council and cross-references are provided when there have been name changes or mergers. Entries in "The People" section of the directory include mailing address, telephone and fax numbers, title, and whether the person is registered as a federal lobbyist. A few entries include an e-mail address. The typeface of the entries is tiny; however, bold headings and subheadings make the volume easy to use.

The *National Directory of Corporate Public Affairs* presents a detailed and fascinating look into the reach of both large and small companies in the public, government, and philanthropic activities in the United States. It would be an excellent addition to the reference collection of nearly any type of library. It will be most useful for a library that serves patrons who are involved in public affairs, governmental affairs, investor relations, or fundraising.—**Sara Anne Hook**

69. **National Directory of Minority-Owned Business Firms.** 11th ed. Thomas D. Johnson, ed. Washington, D.C., Business Research Services, 2001. 1v. (various paging). index. $285.00pa. ISBN 0-933527-77-2.

The directory lists minority-owned businesses throughout the country. It is organized by SIC code number and encompasses virtually all codes. Within each SIC code, users find a geographic classification. Firms are indexed by name and may be listed under multiple SIC codes. Entries include firm name, address, telephone number, contact person, and a description of the services performed. Most entries identify the type of minority owner and alert the user if the business has government contract experience or is certified. A rare number of entries include other information, such as Web address, general sales and employee information, and date of incorporation.

Although the prefatory material explains the criteria for the listings, it is unclear exactly how the list was compiled. Thus, the directory's comprehensiveness is questionable. For example, it is impossible that there is only one minority-owned law firm in Florida—a state with a large, well-established Latino community.

The directory is in its 11th edition and, despite its limitations, serves the useful purpose of providing users with guidance regarding minority-owned businesses. If a library's patrons request this type of information, the directory is a credible and convenient source. It would be difficult to compile a list of minority-owned businesses without the aid of this directory.—**Holly Dunn Coats**

70.   **National Directory of Woman-Owned Business Firms.** 11th ed. Thomas D. Johnson, ed. Washington, D.C., Business Research Services, 2001. 1v. (various paging). index. $275.00pa. ISBN 0-933527-78-0.

This useful title brings together information on businesses in the United States where one or more of the principal owners or the majority of shareholders are women. Additionally, the directory notes if a business is also minority-owned, although the specific minority (black Americans, Hispanic Americans, Asian Americans, Native Americans, Native Hawaiians, or Hasidic Jews) is not given. The main section of the volume is arranged according to the four-digit Standard Industrial Classification (SIC) business descriptions, then alphabetically by state, zip code, and company name. The information was compiled by using various federal, state, and regional organizations and from the listees themselves.

As in earlier editions (see ARBA 95, entry 201; ARBA 91, entry 146; and ARBA 87, entry 189), each entry includes name, address, telephone and fax number, a contact person, and a very brief description of the product. It is somewhat troubling that only an occasional URL or e-mail address is given, even for businesses dealing with computer services. Some entries also include sales information and references. There is a company name index and an alpha industry class index. There is no information given regarding the amount of changes since the last edition. Although users might wish for more consistency in the information given for each entry, this directory serves its purpose well.—**Michele Russo**

71.   **National Trade and Professional Associations of the United States 1998.** 33d ed. Buck Downs, R. Willson Hardy, Nathan L. Cantor, and Nicholas P. Karr, eds. Washington, D.C., Columbia Books, 1998. 733p. index. $129.00pa. ISBN 1-880873-28-1. ISSN 0734-354X.

Published since 1966, this reasonably priced directory continues to be a useful reference tool for public, special, and university libraries. Now encompassing approximately 7,600 active trade associations, societies, organizations, and labor unions, exclusions remain as identified in previous editions (see ARBA 94, entry 54, for a review of an earlier edition).

The introduction, without identifiable author, effectively describes the function, types, activities, and historical development of associations. The concise, alphabetic entries contain basic contact, financial, and activities data. In addition, lists of associations can be retrieved by subject, geography, budget (in 14 categories), executive, and acronym indexes. A separate alphabetic arrangement of management firms completes the volume. New with the 33d edition is the addition of key executives and staff besides the chief executive officer.

This smaller, more focused directory has a place in business reference collections. Although the data collection methods are unspecified, its less complicated format makes it easier to use than the more comprehensive *Encyclopedia of Associations* (37th ed.; see ARBA 2002, entry 41). This edition's extensive coverage of e-mail addresses and World Wide Web sites is a definite plus.—**Sandra E. Belanger**

72. **The Prentice Hall Directory of Online Business Information 1997.** By Christopher Engholm and Scott Grimes. Englewood Cliffs, N.J., Prentice Hall Career & Personal Development, 1996. 524p. illus. index. $34.95pa. ISBN 0-13-255282-5.

The two authors of *Online Business Information*, both business researchers and consultants, set out to provide an "annotated, clearly indexed, and cross-referenced businessperson's guide for really using the business tools available online like we wanted to use them." To meet this goal, they have described more than 1,000 Internet sites in 1-to 2-paragraph evaluative annotations that describe each entry's content, its value to the researcher based on professional needs and level of expertise, and how to most time-effectively use the site. When similar sites exist, the authors compare levels of usefulness. The types of sites described include academic sites; premium online services from such commercial vendors as CompuServe or Prodigy; commercial sites (i.e., "originating in the private sector") that are marketing a product or service; and "Labor of Love" sites, where (usually) a single individual with a passion for something undertakes the assemblage of every existing Internet location for information on that topic.

Topically arranged chapters cover navigational tools, general business resources, career advancement, personal finance, business services, resources by industry, international business resources, business references, and the ever-popular "fun places to go during lunch hour." The core chapters are preceded by 3 introductory chapters that provide a 10-page introduction to the Internet, how it works, and what options (e.g., e-mail) it offers; basic search strategies for business researchers; and 22 survival-tool sites for business researchers (for example, "Addresses and Phone Numbers," "Search Tools," and "U.S. Government") . Each entry notes the site's title, its Internet address, and, in cases where the service charges users a fee, pricing information. Each site is rated (one to five stars) based on content (amount and quality); ease (getting to and getting around within a site); speed (organized for fast and efficient information and retrieval?); and value (worth the time and money involved?). The annotations provide sufficient information to allow business researchers to decide whether a given site will deliver what they need, thus avoiding the dreaded "browsing" downtime. The book's margins allow for plenty of white space, encouraging lots of users' margin notes.

A terrific idea (as are most special-topic Internet directories) with solid, useful content, *Online Business Information* unfortunately lacks those touches that could make its execution as valuable as its content. There are lapses in organizational logic and access points: Edupage, a resource that is focused on educational technology and related issues, players, and companies, is listed within the "multimedia and electronic publishing" section, and has no index listing under "Education" or its *see* reference, "Training/Education." The M. I. S. Research Center, dedicated to research on the use of information technology in management (management information systems), is located under "Management, Consulting, and Human Resources" rather than in the "Information Systems Management" section, with no cross-reference either within the sections or in the index. The work suffers generally from a mediocre index with extremely poor subject indexing. For example, within the text there is a section on "Publishing and the Media" that includes entries for Interactive Age (multimedia industry), Broadcast Professional Forum (television and radio broadcasting), CBS television (television broadcasting), and Electronic Commerce Associates (online mail-order catalogs, online shopping), yet in the index the only place to find these entries is under the heading "Publishing and Media" or alphabetically by site name. A book this valuable deserves generous interchapter cross-referencing and a solid, well-thought-out index that employs useful subject terms.

Despite the need for improved cross-referencing and indexing, *Online Business Information* is nevertheless an extraordinary value for the price. The resource information is updated monthly on the World Wide Web, where one can search by key term. (However, the information offered is much scantier—one-or two-sentence versus one-or two-paragraph annotations.) Unfortunately, the Website continues the print version's occasional errors of misspelling and incorrect alphabetization. However, assuming that the next edition will do a great job of copyediting, cross-referencing, and indexing, this is a publication that one can easily recommend to all business libraries, researchers, academic libraries, and public libraries supporting business research for their communities. [R: LJ, 1 Nov 96, p. 60]—**G. Kim Dority**

73. **Research Services Directory 2001/02.** 8th ed. Lakeville, Conn., Grey House Publishing, 2001. 1309p. index. $420.00; $395.00pa. ISBN 1-891482-83-1; 1-891482-82-3pa.

The *Research Services Directory* (RSD) is a unique source for information on contract and proprietary research companies, as well as corporate research departments, located in the United States and Canada. The directory, which profiles 7,850 companies, employs a broad definition of research that includes fundamental, applied, and developmental studies, in addition to data gathering, analysis, and synthesis activities. RSD primarily focuses on biotechnology and pharmaceutical developers, consumer product research, defense contractors, electronics and software engineers, environmental engineering firms, forensic investigators, independent commercial laboratories, information brokers, market and survey research companies, medical diagnostic facilities, and product research and development firms.

This 8th edition of RSD, which is also available as an online database via the Internet, has been expanded to include more than 1,700 new listings. Data are compiled by direct contact with company officials as well as through Internet research. Thousands of existing entries have been updated to include new e-mail addresses, Websites, and key contacts. A user's guide defines each of the 23 fields of information that a company might choose to include in its entry. While defined fields include items such as principal clients and rates, actual entries often provide only basic directory information.

RSD is alphabetically arranged by company names. Three indexes facilitate access to the descriptive listings: a geographic index that is classified by state, a subject index with cross-references, and an index of principal executives and key contacts. Use of controlled index terms in the company descriptions in the main listing, as well as in the subject index, would make the directory easier to use. The usefulness of the geographic index might also be enhanced by further classifying listed companies alphabetically by city within each state.

Although users will find room for improvement, RSD is a one-of-a-kind information resource. It is most appropriate for corporate and special libraries with scientific or business reference collections. Public libraries will also find it valuable for assisting small businesses in locating companies that can fulfill their research needs.—**Elizabeth M. Mezick**

74. Schraepler, Hans-Albrecht. **Directory of International Economic Organizations.** Washington, D.C., Georgetown University Press, 1997. 460p. index. $65.00. ISBN 0-87840-633-6.

This comprehensive directory covers some 90 main organizations or their groupings, some with additional affiliated organizations. The information includes addresses; the legal basis; objectives; membership; structure; and activities, including publications. The main parts cover the United Nations system, according to its functional divisions; the British Commonwealth regional organizations by areas (with an omission of the Andean Pact); and the banks and funds covered by geographic areas of operation. Separate sections provide more than 300 abbreviations of names of the various international organizations and institutions; historical dates; tables of the membership of major international groupings (demonstrating, among others, the virtual isolation of North Korea); and an index.

The directory is an excellent source of data, although it fails to list bibliographic sources for researchers interested in particular organizations. It is up-to-date, listing as it does various post-Soviet organizations and memberships, and it perceptively indicates the increasing role played by international organizations within the framework of growing global interdependence. The resource is highly recommended for reference libraries, including those of multinational enterprises.—**Bogdan Mieczkowski**

75. **U.S. Business Directory, 1999: 1.1 Million Businesses with 20 or More Employees.** Omaha, Nebr., InfoUSA, 1998. 2v. $795.00/set. ISBN 1-56105-995-1.

The *U.S. Business Directory* is a 2-volume reference work that lists businesses in the U.S. with 20 or more employees. The directory includes the name, address, telephone, SIC code, credit rating code, number of employees, and estimated annual sales of over 1.1 million businesses. The listings are organized by city and state, making them easy to access. Sources for the information contained in the directory include phone directories, the Securities and Exchange Commission, other government agencies and publications, company annual reports, trade journals, business magazines, and newspapers. The directory is a potentially useful reference tool for businesspeople, academic researchers, job hunters, and others. Its cost might make it prohibitive for smaller libraries, but it is recommended for libraries that can afford such a publication.—**Paul F. Clark**

76. **Who Knows What: A Guide to Experts.** 18th ed. Arlington, Va., Washington Researchers, 2000. 588p. $249.95pa. ISBN 1-5848-000-X. ISSN 0894-8801.

This directory provides names, organizational affiliations, and telephone numbers for a wide variety of individuals recognized for their expertise in specific areas. These experts hold positions in industry associations, think tanks, and government offices, although most of the experts included in the volume are, by a wide margin, U.S. government employees.

The bulk of the directory (539 of 588 pages) consists of names and phone numbers for over 16,000 individuals listed by topic—from "Abaca Fibers" to "Madagascar" and "Zymurgy." The number of experts listed under each topic varies. For example, listings under country names often have 10 or more experts, while more arcane topics may list just 1 or 2 names. There is also a "Federal Fast Finder" index listing U.S. government departments and their phone numbers, as well as another short section providing complete directory information for the principal U.S. government agencies.

This 18th edition provides only phone numbers as contact information. The editors justify this in the preface by noting that most people looking for experts are usually operating under tight time constraints and that the telephone is the most appropriate way to contact them. While this is probably true, researchers would also find it very useful to have e-mail addresses available.

In summary, while this is not a necessary directory for every reference collection, it is a useful resource for libraries whose clientele regularly need to identify and contact industry experts —especially those employed by the U.S. government. This guide is recommended for specialized reference collections in public, academic, and special libraries.—**Gordon J. Aamot**

77. **World Business Directory.** Rita C. Velázquez, ed. Farmington Hills, Mich., Gale, 2000. 4v. $595.00/set. ISBN 0-7876-3427-1.

The present edition of the *World Business Directory* (WBD) covers approximately 140,000 companies active in international trade. Some 180 countries are represented and most entries typically contain company name, address, telephone and fax numbers, executive officer, brief financial data, employment figures, products, and industry activities compiled through SIC codes. The information in WBD is also available in a variety of other forms (e.g., on magnetic tape, floppy disk, mailing labels, galley lists, and card files).

The information is not always accurate and occasionally is too brief to be meaningful. Thus for Albania there are only nine entries and for America there are also only nine. Such countries as

Ukraine (with over 50 million people) are not covered at all and information on Belarus or Russia is occasionally not adequate. Nevertheless, this directory provides very comprehensive listings for the countries it covers and hopefully future editions will be updated more carefully for developing countries and Eastern Europe.—**Bohdan S. Wynar**

78.   **World Databases in Company Information.** C. J. Armstrong and R. R. Fenton, eds. New Providence, N.J., Bowker-Saur/Reed Reference Publishing, 1996. 1147p. index. (World Databases Series). \$325.00. ISBN 1-85739-195-0.

This is the 11th title in the World Databases Series that the publisher has issued. This title attempts to provide worldwide coverage of business information databases, with special effort to identify those originating in Australasia, the Far East, Russia, and Europe. The analysis of such a compilation has to recognize the dynamic nature of the business field as the various databases continuously merge, migrate to different formats, change names, create similar but not identical databases in new formats, or simply cease being published. The editors had a formidable task in an area where the research seeks the latest information. The foreword states that the editors want this series to "become the de facto authority on electronically published databases with details of content, size, access and pricing as well as expert commentary on the major databases." They partially succeed at this goal, as the ever-changing nature of business information cannot be successfully documented in a single book. There is no indication that there will be supplements published to maintain the usefulness of this source.

Having noted this, one must also note that the book will be useful as a reference source to identify those less-familiar sources generated outside of the United States. It provides a detailed description of each database using the master record concept, which includes online hosts, CD-ROM publishers, diskette publishers, videotex hosts, and tape producers. The guide does supply some e-mail information, but not as rigorously as other information. Five sections make up the main part of this directory. The first section lists those databases that provide detailed company information; the second gives company directory information; the third segment offers product directory information; the fourth lists directories that identify individuals, and the last section furnishes a list of directories for not-for-profit organizations.

To enhance access to the vast amount of information, four indexes have been included. The first index is a directory of all the addresses referenced in the various entries. The subject index helps to identify specific subject areas within the various databases, the producer index links database names to producers serving as a guide in determining additional products that they produce, and the fourth index gives access by database names. This work is an extensive, detailed look at electronic databases providing company information, and if one uses it as a starting point when looking for information outside of their expertise, it will be of use. The contents of the book will quickly become dated as the migration to World Wide Web sites continues, but it will have value as a retrospective text. This title will be of particular value to large academic libraries and those libraries with a high demand for international trade information.—**Judith J. Field**

79.   **World Directory of Business Information Web Sites 2002.** 5th ed. Chicago, Euromonitor International, 2000. 288p. index. \$690.00pa. ISBN 1-84264-141-7.

This straightforward but expensive directory lists approximately 2,000 business Websites from 133 countries. Sites are chosen from trade associations and trade magazines, stock exchanges, and government offices and NGO's for their utility to the business researcher. The sites emphasize statistical, marketing, and company information as well as agriculture, consumer, industrial, and financial data. Each entry lists site name; originator; Web address; a description of services offered; an outline of the type of statistics (if applicable); and charging structure. This edition appears to list more fee-based sites than earlier editions but the majority of sites are free. There is also an Internet version. Most entries are listed by country, although there are both international and regional chapters. It has both an alphabetical index by name and an index that is alphabetical by country, subdivided by business or service sector. This second index by sector will be very useful for researchers of international statistics. A test comparison of these sites against general searches in Google, Yahoo!, and AlltheWeb found that a little more than half the sites can be found within the first two screens of each of the services, although none were as efficient as using the URL from the sector index. Address accuracy was quite good considering the volatility of the Web. Third world, regional, and international-based sites are a real strength of this work.

As far as content goes, this title is recommended. There are two caveats. Libraries really have to ask themselves if the information is worth $690; only if the agency does serious work in third world or regional economies will the library gets its value. The second caveat is that it has a statement on the verso of the title page that reads, "Reproduction in any form whatsoever is prohibited and libraries should not permit photocopying without prior arrangement. Unauthorized use will result in immediate proceedings against the offending party." Libraries will have to consider if they can live with this restriction.—**Patrick J. Brunet**

80. **World Directory of Trade and Business Associations.** London, Euromonitor; distr., Detroit, Gale, 1996. 430p. index. $550.00pa. ISBN 0-86338-556-7.

This is an expansion of the *European Directory of Trade and Business Associations* (see ARBA 92, entry 245). There are approximately 3,900 entries encompassing international associations and those of 5 world regions and 88 countries, from all business sectors. The publisher compiled the directory through contact with associations and its own research.

The two-page introduction discusses the directory's compilation, coverage, and arrangement. Entries are clustered as follows: first, those for international associations; then, those for seven world regions (Asia, Central and South America, Eastern Europe, the rest of Europe, the Middle East and Africa, North America, and Oceania); and within each region, associations serving the whole region; followed by those of individual countries. Arrangement within sections is alphabetic. There are name and subject indexes, the latter organized into 59 business sectors.

Regional emphasis is on Europe, Asia, and North America, in that order. The top 8 countries (with their number of entries) are the United States (253), Italy (180), the United Kingdom (148), Canada (145), France (141), Japan (131), Spain (111), and Germany (107). Given the relative size of their economies, Japan and Germany seem underrepresented. Ten countries have only one entry.

Entry length varies widely, from 4 lines to half a page, with an average of 11 entries per page. Entries for some countries are typically longer than those for others. The amount of data elements also varies. In addition to address and telephone number, entries usually contain a fax number and names of chief officers. Other elements, in descending order of frequency, are membership size/composition, year established, aims, publications, activities, structure, telex number, and miscellaneous notes. The double-column page layout is attractive and legible. Names in non-roman alphabets have been translated into English. All others are in their original languages.

Some major, well-known associations are missing (e.g., American Marketing Association, Conference Board, OPEC). Occasionally, associations are listed twice. A test of the indexing for 35 entries revealed that 9 were not subject indexed and 4 not name indexed. Some entries are irritatingly alphabetized under "The." The composition and content of 20 association entries were compared with their counterparts in the *Encyclopedia of Associations International Organizations* (37th ed.; see ARBA 2002, entry 42), hereafter abbreviated as EAIO. Both directories have many common data elements, although their content sometimes differs. The directory under review generally gives multiple officer names; EAIO gives only one. EAIO more often supplies information on aims, activities, conventions, and publications. Also, it often has two useful, unique elements: staff size and the association's languages.

Future editions of this directory should address the following: (1) significantly expand the number of entries; (2) balance country coverage better; (3) provide aims, activities, and publication information for many more associations and add staff size and official language data elements; and (4) make name and subject indexing more thorough. The publisher has produced a substantial first effort. Libraries with international business collections may wish to consider this directory, even though the price seems high.—**John Lewis Campbell**

81. **World Directory of Trade and Business Journals.** London, Euromonitor; distr., Detroit, Gale, 1996. 378p. index. $550.00pa. ISBN 0-86338-629-6.

Euromonitor has added a new title to its distinguished series of world business directories, *World Directory of Trade and Business Journals*. This volume replaces previous editions that were limited to European journals. After listing some 60 publications with an international focus, the more than 3,000 remaining entries are distributed into 7 world regional categories. For each region, journals that cover the region are given first. These are followed by journals that are essentially national in focus, by country within each region. Entries include publisher's name and address, as well as telephone and fax numbers. With respect to the publication, information is given on year of establishment, frequency of publication, language, products/industries covered, target readership, circulation, price, and names of both the editor and the advertising manager.

The regional approach simplifies geographic searching, although the distinction in focus among world, region, and country should be taken only as a general guide. Entries are further indexed alphabetically and by business type (pro duct or service covered). Journals serving both industrial and consumer businesses are treated, although there are more of the latter. The large number of journals listed and the broad spectrum of countries covered attest to the comprehensiveness of the volume. Euromonitor editors directly contacted publishers of journals listed to ensure a high degree of accuracy in the entries. The journal synopses are preceded by a table of contents (geographic), a brief introduction, and a list of sectors covered.

This volume can serve as a useful point of departure for obtaining further information on business firms, products, and services. It can also steer advertisers toward appropriate media to reach potential buyers or clients.—**William C. Struning**

82. **World Guide to Trade Associations.** 4th ed. Michael Zils, ed. New Providence, N.J., K. G. Saur/Reed Reference Publishing, 1995. 536p. index. (Handbook of International Documentation and Information, v.12). $395.00. ISBN 3-598-20722-0.

The 4th edition of this work contains 22,000 associations from industry, trade, craft, and service sectors from 187 countries or territories. The countries are arranged in alphabetic order according to the English-language spelling. There are also an alphabetic list of all associations' names, an index of 392 professional fields, and an index of periodical publications. This edition has been expanded to include East European and Asian countries. Chambers of industry and commerce have been left out of this edition and are scheduled to be published in a separate reference work in 1996.

Individual entries contain information, where available, on the association's name, address, telephone and fax numbers, telegram address, telefax, year founded, number of members, names of president and general secretary, area of activity, and regular publication with publication information. This oversized book contains 536 pages on average paper with average binding. The book will be extremely useful for anyone interested in an international guide to trade associations.
—**Herbert W. Ockerman**

HANDBOOKS AND YEARBOOKS

83.　Allen, Larry. **The ABC-CLIO World History Companion to Capitalism.** Santa Barbara, Calif., ABC-CLIO, 1998. 404p. illus. index. $60.00. ISBN 0-87436-944-4.

Using an encyclopedia format, the author shows the evolution of capitalism—from its medieval beginnings through the nineteenth-century's laissez-faire experience to today's current breed and its interaction with socialism, ecological concerns, and social issues. Subjects are presented alphabetically rather than chronologically. A time line provides landmark dates from 1492 with Columbus's discovery of the New World to 1997 and the return of the Labor Party to power in Great Britain.

The selections are concisely written. Key events, laws, policies, and personalities from the United States and major European nations are discussed. Readers see how capitalism has changed over time and across national boundaries. For example, New Zealand initiated minimum wage laws in 1894. It was not until 1911 that Massachusetts enacted similar legislation. The U.S. federal government did not address this issue until 1938. Although the author occasionally preaches, especially on the environment, this is a useful reference for the general student of economic history. —**Adrienne Antink Bien**

84.　**Business Statistics of the United States 1999.** 5th ed. Courtenay M. Slater, Cornelia J. Strawser, and James B. Rice, eds. Lanham, Md., Bernan Associates, 1999. 479p. index. $74.00pa. ISBN 0-89059-213-6. ISSN 1086-8488.

Business managers, students, economic analysts, government officials, and concerned citizens all find it necessary to understand current trends in U.S. business and the economy in which it operates. The most common approach used to describe and analyze the status of business and the economy is to order relevant data by time. *Business Statistics of the United States 1999* provides ready access to the most widely used business and economic time series. The book contains about 2,000 time series, selected largely from the vast flow of data from the federal government. To assist the reader in understanding, a section by Slater overviews and relates the various individual series, while Strawser provides a discussion of current issues and problems involved in measuring economic variables. In addition, extensive notes are included to identify specific sources and to offer further description of each time series. The time series, in tabular format, has been arranged in four categories: the overall U.S. economy, broad industry profiles, historical series that provide annual data back to 1961 (most of the series start with 1970), and state/regional tables. Many sections are preceded by an analysis of trends and their meaning to the current situation. The 1999 edition is the 5th in a series that began in 1995. The publisher revived and expanded an earlier series of publications, *Business Statistics*, that had been made available by the Bureau of Economic Analysis of the U.S. Department of Commerce, but which was discontinued in 1992 after 27 periodic editions. *Business Statistics of the United States* offers a vast array of statistical data in a single volume with source notes to facilitate further investigation and represents an essential reference on recent and historical data on the U.S. economy.—**William C. Struning**

85.　**Economics.** Danbury, Conn., Grolier, 2000. 6v. illus. index. $319.00/set. ISBN 0-7172-9492-7.

The world of economics is presented in this six-volume set, which is designed for use by high school students. The volumes are divided as follows: "Money, Banking, and Finance"; "Business Operations"; "The Citizen and the Economy"; "The U.S. Economy and the World"; "Economic Theory"; and "Economic History."

Each volume, with the exception of "Economic Theory," contains a series of detailed chapters with detailed coverage of specific aspects of the volume's subject. For example, "Money, Banking, and Finance" includes chapters on banks and banking, inflation and deflation, personal finance, and the stock market. "Economic Theory" presents shorter A to Z articles rather than the lengthier chapters of the other volumes. Names of contributors are placed at the beginning of each volume rather than at the end of each chapter. Every volume has an index to the complete set, a glossary, and a bibliography of books and Websites. Cross-references to related articles are included. *Economics* is copiously illustrated and provides charts and diagrams. Chapters are written clearly and provide a helpful introduction on various aspects of the economy to young adults. In addition to its intended audience, this work should be useful to people of all ages who wish to learn more about certain aspects of economics and the world economy. Those looking for concise definitions of terms, such as "elasticity," "monetarism," and "privatization," will find them here. "Economic History" provides those new to the field with an overview of events and key people from ancient times to the present day. This work is recommended primarily to young adult collections in public and school libraries. [R: SLJ, Nov 2000, pp. 88-90; BR, Jan/Feb 01, p. 82]—**Lucy Heckman**

86.   **The Elgar Companion to Classical Economics.** Heinz D. Kurz and Neri Salvadori, eds. Northhampton, Mass., Edward Elgar, 1998. 2v. index. $300.00/set. ISBN 1-85898-282-0.

The editors of this two-volume set are professors of economics at the University of Graz, Austria (Kurz), and the University of Pisa, Italy (Salvadori). The nearly 200 contributors hail from universities in Europe, North America, Asia, and Australia. The volumes are informative, with synoptic entries that end with cross-references and selected bibliographies. The coverage extends to contributions that precede the classical period proper, including references to ancient Greece. Coverage then continues with leading twentieth-century economic theorists, such as Joseph Schumpeter, Piero Sraffa, and Tibor Scitovsky, who have more recently revived the interest in classical economics, as well as those who have interpreted classical thought within the context of twentieth-century economic thought. The books contain diagrams, mathematical formulae, and a broad panorama of criticism, including Marxian.

Several European contributors to these volumes did not seem to want to be bothered with first names of the classical thinkers, such as Frederic Bastiat, who appears somewhat neglected. Authors who were practitioners as well, such as Alexander Hamilton, are not mentioned, although Johann von Thuenen is referred to repeatedly. Interesting areas of classical thought emerge from this work, such as the notion of externalities, the input-output analysis, structural change, and the spread of classical economics to various countries. Contributions of leading individual economic theorists are also included.

This set of two volumes is a valuable reference tool, convenient in its accessibility, its breadth of coverage, and its brevity of treatment. No economics library collection can afford to be without this anthology.—**Bogdan Mieczkowski**

87.   **Encyclopedia of Law and Economics.** Boudewijn Bouckaert and Gerrit De Geest, eds. Northhampton, Mass., Edward Elgar, 2000. 5v. $1,390.00/set. ISBN 1-85898-565-X.

This 5-volume encyclopedia presents 145 review articles and extensive bibliographies on specific topics in the developing field where law and economics intersect, divided (by volume) into "The History and Methodology of Law and Economics," "Civil Law and Economics," "The Regulation of Contracts," "The Economics of Public and Tax Law," and "The Economics of Crime and Litigation." Exactly one-third of the 4,193 pages is devoted to the bibliographies (20,000 entries). The presentation is nonmathematical and generally nontechnical, hence the articles are accessible to generalists and nonspecialists. The classification system is neither European nor American. Instead, the editors invent their own system: methodological and historical; substantial norms (property, transfer of property); voluntary transfer of property between private parties; involuntary transfers between citizens and the state; litigation and evidence law; criminal law; and rules on the production of legal rules. Three examples will illustrate the approach of individual articles. First, "Path Dependence" (closely related to networks, as in telephones and the Internet), by economists Liebowitz and Margolis, surveys the literature well and gives examples (e.g., QWERTY on the keyboard, Beta and VHS, computer operating systems) but without mentioning the Microsoft Antitrust case. Also, their bibliography lists four of their own articles but omits their own recent book (1999). Secondly, corporations and stock markets appear in a nice sequence of articles: "The Theory of the Firm," "Limited Liability," "Separation of Ownership and Control," "The Market for Corporate Control," "Insider Trading," and "Regulation of the Securities Market." Other sequences appear of a similar nature. Finally, the antitrust law article (by two Europeans) admirably summarizes the development of the economic underpinnings of antitrust (competition, S-C-P paradigm, Chicago School, the New I-O); however, the references to specific U.S. cases are at best only suggestive. Generally, the review articles are strong as surveys of the principles of economics and law but scarcely mention relevant cases, and the bibliographies generally stop at 1996 or 1997. No area of the law has remained unexamined and untouched by economic analysis. This encyclopedia successfully meets its goal of providing to scholars and practitioners access to summary statements of the present status of the field of law and economics.—**Richard A. Miller**

88.   **Extractives, Manufacturing, and Services: A Historiographical and Bibliographical Guide.** David O. Whitten and Bessie E. Whitten, eds. Westport, Conn., Greenwood Press, 1997. 523p. index. (Handbook of American Business History, v.2). $115.00. ISBN 0-313-25199-1.

It has been 7 years since the publication of volume 1 of the Handbook of American Business History series (see ARBA 92, entry 206). The original volume focused on 23 manufacturing industries, as defined by the Enterprise Standard Industrial Classification (ESIC). This 2d volume adds 16 industries, including printing and publishing, and 4 chapters on transportation. Each contributor was given tremendous latitude by the editors; the result is a lack of coherence in style, scope, and coverage. The introduction serves as a guide to each chapter and updates the general business history bibliography from the original volume. It mentions the prevalence of computers and telecommunications in today's business environment but fails to provide an update to the industries that were covered in the first volume. Each chapter provides a concise history of the industry with an emphasis on bibliographies. The index is excellent.

Using the industries defined by the largely unknown ESIC is a surprising choice. The use of a more widely used classification system, such as the upcoming North American Industrial Classification System or the International Standard Industrial Classification, would have made the work more compatible with business research. Because of the amount of time passed between volumes, the original entries are now only useful for historical research. If this pace continues, it will take decades for the entire system to be covered. The bibliographies and histories are valuable as a starting point for the junior business historian; however, the series needs much work.—**Bobray Bordelon**

89.   Frumkin, Norman. **Guide to Economic Indicators.** 3d ed. Armonk, N.Y., M. E. Sharpe, 2000. 328p. index. $64.95; $24.95pa. ISBN 0-7656-0436-1; 0-7656-0437-Xpa.

This is an efficient and practical handbook that outlines more than 70 commonly used concepts and statistical measures of economic activity. It outlines the relative significance and application of various economic statistics and terminology used in forecasting macroeconomic activity.

An appealing feature of this handy reference work is that, when appropriate, explanations are provided not only in the context of the U.S. economy but also in an international context. As a reference work it is intended for a general audience, including students, investors, journalists, and other interested laypersons, although it also provides a quick and straightforward handbook for economists and other social scientists.

The alphabetically arranged economic indicators are organized under 551 general categories. Even though some indicators are necessarily cross-referenced, indicators are also organized into 13 broad categories, which is an effective method to demonstrate the interrelationships and correlations between measurements and concepts. The broad categories are economic growth, household income and expenditure, business profits and investment, labor, inflation, production, housing, finance, government, international, cyclical indicators and forecasting, economic well-being, and psychology. Entries initially provide a concise description of the indicator or statistical measure and then go on to provide practical and useful information about the application and relevancy of the indicator or measurement. Knowing where and when the statistics are available, the content of the material released, the methodology used to generate the information, and the accuracy and relevance of the information as well as seeing recent trends in the information and having references from primary data sources helps to make this handbook functional and useful.
—**Timothy E. Sullivan**

90.   **Handbook of Economic Methodology.** John B. Davis, D. Wade Hands, and Uskali Mäki, eds. Northhampton, Mass., Edward Elgar, 1998. 572p. index. $215.00. ISBN 1-85278-795-3.

The editors, who are also contributors to this volume, are respectively from Marquette University, University of Puget Sound, and Erasmus University in Rotterdam. They, and their more than 100 contributors from the United States, Canada, the United Kingdom, Holland, Italy, Denmark, France, Finland, Ireland, Sweden, Germany, Hungary, Cyprus, Australia, and Japan, provide a multidisciplinary perspective on economic concepts and methodology. An extensive index amplifies the list of contributors and their entries, providing easy access for those interested in particular topics or authors. The separate area of economic methodology is new, and is allied to the philosophy of science and the history of economic thought. It also reveals a tendency to expand in a variety of different directions with a wide range of new perspectives. This evolutionary aspect of the field of methodology receives good coverage in the volume. Each entry, averaging three to four pages, is accompanied by a helpful and satisfying bibliography. The entry on "Experimental Economics" is, however, only one page long, and its bibliography includes just three articles, whereas the entry on the "Economics of Science" runs eight pages, and includes notes and a two-page list of references. The quality of entries is high; they are both succinct and readable.

This source is indispensable to historians of economic thought as well as to experts on methodology, and it is useful to those teaching and doing research on any subject in economics. This reviewer found it useful for explanation of concepts even in principles of economics. Scholars in other social sciences may also find this handbook useful and pertinent. The *Handbook of Economic Methodology* is highly recommended.—**Bogdan Mieczkowski**

91.   Harris, Wayne. **CyberTools for Business.** Austin, Tex., Hoover's, 1997. 185p. illus. index. $19.95pa. ISBN 1-57311-025-6.

Hoover's, well known for its directories, has created a basic guide to browsing the World Wide Web. Useful for experienced and novice searchers, the 100 sites described here are well-chosen, stable ones offering both user support and clarity of purpose. Organized in six categories, search engines are explained, and users are directed to news, advice, corporate, and investment data sources. Focused on features and benefits, each clearly written report provides basic information (e.g., URL, value) and an analysis of a site's pros and cons. All required costs are identified along with the benefits to be gained. There is a topical index and a directory of 4,000 corporate Websites, which should increase access to individual, company, and site names. The potential difficulties inherent in most guides to World Wide Web resources have been avoided by limiting content to the more stable sites and emphasizing Web use to save time and money. This volume will prove attractive to libraries at all levels as well as for individual purchase.—**Sandra E. Belanger**

92. **Hoover's Company Capsules on CD-ROM.** [CD-ROM]. Austin, Tex., Hoover's, 1997. Minimum system requirements (Windows version): IBM or compatible. CD-ROM drive. Windows 3.1. 4MB RAM. 20MB hard disk space. Minimum system requirements (Macintosh version): System 7.0. CD-ROM drive. 4MB RAM. 20MB hard disk space. $449.95.

Containing key contact and business industry information on more than 10,000 U.S. companies, this powerful database would fill the needs of every marketing professional, corporate librarian, or business researcher. Developed in Claris's FileMaker Pro, the interface is intuitive, the search capabilities are strong, and the installation is easy. Each listing contains up to 65 bits of information about a company, including several fields the user can customize. The primary information given is company contact information; metropolitan area; the names of the CEO, CFO, and human resources executive; a brief description of the company; fiscal year ending; amount of sales for the previous year; how much the sales changed from the previous year; number of employees; stock exchange; ticker symbol; and primary industry. For a more in-depth analysis of select companies and their histories, one should refer to *Hoover's Company Profiles on CD-ROM* (see entry 93).

Full database capabilities exist. A user can edit, duplicate, and export existing records and import new or revised records. The operator can select which fields to export and choose from a variety of formats. Unfortunately, the headers do not export, and the program truncates the description. The import mechanism allows users to map their information to specific fields in the database before importing the records. All fields can be searched using free-text and wildcard characters; industry description and metropolitan area have drop-down lists. The operator can also sort by one of 10 fields and create address labels or letters for all records, the found record set, or one record.

The most useful and timely feature of the CD-ROM is the hypertext links in the database to a company's homepage on the World Wide Web and to a Website for stock trading information. For example, if a user's Internet connection is active, he or she can click on http://www.hoovers.com, and the Web browser will open to Hoover's Website. Clicking on the stock symbol for Weyerhaeuser Company will take users to DBC Online (http://www.dbc.com) and show the fundamental stock data for that company.—**Susan D. Baird-Joshi**

93. **Hoover's Company Profiles on CD-ROM.** [CD-ROM]. Austin, Tex., Hoover's, 1997. Minimum system requirements: IBM or compatible. CD-ROM drive. DOS 6.0. Windows 3.1. 4MB RAM (8MB for Windows 95). 4MB hard disk space. $449.95/single user; $549.95/2-8 users.

The computer-based version of Hoover's Handbooks (see entries 94, 95, and 96, for example), this product has interesting, lively profiles of about 2,700 public, private, and government-operated companies in the United States and abroad. Four key criteria influenced the selection of the companies: size, growth, visibility, and coverage of each industry. These factors lead to some obvious inclusions, such as Digital Equipment Corporation, UPS, the Big Six accounting firms, Chevron Corporation, and Harvard University. There are some surprising inclusions (the AFL-CIO, The John D. and Catherine T. MacArthur Foundation, Heineken N.V.) and omissions (Adobe and REI).

Like any good reporter, each profile answers the essential questions: who (chief officers and key competitors), what (products or services), when (history), where (location and primary geographic areas of business), why (mission and motivation), and how much (financials for up to 10 years and year-end statistics). Hypertext links point to competitors' profiles, but the links are difficult to activate. Unfortunately, Hoover's buried the subsidiaries, collaborators, and other important business partners in the text instead of putting them in a separate section.

The interface is user-friendly. Fifteen minutes of exploration will get the user up and running quickly. In addition to a sophisticated Find feature, five indexes (company name; headquarters location; industry; keyword; and "sounds like," or Soundex) provide additional entry points into the information. The writing is excellent—funny, irreverent, and full of puns, when appropriate. Microsoft, Inc., is "the 800-pound gorilla of computerdom." The Walt Disney Corporation's "Dumbo-sized acquisition" of ABC, Inc., "left its competitors looking goofy." Aladdin Knowledge Systems Ltd., a Tel Aviv-based company that manufactures hardware to prevent software theft, "sails the cyber seas" to prevent software piracy and keep "the software genie in the lamp." An excellent companion to *Hoover's Company Capsules on CD-ROM* (see entry 92), this product would be a good addition to any marketing group or academic business library 's collection.—**Susan D. Baird-Joshi**

94. **Hoover's Handbook of American Business 2001.** Austin, Tex., Hoover's, 2000. 2v. $159.95/set. ISBN 1-57311-064-7. ISSN 1055-7202.

The aim of the Hoover's company handbooks has always been to provide useful profile information about the companies people have heard of and will want to know more about, at a reasonable price. The 2001 edition of their *Hoover's Handbook of American Business* is no exception. Covering 750 companies, the handbook provides 2-page snapshots of 700 U.S. public companies, more than 30 private companies, and a selection of other large organizations—such as the United States Postal Service and cooperatives like Ace Hardware.

The profiles are presented in alphabetic order and follow a standard format. This format includes an overview of the company's business and history and information on chief corporate officers, locations, and sales for the most recent year; listings of subsidiaries and competitors; summaries of 1999 fiscal year-end information; and 10 years of historical financials and stock price information. For private companies, financial information is much more limited. Also included in volume 1 is a 62-page "List Lovers Compendium." This useful collection includes lists generated from the Hoover database as well as annual lists produced by other sources, such as *Fortune*, *Forbes*, *Business Week*, *Advertising Age*, and other trade journals. The set also indexes entries by geographical location, industry, brands, subsidiary and competitor names, and people mentioned in the profiles.

Many researchers, students, and job-seekers have always found *Hoover's Handbook of American Business* to be a useful starting point—especially valuable are the half-page company histories. Even though much of the financial and directory information is available from other sources, its user-friendly approach and modest cost continue to make it a good value. One question that librarians will want to consider, however, is whether the print or electronic format best fits the needs of their users. This handbook is recommended for all libraries serving users with interests in business.—**Gordon J. Aamot**

95. **Hoover's Handbook of Emerging Companies 2001.** Austin, Tex., Hoover's, 2001. 373p. index. $89.95. ISBN 1-57311-065-5. ISSN 1069-7519.

This edition covers 525 firms, all public companies based in the United States. The publisher aimed to select rapidly growing companies that, in their view, had a good chance of being able to sustain their growth. Each entry contains contact information, a paragraph-length company description, a recent (1999 or 2000) annual sales figure, the number of employees, and the names of key officers and competitors. More than 100 of the companies are covered in greater depth, each receiving a full-page entry that includes an overview of the company's operations, a more complete list of officers and their compensation, a list of the firm's competitors, and limited financial information. The financial data generally include sales; net income; stock price high, low, and closing values; price/earnings ratios; and per-share amounts for earnings, dividends, and book value (all for the most recent six years). The front of the volume offers 11 lists ranking the companies by their rate of growth in sales, earnings, and employment and by several other measures. A dozen lists reprinted from other publications are also included. These lists rank smaller companies in general; firms in specific industries; and ones owned by women, Hispanics, or African Americans. The companies are indexed by industry and headquarter locations. A third index has entries for people, brands, and companies named in the profiles.

Hoover's handbooks, as well as other publications, continue to be well regarded by researchers and librarians for providing a great deal of information in affordable packages. Since the prior edition of this title, the publisher has increased the number of companies included and, of course, updated the content. Although the duplication of content between the capsule and full-page profile sections adds nothing to this volume, the book remains a worthwhile starting point for identifying and obtaining basic information on rapidly growing public companies.
—**Christopher J. Hoeppner**

96. **Hoover's Handbook of Private Companies 2001.** 6th ed. Austin, Tex., Hoover's, 2001. 876p. index. $139.95. ISBN 1-57311-067-1. ISSN 1073-6433.

Hoover's Handbook of Private Companies 2001, now in its 6th edition, is one of many company directories and is one of a 4-volume set that can also be purchased together with an index. The stated mission of Hoover's Inc. is to provide business information of the highest quality, accuracy, and readability at affordable prices. They have achieved this mission with the publication of *Hoover's Handbook of Private Companies*, providing a concise yet comprehensive source of information on a variety of "private" enterprises in the United States that is easy to use and modestly priced. However, this volume is not exhaustive in its coverage of corporate America, choosing instead to focus on only 786 entities. In addition, many of the entities that are included in the volume are not private corporations per se, but are universities, nonprofit organizations, and quasi-governmental agencies (e.g., the State University of New York, the United Way of America, and the United States Postal Service). It is interesting to see the diversity of coverage in the volume, from the Hyatt Corporation to the Green Bay Packers, Inc.

The longer 2-page profiles for 250 companies in *Hoover's Handbook of Private Companies* include an overview and history on 1 page. The text is concise and interesting, pointing out both the key developments and the unusual stories behind each of the companies. This is certainly a welcome change from many of the strictly factual presentations of other business directories and investment reference tools. The opposing page then contains a list of top officers and sometimes even their ages and salaries, locations (including postal address, telephone and fax numbers, URL, and a brief description), a list of products and operations (sometimes with sales or asset information), and a list of competitors. Brief financial and employment information is provided in a historical chart, with a bar graph to indicate changes in net income or sales. Many of the profiles include the company's trademark, while others have additional fiscal information, including debt ratio, return on equity, cash, current ratio, and long-term debt. A typical profile for any of the 786 key private companies, including those with longer profiles, is shorter and much less detailed, with postal address, telephone and fax numbers, URL, an abbreviated list of top officers, type of company, 1999 sales figures, number of employees, fiscal year ending date, a short list of key competitors, and a one-paragraph description. It is puzzling why companies with full profiles are also included in the key private company section with the shorter profiles. It seems to be needless duplication, since the longer profiles are only two pages in length, which is not a great deal more to have to photocopy.

Besides the two types of profiles, which comprise the bulk of the volume, *Hoover's Handbook of Private Companies* includes a number of other interesting features. It has a list of abbreviations, a list of the companies covered by the longer version of the profiles, an introduction, and a two-page overview of how to use the profiles. There are several lists included in a "list-lover's compendium," including a list of the 300 largest companies by sales and by employees, lists compiled by *Forbes* and *Inc.*, and top 10 and top 25 in such categories as universities and U.S. foundations. The volume also includes an index of companies by industry; an index by headquarter location; and an index by brands, companies, and people.

Overall, *Hoover's Handbook of Private Companies 2001* is an interesting and useful volume that presents a wealth of information in one attractive and well-organized volume that is easy to use. It would be a worthy addition to the reference collections of academic, public, and corporate libraries, and the cost is more than reasonable.—**Sara Anne Hook**

97.   **Medieval and Early Modern Data Bank.** [CD-ROM]. Baltimore, Md., National Information Services Corporation, 1996. Minimum system requirements: IBM or compatible 386. CD-ROM drive. 3MB RAM. 480K conventional memory. 2.5MB hard disk space. Color or monochrome monitor. $395.00.

The purpose of *Medieval and Early Modern Data Bank* (MEMDB) is to provide research scholars with the opportunity to access, display, and generate reports of numerical data pertaining to European economic history from 800 to 1815 C.E. MEMDB contains four data banks with more than 210,000 electronic records produced by scanning pages from primary text materials. The databases include all currency exchange quotations compiled by Peter Spufford from his *Handbook of Medieval Exchange* (1986), prices drawn directly from *Inquiry into the History of Prices in Holland* (1946) by N. W. Posthumus, grain prices supplied by Rainer Metz and collected for the print edition of *Getreideumsatz Getreide-und Brotpreise in Koln 1368-1797* (1976-1977) by Dietrich Eberling and Franz Irsigler, and finally monetary data from *Geld, Wahrung und Preisent Wicklung: Der Neiderrheinraum im Europaischen Vergleich: 1350-1800* by Rainer Metz.

The ROMWright bibliographic search and retrieval software, developed by the National Information Services Corporation, provides novice, advanced, and expert search modes with full Boolean, proximity, and truncation capabilities for maximum flexibility in composing a keyword search. For the nonspecialist searcher unfamiliar with the technical language or the subject scope of each data bank, the AUTODEX (AUTOmatic inDEX), available in all search modes, is an indispensable search aid. As words are typed into a search field, the AUTODEX appears automatically with the closest word to the original input highlighted in the index. Each index term in the AUTODEX records the count of records in which the term occurs at least once, which simplifies browsing by revealing the depth to which a topic is covered in the database. The variant search feature expands retrieval by accommodating for plurals, compounds, and British or American spelling alternatives. Systems librarians can customize the software to LAN specifications and modify features of a particular search mode to fit the degree of patron experience with database searching. A variety of output functions allow patrons to tag records in a specified citation display and to choose among several full-record formats for downloading.

Originating as a project at Rutgers University sponsored by Research Libraries Group, MEMDB exists admittedly as an electronic version of previously published print resources. However, the advantage of the electronic version is that it allows the researcher to search all four data banks individually, concurrently, or in any combination, thereby liberating the scholar from the time-consuming tedium of consulting indexes to multiple print titles with multiple volumes often with confusing or clumsy cross-references. Moreover, the original documentation from the print resources is accessible when relevant in the notes field of records displaying numeric data. Consequently, the benefits of the print resources are not lost in the migration to an electronic format. The CD-ROM is recommended for purchase by university libraries with graduate programs in economics or history.—**David G. Nowak**

98. **NAICS Desk Reference: The North American Industry Classification System Desk Reference.** Indianapolis, Ind., JIST Works, 2000. 569p. $24.95pa. ISBN 1-56370-694-6.

The federal government has reported much economic data in the periodic censuses (manufacturers, business, and so on) and elsewhere based on the Standard Industrial Classification (SIC) system, last revised in 1987. The SIC allows the grouping of businesses and establishments into sensible industrial groupings or classifications at different levels of detail ("digits") . In 1997 the SIC was replaced by the North American Industry Classification System (NAICS) that is now in use in Canada and Mexico as well as the United States. This desk reference reproduces most, but not all, of the information in the government manual NAICS. Included are the following: the introductory comments on the background, development, framework, and structure of the system; the titles and descriptions of the industries at the 3, 4, 5, and 6 digit level of detail; the numerical list of short titles; the 1987 U.S. SIC matched to the 1997 U.S. NAICS (allowing a "crosswalk" from the old system to the new); and an alphabetical list of NAICS industries.

The government manual from which this desk reference is derived also contains the 1997 U.S. NAICS matched to the 1987 U.S. SIC (the "crosswalk" going from the new system to the old). The government manual with the full information is available from Bernan Press and the National Technical Information Service in three forms: soft cover ($28.50), hardcover ($32.50), and CD-ROM ($45.00). It is a depository publication. Besides price and the omitted "crosswalk," the third major difference between the NAICS manual and this desk reference is size and weight—the desk reference is smaller and lighter, and also cheaper (but not by much).—**Richard A. Miller**

99. **North American Industry Classification System: United States, 2002.** Lanham, Md., Bernan Associates, 2002. 1419p. index. $45.00; $60.00 (CD-ROM). ISBN 0-89059-566-6; 0-934213-87-9 (CD-ROM).

The North American Industry Classification System (NAICS) was jointly created by statistical agencies in Canada, Mexico, and the United States to enable the three North America Free Trade Agreement (NAFTA) countries to use a common system to collect, report, and compare data on economic activity in the common-trading area. The 2002 revision updates the 1997 NAICS that replaced the Standard Industrial Classification (SIC) code that had been in use since the 1930s as the official U.S. system for classifying and collecting data on economic activity. Many business publishers still use SIC codes for organizing business information. Government agencies such as the Bureau of Labor Statistics (BLS) and private publishers are phasing in data collection and reporting using NAICS. The BLS is only now (Fall 2002) beginning to report data on industry employment, wages, and establishment counts using NAICS. Reformulating the industry classification system provided an opportunity to incorporate activities that had been neglected, such as nonprofit agencies, education, and public administration, and to take into account emerging industries, such as wireless communications, that are playing an increasingly important role in the economic life of all three nations.

The SIC system emphasized the importance of the manufacturing sector of the economy. Manufacturing's share of employment has continued a long decline, while the percentage of people engaged in services now comprise more than 70 percent of the workforce. The NAICS greatly expands the coverage of the service sector that has come to dominate the modern economy and includes new manufacturing sectors such as information technology and services like biotechnology research and development.

NAICS uses a six-digit hierarchy of numerical codes to classify economic activities on the principle that establishments (units of production) are "grouped together based on their production processes." For example, Bed and Breakfast Inns (721191) provide short-term lodging in private homes and converted buildings. They are an instance of Traveler Accommodation (7211) that includes hotels, motels, casino hotels, and all other accommodations for travelers, all of which are included in Sector 72 -Accommodation and Food Services.

Introductory material provides background and explanatory information about the NAICS followed by an outline of the codes. The bulk of the work is taken up with the "Titles and Descriptions of Industries." Cross-references within the entries conveniently refer the user to related industry groups. Superscripts indicate usage in particular countries. For those who gather data and must live by the code, a list of Standard Short Titles for NAICS United States limited to 45 spaces is provided in addition to appendixes matching the 2002 NAICS U.S. to the 1997 NAICS, the 1997 NAICS U.S. to the 2002 NAICS U.S., and a lengthy alphabetic index to the numerical codes.

The NAICS manual is an essential reference work for anyone working with statistics on the U.S. economy. The U.S. Census Bureau maintains a Website (http://www.census.gov/epcd/www/naics.html) to keep users up-to-date with the development of the system.—**Peter McKay**

100. **Small Business Sourcebook: The Entrepreneur's Resource.** 16th ed. Sonya D. Hill, ed. Farmington Hills, Mich., Gale, 2002. 2v. index. $365.00/set. ISBN 0-7876-6762-X. ISSN 0883-3397.

From sign shops, shoe stores, and sewing centers to green houses, gardening centers, and golf shops; animal clinics, art galleries, and auctioneers; calligraphy, campgrounds, and candy shops—more than 300 small businesses are covered in the *Sourcebook*. The *Sourcebook* is a standard reference work for identifying information resources for starting, developing, and growing 341 specific small businesses as well as for finding information on general small business topics and sources of assistance at the state and federal levels and by Canadian province. The *Sourcebook* is divided into four main sections: "Specific Small Business Profiles," "General Small Business Topics," and "State Listings and Federal Government Assistance."

The "profiles" are not narrative descriptions of small businesses but rather directory listings of information sources specific to one of the small businesses covered. For each kind of small business the *Sourcebook* provides start-up information, associations and other organizations, educational programs, directories of educational programs, reference works, sources of supply, statistical sources, trade periodicals, videocassettes/audiocassettes, trade shows and conventions, consultants, franchises and business opportunities, computerized databases, computer systems/software, libraries, and research centers. Many of the entries are enhanced with descriptive annotations in addition to the essential identifying and contact information, including addresses, telephone and fax numbers, e-mail addresses, and URLs for Websites.

The first half of the second volume contains annotated entries on general small business topics arranged in 99 chapters (with up to 14 subheadings) ranging from accounting, business plans, and customer service to electronic commerce, entrepreneurship, management, manufacturing, publicity, venture capital, and workplace safety. The second volume also contains listings of resources for small business development by state, including small business development centers, chambers of commerce, minority business assistance programs, educational programs, and publications. Sections on Canadian and U.S. Federal Government Assistance follow.

The "Master Index" lists alphabetic references to the organizations, publications, products, services, and other materials covered in the 25,000 numbered entries. Other features include a user's guide, a glossary of small business terms, a Standard Industrial Classification Index (SIC), listings for licensing assistance programs, and a guide to publishers that is new to this edition.

The *Sourcebook* is valuable for identifying sources of information but the task of actually locating and accessing the sources is left to the researcher. One must also keep in mind that it is not comprehensive. For example, while there is a listing for the National Restaurant Association Educational Foundation there is not a listing for the National Restaurant Association (www. restraurant.org), which is the leading trade group for restaurateurs. The Association's Website is replete with detailed information in most of the categories covered in the *Sourcebook*. Librarians may use the *Sourcebook* to develop their collections of small business information sources. The strength of the reference work lies in its catalog of resources for specific kinds of small businesses as well as the variety of sources covered and the copious annotations. It will aid entrepreneurs who need both general and specific information to help them solve problems.—**Peter McKay**

101.   **The Value of a Dollar 1860-1999: Prices and Incomes in the United States.** 2d ed. Scott Derks, ed. Lakeville, Conn., Grey House Publishing, 1999. 493p. illus. $90.00. ISBN 1-891482-49-1.

The purchasing history of the U.S. dollar for the last century and a half is interesting to most of us. We can see what the cost of food and clothing in our grandparents' and parents' childhood and young adult lives were, as well as our own lives. This 2d edition of *The Value of a Dollar* records the actual prices of thousands of items purchased from the Civil War to the present time, and provides information about investment options and income opportunities. It has been revised and updated to include chapters on the four-year periods of 1990 to 1994 and 1995 to 1999.

Each five-year chapter contains a chronology of key economic and historic events from each year, a report on per capita consumer prices of the day nationwide, and a selection of investment returns excerpted from Federal Reserve reports. Data in the chapters also include a selection of jobs listed in major newspapers' want ads and a list of national average wage paid for representative jobs traced annually and based on the Bureau of Economic Analysis. There is also a regional report of food prices compiled from the Bureau of Labor Statistics, a selection of prices chosen from the advertisements of the day, a selection of representative items tracked annually, and a selection of anecdotal prices and income reports from publications of the period.

There is an appendix that tracks the prices of the federal gasoline tax rate, the public debt of the federal government, the postal rate for first class mail, public elementary and secondary expenditure per pupil, federal hourly minimum wage, average cost of electricity, college tuition costs and expenditures, and other interesting historical prices.

This book is for high school and college students who are doing historical economic research. It is recommended for high school, college, and public libraries for their social history collections. [R: Choice, Oct 99, p. 316]—**Kay M. Stebbins**

102.   Walker, Juliet E. K. **The History of Black Business in America: Capitalism, Race, Entrepreneurship.** New York, Macmillan Library Reference/Simon & Schuster Macmillan, 1998. 482p. index. (Twayne's Evolution of Modern Business Series). $45.00. ISBN 0-8057-1650-5.

The History of Black Business in America: Capitalism, Race, Entrepreneurship is a thorough, scholarly, and well-researched text. It is also one of the first comprehensive resources on this subject. Prior works have focused narrowly by time, place, or industry. This work covers the span of U.S. history and includes information on major figures, industries and services, and companies. The arrangement of the work is chronological and includes subthemes within sections, such as the influence of discrimination, government policies, culture, and social life on business. Sections on business before the twentieth century are especially valuable because information is scattered and difficult to access for this period. The post-1945 section draws most heavily from the resource

Black Enterprise, compiling information that would require consulting hundreds of issues. Some topics, such as black sports enterprises, that have been covered thoroughly in other resources receive less attention in order to emphasize less well known enterprises. The index is a thorough listing of names, businesses, and themes found throughout the work. This is not an essential purchase for most libraries, but will prove a rich resource for those where there is strong interest in business or African American history.—**Lynne M. Fox**

103.   **World Cost of Living Survey: A Compilation of Price Data....** 2d ed. Robert S. Lazich, ed. Farmington Hills, Mich., Gale, 1999. 618p. $235.00. ISBN 0-7876-2470-5. ISSN 1092-1702.
    This survey is quite a fascinating compilation of data concerning the cost of goods and services around the world. Because the prices are generally given in U.S. dollars, it makes for a very useful way to compare relative costs. While fun for anyone to peruse, its intended audience is people who plan to relocate or travel to another area of the world, or businesses that wish to know the cost of operations in various places around the globe. The information in this volume should also be of value to anyone studying or researching international economic conditions. The data have been drawn from over 500 sources and provide information on 209 countries and 458 cities worldwide for over 30,000 prices on more than 3,900 goods and services.
    Some of the major topics covered are clothing, fuels, health care, entertainment, food, housing, and education. It is important to note that not every geographical location has prices for all the same goods and services, so searching for the comparative costs of a given item can be frustrating. Also, one cannot help but wonder how it was decided that lunch at a snack bar in Kigali, Rwanda, costs, on the average, $12.37. Still, it is doubtful many people outside of Kigali would have a clue about such a cost, so it is useful to have. The data are arranged by country and within each country by city or other geographical entity. The topics are listed in the same order each time, and under each "major topic" are listed specific items. For each item the cost is provided for a given amount (e.g., 1 kg of bananas), the date the cost was ascertained, and a reference to the source from which the information was taken. The data are preceded by a useful introduction, a listing of cities covered, and a listing of items covered (in the same order as found under each country). The list of sources used is found at the end of the book. Most major collections, especially business and research libraries, should find the information in this book invaluable, as it would be virtually impossible to find such an assemblage of information so conveniently arranged anywhere else.—**Paul H. Thomas**

INDEXES

104.   **Business Periodicals Index. Volume 38: August 1995-July 1996.** Hiyol Yang and others, eds. Bronx, N.Y., H. W. Wilson, 1995, 1996. 2v. priced on a service basis rate. ISSN 0007-6961.
    When was the last time you used a Wilson index? Chances are it was not recently. Today's libraries seem to have relegated print indexes of periodicals to use on only two occasions: when the computers are down, or for coverage of the years preceding available electronic indexes. In taking a closer look at the *Business Periodicals Index*, what one sees is a venerable index—solid and reliable, covering more than 400 periodicals. If people are accustomed to computerized indexes, they may be a little surprised to realize the citations are listed in alphabetic order by article title rather than by date, and they may find it restrictive to be limited to only one year's worth of entries.
    Loaded with *see* and *see also* references, the index offers an alphabetic arrangement of subject headings followed by a section at the end giving book review citations. The subject headings can be quirky. The information is not difficult to find; it is just not where users think it will be. For

example, there is no listing for "dress code," although "dress" leads to "clothing and dress," which has a *see also* reference to "Employees—clothing and dress." Most patrons want keyword searching, the ability to print full-text articles, and the immediacy of computerized indexes. Although this index offers none of these features, it remains a quality product. *Business Periodicals Index* is recommended for larger collections.—**Barbara E. Clotfelter**

105. **Forms on File. http://www.fofweb.com/subscription.** [Website]. New York, Facts on File. Prices start at $299.00 (school libraries) and $450.00 (public libraries). Date reviewed: Dec 2001

Facts on File's *Forms on File* is an online database of more than 7,000 forms that are necessary for various private and business activities, including various legal forms. "Government Forms" contains 1,060 entries for forms needed for the armed forces, education, government aid programs, government procurement, immigration and naturalization, patents and copyrights, and much more. Under "Business Forms," users will find 278 entries for forms needed in accounting, human resources, real estate, and sales. College applications and personal finance and property forms are included under "Personal Forms." The sections for government, business, and personal forms all include entries for health and benefits and tax forms.

Users can also access tax forms through a section devoted exclusively to them. With 741 entries, however, this section is difficult to access, even with a high speed Internet connection. Further dividing the entries under more specific individual menus would help alleviate this problem. Potential subscribers should be aware that actual tax return forms are not included in the database. The majority of these entries are for the instructions of the various tax return forms (e.g., 1040, 1040A, 1040EZ).

The largest section of the database is for state forms. Broken down by individual states, nearly 5,000 entries are provided for forms that are relevant to each state. The options to list all forms and keyword search functions are provided for the database as a whole or under the individual sections. An alphabetic index is also provided. Adobe Acrobat Reader is required to view and print the forms. A subscription to this database is highly recommended for all public libraries and business libraries.—**Cari Ringelheim**

106. **Hoover's Handbooks Index 2001.** Austin, Tex., Hoover's, 2001. 340p. $39.95. ISBN 1-57311-068-X. ISSN 1097-7864.

Hoover's Handbooks Index 2001 is the compilation index of the four volumes in the 2001 Hoover's Handbooks series—*Hoover's Handbook of American Business* (see entry 94), *Hoover's Handbook of Emerging Companies* (see entry 95), *Hoover's Handbook of World Business* (see entry 279), and *Hoover's Handbook of Private Companies* (see entry 96). This index is provided to help users quickly locate the desired information on any of the 2,350 companies listed in the series. The work is divided into three indexes: the first listing companies by industry; the second listing companies by headquarter location; and the third listing all brands, people, and companies listed in the series. A page at the beginning of the volume titled "Using the Index" will help users become familiar with the style and alphabetization specific to this index. Libraries owning the entire set of this volume will find this cumulative index most helpful. Those with only one or two volumes in the series can probably get by with using the back-of-the-book indexes in each individual volume. —**Shannon Graff Hysell**

107. **Index of Economic Freedom, 1997.** Kim R. Holmes, Bryan T. Johnson, and Melanie Kirkpatrick, eds. New York, Wall Street Journal and Washington, D.C., Heritage Foundation, 1997. 486p. maps. $24.95pa. ISBN 0-89195-240-3.

The *Index of Economic Freedom, 1997* measures the degree of economic freedom in 150 countries. The authors contend that the most important reason for world poverty is the repressive economic policies of governments and the existence of unequivocal relationships between the degree of economic freedom in a country and its prosperity. Furthermore, they condemn U.S. foreign aid as detrimental to the recipient countries. For each country the economic policy and activity are rated in ten areas: trade policy, taxation policy, government intervention in the economy, monetary policy, capital flows and foreign investment, banking policy, wage and price controls, property rights, regulation, and the black market. Chapter 4 provides a detailed explanation of the method used to construct the index. The findings of the study are illustrated with color-coded maps, statistically correlated curves, and tables that rank each country on each economic factor with cumulative index scores. The five countries ranked as having the greatest economic freedom are Hong Kong, Singapore, Bahrain, and New Zealand, with Switzerland and the United States tied for fifth place. The bottom five countries are Vietnam, Iraq, Cuba, Laos, and North Korea. Chapter 5 contains brief portraits of each country with a discussion of the 10 factors used to rank it.

This is the 3d edition of the *Index of Economic Freedom*, previously published by the libertarian Cato Institute. The index is constructed by the conservative Heritage Foundation and co-published with *The Wall Street Journal*.—**Peter Zachary McKay**

QUOTATION BOOKS

108.   **The Wiley Book of Business Quotations.** By Henry Ehrlich. New York, John Wiley, 1998. 430p. index. $30.00. ISBN 0-471-18207-9.

Could the proliferation of books of business quotations be related to the strong economy? Titles published in the past five years include *Bartlett's Book of Business Quotations* (Little, Brown, 1994), *The Ultimate Book of Business Quotations* (AMACOM, 1998), *Forbes Book of Business Quotations* (Black Dog & Leventhal, 1997), and *Quotable Business* (2d ed.; Random House, 1999).

Now comes another compilation of more than 5,000 quotes taken from the business press, books, television, and speeches. The focus is on themes that have developed over the past 20 years. Topics such as workplace diversity, the Information Superhighway, globalization, business education, e-commerce, deregulation, and the Asian market are included. The importance of the global economy is reflected in sections on Europe and Asia (subdivided by country), NAFTA, and the role of developing countries.

The quotes are organized under 45 main subjects with subcategories under most of them. For the most part, quotes are arranged chronologically. Sections begin with a few historical quotes to illustrate how things have changed. For example, the "glass ceiling" category opens with a turn-of-the-century quote by James Fargo, president of American Express, where he threatens to close the company rather than hire a female employee. The quote is followed by numerous 1990s quotes by women executives. The scope of the quotations is broad, from well-known names such as Bill Gates, Peter Drucker, Ross Perot, Ted Turner ("You're toast") and Bill Clinton to statements by eight-year-olds, college students, and cartoon characters (although Dilbert is not quoted).

Do not look here for the traditional epigrammatic one-liner. Ehrlich admittedly takes liberties with the term "quotation." He includes vignettes, paragraphs from articles and speeches that may contain an idea, lists, and statistics. The context for entries is given, and sometimes crucial, to the meaning of the quote. This is especially true of those quotes that are responses to questions (i.e., "Are you kidding? We reserve that right for the poor, the young, the black and the stupid"). These quotes would be meaningless without elaboration.

The author's approach makes for interesting and entertaining browsing. Speakers at the local Chamber of Commerce searching for an idea for a speech will find the collection useful. But researchers, speechwriters, and students looking for a specific quote or quotes on a topic will be better off using periodical, speech, and transcript databases or Websites that will give more complete bibliographic information. There are a name index of people quoted and a company index, but the table of contents is the only guide to topics. An alphabetic keyword index would have been useful. This is a fun collection but there is nothing here that cannot be found elsewhere.—**Marlene M. Kuhl**

2 Accounting

109. **The History of Accounting: An International Encyclopedia.** Michael Chatfield and Richard Vangermeersch, eds. New York, Garland, 1996. 649p. index. (Garland Reference Library of the Humanities, v.1573). $95.00. ISBN 0-8153-0809-4.

During the last century, many significant monographs have been written on the history of accounting and accounting thought. Landmark encyclopedias and handbooks on accounting also exist. The missing element has been an encyclopedia that focuses on accounting history. One of the closest attempts is R. J. Chambers's *An Accounting Thesaurus* (Elsevier Science, 1995). That work shows the etymology of accounting concepts in a manner similar to the *Oxford English Dictionary* (2d ed.; see ARBA 90, entry 1006).

The work of Chatfield and Vangermeersch is an attempt to fill the gap. Short essays on more than 400 major concepts, laws, cases, individuals, and associations provide concise summaries of the major areas of accounting. Each entry is followed by a brief bibliography. The alphabetic listing is supplemented by *see also* entries and a detailed index. This work is not intended to serve as a dictionary or handbook for the practitioner. Its purpose is to trace the history of accounting and to provide background information on important areas of accounting. As such, it is recommended for scholarly accounting and business history collections. [R: BL, July 96, p. 1845; Choice, Oct 96, p. 253]—**Bobray Bordelon**

110. Siegel, Joel G., and Jae K. Shim. **Dictionary of Accounting Terms.** 3d ed. Hauppauge, N.Y., Barron's Educational Series, 2000. 488p. $12.95pa. ISBN 0-7841-1259-7.

The authors' intention in writing this dictionary is to provide business executives, accountants, or business students with the most up-to-date accounting and financial terms and their definitions. The vocabulary of accounting is constantly changing, with new words and phrases being developed as business and tax laws evolve. Business executives, accountants, or students have to be cognizant of these new terms to be successful in the accounting field.

The standard and the new accounting terms have been gathered from all areas of finance and accounting. Approximately 2,500 terms have been defined concisely and if examples are required for understanding, they are provided.

The entries are alphabetized by letter not by the word. A list of abbreviations and acronyms are provided in the appendix. Cross-references help clarify related or contrasting terms. Special organizations that have played key roles in the field of accounting have been included as entries, such as "American Accounting Association."

The appendix has a table covering compounded values of the dollar and annuities. This little dictionary is a must purchase for academic and public libraries to help provide quick reference for accounting terms. Undergraduate accounting students will find this dictionary a handy reference for their personal research.—**Kay M. Stebbins**

111.   **Wiley Not-For-Profit Accounting Field Guide 2001.** By Richard F. Larkin and Marie DiTommaso. New York, John Wiley, 2001. 258p. index. $24.95pa. ISBN 0-471-38903-X.

Financial accounting for the activities of not-for-profit organizations has always differed in many respects from accounting for business entities and, thanks to new releases from the Financial Accounting Standards Board (FASB), the accounting rules for not-for-profit organizations have grown steadily more complex in recent years. Revised annually, this volume is a small, pocket-sized reference guide to the accounting and financial reporting issues in this area. The guide contains 23 chapters on specific topics and an index. The writing is clear and authoritative; the coauthors collectively have more than 50 years of service in not-for-profit organizations and in major public accounting firms serving such organizations. One coauthor has served on committees of the FASB and the American Institute of Certified Public Accountants that drafted accounting standards and documents advising accountants on financial reporting matters pertaining to not-for-profit organizations.

This field guide will be useful to accounting practitioners working in the not-for-profit area and to libraries that support such practitioners. It should be noted that the *Financial and Accounting Guide for Not-for-Profit Organizations* (2000) from the same publisher, and one of the same coauthors, provides more comprehensive coverage of this area, albeit at a much higher price. Keeping the larger volume current is also more costly as it is revised less frequently (every four or five years) and in the interim is updated with annual supplements, each of which costs considerably more than this guide.—**Christopher J. Hoeppner**

3   Business Education

112. **Barron's Guide to Graduate Business Schools.** 11th ed. By Eugene Miller. Hauppauge, N.Y., Barron's Educational Series, 1999. 812p. index. $16.95pa. ISBN 0-7641-0846-8.

Barron's profiles more than 630 U.S. and Canadian schools that offer graduate business programs in this guide. Each profile states the school's name, address, telephone number, admission contact, Web address, and a short institutional history. The student body statistics include the school's retention rate, while the faculty section describes credentials and average class size. The library and computer lab facilities are discussed. Monetary factors are enumerated in the sections on cost and financial aid. Academics are covered in the sections on admissions, programs offered, course requirements, and average GMAT of accepted applicants. The placement section states the number of companies recruiting on campus, the degrees most in demand, the average and the range of starting salaries, and the percentage of graduates employed within three months of graduation. Preceding the profiles is a sample GMAT, a narrative about pursuing an MBA, and how to choose an institution to fit one's needs. This is a must-have resource for any library that has patrons who are considering graduate business studies.—**Holly Dunn Coats**

113. Gilbert, Nedda. **The Best 80 Business Schools.** 2000 ed. New York, Princeton Review/Random House, 1999. 318p. index. $20.00pa. (w/disc). ISBN 0-375-75463-6. ISSN 1067-2141.

Readers do not expect a reference book about business schools to be extraordinarily informative and relevant but also interesting, engaging, and even a little humorous now and then. The organization of the book, topics addressed, information presented, and style of writing answer the real-world needs of adults who are hoping to make a sound personal and career decision. For those who recognize the importance of the decision they are making, it is undoubtedly frustrating to find sound advice. As graduate students, these are people who are without high school guidance counselors and probably without unbiased and comprehensive advice.

This reference is based upon data collected from 18,500 students, hundreds of admissions officers, dozens of recruiters, and business school graduates. While reporting many critical statistics such as demographic information on students and faculty, other more subjective opinions that are important in the selection process are provided; for example, the opinions of students on topics such as academics, pressure, social life and fellow students, facilities, and placement and recruiting.

For those determined to seek admission to one of these top 80 business schools, there is a wealth of useful information. Common essay questions; case examples of admissions officers from Dartmouth, Harvard, Stanford, and other prestigious institutions who critique winning essays; and 15 surefire ways to torpedo your application are included.

This type of reference usually provides correct information, if you are willing to dig for it, but it is often data without the richness that allows individuals to examine their own lifestyles, needs, and professional goals to make sound, informed, personal and educational decisions. Surely it is important to know faculty-to-student ratios and average starting salary of graduates, but readers might also like to know pertinent information on student life. For those who want guidance and support for selecting and being admitted to a recognized business school, this book is likely to be fascinating and helpful reading. Once the decision has been made (or as part of the decision process), there is also a CD-ROM that contains 59 MBA and 63 LAW program applications.—**Karen D. Harvey**

114. Gilbert, Nedda. **Complete Book of Business Schools 2001.** New York, Princeton Review/Random House, 2000. 571p. maps. index. $21.95pa. ISBN 0-375-76154-3. ISSN 1067-2141.

Princeton Review's newest edition of the *Complete Book of Business Schools* represents a significant expansion over earlier editions and now contains information on 372 business schools. The first eight chapters are devoted to such helpful topics as picking the right business school, reasons for going to business school, the actual business school experience, funding an education, the admissions process, and sample essay questions and critiques. This narrative section runs some 125 pages and provides a comprehensive window on a business school education and what students can expect from application to graduation and beyond.

Each of the business school profiles furnishes data related to institution information, programs, student information, computer and research facilities, expenses/financial aid, admissions information, international students, and employment information. Three indexes listing schools alphabetically, by specific school name and by location, round out this volume. This guide is a solid, well-organized volume of helpful information for business school aspirants, particularly those sections on how to put together a winning application. It is recommended for all undergraduate college catalog collections and for public libraries.—**Arthur P. Young**

115. **MBA Programs 2002.** Lawrenceville, N.J., Peterson's Guides, 2001. 1050p. index. $29.95pa. ISBN 0-7689-0560-5. ISSN 1080-2533.

This is the 7th edition of a guide that was first published in 1995 (see ARBA 96, entry 355). More than 2,900 programs are profiled, although the title is a bit misleading. Not all of the programs are full-blown MBA offerings; some are merely Master's level programs with a relationship to business or with a strong business component (e.g., Information Systems Management, Human Resources Management, Masters of Public Administration, Masters of Science in Management). More than 800 institutions are covered in the guide, including 30 in Canada and 100 in other countries. The guide is arranged according to the usual Peterson's format. There is a 54-page "at-a-glance" section that charts admissions requirements, tuition, and special options for each institution. That is followed by an extensive section of profiles of each business school and MBA program. Each profile contains data on the faculty, student body, costs, degrees offered, financial aid, resources, international students, and application procedures. A smaller number of schools are included in the "in-depth descriptions" section. This section consists of narratives prepared by the institution itself; many contain photographs, information on the faculty, or other special features. Finally, there is an index of schools and of areas of concentration. The guide also offers a variety of introductory essays that cover such topics as "choosing the right program," "surviving the application process," and "going abroad for your MBA." This is highly recommended for all college and university library collections, and is more comprehensive than its chief competitor, *Barron's Guide to Graduate Business Schools* (11th ed.; see entry 112). An accompanying "interactive" CD-ROM provides an easy link to Peterson's MBA Channel Website.—**Thomas A. Karel**

4 Business Services and Investment Guides

BIBLIOGRAPHY

116.   Jiao, Qun G., and Lewis-Guodo Liu. **Internet Resources and Services for International Finance and Investment.** Phoenix, Ariz., Oryx Press, 2001. 540p. index. (Global Guide to Internet Business Resources Series). $49.95. ISBN 1-57356-346-3.

This bibliography includes entries for 3,080 Websites based in 216 countries. Entries are arranged by continent or region, and within each of these headings by country. This organization, while it has the advantage of allowing classes of general finance and investment resources by region, requires a separate index by country, which is provided. Indexes by Website name and by subject are also included. Resources for each country are grouped alphabetically under four broad categories: government agency, stock exchange, business and investment sites, and business and financial/economic news. An initial chapter covers 69 global finance and investment resources. Entries, although brief, are substantive enough to give the reader a general idea of a site's content and, in some cases, to highlight unique or outstanding features. A very large majority of the sites present their content in English and may be accessed free of charge—the annotations clearly note where this is not the case.

Subject bibliographies of Websites, which vary in length, are ubiquitous in the literature of librarianship. But, in-depth treatments of Web landscape in a truly global context are much rarer, and the breadth of this resource is unparalleled in its subject. This work is a recommended reference for any collection that serves investors or financial professionals. [R: BL, 1 Sept 01, p. 154]—**Christopher J. Hoeppner**

DICTIONARIES AND ENCYCLOPEDIAS

117.   **International Encyclopedia of the Stock Market.** Michael Sheimo, Andreas Loizou, and Alison Aves, eds. Chicago, Fitzroy Dearborn, 1999. 2v. illus. $270.00/set. ISBN 1-884964-35-4.

This encyclopedia covers stock markets and subjects germane to them worldwide. Topics include institutions, financial instruments and terms, people, and historical events. It will be a welcome addition to business and general reference collections and relevant special libraries.

Source materials for the entries derive from information supplied by exchanges and regulatory bodies as well as secondary sources. Major banks, brokerages, and other players in markets are also covered, as are commodity and other related markets and international bodies like the International Monetary Fund (IMF). The main text covers 1,191 double-column pages. Alphabetic entries range from a paragraph to more than 15 pages. Estimating from the entry list, there seem to be about 1,800 headings. Stock markets are listed under the country where they are located. Under Canada, for example, there are extensive listings for four stock exchanges—Toronto, Alberta,

Vancouver, and Montreal—including directory information, listing requirements, brokerages, and more. A few major stock exchanges have *see* references from their names, but most do not. Commodity and other non-stock exchanges are listed under their name and under the country heading. Entries range broadly, from people like George Soros or Nick Leeson through specific instruments on Italian exchanges, banking in the ancient world, chaos theory, and scandals to NAFTA and Dresdner Bank. The selection of topics is eclectic and interesting, including such topics as the Japanese organized crime organization, the Yakuza.

In addition to the alphabetic sequence, there are a number of access points besides the list of headings and contents. These include *see also* references in articles and an index. The index has some quirks. It does not include page references for main entries. For example, in the index under "Galbraith, John Kenneth," only other references to him, not the actual article, are cited. The first appendix is an essay on emerging markets. The second provides a world currencies listing (from Afghanistan through Zimbabwe) with the name of the main unit, its abbreviation, and the number of subunits (e.g., 1 pound sterling is 100 pence). An annotated bibliography concludes the work.

This encyclopedia belongs in all major business and economics reference collections. It would be a useful acquisition for appropriate special libraries, individuals in financial services, and smaller libraries where funds and needs warrant. [R: BL, June 99, p. 1881; Choice, Sept 99, p. 119; RUSQ, Fall 99, pp. 93-94]—**Nigel Tappin**

118.   Madlem, Peter W., and Thomas K. Sykes. **International Encyclopedia of Mutual Funds, Closed-End Funds and REITs.** library ed. Chicago, Fitzroy Dearborn, 2000. 367p. index. $65.00. ISBN 1-57958-086-6.

This volume captures a great deal of useful information about mutual funds, closed-end funds, and real estate investment trusts (or REITs). The introductory section gives an informative overview of mutual funds and explains how they issue shares and the various charges that accompany this type of security. Although the authors indicate that load-mutual funds with front-end charges generally do not outperform no-load funds, they are remiss in not stressing the point. The main body of the volume is devoted to tables, which provide information about the various categories of mutual funds. These tables provide the following information: symbol, year offered, manager, tenure, objective, net assets, minimum purchase, maximum sales charge, expense ratio, total return in percent over the last 5 years, yield, beta, alpha index, value, $10,000 invested 10 years ago, and telephone number. This information is furnished for 8 diversified common stock categories, 12 bond and preferred stock categories, and 12 closed-end fund categories. The final section deals with the least known type of investment vehicle, the real estate investment trust. A comprehensive index is furnished to guide the reader to the relevant statistical page. The *International Encyclopedia of Mutual Funds, Close-End Funds and REITs* will find a useful place on the reference shelf as a frontline locator of mutual fund information. A more comprehensive analysis of fund categories, especially performance figures, can only be gleaned through the use of comprehensive Web-based sites, such as *Morning Star*. This work is recommended for academic libraries and business collections in large public libraries.—**Arthur P. Young**

119.   Scott, David L. **Wall Street Words: An Essential A to Z Guide for Today's Investor.** rev. ed. New York, Houghton Mifflin, 1997. 433p. $12.00pa. ISBN 0-395-85392-3.

Since Scott's original dictionary (see ARBA 89, entry 193) was published a decade ago, the Dow Jones has risen 400 percent and many new instruments have appeared. In particular, the derivatives field has exploded. Three hundred new entries have been added to the 3,600 terms in the original edition. Even though some of the newer areas of interest such as inflation-indexed securities and PCS options are absent, this work seems to be the most comprehensive and timely investments dictionary available. By scanning standard professional and popular business serials for terms, Scott clearly defines in simple language most words that an investor would encounter. Although the focus is on investment terminology, the basics of accounting and economics are also treated. Acronyms are cross-referenced to their full terms. In the last few years, a number of similar titles by different authors have appeared. A major competitor is Richard Maturie's *Wall Street Words: From Annuities to Zero Coupon Bonds* (Probus, 1995). Maturi's guide includes more detailed definitions and textbook examples; the drawback is that his work defines about one-sixth the number of terms that Scott's does.

Practical investment tips from industry insiders are sprinkled throughout the guide. In addition, more than 60 case studies help to give the reader real-life examples of the terminology. The book concludes with nearly five pages of technical analysis chart patterns.

The sheer number of clearly defined terms coupled with its low cost make Scott's dictionary a must for all business reference collections.—**Bobray Bordelon**

120.   Shook, R. J. **Wall Street Dictionary.** Franklin Lakes, N.J., Career Press, 1999. 506p. $11.99pa. ISBN 1-56414-402-X.

This is a necessary reference book in any library's collection. Shook has written a complete reference tool for those interested in the definitions of basic to advanced financial terms. Recommended for anyone in need of a reference tool on financial terms.

However, this book is not recommended for financial analysts or special libraries in businesses. This is not a good reference tool for patrons who need complete and detailed explanations of financial terms. Shook's description of terms is frequently short and sometimes inaccurate. Definitions of some terms are no more than a few words. For example, "interest" is defined as "the amount of money a lender loans a borrower to pay for using the borrower's principal." What the author means is that interest is the amount of money a borrower pays to use a lender's principal. It is also the amount of money a lender or bank patron receives for loaning money to a borrower or a bank. "Intangible cost" is defined as "a business cost that is tax deductible." In fact, intangible cost are costs that are difficult to define, such as employee productivity. Finally, many economists would disagree with Shook's definition of the Friedman Theory. Most economists would define the Friedman Theory as a theory of how the money supply influences long-term inflation rates and, while it may have short-term impacts on a country's economy, the money supply has little to do with a country's economic condition in the long term.

More than 5,000 terms are defined in this text. Overall it is a good text for beginning business students or the general population interested in business terms. However, some terms are not fully defined or are misrepresented. This is unfortunate for a reference text that patrons rely on to provide complete and accurate information. [R: LJ, 1 May 99, p. 70]—**Bruce Kingma**

121.   **The Topline Encyclopedia of Historical Charts.** March 1997 ed. Boulder, Colo., Topline Investment Graphics, 1997. 30v. index. $249.00/set looseleaf w/binders.

The Topline Encyclopedia is a 3-binder work comprising 30 sets of charts. The sets may be ordered in any combination at a lower price. Each set consists of 12 charts focusing on a particular variable or data series of interest to investors. These range from economic measures, such as interest rates and consumer prices in various countries, to foreign currency exchange rates, stock indexes, bonds, commodities, precious metals, and more. Each of the 30 sets begins with a detailed explanation of what the chart represents and how the underlying data were obtained and computed. The charts are printed on heavy paper and sold in looseleaf binders for easy copying. The publisher permits unlimited copying of all charts.

For investors and analysts looking for graphic presentations of investment data, this publication is a bonanza the likes of which will not be found elsewhere. Two things would make the encyclopedia even more valuable: presentation of the charts in machine-readable format and inclusion of the underlying data. The publisher maintains that the paper format allows much greater precision than machine-readable formats, and presumably licensing issues may preclude publication of the data. These considerations aside, *The Topline Encyclopedia* will be of real value to investors who want to go beyond tips and newsletters to take a careful, historical look at markets and the variables that impact them.

The publisher has long provided custom charts drawn to order. This publication makes the most commonly requested charts available at a reasonable price. The set is recommended for libraries serving investors, with one caveat—some of the included charts are, arguably, rather esoteric (e.g., Coppock Curves and the McClellan Oscillator), even for relatively sophisticated investors. Some purchasers may want to select a subset of the charts at a lower price.—**Christopher J. Hoeppner**

DIRECTORIES

122.   Bond, Robert E. Thompson, Nicole, ed. **Bond's Franchise Guide, 2001.** 13th ed. Oakland, Calif., Source Book Publications; distr., Emeryville, Calif., Publishers Group West, 2001. 506p. index. $29.95pa. ISBN 1-887137-27-0.

Buying a franchise is a major commitment, involving both time and money. Before selecting a franchise to buy it is essential to locate information about the industry, the franchiser, and what is involved when the franchise agreement is signed. *Bond's Franchise Guide* is designed to provide help in the evaluation process involved in selecting and purchasing a franchise. The guide is designed "to assist in the evaluation phase of the equation: to provide accurate, in-depth data on the many legitimate companies actively selling franchises" (p. 3).

Bond's Franchise Guide provides data on more than 2,150 franchising opportunities and features an in-depth profile on more than 1,000 of these franchises. The in-depth profiles contain a brief description of the franchise, the date it was established, if it is a member of the International Franchise Association, required cash investment, support and training provided, specific expansion plans, projected new units, company contact, Website address, mailing address, and telephone and fax numbers. The shorter entries provide name, address, telephone number, and contact person. Franchises are listed within industry categories. An alphabetic index of franchisers is provided as well.

In addition to its directory section, *Bond's Franchise Guide* contains "30 Minute Overview," an introduction to franchising including definitions of key terms; "How to Use the Data" (which explains how to interpret directory information); "Recommended Reading" (which features an annotated listing of recent books about franchising); "Annual Franchising Industry Overview" (which contains statistical data by industry as of January 1, 2001); and "Franchiser Questionnaire" (which was filled out by officers of establishments listed in the directory). Sorting through the maze of information about franchises is a challenging task. *Bond's Franchise Guide* is a helpful guide for anyone interested in setting up a franchise and deciding which one to purchase. This guide is recommended to reference collections in both academic and public libraries.—**Lucy Heckman**

123.   **Bond's Minority Franchise Guide.** 2000 ed. Robert E. Bond and Nicole Thompson, eds. Oakland, Calif., Source Book Publications, 2000. 268p. index. $19.95pa. ISBN 1-887137-16-5.

Bond's Minority Franchise Guide is intended to expose minorities to business opportunities in the area of franchising. This book features some 400 franchises that actively support recruiting minorities into their business. The book is divided into 39 business categories, which include everything from automotive services and financial services to food services and retail. The information gathered for this book was acquired from a questionnaire issued to franchises throughout the United States. The book provides the company name, address, and telephone and fax numbers; a description of the business; the background of the business (e.g., date established, a breakdown of what percentage of the franchises are owned by which minorities); a brief financial record and terms of the franchise contract; a description of the support and training provided; and any future plans for the franchise to expand. Each franchise receives only about one-third of a page for explanation, which will require an interested party to do further research. Along with the descriptions of the franchise opportunities, this book also offers advice on how to most effectively use the data, recommended readings for those interested in pursuing this career path, advice from the seven corporate sponsors, resources for minority investors, and a sample of the questionnaire.

This directory will be well received in public libraries that serve minority clientele. The book is easy to understand and will answer many preliminary questions that patrons pursuing this type of career will need to know.—**Shannon Graff Hysell**

124. Dauphinais, Marc. **The Incredible Internet Guide to Online Investing & Money Management.** Tempe, Ariz., Facts on Demand Press, 2000. 362p. (The Incredible Internet Guide). $17.95pa. ISBN 1-889150-16-9.

The Incredible Internet Guide to Online Investing & Money Management delivers all that its title promises—a comprehensive guide to managing personal finances via the Internet. Roughly two-thirds of the book lists Internet sites by topic. The remaining pages provide alphabetized profiles of key sites. A brief but adequate introduction offers practical suggestions on accessing Websites. Topics range from broad overviews on such concepts as world financial markets to stock selection and bond markets. There are sites for all levels of experience and expertise, from beginner to those who are more advanced. While most of the included sites are directed toward buying securities and commodity futures via the Internet, a generous number of sites deal with money management (e.g., debt, mortgage, credit, financial planning, retirement, education, tax planning, estate planning, insurance, online banking). This useful book provides a convenient, economical, and user-friendly reference for personal financial management via the Internet—in many cases the information is free. Hopefully, the author will consider future revisions, since new sites are being developed, old sites are withdrawn, and Web addresses change.—**William C. Struning**

125. **Directory of Alternative Investment Programs.** 1998 ed. Steven P. Galante and Keith W. Moore, eds. Wellesley, Mass., Asset Alternatives, 1998. 552p. index. $495.00pa. (w/software); $395.00pa. ISBN 0-9652137-7-3.

Institutional investors, and to a far lesser extent a catch-all category called other investors, invest small portions of their assets in the alternative investment field as a long-term investment strategy. Institutional investors consist of pension funds (both public and corporate), endowments and foundations, banks, finance companies, and insurance companies. The type of alternative investments these investors make varies, including private equity, natural resources, managed futures, hedge funds, and options. Alternative investments are discussed in much detail by authorities in the field in an introductory "Articles" section in this directory. The alternative investments field naturally has many different players ranging from advisors and placement agents to the investors themselves. The remainder of the directory is devoted to these players. One part is a directory of advisors and agents, another a directory of close to 600 institutional investors broken down by category. Still another part analyzes and ranks the assets (and allocations of those assets) of the investors. The final part consists of five useful indexes to the entire directory.

The *Directory of Alternative Investment Programs* is a unique source. It is a companion volume to *Galante's Venture Capital & Private Equity Directory* (see entries 253 and 254), a directory of fund managers who put the institutional capital to work. The *Directory of Alternative Investment Programs* is a required purchase for the libraries of all institutional investors who either invest or intend to invest in the alternative field. It should also be acquired for the business collections of large public libraries as well as large academic libraries.—**Dene L. Clark**

126.   **Directory of Companies Offering Dividend Reinvestment Plans.** 14th ed. Sumie Kinoshita, ed. Laurel, Md., Evergreen Enterprises, 1997. 140p. $32.95pa. ISBN 0-933183-23-2.

Dividend reinvestment plans (DRPs) allow investors receiving dividends to acquire additional shares in the dividend-paying company rather than receiving the amounts in cash. This directory, now in its 14th edition (see ARBA 90, entry 203, for a review of an earlier edition), lists more than 900 companies offering such plans. In addition to contact information, each entry lists the ticker symbol and primary exchange where the company's stock is traded. Costs, eligibility requirements, and minimum and maximum limits on cash purchases, along with other operational details, are also noted. A separate section lists companies based outside the United States that offer American Depositary Receipts (ADRs) in the U.S. market and have DRPs.

In order to participate in a DRP, an investor must first purchase stock in the company. Historically, this has required the use of a broker. In recent years, however, a growing number of companies have taken advantage of a change in federal securities law to offer their stock for sale directly to the public. An appendix provides a list of such companies, accompanied by lists of companies offering individual retirement arrangements and companies offering discounts on shares purchased through a DRP. A bibliography is also included.

Since their origins 30 years ago, dividend reinvestment plans have grown in numbers and in popularity among investors as a low cost way to accumulate shares in publicly traded companies. It should be noted that much of the information included in this directory is freely available via the World Wide Web through such sites as Netstock Direct (www.netstockdirect.com) and the DRP Club (www.cris.com/~Drpclub). However, if a printed directory is desired, this volume is a worthwhile addition to collections serving investors.—**Christopher J. Hoeppner**

127.   **Directory of Companies Required to File Annual Reports with the Securities and Exchange Commission, 1997.** Baton Rouge, La., Claitor's Publishing Division, 1998. 572p. $43.00pa. ISBN 1-57980-189-7.

This directory's coverage is apparent in its title. Approximately 13,000 companies are required to provide annual filings to the Securities and Exchange Commission (SEC). The body of the directory lists these companies alphabetically. The only other items of information provided are the SEC's docket number for the company, the month in which the company's fiscal year ends, and an industry code based on the 1987 Standard Industrial Classification Manual. Codes are assigned based on the major product or service activity of the company as determined from its SEC filings, and the directory's introduction acknowledges that it may "appear to be somewhat subjective" in the case of enterprises with various products or services. A separate section of the directory lists all companies under their respective industry classifications.

This inexpensive directory has long been a mainstay in business collections. In today's environment, however, it is a less important holding than in the past. The SEC now promptly makes public company filings accessible via the EDGAR database at its World Wide Web site, so a user can readily ascertain a company's status as public and the nature of its business in this manner. In addition, of course, many directories from commercial publishers provide more information about public companies than is available in this directory.—**Christopher J. Hoeppner**

128.   **The 100 Best Mutual Funds You Can Buy 2002.** 12th ed. By Gordon K. Williamson. Holbrook, Mass., Adams Publishing, 2002. 310p. index. $12.95pa. ISBN 1-58062-535-5.

129.   **The 100 Best Stocks You Can Buy 2002.** 6th ed. By John Slatter. Holbrook, Mass., Adams Publishing, 2001. 367p. $12.95pa. ISBN 1-58062-536-3.

Williamson's book is now in its 12th edition, while Slatter's is in its 6th, each providing the beginning and veteran investor with a wealth of information regarding possible strategies for redirection of assets. Both authors clearly demonstrate strong backgrounds in investment finance and a vast knowledge of the subjects being treated; and both works are fairly straightforward, using a language that will not lose the average reader or investor. Williamson's treatment of mutual funds is serious, apt, and to the point. Introductory chapters provide guidance in how to use the information presented. The author assumes no base knowledge on the part of the reader, and so begins with brief information regarding what mutual funds are and how they operate, an explanation of categories of funds and fund features, commonly asked questions, and a rationale for the 100 funds selected for this edition. The remainder of the volume profiles each fund under broad categories: aggressive growth, balanced, corporate bond, global equity, government bond, growth, growth and income, health, high yield, metals and natural resources, money market, municipal bond, technology, utility stock, and world bond. Entries for each fund provide directory/contact information (including Web address) and brief treatments of total return performance, risk/volatility, management, expenses, and a summary statement and profile. Fifteen succinct appendixes provide tips and additional information for particular aspects of investing in mutual funds. A brief index is also provided.

Slatter's treatment of stocks is similar in structure of information. Eight introductory chapters review basic terminology, investment strategies, rationales, mistakes, and so on. These chapters are followed by alphabetically arranged profiles of individual stocks. Each profile provides directory and contact information; stock symbol and external rating; a brief overview, history, and company profile; shortcomings to bear in mind; reasons to buy; and a summary financial sheet. Stocks are graded in four categories: income, growth and income, conservative growth, and aggressive growth. There are no appendices and no index. Slatter injects some humor throughout, with a tongue-in-cheek quality that escapes explanation.

For their summary information and the expertise of their authors, both titles are recommended for public and academic libraries. They will assist many potential investors in better understanding the scope of personal finance options.—**Edmund F. SantaVicca**

130.   Robertson, Malcolm J. **The Directory of Listed Derivative Contracts 1996/97.** New York, John Wiley, 1996. 366p. $150.00. ISBN 0-471-96368-2.

Financial researchers often need to know the markets in which an option or future is traded. Although other directories provide exchange listings and products, this work goes a step further by providing not only details about the exchange and its contracts but by including an index of contracts. An international view of the markets for a product is easily obtainable. This biennial directory covers more than 850 contracts traded on 90 exchanges in 40 countries. Individual options on equities are not listed. Because of the exponential growth in the number of contracts, this is a snapshot. Each exchange listing includes standard directory data, trading methods, key exchange methods, key exchange personnel, and an alphabetic list of contracts traded. The contract specifications detail contract size, delivery format, trading months and hours, quotation method, value, daily price limit, position limit, last trading day, and delivery day. For options, type and strike price interval are also given. The directory's easy-to-use format, detailed content, and unique indexing make it an essential tool for any reference collection serving investors or financial researchers.
—**Bobray Bordelon**

131.   **Standard & Poor's SmallCap 600 Guide.** 1996 ed. By Standard & Poor's. New York, McGraw-Hill, 1996. 1053p. $24.95pa. ISBN 0-07-052155-7.

This guide, now in its 2d annual edition, provides investment advisory reports on the 600 companies that compose the Standard & Poor's SmallCap Index. As a group, they typify the universe of 4,800-plus small market capitalization companies and thereby serve as a benchmark against which to measure a small cap mutual fund or company's stock performance. The companies' market caps range from less than $100 million to more than $3 billion, and average $400 million. The industrial, utility, transportation, service, and financial sectors are all represented, as are the 3 major exchanges—276 from the New York Stock Exchange, 18 from the American Stock Exchange, and 306 from NASDAQ.

SmallCap 600 Guide draws 509 reports from the *Standard & Poor's Stock Reports* and 91 from the now-ceased *Standard & Poor's NASDAQ & Regional Profiles*. "Stock Reports" and "Profiles" are arranged alphabetically in separate sections. Each informative, two-page stock report contains a business description; an analysis of recent financial and stock market performance; a summary of important developments; stock performance data and a chart of price movements; earnings, dividend, and balance sheet data; and S&P's quantitative and qualitative measures. Profiles are only one-third of a page and contain a brief business description and stock and financial data. Presumably the stock reports will replace these profiles in the next edition.

Comparison of the work under review was made with well-known investment advisory tools. More than 30 percent of its companies are among those 1,600 covered by the combined *Moody's Handbook of Common Stocks* (see ARBA 93, entry 223) and *Moody's Handbook of NASDAQ Stocks* (Moody's Investors Service). Slightly more than 90 percent (reviewer's conservative estimate) of the guide's companies are among those 3,500 covered by the combined *Value Line Investment Survey, Standard Edition*, and the *Expanded Edition* (Value Line). The Value Line *Standard Edition*'s one-page reports supply more years of data but shorter business descriptions than the *SmallCap*'s stock reports. The Value Line *Expanded Edition*'s one-page reports have relatively little of *SmallCap*'s narrative financial assessment.

The decision to purchase this guide is complex. *SmallCap* is a subset of the *Standard & Poor's Stock Reports*, an expensive service, whose 3 parts cover more than 4,700 companies, with reports revised 3 or 4 times per year. Libraries subscribing to the full set of the *Stock Reports* would gain no coverage with this guide. Those who do not subscribe may find *SmallCap* and its companions, the *Standard & Poor's 500 Guide* (see ARBA 96, entry 214) and the *Standard & Poor's MidCap 400 Guide* (see ARBA 96, entry 215), which collectively cover 1,500 companies, an inexpensive alternative, if they do not mind the merely annual updating. The Value Line title extensively duplicates *SmallCap*'s company coverage and revises reports four times per year. However, libraries subscribing to it, and unable to afford the *Stock Reports*, may find the guide's different emphasis in report content complementary. Libraries owning only the Moody's handbooks would find this guide's added company coverage and report content valuable.—**John Lewis Campbell**

132.   Szuprowicz, Bohdan O. **Online Stockbrokers Directory.** Nyack, N.Y., Todd Publications, 2001. 121p. $50.00pa. ISBN 0-915344-93-9.

Szuprowicz's *Online Stockbrokers Directory* lists more than 100 online brokers. The author takes a minimalist approach, devoting a single page to each broker with no evaluation. Apparently most of the information was gathered from the online broker's Website. For each broker the following information is provided when available: URL; address; telephone number; initial requirements for establishing an account; commissions on stocks, bonds, and mutual funds; margin rates; availability of IPOs; wireless access; after hours trading; incentives; research support; cash balances; and other services. The profiles conclude with a few additional remarks about the broker. The value of this directory is questionable. Although the editor does provide a good introduction to the elements to assess when evaluating online brokers the information provided about the brokers is both limited and dated. There is no evaluative information or rankings to assist in choosing a broker.

There are many resources freely available on the Internet that can help the self-directed investor choose an online broker. Suggested sites for rankings and comparisons of online brokers include Gomez.com (http://www.gomez.com), Money (http://www.money.com), About—The Human Internet (http://onlinebrokerage. about.com/), CyberInvest (http://www.cyberinvest.com), and SmartMoney (http://www.smartmoney.com/). Brokers evaluated on these sites tend to be the more reputable, established firms but they do include a generous number of discounters. Gomez Advisors is a respected, independent consulting firm. Their Website enables side-by-side comparisons of any 2 selected brokers among the 30 that they review. Money has an annual feature ranking the top 24 online brokers. SmartMoney also has an annual survey. About offers a wonderfully detailed guide to online brokerage, including rankings from a variety of sources. CyberInvest has a brokerage center with an alphabetic listing of brokers with key details and a ranking of the top 20.—**Peter Zachary McKay**

133. Walden, Gene. **The 100 Best Stocks to Own in America.** 5th ed. Chicago, Dearborn Financial Publishing, 1998. 383p. index. $22.95pa. ISBN 0-7931-2574-X.

The author recommends using this list of the best stocks to select 10 to 12 companies to study further by requesting annual reports directly and visiting the public library to look up recent articles about the companies and read the latest *Value Line Investment Survey* and *Standard & Poor's Stock Reports.* Walden suggests monitoring the trading ranges for each stock and selecting the four or five that appear to be the best values. He recommends buying and holding a small number of companies, taking advantage of dividend reinvestment and stock purchase plans. Today, of course, one can also visit one or more of the many Internet sites focusing on investments, such as Hoovers Online at http://www.hoovers.com or Quicken.com at http://www.quicken.com.

To select the list, he screened approximately 2,000 major U.S. companies. The primary criteria for selecting companies was record of growth in earnings per share. He also considered revenue growth, stock price performance, and dividend yield. He rated his selected companies by ranking them using 6 categories: earnings per share growth, stock growth, dividend yield, dividend growth, consistency, and shareholder perks. The author sells a twice-yearly newsletter for $12.95 that follows the stocks. Each company report contains the company's name, address, telephone number, ticker symbol, top officers, a chart showing the ratings for each category, a narrative profile of the company, details regarding the rankings, a table listing key financial and market performance data, and a stock chart. Walden's top five picks are Medtronic, Fannie Mae, Gillette, Norwest, and Schering-Plough.

Waldon's approach to stock market investing concentrates solely on individual large company growth stocks with established records. He completely leaves out value stocks, small stocks, newer companies, and international companies. Mutual funds offer an attractive complementary or alternative approach that reduces the risk of stock market investing through greater diversification. As he points out, only 29 companies made his best 100 lists in each of the five editions of his book.—**Peter Zachary McKay**

134. **Walker's Manual of Penny Stocks.** Harry K. Eisenberg, ed. Lafayette, Calif., Walker's Manual, 1998. 500p. index. $45.00pa. ISBN 0-9652088-3-4pa.

Eisenberg, editor of this and other resources for investors such as *Walker's Manual of Community Bank Stocks* (see entry 192) and *Walker's Manual of Unlisted Stocks* (3d ed.; see entry 135), has set out to dispel some of the myths of penny stock investments, such as their high-risk speculative nature and their potential to swindle investors who purchase stocks. Eisenberg's intent is to focus attention on companies that are not well known or that are not followed by institutional investors. In his introduction he notes that he obtained his information from company reports and documents, and that in most cases the information has been audited and filed with governmental agencies. A brief discussion of recent SEC rulings on how stocks are defined and where they are listed helps the reader understand the history and potential investment capabilities of penny stocks. Factors he considered in selecting companies for this manual include profitability, number of employees, longevity and history, financial solvency, and existing revenue stream. Eisenberg also warns the beginning investor to be conservative and to do the research necessary to evaluate potential investment possibilities. A glossary aids the new investor by explaining the terminology of investing and how figures are derived.

There are 500 company profiles, arranged alphabetically, following the introduction. The information is presented in an easy-to-follow chart, and contains information organized into 2 sections. "Per Share Information" includes stock price, earnings and dividends per share, and price/earnings ratio; "Annual Financial Data" includes operating results, balance sheet and performance, and financial condition. A brief one-paragraph company description introduces the data, and a paragraph of comments explains the data. For example, a comment will explain why a stock has behaved in a certain way, what the market situation is for that company's product, advances or setbacks in research and development, refinancing, or incipient bankruptcies. A list of officers and ownership information, along with pertinent information such as the SIC codes, number of employees, auditor and market maker, and contact information, follows.

This manual is intended for the private investor who may be interested in penny stocks (defined by the SEC as stocks that sell for under $5 per share) but is concerned about possible risk and worried about scams. Aside from the company data (always very useful when investing), Eisenberg's guidelines will assist the beginning investor in understanding financial information and analyzing other companies using similar criteria. This manual is recommended for public libraries with business collections and large reference collections.—**Kerie L. Nickel**

135.   **Walker's Manual of Unlisted Stocks.** San Mateo, Calif., Walker's Western Research, 1996. 513p. index. $75.00. ISBN 0-9652088-9-3.

What is the difference between publicly held companies, whose securities are listed and traded on stock exchanges or markets such as the New York Stock Exchange or the National Association of Securities Dealers Automated Quotation System, and those traded through market makers? Although obvious differences are size and number of shareholders, another difference lies in criteria for listing, which include asset base, number of shares publicly traded, and total market value of traded shares. Some companies choose not to list their shares because of high listing fees, annual and quarterly filing requirements by the Securities and Exchange Commission, public exposure on management decisions, and interference by outside investors.

The companies listed in this title are those either sold on regional exchanges (Boston Exchange, Chicago Exchange, Pacific Stock Exchange [now the Pacific Exchange]) or over-the-counter (either through the online bulletin board or the printed Pink Sheets). The profiles include a company description (name, address, telephone number, and a brief note on the company's business); per-share information (stock price for a given year or period, earnings per share, price/earnings ratio, book value per share, price/book value percentage, and dividends per share); annual financial data; compound growth percentages; comments; officers and ownership information; and other information, including the transfer agent, auditor, market maker, broker dealer, location where the stock is listed, and so on. Historical vignettes on eight companies, including the Kohler Co. and Rand McNally, provide additional information on those firms.

There are several indexes: by company name, by geographic locale, by U.S. state, by Standard Industrial Classification code, by total revenues, by market capitalization, and so forth. The introduction, in addition to explaining the tables, discusses considerations for investors, such as performance, financial strengths, products and markets, and ownership. Public libraries, particularly those serving an investment-minded clientele, and business school libraries will find the work useful. Although there is no indication of how often the book will be updated, a compilation on at least an annual basis would be helpful.—**Sue Kamm**

HANDBOOKS AND YEARBOOKS

136.   **The CRB Commodity Yearbook 2001.** By Bridge Commodity Research Bureau. New York, John Wiley, 2001. 316p. $99.95. ISBN 0-471-41267-8.

Compiled by the Bridge Commodity Research Bureau, this useful handbook is a comprehensive almanac of more than 100 domestic and international commodities and futures markets. It offers practical and contextual descriptions of such things as financial statistics, levels of production, and stockpiles of commodities, along with estimated levels of exports and imports. Data are provided for commodities and futures markets, from aluminum to currencies to interest rates to pork bellies to zinc. These data are provided in more than 900 consistent tables and price charts that are well organized and straightforward and, consequently, this reference book should be accessible and helpful to a variety of users. Since data are provided for the last 10 years, this reference work outlines historical and seasonal trends that can be identified and analyzed.

Along with specific commodities and futures markets, this reference work also includes an analysis of the general movement of the futures market and an analysis of commodity price trends through the Bridge/CRB index. Key issues, events, and policies for commodities and futures markets are outlined, along with statistical tables and charts. These succinctly written and informative summaries are useful in providing a contextual understanding of many of the distinctive policies and market activities that have influenced and are likely to continue to influence the availability and price of these commodities. Reports for specific commodities indicate both the source (supply) and the use (demand) of the commodities and provide hints at the continued use or application of the product. All in all, this is a practical and versatile reference work that will be useful to many users.—**Timothy E. Sullivan**

137.   **Cyberstocks: An Investor's Guide to Internet Companies.** Alan Chai, ed. Austin, Tex., Hoover's, 1996. 408p. index. $24.95pa. ISBN 1-57311-011-6.

The explosive growth of the Internet has created a substantial demand for books in the field. Dozens of books have already been published covering almost every aspect of the Internet. Chai's book, however, is unique. *Cyberstocks* is based on extensive research and is packed with excellent information, yet it is concise and extremely easy to read. The guide is directed to investors, but will appeal to all individuals who want to have a basic understanding of the Internet and the players shaping it.

The book consists of five parts and an index. The first four parts provide a simple, but not oversimplified, overview of the hardware, software, and services offered in the Internet market. The fifth part represents the majority of the book. It profiles some 100 companies participating in the industry. Each company profile consists of a brief history of the company, its products, its strengths and weaknesses, its sales and profits, and its future outlook. Recognizing that the fast rate of change in the industry would soon make the book out-of-date, the publishers launched a free Website in conjunction with the release of the book. The Website is updated regularly and is an excellent companion to the book.

Chai has done an excellent service to the industry. His book is highly recommended to anyone who wants to learn from and profit from the Internet.—**Elie M. Dick**

138.   **The Dow Jones Averages, 1885-1995.** Phyllis S. Pierce, ed. Burr Ridge, Ill., Irwin Professional Publishing, 1996. 1v. (unpaged). $95.00. ISBN 0-7863-0974-1.

Charles Dow was a journalist who in 1884 began figuring stock performance averages on a grouping of 11 issues, mostly railroads. Industrials were separated from railroads in 1896 and the two were issued as separate indexes in the first Dow Jones listing in 1897. The current handbook was published by the company in celebration of its centennial year and as an affirmation of the continued importance and workability of its three major indexes today (industrials, utilities, transportation).

The work is simple in design, beginning with a brief introductory segment by an editor of the *Wall Street Journal*, and followed by a comprehensive graph illustrating the monthly averages for a period of 50 years, 1940 to 1990. Five separate graphs then cover the years 1991 to 1995. A chronology dating from July 3, 1884 (Dow's first publication), then traces all changes, additions, replacements, and the like, of all stocks used in each of the indexes, culminating with a 2 for 1 split of International Paper Company on September 18, 1995. The remainder of this large volume is then given to yearly and monthly charts providing daily averages, along with highs and lows for each month from 1885 to 1985.

Primarily for historians or those who love the market, the work offers the most detailed listings to date and provides awareness of such dates as the introduction of stocks not on the New York Stock Exchange and the year that transportation replaced the railroad index. The author is a professional writer with Dow Jones and has served as editor of *Irwin Investor's Handbook* (Irwin Professional Publishing) since 1977.—**Ron Blazek**

139.   **Handbook of North American Stock Exchanges.** 1997 ed. Austin, Tex., Meridian Securities Markets, 1997. 149p. $95.00pa. ISBN 0-9648930-9-6.

The *Handbook of North American Stock Exchanges* provides valuable directory and statistical information for the American Stock Exchange, Mexican Stock Exchange, Montreal Stock Exchange, NASDAQ Stock Exchange, New York Stock Exchange, and Toronto Stock Exchange. Each entry includes name, address, telephone and fax numbers, listing requirements, regulatory agency (e.g., Securities and Exchange Commission), foreign investors, commissions and fees, disclosure requirements, and investor protection information. Directory information, however, does not include Website information for the exchanges; only URLs for regulatory agencies are provided. The publisher should consider listing of Website information in future editions.

Among statistics provided are number of listed companies, market capitalization, share trading, Dow Jones Industrial Average, and top stocks by trading volume. In most cases, statistics presented cover the years 1975 through 1996. Stocks are also ranked by such indicators as trading value, trading volume, price-earnings ratio, dividend yield, and market capitalization. The appendix provides a guide to the calculation of indexes and other performance measures as well as formulas. Data were obtained from the exchanges represented.

The *Handbook of North American Stock Exchanges* is a useful guide that provides a starting point for researching the various exchanges and stock performance. The publisher should consider adding a brief bibliography of additional resources, including citations, for the various publications by each exchange as well as the annual handbooks and other publications. This source is recommended to academic and public library business collections.—**Lucy Heckman**

140.   **Handbook of World Stock Indices.** 1997 ed. Austin, Tex., Meridian Securities Markets, 1997. 434p. $125.00pa. ISBN 0-9648930-5-3.

During the past few years, several directories listing international stock exchanges have appeared. *The Handbook of World Stock and Commodity Exchanges* (see ARBA 93, entry 222) is the most useful for a comprehensive listing of exchanges along with their histories. *The International Guide to Securities Market Indices* (see entry 149) offers the most extensive computational methodology as well as information on a wide range of security instruments.

Handbook of World Stock Indices covers 47 stock exchanges in 42 countries. Arrangement is alphabetic by the name of the exchange; a country index is not provided. Generally 20 years of data chronicles the exchange's monthly high, low, close, and averages. All data were obtained from the stock exchange itself unless otherwise noted. A useful feature is the methodology used to calculate each index along with the number of companies and stocks listed on each exchange. A further breakdown by domestic versus foreign is provided along with number of shares outstanding. A market capitalization profile of each market by industry is also given. Constituent lists are selectively listed.

This work is a subset of another publication, *World Stock Exchange Fact Book* (see entry 155). The fuller version is arranged alphabetically by country and contains additional information on disclosure requirements, restrictions to foreign investors, investor protection, and mergers and acquisitions. The "subset" does provide more data on the number of listed companies—20 years versus 5 years. The most substantial difference is in price: $295 for the *World Stock Exchange Fact Book* as opposed to $125 for this work. Given that most regulatory information can be found on the stock exchange's homepages, this work is clearly the better buy. One will not obtain the comprehensive data available in online services such as Datastream International. The World Wide Web can be hit or miss for data and is typically not archived. This work is an inexpensive means of obtaining summary data in one permanent place.—**Bobray Bordelon**

141. **"How Much Can I Make?" Actual Sales and Profit Potential for Your Small Business.** 2d ed. Genevieve Graves and Minjia Qiu, eds. Oakland, Calif., Source Book Publications, 1997. 446p. index. $29.95pa. ISBN 1-887137-10-6.

This is the 2d edition of a book previously published under the title *Franchising: The Bottom Line*. The body of the work comprises earnings claim statements from 167 franchisers. These statements are financial information presented to prospective investors by franchisers based on the results of franchisees currently in operation. A detailed company profile accompanies each statement. The introductory section offers the authors' commentary on how to critically evaluate an earnings claim statement and worksheets for use in this evaluation, plus an overview essay and annotated bibliography about the franchising industry. Indexes, both alphabetic and by industry, complete the volume.

The author has written extensively about the franchising industry for many years and this work can be thought of as a complement to his *Bond's Franchise Guide* (see entry 122). The *Guide* offers less extensive information on more than 2,300 franchise opportunities, whereas *"How Much Can I Make?"* provides much greater detail on only a fraction of that number. Thus, it is less a directory than a detailed presentation of the type of information an investor needs to consider before making an intelligent decision about pursuing a business opportunity. Even for investors who are not interested in a specific franchiser represented here, it would still be wise to examine others in the same industry for comparative purposes. Also, entrepreneurs who are interested in independently starting a small business that will compete with franchises in a particular industry will be well-advised to consult this book for insights into the economics of their chosen field. This book is recommended for collections serving entrepreneurs and small business owners.—**Christopher J. Hoeppner**

142. Maturi, Richard J. **The 105 Best Investments for the 21st Century.** New York, McGraw-Hill, 1995. 277p. illus. index. $22.95. ISBN 0-07-040939-0.

Maturi, author of five previous investment books and publisher of three investment newsletters, believes the world is changing so fast one must continually evaluate an investment portfolio. Taking the approach that there are no more blue-chip investments, and one can no longer successfully buy and hold stocks for years at a time in light of changes in the global economy, Maturi has listed the investments he feels will be good performers into the twenty-first century.

The investments are categorized into chapters covering stocks, American Depository Receipts, mutual funds, real estate, precious metals, oil and gas, coins, cars, and other collectibles. Each chapter includes an introductory passage giving an overview of the subject, reasons supporting the investment, and occasionally a few caveats. Most of the entries for the 105 recommended investments have brief sections providing an industry review, company profile, description of management talent, financial status, dividend reinvestment plan details, particular strengths of the company, financial statistics, and a final assessment of the investment.

Each of the investment profiles is easily read and understood by the average investor, making this title a useful addition to circulating collections. The book will also appeal to those unaccustomed to monitoring changes in the international, political, and economic environments, and to those seeking to diversify their investments. A glossary and index are included.—**Barbara E. Clotfelter**

143.   **Morningstar Mutual Fund 500.** 1997-98 ed. Betsy Grace and others, eds. Chicago, Morningstar; distr., Burr Ridge, Ill., Irwin Professional Publishing, 1998. 606p. index. $35.00pa. ISBN 0-7863-1090-1.

Since 1984, Morningstar has established itself as one of the most trusted and quoted sources on the mutual funds industry. Today, most business publications regularly feature lists of the top performing or the largest mutual funds. Morningstar has taken a different approach by profiling a wide range of investment choices intended to allow the investor to assemble a portfolio. The principles of successful investing, assembly of a portfolio, and an explanation of its famed ratings system are detailed. An annual industry review, performance summaries by broad type, benchmark averages, various rankings, and a summary of manager and mutual fund name changes are also provided. Most of the work consists of full-page profiles of 450 open-end funds and 50 closed-end funds. Each profile features 12 years of annual and 8 years of quarterly data as well as basic risk analysis, operations information, expenses and fees, and composition. The information presented is a combination of narrative, statistical, and evaluative. One of the most useful features is the detailed user's guide. In addition to standard definitions and methodology, warnings are often given about misuses of data and evaluative items.

Even though only a fraction of the mutual funds in existence are included, the most closely followed funds are presented here. Although sources such as *Investment Company Yearbook* (CDA-Wiesenberger, annual) come close to being comprehensive with basic data, few services offer great detail on any but the largest funds. This source is useful and inexpensive for libraries needing coverage of major mutual funds. Like any investment source, one should consult a variety of sources and always have access to the latest data.—**Bobray Bordelon**

144.   **Mutual Fund Sourcebook 2000.** Don Mills, Ont., Southam, 2000. 2v. $350.00pa./set. ISBN 1-55257-049-5.

The *Mutual Fund Sourcebook* contains detailed information on Canadian mutual funds, including cash and equivalent funds, fixed income funds, balanced funds, global sector funds, and equity funds. Data for this publication were provided by the funds in response to data obtained by Fundata Canada (http://www. fundata.com).

Within its two volumes, the source provides a "Group/Fund Index," which lists the name and address of the fund; its telephone, fax, and toll-free numbers; number of funds in the group;

and volume/page in the sourcebook where a profile of the company appears. Also provided are an index (sorted by fund name); list of portfolio management companies, including the company's objectives; directory of portfolio managers, including brief biographies; auditor directory; survey of mutual funds, measuring their comparative performance; and a 17-year table (simple returns year to year).

Following the sections described above are the "Mutual Fund Pages" (or detailed listings) for each company. The "Mutual Fund Pages" have been subdivided into several categories, including Canadian Market Fund, Foreign Money Market, High Yield Bond Funds, Canadian Mortgage Funds, and Global Balanced and Asset Allocation Funds, to name a few. Each "Mutual Fund page" contains the name; address; telephone and fax numbers; year of fund inception; previous name (where applicable); investment objective; investment strategy; biography of portfolio manager; list of fees; portfolio, including top 10 holdings of the company; and performance of fund, including assets and growth. Also provided are listings of the "Top 50 Mutual Funds," "Top 10 Mutual Funds" (by fund type), and standard deviation statistics for companies.

This set is a comprehensive guide to Canadian mutual funds. Because of its concentration on the Canadian market, it should be part of a comprehensive collection in larger research and academic libraries in the United States. It could also be considered for purchase by academic libraries that support curricula that include the Canadian financial history. It should, of course, be added to business collections in Canadian research, public, and academic libraries.—**Lucy Heckman**

145.   **Plunkett's On-Line Trading, Finance, & Investment Web Sites Almanac.** By Jack W. Plunkett. Houston, Tex., Plunkett Research, 2000. 547p. index. $149.99pa. (w/disk). ISBN 1-891775-08-1.

The intent of the publisher is to provide a selective and convenient list of the most useful financial Websites. The almanac contains comparable descriptions for 200 sites that fall into this category. These descriptions comprise the bulk of the work and occupy 451 pages of the works 547 total pages. Some of the sites covered are completely free of charge, while other sites are a mix of free and fee. The remainder of the pages consist of trends, glossaries, and multiple indexes to the to the sites.

The Website descriptions are standard in format and contain a variety of useful information. Besides basic contact and scope information, each entry lists categories of researchers that might find the site useful, such as day traders or finance professionals, and categories of data elements or features contained in the site. Most of the entries are also accompanied by an image of the Website itself.

Several different indexes provide subject access to the 200 sites. Some indexes, like those recommending use by specific groups of professionals, are useful. Others, however, like geographic location of site headquarters, do not add much to the value of the almanac. The volume is accompanied by a diskette database in spreadsheet format that allows the user to manipulate the data.

Given the dynamic nature of Web resources, there are obvious shortcomings with a print directory of Websites. The authors point this out, however, and continually remind researchers to check the sites themselves for the latest developments. The work is aimed at readers with little Internet experience, but more experienced searchers may also find it useful. It is recommended for public and academic libraries.—**Gordon J. Aamot**

146.   **Ranking of World Stock Markets.** 1997 ed. Austin, Tex., Meridian Securities Markets, 1997. 195p. $75.00pa. ISBN 0-9648930-3-7. ISSN 1096-648X.

This quick reference guide ranks 47 stock exchanges from around the world in terms of size, growth, profitability, liquidity, and volatility as well as other performance measures. Five years of data are presented for 19 of the 21 market measures. The tables give monetary amounts in inflation adjusted dollars (1996), and some also give the corresponding foreign currency equivalents in unadjusted (nominal) amounts. The display varies slightly depending on the ranking. For instance, in the "Per Share Traded" table the numbered ranks are followed by the exchange, then the average price per share traded in U.S. 1996 dollars, and finally the notes (e.g., "includes unit trusts" or "includes equity derivatives") .

Each table has a corresponding bar chart on the facing page presenting the same statistical information in graphic form. The 47 markets covered include American, New York, and NASDAQ from the United States along with a good representation of exchanges in Europe (19), Asia/Pacific (11), and Latin America (7). The rankings include number of listed companies, number of listed stocks, capitalization, company size, trades, dividend yield, and year change.

This is an easy, quick, and efficient tool that adds dimension to directories of exchanges. It provides a more complete and comparative picture of the world's most active and influential stock markets. These rankings are straightforward, uncluttered, easy to read, and dramatize the importance of emerging markets. This source is recommended for any library where there is an interest in investing, especially global investing.—**Gerald L. Gill**

147.   Ricchiuto, Steven R., and Barclays de Zoete Wedd Securities. **The Rate Reference Guide to the U.S. Treasury Market 1984-1995.** Burr Ridge, Ill., Irwin Professional Publishing, 1996. 367p. illus. $55.00. ISBN 1-55738-790-7.

The guide begins with a short overview essay and a dozen graphs charting such data series as real gross domestic product, consumer spending, employment, and prices for the period from 1971 through 1995. The book's main body comprises information on market factors affecting interest rates for the 12-year period in the title. This is done at two levels of detail. First, an annual section looks at the period on a year-by-year basis, enumerating important developments, typically 25 to 50 for each year, and cross-referencing each of these to graphs charting the yields on 3-month bills and 30-year bonds issued by the U.S. Treasury. The last and longest section of the book provides even greater detail using a monthly format. Six to twelve developments are listed and charted for each month. Monthly graphs chart the T-bill and long bond yields on a daily basis, and a third graph tracks the spread between these two yields. Finally, a table gives daily yields on Treasury securities of all maturities.

Because Treasury securities are considered risk-free, their yields serve as benchmarks for interest rates in general. Therefore, the behavior of Treasury yields is of great interest to economic and financial analysts. This book's value, unlike that of many reference works, lies not so much in its content as in its organization and presentation. The events reported in the guide all can be found summarized in such sources as business almanacs and investment newsletters. The yield data and other statistics are also readily available. No other source, however, places in such sharp relief the relationship between economic developments and interest rates. This is a highly revelatory work that merits a place in any business or economics collection.—**Christopher J. Hoeppner**

148.   Ryland, Philip. **Pocket Investor.** New York, John Wiley, 1998. 213p. (The Economist Books). $14.95pa. ISBN 0-471-29597-3.

As its name implies, *Pocket Investor* is a compact volume that is loaded with helpful information about the intricate and sometimes baffling subject of investments. It is one of a series of "pocket" books on management from *The Economist*, a long-standing and highly respected journal. The author is the deputy editor of *Investors Chronicle*. The purpose of *Pocket Investor* is to bring clarity to the complexities and jargon of the investment world. It achieves this purpose by providing a wealth of information in a convenient format that is easy to read. A unique aspect of *Pocket Investor* is that it reflects both U.S. and UK terminology.

Pocket Investor is divided into 3 parts. The 1st presents 4 essays on investing: the returns that can be expected from the market; whether excess returns are really possible; lessons from the most successful investors, such as Warren Buffet and Sir John Templeton; and the flaws in conventional stock market wisdom. These essays are concise, informative, and easy to read. A brief 5th essay describes differences in investment terminology between the United States and the United Kingdom. This is helpful because *Pocket Investor* includes information reflecting both countries' systems. The 2d part comprises the bulk of the volume and is a glossary of investment terms. Definitions are generous, sometimes providing a page or more of text. Figures and tables are included, although the content is primarily text. Interspersed throughout the glossary are quotes from famous people, from both within and outside of the financial world. Some of the terms included are quite advanced and reflect the worldwide investment arena, making *Pocket Investor* a unique and important reference source for patrons who need more than just the basics, although basic terms such as *asset* and *common stock* are also covered. Commonly used abbreviations are cross-referenced, as are country-specific terms. The 3d part is devoted to appendixes, with tables on stock and bond returns, market data, investing formulas, accounting terminology differences between the United States and the United Kingdom, and two pages of references of recommended readings. *Pocket Investor* is small enough for a briefcase, yet the typeset is clear and not too small.

In spite of a wealth of other choices, *Pocket Investor* would be a unique and appropriate addition to any public library's reference collection. Information included in *Pocket Investor* is succinct and easy to read, yet still comprehensive enough to reflect the complexity of the investment field. In addition, *Pocket Investor's* inclusion of more global terms is useful in an investment environment that is no longer confined by geography. *Pocket Investor* would also be a good addition to collections supporting academic business programs and in libraries serving banking, investment, accounting, and consulting personnel.—**Sara Anne Hook**

149.   Shilling, Henry. **The International Guide to Securities Market Indices.** Chicago, Fitzroy Dearborn, 1996. 1030p. $125.00. ISBN 1-884964-48-6.

This interesting and worthwhile directory profiles more than 400 international securities indexes. Each profile contains a performance graph and record for the past 10 years, minimum and maximum values, average annual price return and total return, standard deviation, number of issues, market value, selection criteria, base date, computation methodology, deviation instruments, subindexes and related indexes, background, publisher/producer name, and short editorial comments. The introductory material includes common computational formulas, and examples of the math formulas are found in the 187 pages of appendixes. Any variation from the standard formulas is detailed within the particular profile. Other appendixes cover derivative instruments, a glossary, lists by asset size and country, and brief data on an additional 200-plus supplemental securities market indexes (mainly smaller secondary indexes or benchmarks of special interest).

The principal value of the guide is the coverage of how the indexes are computed. Reasonably priced for this type and size of directory, the work is clearly presented and easy to use. *The Handbook of Financial Market Indexes, Averages, and Indicators* (see ARBA 91, entry 171) also reviews major stock indexes but covers fewer and is dated. A WorldCat search found no other recent title covering the topic. The Fitzroy Dearborn guide is highly recommended for academic and larger public library business collections.—**Patrick J. Brunet**

150.   **Standard & Poor's Stock and Bond Guide.** 1998 ed. Frank LoVaglio, ed. New York, McGraw-Hill, 1998. 461p. $22.95pa. ISBN 0-07-052678-8.

This reference provides financial performance indicators for 14,000 stocks, bonds, mutual funds, and annuities using 1997 year-end data. Previous to this publication, detailed Standard & Poor's information was available only on a subscription basis. The book gives 19 key measures for stocks, such as historic and current price ranges, trading volumes, price to earnings ratios, dividend payments, annual earnings, and the Standard & Poor's rankings. The bond guide provides 18 major data elements, such as long-term debt, capitalizations, debt ratings, yields to maturity, and the like.

The introduction effectively shows the reader how to use the statistics to evaluate a security. The Standard & Poor rating system is also explained. Each section of the guide has detailed definitions for all table headings, abbreviations, and footnote terms. It would be helpful if the publisher had included a table of contents. Without it, the user may not realize the full extent of the resource. For example, tucked in between the sections on U.S. stocks and bonds are notations for foreign bonds and a listing of major underwriters with contact telephone numbers. This reference gives the individual investor pragmatic tools to make informed decisions.—**Adrienne Antink Bien**

151. Troy, Leo. **Almanac of Business and Industrial Financial Ratios 1996.** 27th ed. Englewood Cliffs, N.J., Prentice Hall, 1996. 740p. index. $89.95pa. ISBN 0-13-520503-4.

Business students and investors frequently request industry-wide financial data. These data, often represented in the form of established financial ratios, allow the researcher to benchmark a company's financial performance relative to the performance of its competitors. Of the handful of competing publications offering industry ratios, Troy's *Almanac of Business and Industrial Financial Ratios* stands out as particularly easy to use and attractive in its layout.

Ratios are derived from corporate tax return information from the Internal Revenue Service and are organized according to four-digit SIC codes. For each SIC code, data are presented for 37 key measurements of financial health. For each of the 37 items, data are presented globally for all companies in the SIC code. In addition, the same 37 measurements are listed for categories of company size as determined by assets. This feature is particularly helpful for making meaningful comparisons because a company's size will often influence its financial ratios. An additional feature that proves to be particularly useful is a 10-year historical table showing trends for 13 key measurements. These tables provide a long-term perspective that is sometimes difficult to find in financial reference materials.

This book represents a good value for its price and is recommended for medium and large public libraries and academic libraries.—**David Bickford**

152. **Weiss Ratings' Guide to Bond and Money Market Mutual Funds: A Quarterly Compilation of Mutual Fund Ratings and Analysis Covering Fixed Income Funds, Winter 2000-01.** Palm Beach Gardens, Fla., Weiss Rating's, 2001. 417p. $219.00pa. (single copy); $438.00pa. (4 quarterly editions). ISBN 1-58773-004-9. ISSN 1527-7895.

Weiss Ratings' Guide to Bond and Money Market Mutual Funds is a highly respected and widely utilized source for comparing and analyzing fixed income mutual funds. It provides an independent and unbiased guide to managing an individual or a portfolio of funds. Corporate, municipal, and government bond funds are included, as well as money market funds, but not funds with large investments in equities. Ratings are based largely on performance (i.e., return to investors—recent return is emphasized) and assessment of risk. Past performance represents the primary criterion, however, and comparison among funds also plays a role in making evaluations.

In addition, information on net assets and quality and tenure of fund managers, as well as minimum amounts accepted and load charges, is given for each fund. Further details on rating factors are included for the largest bond and money market mutual funds. Since ratings are largely based on past performance, comments contained in the details are helpful in deciding whither the future of a particular fund will follow past trends. Steps are given to assist investors in making evaluations. Those steps include an investor profile quiz and lists of funds indicating top performing, lowest risk and performance by fund type. The rating scale used in the guide is quite easy to use and to understand (A to F, with plus and minus signs).

Some 4,200 funds are included. Updates are available every three months and emphasis is placed on current data in developing evaluations. This is an extremely useful book for investors, or potential investors, in making investment decisions. While ratings can form an important base, past performance should be supplemented by other factors. This guide is highly recommended. **—William C. Struning**

153. Weiss Ratings' Guide to Brokerage Firms: A Quarterly Compilation of Ratings and Analysis Covering the Major U.S. Stock Brokers, Winter 2000-01. Palm Beach Gardens, Fla., Weiss Rating's, 2001. 429p. $219.00pa. (single copy); $438.00pa. (4 quarterly editions). ISBN 1-58773-005-7. ISSN 1532-1835.

This quarterly guide provides ratings for full service, discount, and online brokerage firms. Where a firm offers services in more than one of these arenas, its entry is repeated (with a different description of services offered). Thus, while the total number of entries is approximately 400, the number of firms covered is lower. Each entry provides an overall rating on an A-F scale, as well as specific ratings, on a 10-point scale, that focus on the firm's range, capitalization, leverage, liquidity, and stability. Also included are contact details, two to four years of recent summarized financial results, commission rates on sample trades, and information on the firm's size.

An index lists all firms alphabetically, and an analysis section summarizes key financial data and the Weiss safety rating for the most recent three years for all firms. These sections include listings for specialty firms and firms serving institutional investors that are not given expanded entries in the other sections. An additional section lists contact details for all firms' branch locations by state. Finally, a short section lists recommended firms (i.e., those with ratings of B+ or higher) in each category. Each section begins with explanatory material useful to readers not accustomed to working with data of this kind.

A well-known and respected organization in financial circles, the Weiss firm has been rating financial institutions since the 1970s. In an era when more and more individual investors have become active in the capital markets and an increasing number of investors have chosen to manage their own holdings through discount and online brokerage accounts, the need for a publication of this kind is greater than ever. This reasonably priced guide is recommended for both academic and public libraries serving investors.**—Christopher J. Hoeppner**

154. Weiss Ratings' Guide to Stock Mutual Funds: A Quarterly Compilation of Mutual Fund Ratings and Analysis Covering Equity and Balanced Funds, Winter 2000-01. Palm Beach Gardens, Fla., Weiss Rating's, 2001. 513p. $219.00pa. (single copy); $438.00pa. (4 quarterly editions). ISBN 1-58773-002-2. ISSN 1527-7909.

The *Weiss Ratings' Guide to Stock Mutual Funds* is published quarterly and provides summary information for more than 6,000 mutual funds. Historical information is provided for the 700 largest funds, as well as additional information regarding fund managers, services offered, and rating factors. Other special sections of the guide include the top 200 stock mutual funds, the bottom 200 stock mutual funds, the 100 best and worst stock mutual funds, and the top performing stock mutual funds by both risk category and fund type.

Oriented toward the general investing public, the guide uses a rating scale of "A" through "F." This system, similar to grades received in school, is meant to be familiar and easy to understand. The ratings are based on both past performance and volatility in the fund's monthly returns, and claim to give an unbiased opinion of a mutual fund's risk-adjusted performance. The guide also includes an "Investor Profile Quiz" to help investors assess their investment needs and risk tolerance. The *Weiss Ratings' Guide to Stock Mutual Funds* is owned by hundreds of libraries in the United States and remains a popular personal investment tool. It is recommended for public and academic libraries supporting strong investment programs.—**Gordon J. Aamot**

155.   **World Stock Exchange Fact Book: Historical Securities Data for the International Investor.** Morris Plains, N.J., Electronic Commerce, 1995. 509p. $295.00 spiralbound; $390.00 (w/disk). ISBN 0-9648930-0-2.

The *Fact Book* provides information concerning stock exchanges in 42 countries, arranged in a standard format by country. The compilers indicate that all data have been gathered directly from the exchanges. The information presented is of two types: textual and statistical. The text consists mainly of bulleted lists outlining stock exchange and government regulations and practices with respect to listing and disclosure, investor protection, restrictions on foreign investments, and mergers and acquisitions. Three types of statistical information are presented: data on the exchange itself (annual trading volume and value, market capitalization, price/earnings ratios and dividend yields); data on one or more stock indexes for each exchange (monthly high, low, closing and average values); and national economic data (annual gross domestic product, balance of trade, interest and exchange rates) for each country. Additionally, the book is available with or without a 3.5-inch diskette containing Microsoft Excel spreadsheet files with all of the statistical data.

Various sources of this type are available. What distinguishes the *Fact Book*? In most cases, the work under review covers only the most prominent exchange(s) in each country—for example, in the United States, the New York and American exchanges and the NASDAQ market are covered, but the Chicago, Pacific, and other regional exchanges are not. In most cases, 20 years of statistical data are provided, much more than in other sources of this type. For most stock indexes, the *Fact Book* provides a list of the component stocks classified by industry. An appendix provides details on the various methods for computing stock indexes and other performance measures. Last but not least, the diskette adds significant value by allowing users to craft their own analyses and readily incorporate selected data into documents and presentations. These features combine to make this book a useful resource for academic and securities industry researchers seeking an analytic tool rather than a comprehensive directory of world stock markets. It is recommended for libraries with clientele of these types. [R: Choice, June 96, p. 1625; LJ, Mar 96, p. 64]
—**Christopher J. Hoeppner**

5　Consumer Guides

DICTIONARIES AND ENCYCLOPEDIAS

156.　**Encyclopedia of the Consumer Movement.** Stephen Brobeck, Robert N. Mayer, and Robert O. Herrmann, eds. Santa Barbara, Calif., ABC-CLIO, 1997. 659p. index. $99.50. ISBN 0-87436-987-8.

Most people today take for granted the assumption that consumers are protected by a safety net of federal laws and regulations. The changes in public awareness and public policies that brought about these protections were, in large part, the result of "the consumer movement," ably chronicled in this important new reference work.

The 198 alphabetically arranged entries cover a broad range of consumer-related topics and represent the editors' attempt to summarize what is known about the consumer movement. Each encyclopedia entry is between 1,000 and 5,000 words and written by an expert with either academic or professional experience in the subject matter. The essays fall into 7 subject categories. There are 9 general essays that discuss topics such as "Consumer Problems in Market Economics" and "U.S. Consumer Movement: History and Dynamics." A selection of 7 entries, such as "Children as a Vulnerable Market" and "Immigrants as Consumers" addresses issues of consumer populations. "Consumer Movement Activities" consists of 20 entries and includes essays on "Boycotts, Consumer" and "Whistleblowers." The largest group, with 66 entries, covers government agencies and consumer organizations. Here one finds long articles on such entities as the Food and Drug Administration and Better Business Bureaus. Four entries are devoted to leaders of the consumer movement, including Ralph Nader. The second-largest amount of coverage, with 51 entries, is devoted to consumer protection. These essays fall into the categories of "Health and Safety," "Economic and Financial," and "Marketing" issues. Lastly, there are 41 essays devoted to international consumer movements, though the emphasis is on Europe.

The editors have done a commendable job in planning the content, recruiting the contributors, and organizing the work itself. Readers will appreciate the subject index, listing by broad subject categories, and the alphabetic list of essays. The editors have also added *see also* references that direct readers to related essays and compiled short bibliographies of supplemental readings for each entry. Its relatively modest price of $99.50 makes it even more appealing. This is a useful, affordable reference work that belongs in both academic and public library reference collections and any special library serving an institution with an interest in consumer issues. [R: BL, 1 April 98, pp. 1344-1345]—**Gordon J. Aamot**

DIRECTORIES

157. **The Catalog of Catalogs VI: The Complete Mail-Order Directory.** Edward L. Palder, ed. Bethesda, Md., Woodbine House, 1999. 567p. index. $25.95pa. ISBN 1-890627-08-9.

The 6th edition of this biennial and respected publication of American mail-order companies includes almost 15,000 entries. This is an increase of over 1,000 listings from the previous edition. The reader will find companies listed under 920 subject categories including 70 that are new to this edition, such as tandem bicycles, pasta sauces, totem poles, paintball, and yo-yos. Each listing includes the name of the company, address, a brief description of the product line, telephone number, and e-mail or Internet address. This title will see a lot of use in public library reference departments for those clients attempting to identify buyers for their product lines or suppliers for their stores. Shoppers will also find this a very tempting book to browse through.

This type of publication is never completely comprehensive or accurate since businesses come and go. The choice of subject categories can be debated, but with 920 subject categories, the editor has attempted to be specific in a way that would be useful to consumers.

Because we do hear about fraudulent mail-order operations and companies changing their names or moving, the compiler requests that users inform him of any problems so that they can be addressed in the next edition. The compiler also provides a few tips on how to shop online.—**Judith J. Field**

158. **Consumer Sourcebook.** 15th ed. Sonya D. Hill, ed. Farmington Hills, Mich., Gale, 2002. 1213p. index. $305.00. ISBN 0-7876-5277-4. ISSN 0738-0518.

Consumers should be able to make informed choices and have adequate recourse if products or services prove to be less than satisfactory. The 15th edition of Gale's *Sourcebook* aims to do just that by providing more than 18,000 references to consumer interest, organized into 17 subject chapters, ranging from general consumerism to education, insurance, health care, and utilities. Groups that primarily promote a single product or industry are excluded. This edition was compiled through contact with the agencies, as well as from government publications and Gale databases, and contains more than 5,000 new entries.

Two informative and useful sections precede the main text. "Chapter Descriptions" informs readers of each chapter's scope, issues, and resources, and "Consumer Tips" offers suggestions for each subject chapter. Individual chapters may include these subsections: "Internet Databases," "Government Agencies," "Associations and Organizations," "Publications," "Multimedia Resources," and "Media and Corporate Contacts." Sequentially numbered entries, although necessarily short, supply sufficient data for identification and, often, a brief description. Two appendixes, dealing with hotlines and clearinghouses and testing laboratories, and alphabetic and subject indexes provide additional access.

The two sections preceding the chapters might be even more useful if incorporated into their respective chapters. Otherwise, the comprehensive nature of this directory makes it a valuable reference tool. As comments are welcome, so are future editions, expanded to accommodate growing consumer issues.—**Anita Zutis**

159. **The Directory of Mail Order Catalogs 2001: A Comprehensive Guide to Consumer Mail Order Catalog Companies.** 15th ed. Richard Gottlieb, ed. Lakeville, Conn., Grey House Publishing, 2001. 1550p. index. $275.00; $250.00pa. ISBN 1-891482-97-1; 1-891482-96-3pa.

This guide to mail order catalogs for the consumer is one of a growing number of business directories from Grey House Publishing. The 2001 edition provides entries for more than 10,000 catalogs published within the United States. It is organized into 44 categories, many of them with subcategories. At a very minimum, entries include the name of the catalog, their address and telephone number, and a brief product description. A substantial proportion of the entries, however, are far more extensive. They typically provide a Web and e-mail address, a fax number, names of the company president and other key individuals, any fee charged for the catalog, number of times the catalog is mailed per year, and a listing of credit cards that the company accepts in payment for orders. A few even list the length of time the company has been in business, its number of employees, a total sales estimate, and size of a typical order.

The directory contains several indexes, including a catalog and a company name index, a geographic index by state, a product index, and a Website index. Because it is considerably more specific, the product index is a useful complement to the classified arrangement of the directory. While the Website index is somewhat redundant with the classified arrangement in that it simply restates categories, titles of catalogs, and URLs, the index could be helpful to individuals who wish to restrict their searching to Websites. In addition to the print format, the directory is available as an online subscription, as an ASCII text file, and in mailing list format. With mail order and Internet shopping becoming increasingly popular, this directory should be a useful addition to public library reference collections.—**Martha Tarlton**

160. **Directory of MasterCard & Visa Credit Card Sources.** 3d ed. Barry Klein, ed. West Nyack, N.Y., Todd Publications, 1999. 71p. $50.00pa. ISBN 0-915344-78-5.

For those unfamiliar with how credit cards work and how they make their money this resource will offer a wealth of information on finding the right card with a low interest rate and how to go about getting approved. The introduction explains the difference between secured and nonsecured cards; offers tips on locating a card with a better interest rate; describes the terms often associated with credit cards (e.g., grace period, annual percentage rate, tiered interest rate); provides names and telephone numbers of secured and nonsecured credit card companies; and provides information on credit card companies that offer low interest rates, no annual fees, and good introductory rates. It also presents companies that offer corporate cards, frequent-flyer cards, and cards for those in national organizations (e.g., AAA cards, Wall Street Club).

The bulk of the directory alphabetically lists directory information of companies issuing credit cards. The information provides the company's name; where their cards are offered; telephone number and address; the annual membership fee, annual interest rate, minimum income required, and credit line range for both regular cards and gold cards; and the grace period, any additional charges, and extra benefits. This volume, along with forthcoming editions, will be valuable additions to the business or finance collections of public libraries. Because so many Americans are using credit cards and trying to find the best deals, this work can answer a lot of questions at the reference desk.—**Shannon Graff Hysell**

161. **The Directory of Overseas Catalogs, 1997.** Lakeville, Conn., Grey House Publishing, 1996. 522p. illus. index. $199.00; $165.00pa. ISBN 0-939300-36-2; 0-939300-75-3pa.

This directory lists alphabetically by country 1,327 mail order catalogs from 41 nations other than the United States. The majority are from Canada, the United Kingdom, and Europe, with representation from other parts of the world. Each entry has a short description of the products carried and address information including telephone and fax numbers and e-mail addresses. Key contact names, specific credit cards accepted, cost of the catalog, circulation, frequency of publication, how long the company has been in business, and the number of employees are given, when available. Catalog specifications are provided as to the number of pages, type of stock, and how it is bound. The reader is also told if the company imports, exports, or does business in the United States.

The book is indexed by type of product and also alphabetically by catalog or company name. This easy-to-use reference is also available in an electronic format that can be merged with several database software programs. The publication yields a fascinating potpourri of products. Many of the catalogs are narrowly defined and have long histories. Entries range from industrial products to Bunka With Flair (this Canadian company sells Japanese punch embroidery kits and has been in business for 16 years).

U.S. catalogers looking for international mailing lists or strategic partners for expansion into the global market will be the primary users of this directory. It will be helpful also to the general reader with a passion for a specific product, such as Scottish woolens or South African plants.—**Adrienne Antink Bien**

162.   **The National Directory of Catalogs 1997.** New York, Oxbridge Communications, 1997. 1159p. index. $495.00pa. ISBN 0-917460-85-5. ISSN 0163-7010.

This 7th edition of *The National Directory of Catalogs* contains close to 9,000 entries for business-to-business and consumer mail-order catalogs. The 1990 premier edition (see ARBA 91, entry 194) held slightly more than half that number of entries (approximately 5,000) and cost a mere $145.

The directory is arranged in 200-plus subject categories. Each entry lists catalog company name followed by catalog name, address, telephone and fax numbers, description of product carried, target audience, sales volume, catalog circulation, list rental information, payment information, frequency of catalog issue, number of pages and size of catalog, use of color, type of binding, paper stock, key staff names (including buyers), and name and address of management company if catalog is handled by an outside firm. A company name index; a catalog title index; and an index to companies by state, including Canadian provinces and Mexican states, are included. This directory is essential for businesses engaged in mail order, businesses wanting to start mail order, and businesses wanting to place products in the most appropriate catalogs. Special libraries in this arena will want to purchase this new edition if they do not have a recent edition. The *National Directory of Catalogs* is substantially more comprehensive than either the *Catalog of Catalogs* (see entry 157) or the *Directory of Mail Order Catalogs* (see entry 159).—**Thomas K. Fry**

HANDBOOKS AND YEARBOOKS

163.   Achar, Rajani, and others. **Shopping with a Conscience: The Informed Shopper's Guide to Retailers, Suppliers, and Service Providers in Canada.** Etobicoke, Ont., John Wiley & Sons Canada, 1996. 434p. index. $18.95pa. ISBN 0-471-64172-3.

Aimed at conscientious shoppers in Canada, this volume, produced by EthicScan, Canada's oldest and largest corporate social responsibility research firm, advances concentrated information about 10 major ethical concerns that can affect purchasing policies of individuals and organizations for 16 major service sectors. These concerns include gender and family issues, community responsibilities, progressive staff policies, labor relations, environmental performance, environmental management, management practices and consumer relations, sourcing and trading policies, candor, and Canadian content (the degree to which company decisions are made in Canada).

The text, directed at both potential customers and students of consumer studies, is well organized and highly accessible. The introductory information discusses the criteria used to formulate the ratings and the businesses included in the study and offers table summaries of the social, labor, and environmental performance of the individual companies analyzed. The assessment of these individual businesses, organized alphabetically within the service sectors, are then discussed in greater detail. Each entry includes background information on the company and its history in Canada, a brief summary of the findings for each of these issues, and the raw scores they obtained in the study. These scores are compared in rating tables within each sector. The service sectors are introduced with a brief discussion of the particular ethical challenges that they face. The policy of the authors is not to tell their readers what to think, but "just to offer the information." This tactic is carried out well, notwithstanding that some of the material is already dated; one of the major companies discussed, Consumers Distributing, is no longer in business.—**Gail de Vos**

164.   **Better Buys for Business: The Independent Consumer Guide to Office Equipment.** Santa Barbara, Calif., Better Buys for Business, 1996. 10v. illus. $125.00/set/yr.

Not everyone needs a copier to print a million copies per month at a speed of 135 copies per minute, but for office equipment buyers who do, *Better Buys for Business*, published since 1986, is the definitive consumer guide. Formerly known as *What to Buy for Business*, this resource is published 10 times a year, with each issue focusing on one type of office equipment. Evaluations have low-, mid-, and high-volume copiers; business telephone systems; computers; postage meter systems; fax machines; and laser and LED printers. For ease of use, issues are organized similarly into four main sections and are intended to give buyers all the facts to make the best choice.

Discussions cover a general overview of the machine; pros and cons; how to purchase the machine; the technology in plain, easy-to-understand English; hookup and networking considerations; future developments; and advance information on new machines that will be entering the market. Vendor information and profiles with company track records and comparisons of service and customer support policies should be valuable for long-term maintenance of the machines. The last section reviews specific machines and follows it with a summary chart of all models in grid format including price and features. Recommendations are made from research and analyses of the products and are unbiased.

The past 10 years have verified the trend toward more and more automation in the workplace with the advent of such machines as computers, fax machines, laptops, and color printers. One would expect there to be other guides such as this one. However, it was difficult to find any that were this comprehensive. The only book that might even compare is *The Office Equipment Adviser* by John Derrick (3d ed., What to Buy for Business, 1995), which is a condensation of the *Better Buys for Business* series into one paperback and does not include any price information. —**Elizabeth D'Antonio-Gan**

165.   **The Essential Business Buyer's Guide.** By the Staff of *Business Consumer Guide.* Naperville, Ill., Sourcebooks, 1997. 436p. index. $18.95pa. ISBN 1-57071-130-5.

The staff of the *Business Consumer Guide* has created a handy volume filled with helpful and friendly advice regarding more than 110 business products and services. Although designed as an aid for the buying process, it also gives purchasers one less thing to worry about by identifying potential blunders. For instance: Some cordless telephones will not work during a power outage; if buying a paper shredder, one must be sure the power switch is easily accessible because neckties can become entangled; the U.S. Postal Service is the only business that can deliver to military addresses or post office boxes; and if a company uses a music-on-hold system, it should not play a radio station unless it has checked to be sure a competitor does not advertise on the same station.

The table of contents lists the topics alphabetically. Topics covered include 401(k) plans, beverage services, chairs, ground shipping, international callback services, off-site storage, recycling, safes, telephone systems, trade show displays, and video conferencing services. Each profile for the business product or service begins with a brief introduction, followed by a chart listing the major vendors. Buying points, pricing, and special tips are discussed and, depending on the topic, words or phrases unique to the topic are defined. An exhaustive index is provided, as well as a list of topics by category.

The staff of the *Business Consumer Guide* has also developed BuyersZone, a World Wide Web site. The icon for BuyersZone is included at the end of many of the profiles to indicate that additional purchasing information, vendor links, and user forums can be found on the Web. This title is practical, well planned, and affordable. It is recommended to all libraries.—**Barbara E. Clotfelter**

166.   Kent, Cassandra. **Household Hints & Tips.** New York, DK Publishing, 1996. 192p. illus. index. $19.95pa. ISBN 0-7894-0432-X.

Divided into 9 sections, this little handbook dispenses wisdom with "more than 2,000 ingenious solutions to everyday problems in and around the home." It covers the basics of house cleaning, stain removal, clothes and laundry, care and repair, home improvements, home maintenance, food and drink, housekeeping, and health and safety. The neophyte is sure to appreciate this collection, and the more experienced will enjoy the convenience of having new and old tips collected together.

Copious illustrations and photographs are used throughout, whether necessary for clarity or not. For instance, lists of stain removal cleaners and solvents would probably fit the bill just as well as titled pictures of plain bottles and accessories. The pictures do make the book less text intensive and, therefore, probably more enjoyable for most readers. In other words, this book is arranged in typical DK format.

Special features include a quick reference box that denotes chapter contents at the beginning of each section and boxes with traditional tips, warnings, and safety information scattered throughout the text. In addition, there are five icons that pop up from time to time, presenting traditional wisdom, moneysaving and timesaving tips, bright ideas, and green alternatives that make chores go quicker, easier, or more efficiently. One of the most important features is the "Getting Organized" section at the beginning of the book, which points out the necessity for a home log book—one of the best tips for the busy household of today.

There are a few tips that the author might want to reconsider before another printing of this book. Of primary importance is the addition of a warning concerning the cold mixture recommended on page 179. Doctors warn that honey should not be given to children under the age of one due to the risk of botulism spores that their little bodies are unable to metabolize. Another item suggests a method for reviving dried mascara, which ophthalmologists recommend throwing out.

Although this book does not answer all house questions, it is a good overview of solutions to common problems. It is great for someone going "out on their own" for the first time or for anyone who would just like to have answers to a lot of life's little household problems in one book.—**Jo Anne H. Ricca**

167.   Krantz, Les, and Sharon Ludman-Exley. **The Best of Everything for Your Baby.** Paramus, N.J., Prentice Hall, 2000. 334p. illus. index. $15.00pa. ISBN 0-7352-0032-7.

The Best of Everything for Your Baby is more than just a buying guide for infant and toddler necessities; it also provides tips and advice for novice parents. The guide covers essential purchases that babies and toddlers need as well as a few convenient and playful items. The authors have drawn on their own experiences, along with opinions from other parents, to provide sound advice for new parents no matter what their budget is.

The first section of the guide directs readers in purchasing items that are necessary before the baby arrives. Tips are given about what features to look for on items such as cribs, monitors, changing tables, and playpens. This section also lists accessories that are not necessary, but they are recommended. The second section covers items that parents will need after the baby arrives, such as nursing and bottle feeding items, highchairs, toiletries, and bath gear. The third section lists educational and stimulating toys for infants and toddlers as well as videos, music, software, and books. The last section features items for traveling, such as car seats, carriers, and strollers. This section also provides safety tips for staying at hotels, shopping, and air travel. The appendixes list toll-free numbers for consumer relations departments at a number of manufacturers and Websites for shopping and information.

Overall, this guide offers more advice on what to buy and what to look for than actual reviews of products. Safety is a key issue that is continuously stressed throughout the work. This is a highly recommended guide for novice parents. It gives good advice about a number of basic concerns for new parents. [R: LJ, 1 Oct 99, p. 82]—**Cari Ringelheim**

168.   McBroom, Michael. **McBroom's Camera Bluebook: A Complete, Up-to-Date Price and Buyer's Guide for New and Used Cameras, Lenses, & Accessories.** 6th ed. Buffalo, N.Y., Amherst Media, 2000. 323p. illus. index. $29.95pa. ISBN 1-58428-013-1.

This is the 6th edition of *McBroom's Camera Bluebook*, the 1st edition of which was published in 1990 under the title *Price Guide to Modern Cameras, Lenses, and Accessories*. It has become the standard handbook for new and used cameras. The bluebook is arranged by camera format: 35mm, advanced photo system (APS), panoramic, medium, multiformat, large, and digital. Strobes and exposure meters are also covered. Each section is further arranged by manufacturer (e.g., Nikon, Cannon, Hasselblad, Kodak) with specific information, description, and prices for individual camera models. The features for each model are listed along with dates of manufacture and a range of prices for new, mint, excellent, and user condition examples. The narratives for each camera are very informative and give the reader insight into the improvements for specific models. McBroom gives excellent advice on the use and value of each model, both as a collectable and as a current user camera. There is also an introductory section on tips for buying along with an index and a glossary.

Prices are about average—some examples are listed a little high, while others are bit low and might actually be more typical of what the reader would expect to pay at a local camera store. Mail order stores that advertise in *Shutterbug* magazine tend to have examples on sale at lower prices. Also, private owners sometimes will sell examples for less than the prices listed here. While the press date of this volume is 2000, prices appear to be from early in that year. There is some seasonal variation in camera prices (they tend to be higher during the October-December period), but McBroom appears to capture the average retail price. In fact, in a number of cases he sees prices for some classic models as stable over time. The volume is a well-designed paperback. Most libraries will want to purchase this book for their general readers and camera collectors.—**Ralph Lee Scott**

169.   Norrgard, Lee E., and Julia M. Norrgard. **Consumer Fraud: A Reference Handbook.** Santa Barbara, Calif., ABC-CLIO, 1998. 338p. index. (Contemporary World Issues). $45.00. ISBN 0-87436-991-6.

Part of ABC-CLIO's award-winning Contemporary World Issues series, this work reveals the spectrum of consumer fraud, from work-at-home and investment scams to credit issues and high tech merchandising. By learning what consumer fraud involves, how society is affected, and what tactics are used to combat it, readers may be able to understand their own vulnerability and avoid being taken. However, everyone pays for consumer fraud in the increased prices businesses must charge to recover their loses.

This vast, ubiquitous topic begins with a chronology starting from Hammurabi in 1800 B.C.E. and continues through telemarketing and car leasing on the brink of the twenty-first century. Brief biographical sketches of men and women, including three presidents, who either made consumer issues a career, or in the case of the presidents, played a critical role in governmental policy and legislation are included. Chapter 4 is titled "Documents, Laws, and Regulations"; "Directory of Agencies and Organizations," which is arranged alphabetically by state, is the 5th chapter. The final two chapters are annotated bibliographies of print and nonprint resources. Especially noteworthy are the 29 Websites listed.

A short glossary, a print advertisement that has the appearance of a news story or editorial, and a detailed index complete the volume. This unique, authoritative reference resource should be found in most public libraries and in business collections. Citizens, activists, students, and researchers will find a lot of information here. [R: Choice, June 99, p. 1765]—**Susan C. Awe**

170.   **Orion Blue Book: Camera 2000.** Scottsdale, Ariz., Orion Research, 1999. 443p. $144.00. ISBN 1-892761-04-1. ISSN 1046-3861.

Orion Blue Books have long been a useful reference tool for retail dealers, insurance companies, pawnbrokers, manufacturers, and libraries. The *Orion Blue Book: Camera* begins by presenting guidelines to camera salespeople by stressing the importance of knowing their product in terms of testing trade-ins, knowing which products are collectibles, inspecting cosmetic condition, and getting a profit on trade-ins. It then defines the terms listed in the book and defines the codes used. The bulk of the book lists cameras alphabetically, first according to brand name and then by type. For each camera the following are listed: type name, year it was released for sale, name of manufacturer, f-stop, lens size, model, retail sale price, used sale price, wholesale mint condition price, and wholesale average price. The alphabetic layout of the work makes it easily accessible. A directory of camera manufactures is included, which provides the companies address and telephone and fax numbers. This volume, along with the other *Orion Blue Books*, will be a useful only to public libraries that often have reference questions pertaining to merchandise value.—**Shannon Graff Hysell**

171.   **Orion Blue Book: Computer 2000.** summer ed. Scottsdale, Ariz., Orion Research, 2000. 790p. $516.00 (annual); $129.00 (quarterly). ISBN 0-932089-65-8 (annual); 0-932089-17-8 (summer). ISSN 0883-4881.

This volume is the computer industry equivalent of the *NADA Blue Book* for used car prices. Retail and wholesale prices are given for used desktop computers, notebooks, monitors, printers, plotters, digital cameras, disk drives, and much more. Some of the equipment listed here dates back to the early 1980s. Prices are derived from national surveys of dealers. Orion also publishes price guides for audio equipment, cameras, car stereos, copiers, musical instruments, guns, power tools, and videos and televisions.

According to the FAQ in this book, "retail dealers, insurance companies, manufacturers, libraries, pawnbrokers, freight adjusters, law enforcement personnel, divorce and probate attorneys, and the Internal Revenue Service" (p. 8) will benefit from the information provided in this guide. Most of that makes sense, but for libraries this is a stretch. After factoring in the price—same cost annually or quarterly—it clearly makes no sense for any library.—**John Maxymuk**

172.   **Orion Blue Book: Guitars & Musical Instruments 2000.** Scottsdale, Ariz., Orion Research, 1999. 1102p. $179.00. ISBN 1-892761-02-5. ISSN 1046-3880.

In the early 1970s, Roger Rohrs compiled the *Orion Trade-in Guide* for use in his stereo stores for pricing used equipment and as a training tool for his staff. In 1979, he became the exclusive owner of the guide and has since developed it into a product line of a dozen blue books (in print and CD-ROM) covering audio, professional sound, video, and television equipment; cameras; car stereos; computers; copiers; guns; pianos; power tools; and vintage guitars and collectibles. The guidelines provided in the beginning of the book are certainly those of a profit-driven professional in a field where the purchase and sale of used equipment can be more profitable than in dealing only with the brand new. The noted importance of such things as regional pricing, the collectible factor of certain vintage brands and models, the cosmetic condition of the instrument, and so on can work to the advantage of both the dealer and the seller (or buyer). It seems that the compiler has tried to provide a tool for fair transactions.

The bulk of the book is an alphabetic listing by company of manufacturers of musical instruments. Instruments of all types are included and are of the types found in towns and cities across the United States. Under each company the information is given in grid format, making it easy to use. Each entry gives instrument, manufacturer and year made, power (if appropriate), and model. This information is followed by four dollar value categories: new list (manufacturer's suggested price), retail used (sale price if sold within 30 days), wholesale mint (price to seller of used equipment in perfect condition), and wholesale average (average of prices paid to customers for this specific model). These figures are determined by dealer surveys so that they come directly from the marketplace.

These guides must be very useful to those buying and selling as well as for other uses, such as insurance companies, pawnbrokers, divorce and probate attorneys, and the IRS. A directory of manufacturers is also given with full addresses and telephone and fax numbers (a useful feature in itself). This guide is of invaluable use to large retail establishments selling this merchandise, but is probably more apt for business libraries than to music libraries.—**George Louis Mayer**

173. **Orion Blue Book: Video & Television 2000.** Scottsdale, Ariz., Orion Research, 1999. 596p. $144.00. ISBN 1-892761-05-X. ISSN 1046-3861.

Orion Blue Books have long been a reliable source for obtaining the value of merchandise. This volume focuses on video equipment and television. The work begins with an introduction explaining how to use the information it contains. It then provides the addresses and telephone and fax numbers of the manufacturers presented in the volume. The bulk of the book is listings of television and video equipment. The equipment is listed alphabetically by the manufacturer's name and includes information on the type of equipment, the year it was released for sale, the model number or name, the retail price of the item new, the retail price of the item used, the wholesale price of the item in mint condition, and the wholesale price of the item in average condition. Once one becomes familiar with the layout of the book, the information provided is easily accessible.

This volume, along with the other volumes available, is valuable to retail dealers, insurance companies, attorneys, and the Internal Revenue Service. Public libraries should have these volumes on hand for reference questions from people in these professions as well as clientele seeking information on their own.—**Shannon Graff Hysell**

174. **Orion Blue Books 2001.** [CD-ROM]. Scottsdale, Ariz., Orion Research, 2001. $29.95 (trial basis).

Orion has published price books for used equipment since 1973. Their blue books appear in print, on floppy disks, and now in a CD-ROM format. The CD-ROM can include up to all of the books available from Orion on audio equipment, cameras, car stereos, computers, copying machines, musical instruments, guns, professional sound equipment, video equipment and televisions, and collectible musical instruments. Price guides for pianos/keyboards and power tools will be published soon.

Products range from very inexpensive to high-end, such as the Hohner A-8 Tremolo 22/8 accordion for $125 and the Hohner Alpina IV Continental 42/120 accordion for $10,725. Some books include more manufacturers than do others. For example, no omission was found among the 8,106 records for acoustic guitars. On the other hand, the 206 records for accordions did not include Italo-American or Weltmeister accordions. The range of models priced in most books, however, is impressive.

The search screen is easy to use. Drop-down lists for manufacturers and product types allow beginners quick results. A type-in search box for model number is also available. Highlighting an item on a results list displays the manufacturer's suggested retail price, used retail price, and wholesale price (mint and average conditions) above the search area. The disc has its own tools for printing, switching books, setting security, and so forth. A tutorial is available on the disc and on Orion's Website (http://www.orionbluebook.com). Helpful technical support is available by telephone or by e-mail.

Orion establishes prices by surveying retailers throughout the United States and calculating the average price of a product. Boards of advisors, who include retailers and other experts, review the survey data. Orion also lists the IRS as one of its customers, although an IRS representative was unable to confirm the claim. Orion does not have a direct competitor for its CD-ROM of 10 books. However, competing print price guides exist for specific products, such as *McBroom's Camera Bluebook* (6th ed.; see entry 168). Orion's CD-ROM is recommended for public libraries, appraisers, and retailers of used equipment.—**Nancy L. Van Atta**

175.   Rudman, Theo. **Rudman's Cigar Buying Guide: Selecting & Savoring the Perfect Cigar for Any Occasion.** Chicago, Triumph Books, 1997. 394p. index. $14.95pa. ISBN 1-57243-233-0.

176.   Rudman, Theo. **Rudman's Complete Guide to Cigars: How to Find, Select, & Smoke Them.** 4th ed. Chicago, Triumph Books, 1997. 376p. index. $14.95pa. ISBN 1-57243-245-4.

These two guides overlap, but are not identical. The *Complete Guide* contains more than 100 pages introducing readers to the history, production, selection, and smoking of cigars. The remaining two-thirds of the work contain a country-by-country list of the major cigar brands. The list uses a 5-star system to evaluate more than 900 of the 4,500 cigars included. This 4th edition has been updated by 47 pages of new brands. This new information is not integrated into the main list. Rather, the new brands are listed on colored pages at the beginning of the work.

The *Cigar Buying Guide* includes a 16-page section, "Smoking for Pleasure," giving guidance on how to select, keep, and smoke cigars. The vast majority of the work comprises lists—a quality rating index, a cigar-sized index, and a "world directory" of cigars. The rating index evaluates more than 500 cigars using the "the author's subjective" 5-star rating system. The price index rates more than 2,000 cigars into 6 categories (below $1 to more than $20). The size index lists more than 3,700 cigars in 16 size categories. The directory lists more than 3,700 cigars by country and brand and includes the quality and price ratings, a brief overview of cigar making in each country, and brief descriptions of most brands listed, with an index identifying cigar brands by country.

The author is a South African cigar connoisseur and, hence, has much more access to Cuba and Cuban cigars than any U.S. citizen. Both works include extensive coverage of Cuban cigars, considered by most experts to be the best in the world, and the *Complete Guide* includes a short summary of the laws pertaining to Cuban cigar imports into the U.S. (an officially licensed traveler to Cuba may bring back less than $100 worth, but Cuban cigars may not be brought into the U.S. from any other country, and anyone illegally trading or dealing in Cuban cigars is liable for a $50,000 fine or imprisonment or both).

Although each work contains lists called "directories," they cannot be considered true directories because the lists do not contain addresses, telephone numbers, fax numbers, or e-mail address. The works are both relatively inexpensive paperbacks and are not made to stand up to heavy reference use. This should not be considered a fatal defect because they also contain a large amount of quality and price information that is sure to be rapidly outdated. Both of these guides are suitable for libraries needing to provide reference works to meet the needs of the currently increasing number of cigar smokers. Of the two, the *Complete Guide* is the work of choice for most libraries because it contains the most general information on cigars and cigar smoking and includes the quality ratings; it lacks only the price and size ratings of the *Cigar Buying Guide*.—**Richard H. Swain**

INDEXES

177. **Consumers Index to Product Evaluations and Information Sources. Volume 24, Number 2, April-June 1996.** C. Edward Wall and others, eds. Ann Arbor, Mich., Pierian Press, 1996. 163p. index. $129.00pa./yr.

Consumers Index, published quarterly and cumulated annually, is an index to articles in more than 110 periodicals, services, and World Wide Web sites. The index is geared to the general consumer and the educational/library community. It is divided into 17 main subject groupings under such headings as "Finances, Employment, Insurance and Investments," "Transportation," and "Sight and Sound." There are divisions under each of these principal headings; for example, "Sight and Sound" has subheadings for audio equipment, television, video equipment, photography, and optics. These subgroupings are further subdivided as appropriate. Articles that survey the topic as a whole appear first, followed by headings for specific products, services, or topics. Next are articles discussing alerts and warnings and articles on *National Highway Traffic Safety Administration News Releases* that detail safety recalls.

If all the sections and subdivisions give one the impression the index must be cumbersome and hard to use, such is most certainly not the case. The inside of the front cover gives a useful "how-to" explanation. This is followed by a detailed table of contents. After this is a helpful alphabetic subject index. The other indexes are by product name/manufacturer and manufacturer/product name, by recall, and by alerts and warnings. There are other periodical indexes that index product evaluation articles within a given field, but only *Readers' Guide to Periodical Literature* (see ARBA 92, entry 60) begins to offer the breadth that *Consumers Index* provides, and the *Readers' Guide* pales by comparison. The title under review is strongly recommended for public libraries of all sizes and all but the most specialized academic libraries.—**Dene L. Clark**

6   Finance and Banking

DICTIONARIES AND ENCYCLOPEDIAS

178.   Allen, Larry. **Encyclopedia of Money.** Santa Barbara, Calif., ABC-CLIO, 1999. 328p. illus. index. $75.00. ISBN 1-57607-037-9.

Written for the general reader rather than for the scholar, this compilation of some 300 brief essays (500 to 1,000 words in length) presents a variety of historical information regarding important monetary experiences that have influenced the evolution of money and banking. Although the author indicates an intent not to dwell on proving or disproving any specific theories of monetary economics, it is evident that certain exceptions prove the rule. Likewise, theories are brought into discussion only when they result in bringing some order out of chaos. In essence, the guiding principle is identification of the common characteristics that are shared within and between various monetary systems.

The work opens with an alphabetic list of entries, followed by a brief preface and introduction. Some entries include illustrations and all include cross-references and a brief bibliography of resources. A full bibliography and index supplement the main text.

To trained economists, this work might prove too vague and unrewarding. However, to the general reader, armchair historian, and seeker of curious facts, the work should be quite fulfilling. High school, public, and college library users might benefit from the clarity of discussions. [R: BL, 15 Nov 99, pp. 649-652] —**Edmund F. SantaVicca**

179.   Clark, John. **International Dictionary of Banking and Finance.** library ed. Chicago, Glenlake and Chicago, Fitzroy Dearborn, 1999. 352p. $55.00. ISBN 1-57958-160-9.

This title provides short definitions for an estimated 4,500 acronyms, keywords, terms, and proper names in the broad field of banking, finance, investments, savings institutions, and stock exchanges. Selection of entries is based heavily on UK terms with some U.S. terms and a very few continental European terms thrown in. It is strong for acronyms but weak for insurance. Any library with active business clientele will benefit from updated subject dictionaries and this one is clearly written, and UK terminology aside, easily understandable. At $55, however, it is overpriced for U.S. libraries who would find Thomas Fitch's *Dictionary of Banking Terms* (see entry 181) at $12.95 and Jerry M. Rosenberg's *Dictionary of Banking* (see ARBA 94, entry 207) at $19.95 provide better coverage for less cost. In addition, the *American Bankers Association's Banking and Finance Terminology* (1999) costs $49 but is twice as long. Edward Hinkelman's *Dictionary of International Trade* (3d ed.; see entry 247) at $16.50 is an acceptable choice for international banking terms. If Canadian banks use UK terminology, then this would be an acceptable purchase for larger academic and public libraries in Canada or for U.S. libraries that feel the need for a British take on banking terms. Otherwise, the other titles mentioned are better for U.S. libraries.—**Patrick J. Brunet**

180.   **Elsevier's Dictionary of Financial Terms in English, German, Spanish, French, Italian, and Dutch.** rev. ed. Diana Phillips and Marie-Claude Bignaud, comps. New York, Elsevier Science, 1997. 644p. $230.00. ISBN 0-444-89950-2.

This dictionary is comprehensive and easy to use. It includes terms from various areas of economics and finance as well as allied ones from accounting, law, and insurance. It has a "Basic Table" in which terms in English, their synonyms, and related expressions are translated into the five other languages of the dictionary in alphabetic order. This extensive section is followed by a six-part list of terms in each of the six languages, with reference to the page(s) in the "Basic Table." The pages of the latter contain two columns, and those in the six-languages part contain three columns, indicative of the large volume of material covered in this book. Abbreviations include grammatical categories and gender. A spot check revealed an impressive collection of synonyms and alternative translations that will be of great service to the user of this volume. In view of the increasing globalization of economic relations and existence of the European Union and other preferential trading blocks, this book is of great value to translators and business practitioners as well as to academics. This dictionary is highly recommended.—**Bogdan Mieczkowski**

181.   Fitch, Thomas P. **Dictionary of Banking Terms.** 3d ed. Hauppauge, N.Y., Barron's Educational Series, 1997. 527p. (Barron's Business Guides). $16.95pa. ISBN 0-8120-9659-2.

More than 3,000 terms related to the banking and financial services industry are defined and described in the latest edition of the *Dictionary of Banking Terms.* Included, in addition to definitions of such terms as *bank credit* and *common stock,* are entries for organizations (e.g., New York Stock Exchange) and key legislation (e.g., Glass-Steagall Act). Provided with some of the definitions are illustrations, charts, and graphs. Cross-references are also included.

The dictionary has been updated to reflect changes since the 1993 edition, notably developments in global banking, electronic banking, and legislation. Additionally, several obsolete terms have been deleted, and the list of abbreviations and acronyms has been expanded since the last edition. *Dictionary of Banking Terms* is highly recommended to business reference collections in academic, special, and public libraries. This reference source is comprehensive and contains clear explanations of terms.—**Lucy Heckman**

182.   Rider, A. J. **The International Dictionary of Personal Finance.** Harrogate, England, Take That; distr., North Pomfret, Vt., Trafalgar Square, 1999. 188p. $11.95pa. ISBN 1-873668-54-6.

The number of financial and business dictionaries published each year can be overwhelming. Since most libraries cannot buy them all, finding the ones that are best for specific clientele can be very challenging. Many focus on the United States or try to cover the international scene comprehensively. Rider's new paperback dictionary focuses on two major markets: the United States and the United Kingdom. However, common terms exclusive to other parts of the world are occasionally included. It is written for the consumer and focuses on annuities, banking, bonds, business, equity-based investments and mutual funds, insurance, pensions, taxation, and wills. If a term is used exclusively in one country, it makes this distinction. The definitions are concise and sometimes include usage, but can be overly simplistic. While a number of less familiar financial terms (contango, kangaroos, peppercorn rent) are covered, some that appear regularly in the business press (hedge funds, poison pill) are not. A peculiarity is using British spellings when referring to exclusively American terms. A more comprehensive, albeit more dated and expensive alternative is *The Handbook of International Financial Terms* (see entry 190). Recommended only for comprehensive investment research collections or libraries requiring an inexpensive international financial dictionary.—**Bobray Bordelon**

183.   Salda, Anne C. M. **Historical Dictionary of the World Bank.** Lanham, Md., Scarecrow, 1997. 281p. (International Organizations Series, no.11). $68.00. ISBN 0-8108-3215-1.

The International Bank for Reconstruction and Development (World Bank) plays an influential and often high-profile role in the economic development of many contemporary developing countries. Not only does it lend money, provide technical assistance, and influence economic and financial policies to these countries, but the adoption of its programs is seen as a stamp of approval that opens access to private international capital for a country. Despite this high-profile and often controversial role played by the bank, there are few sources that provide adequate information about the history, structure, and operation of the bank and its affiliate institutions. *Historical Dictionary of the World Bank* fills this gap. The 281-page book provides copious information about the World Bank that has hitherto not been available in any single volume.

The majoring of the book, covering pages 26 to 207, is devoted to the dictionary itself. This section provides entries on the World Bank's activities from such subjects as acquired immunodeficiency syndrome (AIDS) to world tables. Each entry gives sufficient detail and is put in a historical context that makes it understandable and enjoyable to read. Part 3 of the book is a statistical appendix that furnishes information on membership, capital subscription, and lending activities of the bank. Part 4 is a comprehensive list of the bank's publications. Perhaps the most interesting and informative part of the book is the introductory chapter covering the first 25 pages. In this short section, the author brilliantly describes the historical context within which the bank was created; the major personalities behind its creation; objectives of the bank, its growth, and changes in objectives; the structure of the bank; and how some of its affiliates came to be created. The historical chronology of events that precede the introduction makes the book user friendly. The book is also well written.

By putting the activities of the World Bank in a historical context, this book will do more to educate the public about the bank than any effort the bank itself may produce. The dictionary is recommended for all who are interested in the activities of the World Bank.—**Kwabena Gyimah-Brempong**

184.   Spurge, Lorraine. **Money Talk: From Alphabet Stock to the Naked Sale; The Words and Phrases That Control Your Money.** New York, Hyperion, 2001. 316p. $12.95pa. ISBN 0-7868-8498-3.

This dictionary defines several thousand business, finance, stock market, accounting, and financial investing terms. The intended audience is uninformed or inexperienced individuals who take an interest in managing their own financial assets. As a result, the definitions are easy to understand, straightforward, and accurate, with many helpful examples. The cost is in breadth and depth of coverage: other such dictionaries contain more entries, each in greater detail than *Money Talk*. But *Money Talk* is more easily understandable for individuals who are novices at understanding the complexities of financial terms. Only occasional errors creep in: *Value Line* now tracks 3,500 companies not 1,700 (p. 302), tax-free amount for estate tax calculations is currently (2001) $675,000 not $600,000 (p. 292), and simple interest is miscalculated (p. 44). An editing sweep through the entire volume would have caught these minor slip-ups, mostly requiring updates of obsolete information, in an otherwise excellent volume that serves its audiences with great clarity. [R: LJ, 1 Feb 01, p. 82]—**Richard A. Miller**

DIRECTORIES

185.   Blum, Laurie. **Free Money from the Federal Government for Small Businesses and Entrepreneurs.** 2d ed. New York, John Wiley, 1996. 358p. index. $16.95pa. ISBN 0-471-13009-5.

The majority of people in the United States are not aware of the fact that billions of government dollars are available for small businesses and entrepreneurs. These funds can be obtained from a large number of federal, state, county, and city agencies. They can be used in a wide variety of programs. The few who know about the availability of these funds do not know whom to contact and how to go about getting help.

Blum's book is an excellent attempt to help individuals and small businesses in locating the right agency to get them going. The book covers almost all types of grants in almost all fields. This includes agriculture, community development, energy, the environment, research and development, housing, and minorities. Blum ensured that addresses are complete with names of contacts and telephone and fax numbers. All entries are arranged by state and by field. Many entries are duplicated, but only to ensure simplicity and ease of use. Finally, the author goes the extra step to help the reader with instructions on how to apply and how to write winning proposals. *Free Money from the Federal Government for Small Businesses and Entrepreneurs* is highly recommended to all public libraries, university libraries, and small businesses. [R: Choice, July/Aug 96, p. 1768]—**Elie M. Dick**

186.   **Directory of Venture Capital Firms, 2000: Domestic & International.** 4th ed. Lakeville, Conn., Grey House Publishing, 1999. 1227p. index. $295.00. ISBN 1-891482-95-5.

The *Directory of Venture Capital Firms*, formerly published by Fitzroy Dearborn and titled *The International Directory of Venture Capital Funds*, has been extensively updated since its last publication in 1997. The directory lists 1,800 venture capital firms—1,270 domestic firms and 574 international firms. The data provided for each firm include contact information, education and professional background of the firm's management, a mission statement, when the firm was founded, geographic preferences, fund size, average amount of investment, portfolio companies, and investment criteria. Not all firms listed provide all of the information; some firms are more thoroughly represented than others. The 5 indexes offered here will help researchers explore the directory to their best advantage. They include a geographic index, an executive name index, a portfolio company index, an industry preference index, and a college and university index. This work will find much use in business libraries and the finance collection of many public libraries. —**Shannon Graff Hysell**

187.   **Fitzroy Dearborn Directory of the World's Banks.** 11th ed. Compiled and edited by Euromoney Books. Chicago, Fitzroy Dearborn, 1996. 1186p. $150.00. ISBN 1-884964-84-2.

For the past 10 years, this directory was published by *Euromoney* magazine for its subscribers. Fitzroy Dearborn has now begun publishing a hardbound annual edition, compiled by the same editors, for general distribution. The directory includes more than 10,000 financial institutions in 211 countries. The entries are organized by country and provide contact information, names of key executives, correspondent banks, subsidiaries and affiliates, ownership details, and the number of employees and branches. Indexes by bank name and by city are provided. An additional useful feature is a ranking (based on assets) of the leading 250 institutions in each of 4 regions (Europe, the Americas, Africa/Middle East, and Asia/Pacific).

The *Fitzroy Dearborn Directory* is considerably less comprehensive in coverage than are the *Thomson Bank Directory* (Thomson Financial, semiannual), *Polk's World Bank Directory* (R. L. Polk, annual), and *The Bankers' Almanac and Yearbook* (West Sussex, England: T. Skinner

Directories, annual), each of which discusses in excess of 20,000 institutions. The Fitzroy Dearborn title also lacks the summarized financial data included in the Thomson and Polk directories. In fairness, it has a much lower price than these other sources. The Fitzroy Dearborn publication is apparently not primarily intended as a directory of North American financial institutions; it contains only about 100 pages of United States listings and 15 pages of Canadian listings. Finally, as in many business directories, the amount of information in the entries varies considerably. Many entries include lengthy lists of officers, subsidiaries, and corresponding institutions, while others provide contact information only. Libraries not subscribing to one of the above-named publications may want to consider this directory as a low-cost alternative for international bank information.
—**Christopher J. Hoeppner**

188. **Fitzroy Dearborn International Directory of Venture Capital Funds 1998-99.** Jennifer Schellinger, Patrick Heenan, and Monique Lamontagne, eds. Chicago, Fitzroy Dearborn, 1998. 1886p. index. $175.00. ISBN 1-884964-87-7.

This monumental directory is prefaced by a review authored by specialists in the field of entrepreneurial finance. Immediately following are authoritative essays that examine the ways in which entrepreneurs ought to target and attract the financing they need. A final essay provides information on venture capital funds in Europe, Asia, and the Pacific Rim. Most of this work is a directory for entrepreneurs electing to seek out the venture capital market. Firms are listed within one of five sections, each in alphabetic order. The first four sections include funds in the U.S. and Canada and are broken down as follows: "General Companies"; "High Tech/Medical Funds"; "Minority and Socially-Useful Funds"; and "Strategic Partners." These are followed by a section that lists venture capital funds outside the United States and Canada. Four indexes round out the directory. They include an alphabetic list of all companies, an index of fund executives and their company affiliation, a geographic index, and a category index that lists funds according to their investment preference.

Each listing includes standard directory information, such as name, address, telephone and fax, other office locations, mission, fund size, year of founding, average investment, minimum investment, investment criteria, industry group preference, and companies in portfolio. An interesting feature is names of officers, executives and principals, occasionally including the universities they attend and the degrees they attained.

The only directory as comprehensive as the *International Directory of Venture Capital Funds* is *Pratt's Guide to Venture Capital Sources* (see ARBA 93, entry 197). With minor differences, both works provide comparable information, along with multiple indexes. *Pratt's* arrangement is different in that it lists U.S. companies in alphabetic order under state. Foreign firms appear in a separate alphabetic list. Library patrons should find each directory's arrangement to be equally useful with a little practice on their part. Business collections in mid-sized academic and public libraries need to carry one directory or the other; business collections in large academic and public libraries should carry both directories. Likewise, economic development agencies should carry both directories.—**Dene L. Clark**

HANDBOOKS AND YEARBOOKS

189. Lester, Ray. **Information Sources in Finance and Banking.** New Providence, N.J., Bowker-Saur/Reed Reference Publishing, 1996. 818p. index. (Guides to Information Sources). $125.00. ISBN 1-85739-037-7.

This compendium of banking and finance resources is extremely ambitious. In its more than 800 pages, the author lists a tremendous variety of business resources from all corners of the globe and in many different media. Also included is detailed analysis of where business information originates, how value is added to it, and what form it may take as newer electronic media proliferate. Unfortunately, the result is an unwieldy tool that seems half resource directory and half library science textbook. Neither role is fulfilled adequately.

The book's most obvious problem lies in its organization. Instead of grouping information sources by such topical rubrics as "interest rates" or "money supply," the book focuses on just a few broad and ambiguous headings. Chapter names such as "approaches to structure" and "scholarly research and study" are simply not helpful to a researcher looking for a quick way to locate a source for a particular fact or statistic. The organizational problem is compounded by the book's lack of sufficient indexing. Although there are indexes of organizations and serials, there is no subject index. Hence, a researcher looking for guidance regarding industry averages of balance sheets and income data, a popularly requested business reference topic, would have to know to look in the chapter "Financial Institutions and Markets." Assuming the user was able to guess the correct chapter, he or she would then have to wade through 145 pages of text to find the entry for Robert Morris Associates's *Annual Statement Studies.*

Despite its shortcomings as a researcher's aid, this book does contain some interesting essays on the nature of information in finance and banking. However, these insightful passages are awkwardly interrupted by voluminous listings of actual information resources. As a result, using this guide as a library science textbook would be difficult as well. The limitations of this compendium seem to be inherent in the Bowker-Saur series of which it is part; other titles in this series dealing with different subject disciplines seem to have the same structural problems. The author is certainly to be commended for the extraordinarily thorough research and documentation of his work. Despite Lester's completeness, however, *Information Sources in Finance and Banking* is recommended only for special libraries in financial institutions and comprehensive academic libraries supporting a graduate-level business curriculum. For most general college and university libraries, as well as all public libraries, the amount of useful and easily retrieved information simply does not warrant the book's hefty price. [R: Choice, July/Aug 96, p. 1775]—**David Bickford**

190.   Moles, Peter, and Nicholas Terry. **The Handbook of International Financial Terms.** New York, Oxford University Press, 1997. 605p. $95.00. ISBN 0-19-828885-9.

Authors Moles and Terry, members of the finance faculty at Edinburgh University Management School, have produced a first-rate reference volume covering 14,000 definitions of terms, concepts, laws, and institutions relating to financial markets around the world. Definitions are clear and usually concise. Common terms (e.g., callable, Paris Bourse, risk premium, expected value, index fund, Beta) are augmented by less common terms (e.g., binomial option pricing model, vertical bull spread, masharaka, facultative reinsurance), colloquial terms (e.g., beamer, repos, G-hedge, Baba, box, strips), and financial institutions (e.g., ICC, SVT, CVM). Several entries go well beyond definitions. These are particularly good and of greater length: risk, options pricing, options strategies, stock index, and Federal Reserve (of the United States). About 1,600 abbreviations and acronyms are listed and identified in a separate section; most are defined in the main text. Over 200 international currencies are listed by country separately—lek, pula, and dirham for Albania, Botswana, and Morocco. An excellent 24-page essay titled "Getting Going with the A to Z of Entries" introduces some operations of international financial markets.

Entries on the tools of statistics are understandably short, and thus the reader may require additional references. The *McGraw-Hill Pocket Guide to Business Finance* (see ARBA 93, entry 241) provides the coverage of the quantitative tools that this handbook lacks. A less complete and less expensive dictionary is Barron's 4th edition of *Dictionary of Finance and Investment Terms* (see ARBA 96, entry 220), which lacks the international scope of this book.—**Richard A. Miller**

191. Plunkett's Financial Services Industry Almanac 2000–2001. Jack W. Plunkett, ed. Houston, Tex., Plunkett Research, 1999. 754p. index. $179.99pa. ISBN 1-891775-03-0.

This almanac provides information on 500 leading firms in investment banking, insurance, commercial banking, and financial information. One-page summaries ("individual data profiles") for each of the 500 include the following: services in investments, banking, technology, and credit cards; types of business (e.g., auto, liability, property, insurance); divisions, brands, and affiliates (with a handy index); executives; address, telephone, and fax numbers; annual sales and profits for recent years; and 200-word summaries of plans and special features. These 500 pages provide the bulk of this almanac. In addition, it has an array of helpful, general data pertaining to finance, generally annual for the past 30 or more years, such as household data on consumer credit earnings, income, and consumption; private and government saving and gross investment; national income and its components; and unemployment rates and hourly compensation for seven developed countries. The CPI, government debt, interest rates, federal budget data, capacity utilization rates, business failures, and corporate profits (all 30 or more years) are also included. Foreign data provide U.S. exports and imports; international reserves (22 countries, 10-year intervals); exchange rates (30 years, 10 countries); U.S. foreign investment (10 years); industrial production and consumer prices (7 countries and the European Union, 28 years). Also included are data on housing starts, new construction, and mortgage debt (30-40 years). Unfortunately, most of the data end in 1998. Websites for ISO data and information services (with descriptions) and for 300 mutual funds, securities groups, regulators, and insurance associations are provided. Eighty pages of text describe banking, insurance, mutual funds and retirement plans, online financial services, residential mortgages, and careers in finance. A CD-ROM version is available.—**Richard A. Miller**

192. Walker's Manual of Community Bank Stocks. Lafayette, Calif., Walker's Manual, 1997. 1v. (various paging). index. $100.00. ISBN 0-9652088-7-7.

Community banks are often the lifelines of small towns. They provide a source of investment for local inhabitants and loans for area businesses and citizens and, according to *Walker's Manual of Community Bank Stocks*, can be good investments that supply consistent returns. The manual covers 502 community banks that are traded over-the-counter. As a handbook, the manual serves two possible functions: as an investment analysis guide and as a local banking directory.

The manual does not try to give investment advice. Instead, it provides ownership and officer information, loan mix, per share information, annual financial data (1993-1996), and financial comments. This information can be used to measure performance and financial strength. Indexes by financial measures and ratios also give useful financial information. For some of the banks, the data can be easily obtained from Securities and Exchange Commission (SEC) information. However, many of the banks do not have to file with the SEC, and the data are more difficult to obtain. The profiled companies are not ones that services such as Value Line normally cover. As with any handbook, one would have to supplement the information furnished with other sources.

The majority of the banks are listed in major comprehensive banking directories. Standard directory information is given. A brief profile is supplied with the founding date. In addition to the financial indexes, there are indexes by geographic area and additional company name cross-references. An appendix lists World Wide Web addresses for approximately 10 percent of the companies. *Walker's Manual of Community Bank Stocks* is more appropriate for libraries providing investment advisory services than research libraries.—**Bobray Bordelon**

193. Weiss Ratings' Guide to Banks and Thrifts: A Quarterly Compilation of Financial Institution Ratings and Analysis, Spring 2001. Palm Beach Gardens, Fla., Weiss Rating's, 2001. 421p. $219.00pa. (single copy); $438.00pa. (4 quarterly editions). ISBN 1-58773-007-3. ISSN 1049-5673.

This volume reports Weiss's 2000 safety ratings (also 1998 and 1999) for almost 20,000 banks and thrift institutions. All U.S. federally insured commercial banks, savings banks, and savings and loans are reported in alphabetic order. This guide is a quarterly compilation. The ratings range from "A+" (excellent financial security) to "E" (very weak) and "F" (failed).

Ratings are based on many factors (emphasizing capitalization, asset quality, profitability, liquidity, and stability) that are measured by an index. Supporting data include size (total assets), growth (one year), asset mix, a capitalization index (downside risk), financial leverage, capital ration (capital divided by assets), an asset quality index, nonperforming loans (percent), ratio of nonperforming loans to capital plus loan reserve, a foreclosure ratio, a profitability index, net income, return on assets, return on equity, net interest spread, overhead divided by total reserve less interest expense, a liquidity index, liquidity ratio, a hot money ratio, and a stability index. The elements making up each index are indicated, but no weighting (e.g., algebraic weighted average) scheme is revealed.

In a separate part, institutions rated "B+" or higher are listed state by state. A third part alphabetically lists upgrades and downgrades during the spring 2001 quarter. An appendix lists recent bank and thrift failures (1997-2000). Of the 19 failures reported, all but one had low Weiss ratings. The exception had an "A-" rating (nonperforming loans were very large). This guide provides excellent, but not infallible, ratings for banks and thrifts.—**Richard A. Miller**

7 Industry and Manufacturing

DICTIONARIES AND ENCYCLOPEDIAS

194. **Encyclopedia of Emerging Industries.** Jane A. Malonis and Holly M. Selden, eds. Farmington Hills, Mich., Gale, 1998. 580p. illus. index. $249.00. ISBN 0-7876-1863-2. ISSN 1096-2433.

Encyclopedia of Emerging Industries (EEI) is the 1st edition of a planned annual series identifying, describing, and assessing the outlook for U.S. industries that show the greatest potential for growth. Twenty-one contributors, whose efforts were guided by the skilled editing of Jane A. Malonis and Holly M. Selden, have detailed essential facts on 88 U.S. industries. Some of the included industries, cigars for example, have been active in the economy for many years, but have recently experienced a resurgence of growth. Others, like artificial intelligence, have exploited recent technological developments in capturing or promising rapid growth. Industries are arranged alphabetically, listed in a table of contents, and cress-referenced in a comprehensive general index. Also, industries are indexed by SIC codes, with a conversion guide to NAICS codes. Thus, it is quite convenient to search for specific business sectors and major organizations. Each industry profile averages 3,000 words and includes current size, present status, and organization, as well as historical background and prospects for the future. In addition, leading companies are sub-profiled, industry pioneers recognized, and employment opportunities provided. Suggestions for further reading accompany each profile. Nearly 200 charts, graphs, and tables increase readability and understanding. Although a reference volume, the book should interest a broad audience—certainly business students and practitioners, but students from other fields as well, seeking trends in current U.S. business activity. [R: RUSQ, Summer 98, p. 352]—**William C. Struning**

195. **Encyclopedia of Tourism.** Jafar Jafari, ed. New York, Routledge, 2000. 683p. index. $140.00. ISBN 0-415-15405-7.

This timely reference work is the joint effort of an extensive editorial team and a long list of contributors and was five years in the making. Because this field of study is relatively new when compared to others there are few scholarly reference books on the subject, making this work especially valuable. There are more than 1,200 alphabetically arranged entries listed here, all of which are signed by the contributor. The entries range from a full page for often-used words (e.g., marketing, destination, recreation) to a few sentences (e.g., manpower development, collaborative education). Words appearing in the entries that have their own entry elsewhere in the volume are set apart in bold typeface. Many of the entries also contain *see also* references and a list for further reading. The editor points out in the introduction of this work that there are a few problems within the volume. Namely, because entries were written by many different contributors there tends to be an overlap of information in many of the entries. Also, subject areas tend to be unevenly represented, with some less-important entries receiving a more detailed description than the more important entries. Another drawback for American researchers is that British spellings are used instead of American English.

In spite of these few problems, this work will fill a niche in the field of tourism and travel. It is highly recommended for academic libraries offering classes in the field of tourism and the hospitality industries. [R: LJ, Jan 01, p. 88]—**Shannon Graff Hysell**

DIRECTORIES

196. **American Manufacturers Directory, 1999.** Omaha, Nebr., American Business Directories, 1999. 2v. $595.00/set. ISBN 1-56105-998-6.

Making things is out of fashion. Yet companies that manufacture products are the backbone of the economy. Everything from the food we eat and the appliances we use to prepare it, to the clothes we wear, the cars we drive, and the pumps used to fill their tanks with gasoline to power them are made by someone. The *American Manufacturers Directory* lists everyone in the U.S. supply chain, from printers to publishers to pulp and paper mills. More than 168,000 manufacturers are included.

The 2-volume print directory is arranged into 3 sections: alphabetically by company name, manufacturers by city, and manufacturers by SIC code. A final section provides counts by SIC code. Main entries are brief. A typical entry lists the manufacturer's name, address, telephone and fax numbers, a contact name and position, number of employees, estimated sales, SIC codes, a credit score, and a year code. Among the significant omissions are URLs for company Websites and company/subsidiary/affiliate/location relationships. There are no indications whether a company is publicly traded or if it is a headquarters location.

The directory's origin as a source for mailing lists compiled from yellow pages and business white pages telephone directories limits its usefulness as a reference work for manufacturing companies. Unlike Thomas Register of American Manufacturers (http://www.thomasregister.com), there is neither a trade name nor an alphabetic product name index. The entries do not offer any detail on the specific products made. To find companies that make a product one must first figure out the appropriate SIC code. The SIC definitions provided are minimal. The price advertised on InfoUSA's Website (http://www.infousa.com) is $595.00 for a subscription to the print directory with a CD-ROM version. The company also sells the data on mailing labels, magnetic tapes, and diskettes.—**Peter Zachary McKay**

197. **The American Manufacturers Disc.** 2000 library ed. [CD-ROM]. Omaha, Nebr., InfoUSA, 2000. Minimum system requirements: IBM or compatible PC. Double-speed CD-ROM drive. Windows 95, Windows 98, or Windows NT 4.0. 8MB RAM. 15MB hard disk space. $695.00.

Manufacturing is both the foundation and measure of industrialization within most modern economies. According to recent estimates, American manufacturers now employ more than 18.6 million laborers and produce approximately $1.4 trillion worth of products. Manufacturers are defined as those establishments that process raw materials into finished products, but the number of establishments can be difficult to count since a single firm can have many plants, branch operations, and subsidiaries. This comprehensive reference work provides an updated electronic listing of more than 645,000 American manufacturers.

Entries can be sorted, searched, and thus evaluated by a variety of useful measures. A basic method of organization is to search and arrange the database by a company's name or its type of business. The records of manufacturers are organized and can be searched by recognizable structures, such as the U.S. Office of Management and Budget's *Standard Industrial Classification*

Manual (SIC). Geographical searches can be conducted by zip code, city, county, state, metropolitan area, and area code. Companies can also be searched and arranged by sales volume and the number of employees. Financial information can be searched since credit ratings for many firms are available along with stock exchange listings from the New York Stock Exchange, NASDAQ, and the American Stock Exchange.

Because this reference work is available in an electronic format, searches can also be carried out with partial information. For example, even with partial names, addresses, and descriptions the CD-ROM's database can return a list of potential matches that are easily reviewed. As a reference work it is easy to use and provides concise information. Its most useful feature is its ability to combine various search criteria that provide users with more practical information. —**Timothy E. Sullivan**

198. **American Wholesalers and Distributors Directory: A Comprehensive Guide Offering Industry Details on Approximately 27,000 Wholesalers....** 7th ed. Rebecca Marlow-Ferguson, ed. Farmington Hills, Mich., Gale, 1999. 1668p. index. $195.00. ISBN 0-7876-2430-6. ISSN 1061-2114.

The subtitle of this book characterizes it as "a comprehensive guide offering industry details on approximately 27,000 wholesalers and distributors in the United States." Covering 61 major product categories, with extensive cross-listings of product types, plus both geographic and SIC-code indexes, it earns the "comprehensive" portion of this claim.

It is, however, somewhat sketchy on the "details" part. The typical entry is a company name, address, and telephone, combined with a vague description of the product lines offered, one or a few SIC codes, and sometimes some miscellaneous information (officers' names, date founded, and so on).—**Ray Olszewski**

199. **Brands and Their Companies: Consumer Products and Their Manufacturers with Addresses and Phone Numbers.** 18th ed. Jennifer L. Carman and Christine A. Kesler, eds. Farmington Hills, Mich., Gale, 1998. 2v. $805.00/set. ISBN 0-7876-2286-9. ISSN 1047-6407.

Who makes Wonderbras? (Sarah Lee). What are Wooly Boogers? (tires). Gale's *Brands and Their Companies* (BTC) answers these questions and 365,000 more about consumer brand names and who makes them. Branding distinguishes a product in the marketplace, provides assurance of consistent quality, and serves as a focal point for advertising and marketing. Glancing through the entries, one is struck by the many uses to which a name can be put. For example, "American Beauty" is a pasta and also a candy, a cigarette, giftware, greeting cards, seafood, soldering irons, wallpaper, and wet mops all made by different companies. BTC covers only consumer products.

There are so many brand names it is necessary to publish them in 2 hefty volumes at a hefty price ($805 per year). This edition includes more than 365,000 consumer brands by over 77,000 manufacturers and distributors (20,000 brands are new). The work is updated with a midyear supplement and is revised annually. The sources used to compile it are company literature, the United States Patent and Trademark Office (PTO), and trade journals and directories. BTC is arranged in two separate sections: brand listings and company listings. Numerical brands precede an alphabetic listing by brand name. Entries include the trade name, description, and manufacturer or distributor. Symbols indicate companies that are out of business, brands that are no longer produced, and brands that are currently considered generic. Brands not registered with the PTO as well as imported products are included. Company listings include name, address, phone, and fax. URLs, e-mail, and toll-free numbers are included as available.

BTC is the most comprehensive listing of consumer brand-name products in print. It is derived from a database maintained by Gale and is available on tape or diskette, CD-ROM, online, and through GaleNet. Other sources for brand names commonly held by libraries include the *Standard Directory of Advertisers* (1993 ed.; see ARBA 94, entry 296) and the *Thomas Register of American Manufacturers* (87th ed.; see entry 207). If readers want to know all of the brands a company makes, they will have to consult Gale's companion volumes, *Companies and Their Brands* (18th ed.; see entry 200).—**Peter Zachary McKay**

200.   **Companies and Their Brands: Manufacturers, Their Addresses and Phone Numbers, and the Consumer Products They Produce.** 18th ed. Jennifer L. Carman and Christine A. Kesler, eds. Farmington Hills, Mich., Gale, 1998. 2v. $515.00/set. ISBN 0-7876-2527-2. ISSN 1047-6407.

This massive set is an alphabetic list of U.S. companies, containing under each company entry contact information for the company (e.g., address and telephone numbers) and the brand names of the products it produces. If the user knows a company name and wants to find out what it makes, this is a key reference. It is extensive, apparently comprehensive, and includes entries for defunct companies and product lines. If one knows a brand name and wants to find the company that makes it the companion to this volume, *Brands and Their Companies: Consumer Products and Their Manufacturers with Addresses and Phone Numbers* (see entry 199), will need to be consulted

For more specialized users, such as investors, market researchers, and providers of business services, the book can contribute usefully to the development of company profiles. Overall, this is a database that invites delivery as a searchable, computer-based product, not a paper text, and most libraries would find a CD-ROM-based product of similar scope more useful than this set. The set also includes a brief directory of industry-specific information sources.—**Ray Olszewski**

201.   **Business & Industry.** [CD-ROM]. Beachwood, Ohio, Responsive Database Services, 1997. Minimum system requirements: IBM or compatible 386. CD-ROM drive. DOS 3.0. Windows. 8MB RAM. 7MB hard disk space. $2,397.00/yr. (single user). (Other pricing options available.)

Business & Industry is an extensive and practical electronic database of some 350,000 records outlining business information that has been compiled from more than 700 business trade magazines, regional newspapers, newsletters, international trade journals, and business dailies from more than 30 countries. Approximately 60 percent of these records contain the full text of articles, and the remaining records are abstracts. Despite covering a diverse array of business publications, entries within this database seem to consistently gather together the various facts, figures, and events contained within these published articles. Data, tables, and rankings are provided in a concise and factual manner for a great many companies, products, markets, and industries. As a CD-ROM, this is a handy reference device because users can readily search this large database by word, business subject, company, industry, brand names, and slogans as well as by publication date, journal name, and geographic areas.

A variety of users may benefit from and use this database in alternative ways. Academic users will most likely be interested in developing and comparing case studies and research papers. The relevant and timely material will be useful and necessary for consultants. Practitioners, investors, and prospective job candidates can review and evaluate companies, markets, and industries. Searches can be modified to detect specific information, as well as providing the ability to survey large amounts of data quickly and efficiently. The database's search engine also sorts the results by the frequency of selected search terms. Another useful and practical feature of this database is its ability to display a search history, which is invaluable to any user conducting multiple searches. [R: LJ, 15 June 97, p. 107]—**Timothy E. Sullivan**

202. Clarke, Norman F. **Recreation and Entertainment Industries: An Information Sourcebook.** 2d ed. Jefferson, N.C., McFarland, 2000. 286p. index. $55.00pa. ISBN 0-7864-0797-2.

This well-organized, annotated bibliography has been extensively revised to take into account name, title, and address changes; cessations; and industry classification revisions that have occurred in the decade since the work's initial publication. This new volume also incorporates many Websites along with e-mail and fax addresses, thus taking account of the new trends in information provision since the 1st edition. The focus is on North America, but there is wide coverage of international, especially European, organizations and sources.

The main body of the work is divided into 30 groupings of industries, from fitness and skiing to recreational vehicles, gifts, musical instruments, accommodations, and travel. Each chapter has sections for one or more North America Industry Classification System (NAICS) industries, replacing the older Standard Industrial Classification used in the earlier edition. Each industry section lists materials under several standard headings, including directories, management, industry, market, associations, periodicals, and databases. Citations themselves include bibliographic details, address and contact information where appropriate, and a sentence to a paragraph characterizing the source's usefulness.

Another feature is an appendix on basic reference sources. It uses the same headings and annotation format as the industry sections. The index gives access by title or organization to entry numbers. Contents list the chapters and NAICS industries covered. This work is recommended for academic and larger public libraries collecting on this dynamic sector.—**Nigel Tappin**

203. **The Directory of Business to Business Catalogs 2002.** 10th ed. Lakeville, Conn., Grey House Publishing, 2002. 752p. index. $190.00; $165.00pa. ISBN 1-930956-12-6; 1-930956-11-8pa.

This directory will be useful in large public libraries with business clientele as well as large corporate libraries with purchasing departments. It provides contact information for more than 6,100 catalogs in 39 industries. The industries range from agriculture and book publishers to office products and telecommunications. A general entry includes the company's address, telephone and fax number, toll-free number, e-mail and Website address, a brief description of the business, key personnel, number of years in business, credit cards accepted, number of employees, and price of catalog (if any). Not all of this information is provided for each company; the amount of data provided varies greatly. The book includes a catalog index, a geographic index, and a Website index. The names of catalog companies are in bold typeface.

This directory is also available online. The same 6,100 business-to-business catalogs are listed but the user can search the site by entering the product type, geographic location, sales volume, printing information, or product keyword. The database can help users determine the catalog companies that meet their sales volume or criteria as well as the names of personnel that can help with their business venture. The online database is significantly more expensive than the book volume; however, with the purchase of the online version one receives the book edition free.—**Shannon Graff Hysell**

204. **Directory of Contract Electronics Manufacturers, 1999.** North Americ ed. Kathleen Fitzpatrick and others, eds. San Francisco, Calif., Miller Freeman, 1998. 368p. index. $295.00pa.

Listing almost 1,400 electronics manufacturers who work under contract, this directory provides information necessary to identify companies with the capabilities to match specific needs. It opens with a review of the contract electronics manufacturers industry, followed by a state-by-state list of companies. Each listing has the address; year founded; top officers; types of board assembly; production data (e.g., plant size, capacity, specifications on work done, end products); assembly equipment; test equipment; materials procurement (e.g., consignment, turnkey); and other services. Several indexes organize manufacturers regionally by type of component preparation. There is a list of associations and trade shows as well as an alphabetic list of companies.

This directory is a straightforward list of and information on contract electronics firms that do customized work to specifications. However, the terminology used for individual companies is technical, and it is assumed that the reader is familiar with it. This source will be valuable in settings where users, probably local technology firms, will need to identify possible suppliers. *Directory of Contract Electronics Manufacturers, 1999* is recommended for libraries that serve a high technology clientele from the local community.—**Gerald L. Gill**

205. **Directory of the Steel Industry and the Environment.** By the Economic Commission for Europe. New York, United Nations, 1996. 90p. $52.00pa. ISBN 92-1-116654-3. S/N E.96.II.E.22.

Sponsored by the United Nations Economic Commission for Europe (UN/ECE), the *Directory of the Steel Industry and the Environment* comprises five categories: United Nations commissions and programs; international financing organizations; international governmental organizations; international nongovernmental organizations; and governments, associations, and steelmakers of all the ECE member countries and other major steel-producing countries. This is a broad and diverse group. For example, in the last category, U.S. listings include groups within the Department of Commerce, the Environmental Protection Agency, the Department of Energy, and the International Trade Commission; the American Iron and Steel Institute, the American Welding Society, the United Steelworkers of America, and the Steel Recycling Institute; plus 12 of the nation's largest steelmakers. Generally, the entries include name, address, and telephone and fax numbers, but occasionally some of these data are absent. Some entries provide a Website or telex number, but there is no other information as to mission or history. As the author states, the directory is far from exhaustive, so it will be of interest primarily to those involved in the work done by the sponsoring organization.—**G. Kim Dority**

206. **The Harris Manufacturers Directory 2000.** national ed. Frances L. Carlsen, ed. Twinsburg, Ohio, Harris InfoSource International, 2000. 2v. $565.00/set. ISBN 1-55600-709-4. ISSN 1061-2076.

This is an extensive and hefty reference work that is an updated directory of American manufacturers, compiled in cooperation with the National Association of Manufacturers, which provides useful and practical data in a handy and efficient format. Statistical summaries are provided for nearly 47,000 American manufacturing establishments that employ a minimum of 100 employees. A representative entry lists such things as the establishment's mailing address, telephone and fax numbers, the names and titles of key corporate personnel, the number of employees onsite, primary and secondary SIC codes along with product descriptions, estimates of foreign trade and annual sales, whether or not the firm is publicly or privately owned, the year the company was established, and referrals for companies that have changed their name or moved. The first and larger of these two volumes contains this statistical information for these manufacturers and is arranged as an alphabetic listing. The second volume is arranged into four distinct and practical listings: geographic, by SIC code, by rank order, and by industrial product.

Users may find the second volume more useful for local and product-oriented analysis. The geographic section alphabetically lists manufacturers by state and cities within those states. County and city tables and state maps are provided to facilitate analysis of establishments in proximity to each other or to market areas. The SIC section lists and cross-lists firms under more than 500 four-digit classification codes. The products of these manufacturers are listed under some 5,000 product and manufacturing service categories. Rankings are provided on both the national and state levels. National rankings list the 1,000 leading manufacturers ordered and grouped by employment levels. State rankings list the top 100, or as many as possible, manufacturing establishments for each state and sorted by employment levels by location.—**Timothy E. Sullivan**

207. **Thomas Register of American Manufacturers, 1997.** 87th ed. New York, Thomas Publishing, 1997. 33v. illus. index. $210.00/set.

208. **Thomas Register on CD-ROM, 1997.** [CD-ROM]. New York, Thomas Publishing, 1997. Minimum system requirements: IBM or compatible 486. Windows-supported CD-ROM drive (double-speed or faster recommended). DOS 3.3. Windows 3.1. 16MB RAM. 5MB hard disk space. VGA monitor. Windows-supported mouse. Windows-supported printer. $210.00.

The *Thomas Register* is an extensive and comprehensive inventory of the many and diverse products and services available from U.S. manufacturers. Volumes 1 through 22 contain more than 56,000 alphabetically listed product and service headings. Within each of these headings is a list of manufacturers and suppliers arranged alphabetically by states as well as by cities within individual states. Scattered throughout these listings are advertisements that provide comparative details about various manufacturers and suppliers. Volumes 23 and 24 provide company profiles on some 152,000 alphabetically arranged U.S. firms. In a typical entry, the company's name is followed by a concise list of the firm's products, along with contact information, asset ratings, data on subsidiaries, and even if the company provides export services. Volumes 25 through 33 contain alphabetically arranged catalog descriptions, pictures, technical sketches, and diagrams of product lines for some 2,400 companies. Entries throughout this ample and impressive register are cross-referenced and indexed, which makes it a practical albeit weighty directory of the distribution, location, and activity of U.S. manufacturers and suppliers.

This directory is also available on CD-ROM. In its electronic format, the directory permits users to more easily search and compare information because items are indexed and cross-referenced. The CD-ROM contains an interactive tutorial to guide users through the practical features of the register. Users can not only search by types of products and services available, by company name, and by brand names, but also attach and edit notes to a specific record or company.—**Timothy E. Sullivan**

209. **USA Oil Industry Directory 1998.** 37th ed. Margaret Acevedo, ed. Tulsa, Okla., PennWell Publishing, 1998. 344p. index. $165.00pa. ISSN 0082-8599.

This directory lists more than 3,000 oil and gas companies involved in various activities, such as drilling, exploration/production, pipeline gathering, and refining/petrochemicals. In addition to production company information, this directory includes the names of brokers and dealers, marketing companies, and national associations affiliated with the petroleum industry. The purpose of this directory is to provide a complete listing of contacts for decision-makers in the petroleum industry who depend on them.

The directory is divided into industry segments with listings organized alphabetically by company name. Each entry includes company address, telephone and fax numbers, e-mail addresses (when applicable), names of key executives, plant information, and pertinent descriptions. Each main company name is designated with a black box (bullet) and is in all capital letters. Subsidiary companies are listed under their corporate parent but are referenced in the company index. Companies that are new to this year's edition, such as ROC Gases, are listed with an asterisk. The 2d section, entitled "Index/Surveys," is arranged alphabetically by state and then by plant name. In addition to the geographic index, there are company and personnel indexes. Also included is a survey, entitled "OGJ200," that is reprinted from the *Oil & Gas Journal.*

This edition incorporates industry changes, mergers, and acquisitions as provided by the companies at the time of printing. Hence, Burlington Resources Inc. appears on this year's list as the parent company instead of Meridian Oil Inc. Amoco's merger with British Petroleum is not listed, however. The publisher promises that the directory will be continuously updated. This useful, comprehensive reference source is recommended for engineering students and employees of the petroleum industries.—**Marilynn Green Hopman**

210.   **World Cosmetics and Toiletries Directory 1999.** Chicago, Euromonitor International; distr., Farmington Hills, Mich., Gale, 1999. 589p. $990.00pa. ISBN 0-86338-808-6.

Marketing information is supplied on 6,000 leading cosmetic companies in nearly 60 countries along with statistical marketing information data in this volume. This book has an introduction with world and area rankings of the major companies according to sales. This is followed by major companies separated into country categories and contains such information as company name and full headquarters address, telephone and fax numbers, Website and e-mail addresses, year established, main activity of company, parent holding and ultimate holding company together with details of shareholding, major subsidiaries at home and abroad with details on any shareholding, key personnel, number of employees for latest year, details of main products and brands of the manufacturing and marketing companies, number of trading names, and size of outlets for retailers. Financial data, including financial year-end turnover and profit in the last three to four years, details on sales geographically and manufacturing capabilities, general notes covering company news and development, and company products and brands market shares are included where available. This is followed by a section on official organizations, again subdivided into countries, and another section including major trade and business associations followed by a section on major trade and business journals. There are several indexes that break down the countries of the world and give sales figures on various commodities, usually from 1992 to 1996. These are followed by a general index and information source sector index. The book should be useful for personnel trying to locate potential partners, identify and find competitors, generate sales leads, and access expert insights into new markets. It also provides useful information on finances, brand and company shares, and recent developments. This should be an essential book for people interested in the toiletries and cosmetics marketing industries.—**Herbert W. Ockerman**

211.   **World Drinks Marketing Directory 1999.** Chicago, Euromonitor International; distr., Farmington Hills, Mich., Gale, 1999. 859p. index. $990.00. ISBN 0-86338-807-8.

This latest Euromonitor directory expands on material found in the well-received *European Drinks Marketing Directory* (see entry 338). The new title covers 4,000 companies, approximately twice as many as the earlier version, costs twice as much, but covers the drinks industry worldwide. Drinks are broadly defined as mineral and sparkling waters, fruit juices, soft and carbonated drinks, iced tea, sport drinks, beer, wines, and spirits. Most of the companies are from 60 First World countries, but tables providing various rankings list up to 150 countries. It is divided into four parts. The first and largest part lists companies by country with some or all of the following data: company name, full address, phone, fax, telex, year established, main activities, parent and subsidiary holdings, key personnel, number of employees, outlets/operations, brands (with notes on important brands), market share, and brief financials (i.e., turnover, profit, operating revenue). Also included are general notes that can run up to 500 words of text, though most notes are only a few sentences long.

The second section gives approximately 800 sources of information such as associations and statistical locations or sources. Of particular value is the inclusion of leading market research companies for non-U.S. or U.K. markets, though it is surprisingly weak for U.S. market research companies. Other minor sections include trade and business journals, Web addresses, and nongovernmental statistical sources. The 3rd section is 37 pages of tables on per capita value and sales volume by type of drink for 50 or so of the largest economies. The last section consists of company name and type of beverage indexes, but does not include a brand name index.

This work, like other Euromonitor directories, is notably strong in non-U.S. and U.K. companies, weak in financials, and pricey. To be fair, getting accurate financial data for non-European businesses is very difficult. Although it is published in England, virtually all the terminology is understandable. Readers may also want to look at the *Food and Beverage Market Place* (1997/98 ed.; see ARBA 99, entry 1339). It is an excellent complement to the more costly and more detailed worldview provided by the equally fine and unique *World Drinks Marketing Directory 1999*. Libraries serving the drinks industry would do well to have both.—**Patrick J. Brunet**

212. **World Food Marketing Directory 1999.** Chicago, Euromonitor International; distr., Farmington Hills, Mich., Gale, 1999. 2v. index. $990.00/set. ISBN 0-86338-809-4.

In this extensive directory, the publisher expands the scope of an earlier publication, *The European Food Marketing Directory* (1994 ed.; see ARBA 95, entry 279), from regional to worldwide coverage. The directory has 4 sections. Section 1 includes profiles of approximately 6,000 major food companies in some 60 countries. Most company entries contain company name and headquarters address; telephone and fax numbers; Website and e-mail addresses, if available; year established; main activity of the company; parent or holding company, if applicable; major subsidiaries; key personnel; number of employees; main products and brands; number, trading names, and size of outlets for the retailers; financial data; sales geography and manufacturing capacity, if applicable; general notes on company news and developments; and company product and brand market shares, if available. Volume 1 lists rankings of leading international food manufacturers and retailers in the front of the volume, and each country has a similar ranking prior to the country's listing. The last three sections of the directory contain supportive material on food marketing and can be located in volume 2. Section 2 lists more than 2,000 sources of information related to food marketing, including journals, online sources, and business information Websites. Section 3 provides the reader with useful statistics, such as total consumer expenditures as well as expenditures on specific food products, for the past 5 years. Section 4 enhances access to the publication with general and sector indexes. This directory on food marketing comprises a comprehensive source of information for pertinent business and large public and academic libraries that have a demonstrated a need in this area. [R: Choice, Sept 99, p. 124]—**O. Gene Norman**

213. **Worldwide Offshore Petroleum Directory 1998.** 30th ed. Margaret Acevedo and Elizabeth Arceneaux, eds. Tulsa, Okla., PennWell Publishing, 1998. 528p. index. $165.00pa. ISSN 1096-1356.

Formerly known as the *Worldwide Offshore Contractors & Equipment Directory*, this volume is in its 30th edition. PennWell Publishing proudly points out that this is not a directory of advertisercompanies do not pay to be listed. Companies are listed because they answered an annual questionnaire that updates and verifies each entry for changes caused by mergers, acquisitions, or personnel changes.

The directory is divided into industry segments with listings arranged alphabetically. Segment examples include exploration and production, services companies, and suppliers and manufacturers. The entries are arranged by parent company. Parenthood is designated by a black box above the all-capital-letter entry. Under each parent, in smaller typeface, is a list of the relevant subsidiaries. New companies or those with significant changes are marked with a star.

The directory has two major indexes, alphabetic and geographic. The alphabetic index lists all entries from parent to subsidiary in one listing. This arrangement makes it possible to find a subsidiary without knowing the parent company's name—a useful feature. Access is also possible by state or country using the geographical index. This directory is "the" directory in this field and as such is useful for any library serving users interested in the petroleum industry.—**Susan B. Ardis**

214. **Worldwide Petrochemical Directory 1998.** 36th ed. Anne K. Rhodes and Margaret Acevedo, eds. Tulsa, Okla., PennWell Publishing, 1998. 295p. index. $165.00pa. ISSN 0084-2583.

This volume is the 36th edition in a series of petroleum industry directories published by PennWell Publishing. As usual, the issue is divided into regions (continents and countries) with listings arranged in alphabetic order by company. Each main company is designated with a black box and is in all capital letters. Subsidiary companies are listed under their corporate parent but are referenced in the company index. Companies that are new to this year's edition or have had significant changes have been designated with a star. The contents of the directory are as follows: geographic regionsUnited States, Canada, Latin America, Europe, Asia-Pacific, Middle East, and Africa; supplementary information on engineering and construction; a company index; a geographic reference; and statistical surveys.

This issue is entirely new, having been updated by questionnaire research in return for a free company listing. Included information has been verified and incorporates all industry changes, mergers, and acquisitions as provided by participating companies at the time of printing. The directory is the standard reference guide to the petroleum industry; it contains the most reliable and compatible information from one of the world's leading providers. Therefore, this edition can be recommended as a book of ready-reference for all decision-makers involved in the petroleum business.—**Ludmila N. Ilyina**

HANDBOOKS AND YEARBOOKS

215. **Agriculture, Mining, and Construction USA: Industry Analyses, Statistics, and Leading Companies.** Arsen J. Darnay, ed. Farmington Hills, Mich., Gale, 1998. 1133p. maps. index. $205.00. ISBN 0-7876-2827-1.

Gale continues its USA series by adding the three sectors of the economy in *Agriculture, Mining, and Construction USA*. The work includes 77 industries as defined by the 1987 Standard Industrial Classification (SIC) code. Primary data from the *Economic Census of the United States* (1977, 1982, 1987, 1992) are supplemented by establishment, employment, and compensation data for 1993-1995 from *County Business Patterns* (Gordon Press, 1995). Projections are made through 1998. Statistics on 127 agricultural commodities are derived primarily from *Agricultural Statistics*. Individual company information comes from *Ward's Business Directory*. Finally, data on 100 occupational groups as defined by the Bureau of Labor Statistics *Industry-Occupation Matrix* are included. With the exception of *Ward's Business Directory*, all of the sources are governmentally produced and available in depository libraries. The value of this book comes from its combining of sources and footnotes, allowing the researcher to easily discern the original sources. The first part of this work presents national and state data organized by sector and SIC code. The second part presents state and county data.

When combined with the other volumes in the series, a detailed portrait of U.S. industry can be obtained. With the 1997 *Economic Census* (construction, mining) and the *Census of Agriculture* (the 1997 edition being conducted by the U.S. Department of Agriculture and not the Census Bureau) scheduled to debut in the spring of 1999, this volume will soon be useful for historical purposes only. As Gale begins to provide updates to the series using the 1997 censuses, it should include both the North American Industry Classification System (NAICS) as well as the SIC codes along with a concordance. This work will be useful for ready-reference purposes in business library collections. [R: BL, 1 Dec 98, p. 698]—**Bobray Bordelon**

216.   **By the Numbers: Emerging Industries.** Lazich, Robert S., ed. Detroit, Gale, 1998. 534p. index. $79.00pa. ISBN 0-7876-1859-4. ISSN 1096-4967.

By the Numbers is a series of four volumes of statistical data about various industries. This volume, *Emerging Industries*, mainly covers computers (hardware and software), other electronics, and biotech

Market research is a valuable commodity, so it comes as little surprise that the good information is generally not cheap, and the cheap information generally not good. This is the case with this volume. Aside from some tables drawn from U.S. government sources (and readily available elsewhere), this collection is a haphazard mishmash of tables and summaries drawn from various publications. Usually the ultimate source of the data is a well-known research firm such as IDG or Dataquest, but the actual data can come from anywhere, including trade publications, daily newspapers, and financial newspapers and magazines.

Little care is taken with even the basic requirements of documentation for the tables. For example, what products do the terms *hand-held computer*, *electronic organizer*, and *PDA* cover? Separate market share reports for these three categories appear as tables but provide no explanation of how the definitions differ.

Even more egregiously, the tables do not distinguish historical data from estimates of the future, requiring a careful look at the source citation to give one guidance in this area. Table 39, for example, lists market shares for the "global multimedia market" (another undefined term) for 1994, 1997, and 2000. Although one can assume the year 2000 data are estimates, one needs to note that the cited source has a June 1997 date to infer that the 1997 data are at least partly projected. Not clearly marking estimates as such violates a basic rule of data presentation

Researchers with a professional need for market research in these areas should not rely on the odd assembly of tables provided here; for them, more systematic (and costly) reports are available. This collection may suffice to assuage casual curiosity, but not more than that. [R: Choice, Nov 98, p. 499]—**Ray Olszewski**

217.   **Dun & Bradstreet/Gale Group Industry Handbook: Entertainment and Hospitality.** Jennifer Zielinski, ed. Farmington Hills, Mich., Gale, 2000. 600p. index. $135.00. ISBN 0-7876-3774-2. ISSN 1521-6640.

This handbook is one in a series of collaborations between Dun & Bradstreet and the Gale Group that mostly repackages and combines information from their other, more established, publications. The handbook is divided into two parts covering the entertainment industry and the hospitality industry.

Each part is subdivided into a foreword and 10 chapters. The foreword introduces the industry with brief sketches of the major industry segments highlighting recent trends. By including so many varied activities—motion pictures, television, video games, radio, race cars, music bands, professional sports, arcades, dance studios, adult entertainment, zoos, and so on—the essays lack coherence. The first chapter presents an industry overview structured like those found in Gale's *Encyclopedia of American Industry*. The overview includes an industry snapshot, organization and structure, background and development, pioneers in the industry, current conditions and future projections, industry leaders, workforce, a section on North America and the World, and one on research and technology. Because so many lines of business are brought together under the heading of "Entertainment" this section markedly lacks the detail and depth of Gale's encyclopedia. The second chapter reprints data tables from *Service Industries*

USA, which has reprinted tables from the *U.S. Census of Service Industries* and other federal government statistical publications. In some cases, an entire page is devoted to three or four lines of data. The third chapter provides three years of financial data and ratios by SIC code from Dun & Bradstreet's *Industry Norms and Key Business Ratios*. This is followed by the fourth chapter's directory listings for 1,000 companies in the industry. No reasons are given for including or excluding companies. The most significant omission is the virtual absence of any Internet companies. The fifth chapter has two ranked lists of all 1,000 companies by sales and by employment. There is no division by type of business. The sixth chapter discusses mergers and acquisitions in the entertainment industry, listing significant deals. The last four chapters list associations, consultants, trade information sources, and trade shows derived from other Gale publications. These lists are alphabetical with no breakdown by industry sector.

A master index lists names of companies, organizations, individuals, SIC industry names, and terms with corresponding page numbers. A company index by SIC does list the companies in the directory by SIC code. A geographical company index lists companies by state. The work concludes with an appendix converting SIC codes to NAICS and NAICS to SIC.

Library patrons, reference librarians, and other users may find the repackaging of this disparate information convenient. But, overall, the volume lacks depth, detail, timeliness, and coherence. The Gale and Dun & Bradstreet brand names on the cover and in the title indicate a quality that is sadly lacking. [R: LJ, 1 April 2000, pp. 88-90]—**Peter Zachary McKay**

218. Dun and Bradstreet/Gale Industry Reference Handbooks: Hospitality. Stacy A. McConnell and Linda D. Hall, eds. Farmington Hills, Mich., Gale, 1999. 722p. $99.00pa. ISBN 0-7876-3776-9.

This survey is one of nine planned to be published covering the most popular industries. Each will be updated annually. The information is a compilation of other Dun and Bradstreet and Gale reference books and as such represents material that is already owned in many libraries, but is collected here for convenience.

The opening chapter is an overview that describes the industry, its history, its key players, its workforce, and the relevance of the data collected. Particularly useful are the surveys of trends and future expectations of the industry. Next are the performance indicators and industry norms that compare a variety of data (employees, solvency ratios, profitability, and so on) by SIC code (Standard Industrial Classification). Data are from 1995 to 1997.

The largest section is an alphabetic company directory with address information, sales, employees, and private and public status. The data are similar to those of any Dun and Bradstreet directory. This is supplemented with ranking lists by sales (from 1st to 4,859th) and by employment. Next is a section chronicling merger and acquisition activity during 1997 and 1998, arranged by company, with a citation of the announcement from *Nation's Restaurant News*, *PR Newswire*, and other sources.

The associations list is selected from the *Encyclopedia of Associations* (37th ed.; see ARBA 2002, entries 41, 42, and 43) and seems unnecessary here. The usual hotel and restaurant associations and unions are suitable, but the Bob Crane Memorial Fan Club seems to be a curious inclusion. The consultants and trade publications sections are adapted from more of Gale's commonly available reference books.

The indexes are essential for a collection like this, and the master index does cover each of the above sections. The geographic index is by state, not city and state, and there are very useful conversion lists of SIC to NAICS (North American Industrial Classification System, the successor to Standard Industrial Classification) and from NAICS to SIC.

This work is a useful compilation combining many features from two of the best-known reference publishers, and can be recommended for libraries that are willing to acquire it annually, either selectively or as an entire series. However, the majority of this information will already be available in a reasonably equipped reference collection, and each library will have to decide the ultimate cost of convenience.—**Gary R. Cocozzoli**

219. **Energy & Environmental Industry Survey 1997.** Ruth M. Bennett, comp. and ed. Lilburn, Ga., Fairmont Press, 1997. 109p. $95.00. ISBN 0-88173-281-8.

The 8,200 members of the Association of Energy Engineers were polled on their opinions of the energy and environmental marketplace and asked to provide salary data. The return rate was 8.6 percent, and this work is based on the returned surveys. They were asked to evaluate products and detail purchasing trends for energy management systems, lighting, motors, and drives. Other questions involved cogeneration and independent power production, energy services, and demand-side management.

A reproduction of the original questionnaire serves the purpose of an index, and the overall work acts as both a codebook and source of data. This highly specialized study is written for industry insiders and makes no attempt to explain terminology or acronyms. Researchers investigating the energy and environmental industry who need technical information and human resource executives seeking specialized compensation data may also find this survey useful. Results are only given for the current year; a time series would make the data more useful for comparative purposes. It is not mentioned when this annual survey was first conducted or if the data are available in machine-readable form. This work is recommended for special libraries in the energy and environmental industry and research libraries that have a strong interest in this field.—**Bobray Bordelon**

220. **First Stop for Jobs and Industries.** Jennifer A. Dupuis, ed. Farmington Hills, Mich., Gale, 2000. 1483p. index. (Gale Ready Reference Handbook Series). $125.00pa. ISBN 0-7876-3950-8. ISSN 1526-2758.

The 1st section of this work, "Jobs," is a blending of the U.S. Department of Labor's *Occupational Outlook Handbook* (see entry 402) and essays written by the Gale Group. All entries begin with a brief section that includes salary range, Dictionary of Occupational Titles (D.O.T.) codes, and preferred education. Following the *Occupational Outlook Handbook* format, the nature of the work, job outlook, earnings, and related industries are provided. The 2d section, "Industries," offers excerpts from Gale's own titles—the *Encyclopedia of American Industries* (see ARBA 95, entry 236) and the *Encyclopedia of Emerging Industries* (see entry 194). A snapshot of each industry is given, along with a list of the major players in that industry. Two appendixes present a numerical listing of the D.O.T. codes, along with their corresponding federally recognized job titles and a listing of the Standard Industrial Classification (SIC) codes. No mention is made of NAICS (North American Industrial Classification System). Like most Gale products, the index is extremely helpful and comprehensive. The repackaging is well done and is useful for libraries that do not have the space for the original sources, but the work provides no real added benefit because it consists largely of extracted material and has minor original content. The price is rather steep for a paperback of reformatted information. This volume is recommended only for libraries willing to pay extra for the convenience of providing a one-stop source for job-hunters. [R: BR, Sept/Oct 2000, p. 76]—**Bobray Bordelon**

221. **Handbook of North American Industry.** 2d ed. John E. Cremeans, ed. Lanham, Md., Bernan Associates, 1999. 644p. maps. $89.00. ISBN 0-89059-157-1.

In 1998, the 1st edition of the *Handbook of North American Industry* appeared (see ARBA 99, entry 220). The work has now been updated and, although the amount of new information is relatively small, all that made the 1st edition win prestigious library awards remains true. While the focus is the impact of the North American Free Trade Agreement (NAFTA), the benefit of this work is its pulling together of industry and employment data from numerous U.S., Canadian, and Mexican sources to present a unified and comparative statistical analysis of the North American economy.

This edition updates some of the features found in the 1st, such as a review of NAFTA; employees, benefits, and wages in North America; and the "Free Trade Area of the Americas Initiative." The added feature is on labor unions in North America. The majority of the work is statistical in nature. Standardized chapters make it easy to gain a grasp of industry. Textual analysis is based on the statistics. With the United States being the dominant economy, more information is available on it than on its partner countries. A useful feature is a comparative table at the end of each chapter showing NAFTA's impact on each nation. Although the North American Industrial Classification System (NAICS) scheme is included in the appendix, the United States Standard Industrial Classification System (SIC) is used to present data since NAICS data are not yet available. With data from the 1997 Census not yet available, much of the data for the United States are derived from the 1992 economic census. Various statistical agencies help update the data to 1997 (with some key data as recent as 1998) and in some cases projections to 2006. Canadian data tend to end with 1996 and Mexican data usually end around 1997. In all cases, data back to 1988 are available. Additional appendixes include an overview of NAFTA's predecessor—the Maquiladora program and governmental infrastructure information.

Although more current information can be obtained from other sources, this inexpensive work makes it easy for the researcher to get a quick overview and know which sources to turn for further information. If one has the 1st edition, this is a nice but not essential update because it only has one more year of information. All business collections could benefit from this work, whether the current or the 1st edition.—**Bobray Bordelon**

222.   **How Products Are Made, Volume 4: An Illustrated Guide to Product Manufacturing.** Jacqueline L. Longe, ed. Farmington Hills, Mich., Gale, 1999. 489p. illus. index. $90.00. ISBN 0-7876-2443-8. ISSN 1072-5091.

How Products Are Made: An Illustrated Guide to Product Manufacturing provides concise descriptions of the manufacturing process for 103 common products. The products include foods (e.g., rice cakes, licorice), toys (e.g., kazoos, model trains), household items (e.g., shellac, vinyl floor covering), vehicles (e.g., motorcycles, armored trucks), clothing (e.g., spandex, wet suits), and a number of other assorted products. The descriptions are clearly written and nicely illustrated so that little, if any, technical knowledge is needed to understand the processes. This volume is part of a series of similar volumes. The index in this volume gives references on the products included in this publication as well as the products discussed in other volumes. This reference work will be a useful inclusion in any engineering, science, or business collection. It will have limited usefulness in more general collections.—**Paul F. Clark**

223.   **Industrial Commodity Statistics Yearbook, 1998: Production Statistics (1989-1998). Annuaire de Statistiques Industrielles par Produit.** By the Department of Economic and Social Affairs, Statistics Division. New York, United Nations, 2000. 889p. $115.00. ISBN 92-1-061188-8. ISSN 0257-7208. S/N E/F.01.XVII.3.

The 32d edition under review provides up to 10 years of production figures for almost 530 commodities divided into 3 broad categories and 26 subcategories: mining and quarrying (4 subcategories); manufacturing and food (20 subcategories), and electricity and gas (2 subcategories). Data cover 1989-1998 and are displayed by continent and then by country, with many footnotes detailing qualifications and sources. Commodities include such traditional goods like grains, cotton, coal, and so on, but also such items as rubber footwear, washing powders, men's underwear, and cigars. All notes, as well as the brief introduction, are in both English and French. Both International Standard Industrial Classification (ISIC) and Standard International Trade Classification (SITC) numbers are linked to each commodity and there is an index that translates the numbers between the systems. The index does not list page numbers, but rather the ISIC/SITC numbers, even though they are not presented in exact numerical order in the body of the work.

Comparing this title to other works on commodities, the coverage is very good. The U.S. government document, *Minerals Yearbook* is a major source with statistics reported verbatim. The U.S. produced *Agricultural Statistics* is cited less frequently, but is generally one year more current although it covers fewer countries. The *CRB Commodity Yearbook* (see entry 136) provides more tabular data, but for only about 120 commodities. The *World Commodity Survey* covers only 70 commodities, but provides extensive textual explanation of the state of the commodities and is one to three years more current. The *CRB Commodity Yearbook* (CRB), *World Commodities Survey* (WCS), *Minerals Yearbook*, *Agricultural Statistics*, and the *Industrial Commodities Statistics Yearbook* (ICSY) are far more complementary than competitive. The ICSY benefits from the authority of the United Nations but, like most UN produced statistical sources, suffers against the other titles in not being as current. Since the CRB and the WCS offer textual description for the current state of affairs for the commodities they cover and the ICSY is tabular, they are particularly good choices for academic and larger libraries seeking good coverage on commodities. Very small libraries could easily get by with *Agricultural Statistics.*—**Patrick J. Brunet**

224.   **Manufacturing Worldwide: Industry Analyses, Statistics, Products, and Leading Companies and Countries.** 3d ed. Arsen J. Darnay, ed. Farmington Hills, Mich., Gale, 1999. 885p. index. $210.00. ISBN 0-7876-2447-0. ISSN 1084-8738.

The 1st edition of this title was issued in 1995 as a companion title to Gale's established series on U.S. industries. This edition provides industry statistics for 190 countries gathered from the United Nations Industrial Development Organization Industrial Statistics Branch. The United Nations Statistical Division's *Industrial Commodity Production Statistics* was the source for the commodity data. Some of the company information was also retrieved from Gale's *World Business Directory*. These data cover the period from 1990 through 1995 except for commodity data, which are current through 1996. Only 133 manufacturing countries from the above databases had information current enough to be included for the general statistical profile section. Part 1, which is 90 percent of the book, includes nearly 500 product categories produced by more than 4,000 companies. In addition to providing statistical summaries of each product category, there is a list of representative companies for each sector, which provides standard contact information.

The country profile section provides a half-page summary of the manufacturing activities for the years 1990 to 1995 in 16 categories, such as number of establishments, total employment, and capital investment. The index provides both country and company references. For libraries fielding questions about doing business overseas, this book will be a useful addition. It will serve as a beginning point in understanding the size of the markets in other countries.—**Judith J. Field**

225.   **Market Share Reporter, 2000: An Annual Compilation of Reported Market Share Data on Companies, Products, and Services.** Robert S. Lazich, ed. Farmington Hills, Mich., Gale, 1999. 595p. illus. index. $245.00. ISBN 0-7876-2449-7. ISSN 1052-9578.

This volume (the 10th edition) presents 2,000 entries in 500 SIC codes on "market" shares as reported in numerous sources (979), such as trade journals and Internet sites. All of the data are either new or updated from the 9th edition and cover North America, although the entries are primarily for information pertaining to the U.S. rather than Mexico and Canada. Entries are by firms; by products, commodities, and services; and by geographic areas. The coverage is wide: snowboard makers, agriculture banks, hotel companies, casket makers, charitable donations, gasoline stations by state, and largest grocers in various cities. Data are also provided for the 1997 Internet browser market (Netscape Navigator, Microsoft Internet Explorer, AOL, and others) and the 1998 operating systems market (Windows 98 and Windows NT). The excellent indexes include sources (979); place-names (more than 250); products, services, names, and issues (1,980); companies (4,000); brands (1,250); SIC coverage; SIC to NAICS conversion; NAICS to SIC conversion; and an annotated list. This resource is available on tape, diskette, online (LEXIS-NEXIS), and on CD-ROM. It is not a substitute for data available from the Bureau of the Census.—**Richard A. Miller**

226. **Plunkett's Retail Industry Almanac 1999–2000.** By Jack W. Plunkett. Houston, Tex., Plunkett Research, 1999. 648p. index. $179.99pa. ISBN 1-891775-05-7.

This is a directory of U.S.-based and mostly publicly held retailers, where retailers are broadly defined to include retail chain stores and retail service companies as well as the growing number of nonstore retailers. Given the pervasive significance and influence of consumer spending, this is an industry that clearly has a meaningful effect on both the U.S. economy and American culture. It is an industry that not only had sales of nearly $2.7 trillion in 1998 but is also changing over time and thus is typically redefining itself. Accordingly, this is a useful and informative guide to current conditions in U.S. retailing rather than merely for select firms or for particular retailing activities. It provides statistical and descriptive information for 500 companies. It consolidates into one general reference guide information on acquisitions and consolidations, data on sales and profits, the numbers of personnel in various occupations, and the names and addresses of officers and other significant contacts, as well as the names and descriptions of brands, divisions, and affiliates for these firms.

This reference work also helps provide a historical context to American retailing. There is a brief descriptive passage for each of the 500 profiled retailers, outlining growth plans and other special features of the firm. Appendixes to the guide also include three years' worth of monthly retail trade surveys along with the Web addresses needed to retrieve current census surveys. The almanac also contains a glossary of retailing terms, definitions of the business classification used by the Department of Commerce, a short list of notable industry-wide retail and retail-related contacts (postal and Web addresses, telephone numbers), along with state and regional indexes of company headquarters. This is an easy-to-use and informative reference work that will be helpful to a variety of users.—**Timothy E. Sullivan**

227. **Plunkett's Telecommunications Industry Almanac.** Jack W. Plunkett, ed. Houston, Tex., Plunkett Research, 2000. 653p. index. $179.99pa. (w/CD-ROM). ISBN 1-891775-06-5.

This guide is a comprehensive overview, from a business and investment perspective, of the companies participating in the worldwide telecommunications industry. Overall an excellent guide to the industry, it has two main components. About the first quarter of the book is a discursive guide to industry trends—discussing market trends, historical and projected for the next five years, by category of service. It discusses worldwide variation in the technologies used, the potential market, and the degree and character of government involvement. The role of new technologies and products and select lists of companies that might be attractive investment opportunities are also covered. Overall, this coverage is careful, complete, and accurate. Occasionally, the writer gets a bit too enthusiastic, as when he describes the Sony Playstation 2. But these flaws are few. This section provides a good, balanced look at the range of telecommunications technologies in use, the firms that provide them, and the markets they serve.

The second section, provided in both print and CD-ROM form, is a database of the "Telecom 400," a listing of 455 companies chosen specifically for their prominence in telecommunications and related support industries. Each gets (in the print version) a one-page listing, including company contact information, a narrative description of the company's lines of business, revenues and profits for the past five years (1995-1999), and a few more details. Company selection seems good. The company descriptions are generally informative, but the financial detail is a bit sparse when contrasted with, for example, the sorts of details provided in similar one-page profiles created by Value Line.

This directory is the first of what is promised to be an annual compilation, so by the time this review is read, release of the 2001 edition will either have occurred or be imminent. Judging from the quality of this 1st edition, the current edition will be a good purchase.—**Ray Olszewski**

228.   **Researching Markets, Industries, and Business Opportunities.** 6th ed. Arlington, Va., Washington Researchers, 1999. 245p. index. $275.00pa. ISBN 1-56365-051-7. ISSN 1067-0394.

This manual for managers is issued by a Washington-based research firm. Its stated aim is to guide decision makers in planning and research. The introduction indicates it shows users how to research markets and industries worldwide, but assessed resources are heavily weighted to U.S. ones, suggesting it will be most useful to American-based researchers. The brief introduction profiles Washington research and identifies the first two chapters on selecting sources and profiling markets and industries as starting points. These chapters provide suggested methodology and a brief introduction to, and lists of, business information sources from association, newsletter, manufacturer and periodical directories, and indexes to research report databases and include a table matching information categories with corresponding print, people, and electronic sources. Material cited will be familiar to library staffers trained on large business collections.

The next 4 chapters cover Internet use, print and databases, experts, and international sources in only 57 pages. Each chapter has a one-to a few-page introduction followed by classified, annotated lists of resources with bibliographic and directory information (including numerous Internet addresses). Some subsections start with added instructional material. Over half the book is devoted to five chapters on U.S. administration, congressional, judicial, and state government resources.

An appendix gives addresses of about 76 information vendors and publishers—only 8 outside America (all but 1 of those English). A table of contents, an index, and boldfaced subheadings provide access. This introductory manual and resource list, while hardly unique, will be of interest to larger business collections and appropriate special libraries.—**Nigel Tappin**

229.   **U.S. Industry and Trade Outlook '98.** New York, McGraw-Hill, 1998. 1v. (various paging). index. $69.95pa. ISBN 0-07-032931-1.

From 1959 through 1994, the U.S. Department of Commerce published annual editions of a much respected and consulted reference, *U.S. Industrial Outlook* (see ARBA 94, entry 218, for a review). Recent developments and trends in major segments of U.S. industry were captured in a single, convenient volume, providing authoritative insights and guidance for business practitioners, researchers, students, and the general public. Following a hiatus of several years, in 1998 the Commerce Department and McGraw-Hill combined their considerable talents and resources to revive the former series under the title of *U.S. Industry and Trade Outlook '98*. The resulting volume breaks total U.S. industry into 50 broad categories, each containing historical data from 1989 and prospects for the future. Each category is supported by references for further investigation and, where helpful, a glossary. Significant trends of each industrial segment are highlighted by charts and tables. An overall prospective of U.S. industry is presented in preliminary chapters as well as a world economic outlook that underlines a pervasive theme of the book, the increasing dependence of U.S. industry on exports. The table of contents and a detailed index ease efforts to locate specific information of interest to a particular reader. This work provides a great deal of information in one place and will also be useful as a point of departure for further research. [R: Choice, Sept 98, p. 102-104]—**William C. Struning**

230. **WEFA Industrial Monitor 1999-2000.** Priscilla Trumbull and Frantz R. Price, eds. New York, John Wiley, 1999. 1v. (various paging). $59.95. ISBN 0-471-33320-4. ISSN 1093-6580.

Wharton Econometric Forecasting Associates (WEFA) is part of the PRIMARK organization and is one of the country's foremost economic forecasting and consulting firms. The *WEFA Industrial Monitor* covers more than 130 major industries. Each 3-to 5-page industry chapter gives an industry overview, sales data for the past 10 years, and estimated annual industry growth rates to the year 2007. Information in each chapter is presented using a mix of narrative and graphics and follows a uniform organizational scheme.

The introduction provides brief reviews and forecasts of U.S. and world economies. It also has a useful table with forecast highlights for the top growth industries. Parts 1 through 6 of the work contain the industry chapters. They are organized into the following categories: agriculture, forestry, fishing, and the environment; mining, construction, and energy; light and heavy manufacturing; transportation and communications; wholesale and retail trade; finance, insurance, and real estate; and healthcare, education, entertainment, law, and other service industries. An industry index provides access to individual industry entries.

The 1st edition of the *WEFA Industrial Monitor* was published in 1997 (see ARBA 98, entry 198). This 2d edition, published in March 1999, also provides outstanding value at a surprisingly modest price. Its combination of solid coverage and affordability should make it quite appealing to business librarians, especially if the publisher continues to update it on a regular basis. This work is recommended for all reference collections serving clientele with business information needs. [R: Choice, Oct 99, p. 316]—**Gordon J. Aamot**

231. Whitten, David O. Whitten, Bessie E., ed. **Infrastructure and Services: A Historiographical and Bibliographical Guide.** Westport, Conn., Greenwood Press, 2000. 600p. index. (Handbook of American Business History, v.3). $115.00. ISBN 0-313-25198-3.

This is the 3d and final volume in the Handbook of American Business History series by the same editors. Volume 1, *Manufacturing: A Historiographical and Bibliographical Guide* (see ARBA 92, entry 206) and volume 2, *Extractives, Manufacturing and Services: A Historiographical and Bibliographical Guide* (see entry 88), appeared in 1990 and 1997, respectively. Volume 3 focuses on services, but also contains a chapter on the zinc industry that was to be published in volume 2, but was not received in time to be included.

The handbook is intended to be a consolidated business history of the United States. Volume 3 covers the following industries: zinc, telegraph communications, radio and television broadcasting, electrical services, gas production and distribution, lumber and other construction materials wholesaling, shoe stores, federal reserve banks, mutual savings banks, clearinghouse associations, mortgage bankers and brokers, medical service and health insurance, hotels, funeral service and crematories, advertising agencies, nursing and personal care facilities, health maintenance organizations, educational services, social services, business and professional organizations, and public administration.

The editors and contributors are all academics and the content reflects their scholarly approach. The chapters are approximately 15 to 20 pages in length and are heavily documented. Each chapter concludes with a short bibliographic essay and a supplementary list of references. A detailed index provides subject and publication title access to the volume.

The 21 industry chapters each contain useful historical information, but the selection of industries in the volume is very uneven. For example, a huge sector like retail is represented only by the shoe store industry. Another missing piece, acknowledged by the editor in the preface, is the telephone industry. On balance, however, this final volume of the Handbook of American Business History series is a valuable addition to the set. It can stand alone, but librarians may want to consider also purchasing the first two volumes if they do not already own them. This volume is recommended for large research collections with a strong interest in American business history. [R: Choice, Dec 2000, p. 691]—**Gordon J. Aamot**

232. **Yearbook of Tourism Statistics.** 50th ed. Lanham, Md., Bernan Associates, 1998. 2v. $150.00pa./set. ISBN 92-844-0259-X. ISSN 1011-8977.

This comprehensive summary of world tourism presents its contents pages and explanatory notes in English, French, and Spanish. The titles and headings of the tables are in English only. Countries are classified in English in alphabetic order. The information, which the World Tourism Organization has been gathering annually for 50 years, comes from data obtained by questionnaires sent to governments and from official national publications. Volume 1 presents an overview of worldwide trends in tourism, with country rankings for top destinations, earners, and spenders, among other things. These are followed by regional summaries for Africa, the Americas, East Asia and the Pacific, Europe, and the Middle East. Volume 2 presents details for selected countries and territories on total arrivals and overnight stays by country of origin.

This publication is a standard reference for tourism officials. Large urban public libraries and colleges and universities that provide public administration courses may want to consider its purchase, but it is probably too arcane for most.—**Susan B. Hagloch**

8 Insurance

DICTIONARIES AND ENCYCLOPEDIAS

233. Clark, John. **International Dictionary of Insurance and Finance.** library ed. Chicago, Glenlake and Chicago, Fitzroy Dearborn, 1999. 341p. $55.00. ISBN 1-57958-161-7.

This dictionary provides definitions of thousands of terms from insurance, banking, and finance. The definitions are firmly from the perspective of the United Kingdom financial services industry. The target audience is financial services professionals and students.

The arrangement is alphabetic and entries are brief, mostly one or two sentences. More complex terms have a longer paragraph or two devoted to them. The thorough cross-references are indicated by bold typeface in entries.

Although the dictionary is billed as international, many definitions of general terms are definitely focused on the United Kingdom. For example, *whistle blowing* is shortly and narrowly defined with respect to the *1995 Pensions Act,* and *tax return* is characterized as a document submitted annually to the *Inland Revenue.* UK *individual savings accounts* are defined, but U.S. *individual retirement accounts* are not. The institutions listed, such as the Confederation of British Industry, also have a clear UK bias, although some U.S. and many international bodies are included. Although the status of the city of London as a major financial and insurance market makes UK usage and organizations important, lack of broader context is a major limitation in a purportedly international tool. Still only a minority of terms suffer from this obvious UK bias.

Prefatory materials are limited to a paragraph-length preface and a three-paragraph blurb on the back cover. No characterization of the author's qualifications or affiliations is given, although the copyright being held by the Chartered Institute of Bankers provides a clue. This dictionary is recommended for libraries and individuals collecting material on the UK financial and insurance industry, or the international sectors where its uses are important. More narrowly focused business collections will find it less appealing.—**Nigel Tappin**

234. **Elsevier's Dictionary of Export Financing and Credit Insurance in English, German, and French.** 2d ed. Peter Dorscheid, comp. New York, Elsevier Science, 2001. 297p. index. $148.00. ISBN 0-444-50533-4.

Readers should not consult this book if what they need is a formal definition of a word or phrase related to the fields of export financing or credit insurance. Instead, readers should consult this list of terms if they need to know the English, German, or French equivalent of a particular word or phrase. The 1st edition of this work was published in 1989 and included 6,500 terms (see ARBA 91, entry 264). This edition includes 14,000 terms in 3 languages, showing how much this field has grown in the last 12 years.

It is easy to find terms in this book. The first and largest section is an alphabetic list of the terms in English. Each entry has been numbered and includes the German and French words for the term. This section is followed by an alphabetic list of the German terms that include reference to the English entry, and this format is repeated for the French terms. This dictionary is a very specialized reference work that will be most useful to firms, government agencies, or academic institutions that are heavily involved in international business.—**Judith J. Field**

235.   **Glossary of Insurance and Risk Management Terms.** 6th ed. Edited by the Staff of International Risk Management Institute. Dallas, Tex., International Risk Management Institute, 1996. 161p. $18.00pa. ISBN 1-886813-23-X.

Regardless of subject, dictionaries and glossaries share many similarities. Obvious similarities include arrangement and purpose, but generally there is another unintended similarity—one source is not sufficient. Such is the case with this title. While it definitely provides clear and practical definitions, the focus is directed toward those working with the industry in a professional capacity, as evidenced by the inclusion of such terms as *factory firm, rainmaker,* and *30(b)6 deposition.* Unlike most dictionaries, this title frequently goes beyond the standard definition and gives a sentence or two of expert advice, highlighting advantages or disadvantages, passing along pointers, or giving warnings regarding limitations. For instance, the entry for *whole life insurance* provides a definition plus a comparison to term life. Under *flood coverage,* the entry goes on to list how coverage may be obtained.

The glossary is supplemented with a list of state insurance commissioners' addresses and telephone numbers; a directory of offices involved with workers' compensation; a list of states not permitting private insurance companies to write workers' compensation insurance and a list of states that do, along with the organization's contact information; and a list of risk management and insurance organizations. This would be a good addition to collections serving attorneys or insurance professionals.—**Barbara E. Clotfelter**

236.   Rubin, Harvey W. **Dictionary of Insurance Terms.** 3d ed. Hauppauge, N.Y., Barron's Educational Series, 1995. 531p. $10.95pa. ISBN 0-8120-3379-5.

The price of the 3d edition of this useful pocket-sized insurance reference book is 10 percent higher than its predecessor, but still a bargain at $10.95. For the extra money, the reader gets a raft of new entries such as "Addendum: addition to a written policy"; "Ad infinitum: continuing on an indefinite basis"; "Adjacent: that which adjoins"; "Egress: exit, act of leaving or going out." Most entries are taken verbatim from the 2d edition (see ARBA 92, entry 210), including outdated entries (e.g., a page-and-a-half on the Medicare Catastrophic Coverage Act that was repealed in 1989). As with previous editions, the 3d edition is relatively strong in areas of life, property, and casualty insurance, and weak in health insurance.—**Bruce Stuart**

HANDBOOKS AND YEARBOOKS

237.   **Standard & Poor's Insurance Company Ratings Guide.** 1995 ed. By Standard & Poor's. New York, McGraw-Hill, 1996. 398p. $19.95pa. ISBN 0-07-052101-8.

Standard & Poor's Insurance Company Ratings Guide is a strong addition to any consumer education collection. The goals of the book are clearly stated: to "cut through the peculiarities of accounting in this industry" and "to provide you with the highest-quality, most timely, and in-depth insurer ratings." Its strength lies in the explanatory sections preceding the actual company ratings. This information alone is worth the price of the book for consumer reference.

The contributors from McGraw-Hill and Standard & Poor's present an excellent explanation of terms and an equally excellent explanation of rating terminology and information. Due to the degree of analysis, the data are not the most timely. However, that is a technical point most valuable to the insurance industry researcher who needs the latest possible rating for a given company. For the consumer, the careful delineation of rating grades, acronyms, and relevant accounting terminology should prepare average readers for deciphering the ratings assigned to companies with whom they may consider doing business.

Parts 1 and 2 contain the "Insurance Company Rating Reports" and the "Insurance Company Rating List," respectively. Entries in part 1 provide the consumer with anecdotal and brief financial information, with up to 5 years of historical figures for 300 life, health, auto, fire, commercial, annuity, and reinsurance companies. Part 2 simply lists more than 3,000 companies alphabetically, with the most current rating as of publication. Not all consumers will find their companies of choice in part 1. However, any consumer who reads the explanatory sections will have a basic knowledge of rating criteria to apply to any insurance company report. [R: RBB, 1 April 96, p. 1390]—**Deborah K. Scott**

238. **Weiss Ratings' Guide to HMOs and Health Insurers: A Quarterly Compilation of Health Insurance Company Ratings and Analysis, Winter 2000-01.** Palm Beach Gardens, Fla., Weiss Rating's, 2001. 491p. $219.00 (single copy); $438.00 (4 quarterly editions). ISBN 1-58773-003-0. ISSN 1081-2318.

Intended to provide consumers with a reliable source of company ratings and analysis, this guide analyzes more than 1,200 insurers, including major companies (e.g., Blue Cross Blue Shield) and health maintenance organizations (e.g., Kaiser Foundation). The Weiss method for acquiring accurate, unbiased ratings is explained with a table comparing the system to those of other providers.

Organized into eight sections, each begins with an explanation of the data provided, its categories, acronyms, and instructions on reading the tabular data. The name index, which appears first, offers the safety rating, company type, brief financial data (e.g., total assets and health premiums), and two ratios for risk-adjusted capital. The second, "Analyses of Largest Companies," has 22 categories of information from the basics (e.g., name and address) to membership numbers, ratings factors (e.g., capitalization and profitability), and specific ratios (e.g., medical loss ratio). An interesting statistic is the percentage of a company's business devoted to Medicaid, Medicare, and other types of business, such as dental. Five years of background data and ratings are shown in a table and chart. The remaining sections cover recommended companies (by name and state), long-term care insurers, Medicare, complaints, and recent changes (upgrades and downgrades). Three appendixes complete the volume, with an explanation of risk-adjusted capital, a glossary, and a list other available products.

This work is one of many focused printed reports and guides produced by Weiss. While they are described along with the company's 800 number, the Weiss Website (http://www.weissratings.com/) is not identified. Some current information is available online along with the availability of online purchasing and subscriptions. The guide is recommended for libraries supporting insurance programs or strong consumer affairs collections. Other libraries, particularly those with budget considerations, will have to compare the Weiss product line to that produced by other vendors, such as *Standard & Poor's Insurance Company Ratings Guide* (1995 ed.; see entry 237).—**Sandra E. Belanger**

239. **Weiss Ratings' Guide to Life, Health, and Annuity Insurers: A Quarterly Compilation of Insurance Company Ratings and Analysis, Spring 2000.** Palm Beach Gardens, Fla.,

Weiss Rating's, 2001. 393p. $219.00pa. (single copy); $438.00pa. (4 quarterly editions). ISBN 1-58773-006-5. ISSN 1079-7815.

The purpose of the Weiss insurance guides is to provide the consumer with information about various insurance companies that will enable them to make wise choices for their insurance needs. The Weiss Guides cover only U.S. companies and are updated on a quarterly basis. Weiss Ratings do not accept money for recommendations. Therefore, the ratings are unbiased and are recognized as the insurance industry's leading consumer advocate. The Weiss Ratings range from A-F, with "A+" being the best rating and "F" signifying failure of the company. The volume is divided into "Index of Companies," "Analysis of Companies," "Weiss Recommended Companies," "Weiss Recommended Companies by State," "All Companies Listed By Rating," "Rating Upgrades and Downgrades," "Appendix with State Insurance Commissioners' Departmental Phone Numbers," and a glossary of terms. This rating guide is recommended as a priority purchase for large public libraries and academic libraries.—**Kay M. Stebbins**

240.   **Weiss Ratings' Guide to Property and Casualty Insurers: A Quarterly Compilation of Insurance Company Ratings and Analysis, Winter 2000-01.** Palm Beach Gardens, Fla., Weiss Rating's, 2000. 453p. $219.00pa. (single copy); $438.00pa. (4 quarterly editions). ISBN 1-58773-001-4. ISSN 1080-6881.

The Weiss Ratings' Guide's purpose is to provide insurance consumers with a reliable source of timely ratings and analysis of U.S. insurance companies. The primary focus is on the insurance companies ability to pay their current claims, even in depressed economic times. The *Weiss Ratings' Guide to Property and Casualty Insurers* covers only U.S. insurance companies for homeowner, business, auto, workers compensation, product liability, medical malpractice, and other professional liability insurance coverage.

The guide has a user-friendly chapter entitled "How to Use This Guide." The guides are updated frequently and issued on an annual and quarterly basis. The ratings range from strong to weak on a scale of A-F, with "A+" being the best rating and "F" signifying a failing company. The primary indexes for evaluation of companies are risk adjusted capital, reserve adequacy, profitability, liquidity, and stability.

The General Accounting Office of the United States has stated that only Weiss has rated more than half of all health insurers. Weiss outperformed A.M. Best three to one in warning of coming financial troubles with Weiss' warning coming an average of eight months earlier than Best's.—**Kay M. Stebbins**

9 International Business

GENERAL WORKS

Bibliographies

241.   Liu, Lewis-Guodo, and Robert Premus. **Global Economic Growth: Theories, Research, Studies, and Annotated Bibliography, 1950-1997.** Westport, Conn., Greenwood Press, 2000. 342p. index. (Bibliographies and Indexes in Economics and Economic History, no.19). $85.00. ISBN 0-313-30738-5.

Almost 1,300 annotated entries make up this bibliography aimed at serious economic scholars who study global economic growth. The first chapter provides entries that give an overview of research in the topic, including historical perspective and various economic models found within. The remaining chapters are arranged by continent, then by country. Entries from books, articles, dissertations, conference proceedings, working papers, and government and nonprofit reports provide descriptive, but not evaluative, annotations running from three to eight lines, with an average length of five lines. To be included, the work must deal with theoretical, methodological, or empirical economic growth with an emphasis on literature reviews of the topic. There are very few descriptive articles. The compilers particularly sought locally produced material, but still the majority of material is from the First World. The author, country, and subject indexes are adequate and economic concepts are indexed under the affected country. Works like this have a very limited audience: practicing economists, university faculty, and economic graduate students. Libraries serving that clientele may find this $85 bibliography worth the cost, especially for its hard-to-find Third World coverage. All other libraries will find it overpriced and too specialized.—**Patrick J. Brunet**

242.   Schreiber, Mae N. **International Trade Sources: A Research Guide.** New York, Garland, 1997. 327p. index. (Research and Information Guides in Business, Industry, and Economic Institutions, v.12; Garland Reference Library of Social Science, v.1068). $55.00. ISBN 0-8153-2109-0.

Adding a title dealing with international trade should enhance the scope of Garland's Research and Information Guides in Business, Industry, and Economic Institutions series. Unfortunately, this title has only a slightly broader scope than Ruth Pagell's *International Business Information* (see entry 285), but is not as comprehensive, accurate, or as detailed as this award-winning title. The one strength that the title at hand has over the Pagell title is the number of Websites that have been included.

The subtitle states that the volume is a research guide, but it is not a good resource for a researcher. Many of the titles listed do not indicate that they are 2d or 3d editions, others do not indicate that they have ceased publication, and some of the annotations are not very descriptive or at best incomplete. References to the Standard Industrial Classification (SIC) code have been included, although no mention is made that it has been superseded by the North American Industry Classification System (NAICS). This change has long been known, but Websites to NAICS have only recently been mounted. Some of the Websites that the author has included here have changed, but this is to be expected as the migration toward electronic resources continues.

Libraries that own the 1st edition of the Pagell title should wait for the new edition that is in preparation rather than acquiring this title. If there is a need for electronic addresses for government sites, there are books published by the National Journal or Congressional Quarterly that are published more regularly. Interest in international business is increasing, and resource publications in this area are multiplying. Unfortunately, this book does not serve its intended clientele well.—**Judith J. Field**

Dictionaries and Encyclopedias

243.   Capela, John J., and Stephen W. Hartman. **Dictionary of International Business Terms.** Hauppauge, N.Y., Barron's Educational Series, 1996. 584p. (Barron's Business Guides). $12.95pa. ISBN 0-8120-9261-9.

This is an excellent, practical, and comprehensive source of information for students; practitioners in management, marketing, trade, finance, and foreign exchange; and the general public. The terms covered include specialized concepts, abbreviations and acronyms, geographic/institutional terms, military phrases, some foreign expressions, monetary units, Internet terminology, legal jargon, and so on. Cross-referencing is meticulous, the size is eminently portable, and the price is surprisingly low. Twelve appendixes provide international acronyms, Internet acronyms, contacts for major foreign markets, International Trade Commission offices, Department of Commerce information, customs information, a six-language dictionary of basic terms, weights and measures conversions, a list of currencies, and fax-back services. The dictionary is highly recommended.—**Bogdan Mieczkowski**

244.   **Economics, Trade and Development: English-Spanish General Terminology (with a Spanish Index). Terminologia General de Economia, Comercio y Desarrollo, Glosario Inglés-Español.** New York, United Nations, 2001. 613p. index. $60.00pa. ISBN 92-1-101033-0. S/N GV.E/S.01.0.4.

This is a glossary of words that have appeared in works published by the Terminology and Technical Documentation Section of the Languages Service of the United Nations. The terms have been gathered from these works' glossaries to create a comprehensive source for Spanish-speaking users. J. Anllo, a former member of the Spanish Translation Section, served as the glossary's compiler. The foreword is written in both Spanish and English and explains the topics covered in the glossary: poverty alleviation, banking, stock exchange, debt trade efficiency, trade measures, privatization, insurance, information services and technologies, and international financial terms, just to name a few. For each term the English and Spanish version is presented; no definitions are given. Because the bibliography and the index to the volume are both in Spanish this work will only be appropriate for libraries needing this specific type of information that have a Spanish-speaking clientele base.—**Shannon Graff Hysell**

245. **Encyclopedia of Global Industries.** Diane M. Sawinski and Wendy H. Mason, eds. Detroit, Gale, 1996. 1034p. index. $395.00. ISBN 0-8103-9767-6. ISSN 1084-8614.

This encyclopedia is a new and needed entry in the international business information field. Much of the information included in this title is available industry-by-industry in many other, far more expensive resources, so this compilation of international industry information in one volume will be seen as a welcome addition to most business reference collections. Summary information from 7 to 12 pages is provided for the 115 international industries. This includes a narrative description for each industry similar to what one would find for U.S. industries in *Standard & Poor's Industry Surveys,* brief analysis on the general outlook for the industry with projections, a general background section that provides brief descriptions of the industry in particular countries or regions, information related to research and development, and many graphs and charts used to list the major players in each industry.

Each section concludes with a reading list of industry information sources. This section could have been made more useful by referencing many of the special issues on industry outlook that trade magazines publish. These reading lists also do not always refer to the latest annual publications, and many of the general periodical articles selected do not necessarily reflect current issues. This is a minor shortcoming that one hopes will be corrected when a new edition of the title comes out. The indexes provide access to the contents by the Standard Industrial Classification (SIC) code, by the Harmonized System code, or by geographic location. Because 1997 will see the Harmonized System code replacing the SIC code, this book will not be quickly outdated.

The information here is timely and provides the reader with a useful overview of those industries with international importance. If one needs company information, other sources should be consulted, as those companies that are included are merely mentioned. This is not a shortcoming of the book, but many readers will want to do one-stop searching. This book is a valuable resource and is a must-acquisition for those libraries serving clienteles interested in international business or for academic libraries with a business administration program. [R: Choice, Oct 96, p. 250; RBB, Aug 96, p. 1924]—**Judith J. Field**

246. **Exporting to the USA and the Dictionary of International Trade.** 1996-97 ed. [CD-ROM]. San Rafael, Calif., World Trade Press, 1996. Minimum system requirements: IBM or compatible 386. CD-ROM drive. DOS 3.3. Windows 3.1. 8MB RAM. 10-20MB hard disk space. VGA 640 x 480 monitor (SVGA recommended). Windows-compatible mouse. PostScript or PCL printer and ATM or TrueType font manager (for printing). $149.00.

The CD-ROM is divided into nine parts or "books." First is the commodity index, containing an overview of import regulations and requirements for a complete range of products arranged according to the 99 chapters of the Harmonized Tariff Schedule. Next comes a section on international law, covering a wide range of legal issues. The part on international banking contains sections on banking services and letters of credit. The customs entry segment covers regulations for U.S. Customs entry and clearance. Customs forms include 30 forms from the Customs Service and other U.S. government agencies (these forms can be printed for use, but should only be used after consulting with the Customs Service). A container packing section contains a complete guide from Happag-Lloyd on how to pack shipments. Details on shipping containers include an excellent description by Happag-Lloyd on standard containers. A section on insurance provides detailed information from Insurance Company of North America (INA) and CIGNA on ocean cargo insurance. Finally, the part called "Info Lists" includes 30 sections on a range of topics, such as brokers, attorneys, General Agreement on Tariffs and Trade and the North American Free Trade Agreement. Also contained on the CD-ROM is the complete text of *Dictionary of International Trade* by Edward G. Hinkelman, which is accessible at any time from any of the books and from the main menu. The dictionary includes definitions of terms, a list of acronyms, a description of currencies of the world, an International Dialing Guide, resources for international trade, weights and measures, and a detailed table of contents.

The CD-ROM is straightforward and easy to install. The display is meant to be about 10 inches (25 cm) on the diagonal, which means that it will be smaller than most desktop or laptop screens. Nonetheless, the display is clear, distinct, and reasonably easy to read. The interface is consistent throughout all the parts of the CD-ROM, but it is somewhat cumbersome. In addition to a standard Windows pull-down menu, from the main menu one may click on an icon for any one of the nine books, or click on a button for a complete index, the dictionary, Help, or to exit the CD-ROM. After entering any one of the nine book sections, one may click on a table of contents or an index to all nine books. Also, the user always has the option to choose another book, the dictionary of terms, the dictionary of acronyms, or a list of addresses of U.S. regulatory agencies. The navigation buttons are the same within every book. Unfortunately, there is no search function allowing a user to type in a word and go to it. Instead, one must page through all the entries in an index or table of contents until coming to the desired item. In addition to the standard set of navigation buttons, there are hypertext links allowing the user to jump to related concepts.

This CD-ROM is notable for its exhaustive and authoritative coverage of importing goods into the United States. It has a serviceable interface and consistent navigation tools. This is an extremely useful source for any library serving patrons or businesses interested in importing into the United States, and the price is reasonable considering the comprehensiveness of the information provided.—**Richard H. Swain**

247.   Hinkelman, Edward G. **Dictionary of International Trade: Handbook of the Global Trade Community.** 3d ed. San Rafael, Calif., World Trade Press, 1999. 412p. illus. $32.00pa. ISBN 1-885073-82-8.

Precise communication and understanding are essential to the conduct of international trade. To enable transactions to flow efficiently and rapidly, specialized terms and concepts have evolved. It is necessary to understand those terms and concepts in order to engage in foreign commerce or to evaluate international transactions. *Dictionary of International Trade* by Hinkelman, an international economist, author, and experienced importer/exporter, provides a concise, yet comprehensive, reference for locating appropriate terms for verifying one's understanding of concepts. More than simply a dictionary, the book contains useful appendixes that include data on acronyms, abbreviations, international dialing codes, maps, world currencies, types of business entities engaged in international trade, weights/measures, incoterms (i.e., terms of trade), letters of credit, and ocean/air freight containers. The author has included extensive lists of resources for those requiring more detailed information as well as lists of service providers. The dictionary represents a single source for obtaining much basic information on international trade. It should prove useful to importers, exporters, insurers, bankers, shippers, students, economists, and government officials, as well as readers who have a general interest in world commerce.—**William C. Struning**

248.   Johnston-Des Rochers, Janeen, Inés Barry, and Maguy Robert. **Export Financing and Insurance Vocabulary. Vocabulaire du Financement et de L'assurance à L'exportation. Vocabulario del Financiamiento y Seguro a la Exportación.** Quebec, Canada Communication Group, 1996. 572p. (Terminology Bulletin, no.230). $36.95pa.(U.S.). ISBN 0-660-59978-3.

This is one of a series of Terminology Bulletins published by the Translation Bureau on various topics. It contains 1,400 entries in English, French, and Spanish concerning export financing and insurance and includes 470 definitions and notes. These entries are filed alphabetically in each of the three languages, with the filing language in the first column and the interpretation into the other two languages listed in the second and third columns. Below these terms (in the English listing only) one finds definitions and notes in the three languages running across the page. Synonyms in the same language are frequently included and are found in both alphabetic places in the same listing. In the English listing, however, *see* references are used from synonyms to the main listing. A bibliography is found at the end of the book.

The printing is clear and easy to read. The terminology is in bold typeface, while the definitions and notes are in regular typeface. The choice of words is satisfactory and the translations and definitions are accurate. The work was prepared by experts in the field and is especially valuable and useful for those involved in export financing and insurance.—**Barbara E. Brown**

249.   Shim, Jae K., Joel G. Siegel, and Marc H. Levine. **The Dictionary of International Business Terms.** Chicago, Glenlake and Chicago, Fitzroy Dearborn, 1998. 317p. $45.00. ISBN 1-57958-001-7.

This dictionary contains a variety of words and terms from business and economics. Although the basis for inclusion is not explained, the terms include those related to business, such as *bearer bond* and *matrix structure*; to economics, such as *near money* and *imperfect market*; to international activities, such as *currency basket* or *most favored nation*. The definitions are generally short. Of particular value are the listings of acronyms both as an acronym referenced to the full wording and with the entry for the full term. There are six appendixes, the first on export periodicals with address, telephone number, and cost. Other information sources are listed in another appendix along with hotline numbers. There is also an appendix on very general sources of statistical information. The appendix on Internet sites for international business and trade is slightly annotated. Although the dictionary contains names of the currencies for some countries, a more complete list of countries, territories, and islands with the currency name and symbol is in a separate appendix. The last appendix gives 12 organizations that could be contacted for sources for assistance in conducting business.—**J. E. Weaver**

Directories

250.   **Companies International.** [CD-ROM]. Detroit, Gale, 1996. Minimum system requirements: IBM or compatible 386 (486 recommended). Double-speed ISO 9660 CD-ROM drive with MS CD-ROM Extensions 2.2. DOS 5.0. Windows 3.1. 4MB RAM (8MB recommended). 5MB hard disk space. VGA monitor and graphics card. Windows-compatible mouse. Printer (optional). $2,495.00. ISBN 0-8103-5148-X.

This is a Windows Version 2.0 CD-ROM of *Companies International*, a semiannually updated directory of U.S. and foreign companies derived from databases underlying *Ward's Business Directory* (see ARBA 93, entry 198) and *World Business Directory* (WBD; see ARBA 93, entry 261). The number of companies has increased since the last review (see ARBA 95, entry 245) to more than 325,000. There are 140,000-plus U.S. companies, with the other 191 countries represented proportionately to their world trade involvement. Companies in WBD were selected "for their interest in international trade" (1996 WBD front matter). There are no stated selection criteria for *Ward's*, other than companies being "culled from more than 4,000 business publications" (1997 *Ward's* introduction). All company sizes and business sectors are present.

There are 28 record fields. A close examination of 368 sample records reveals that—beyond the standard address, telephone number, and industry/product codes/descriptions fields—the following are often present: officers, number of employees, fax number, date founded, revenue, company type, fiscal year ends, and importer/exporter designation. The year of the data is consistently indicated for revenue, less so for number of employees. U.S. companies have revenue, number of employees, and company type data more frequently than foreign ones. A search for companies in the United Kingdom discovered 471 virtually "empty" records, containing, at maximum, the company name, country, and company type. Many of these were for parent or holding companies mentioned in other records. In addition, revenue for some publicly held companies is from 1993—surprising, considering the easy accessibility of more recent data.

The interface accommodates different user needs and experience, offering five search modes. Searching by company name allows browsing of an index and keyword searching of words/phrases in names. A search by industry/product grants browsing of Standard Industrial Classification and Harmonized Commodity codes and descriptions. Searching by location affords browsing of city, state/region, postal code, area code, and country indexes. Extended and expert modes of searching possess Boolean and truncation capabilities. Extended mode allows the combination of 2 or more of 21 fields arranged thematically on a series of 4 cards (contact, industry/product, location, and scope) and free-text searching of words/phrases in any text field. Clicking on the field name in a card produces either a box for entering ranges of values or an index list. Limiting to either *Ward's* or WBD records is also possible. Expert mode involves input of commands and field labels and creation and manipulation of search sets. Two difficulties were encountered: Searching by state resulted in an error message, even when trying the example from the user's manual, and searching for a word/phrase in company names retrieves only those companies having the word/phrase as their entire name, not as part of their name.

To view full records for companies, users must select names from an alphabetic list. Other formats are mailing label, telemarketing card, and customized. Users can sort records in seven ways in addition to company name. Unfortunately, there is no way to print lists, other than short ones. Screens are uncluttered, with typing areas well demarcated and clickable buttons clearly labeled. The Windows Menu Bar has five options: File, Edit, Search (which allows rapid switching to different search modes), Format, and Help. Both online Help and the substantial user's manual provide clear instructions.

Records for 50 U.S. companies were compared to their counterparts on the fourth-quarter 1996 disc of *Dun's Million Dollar Disc* (MDD) (Dun & Bradstreet) a database covering only U.S. companies. Both fairly consistently report data for fields they have in common. However, they significantly disagree on revenue and number of employees for some private companies, even allowing for the slightly greater currentness in MDD.

This reviewer is unaware of a comparable single-disc international directory. Although MDD and *Principal International Businesses* (Dun & Bradstreet), combined would provide international scope, their selection criteria emphasize larger companies. The *Ward's* records are also available in *Gale Business Resources*, as part of a Galenet subscription. Although the unusual records and the two search difficulties mentioned above are cause for concern, business collections would profit from *Companies International*'s global scope and well-designed interface. A network license is also available.—**John Lewis Campbell**

251. **Directory of American Firms Operating in Foreign Countries.** 14th ed. New York, Uniworld Business Publications, 1996. 3v. (A World Trade Academy Press Publication). $220.00/set. ISBN 0-8360-0041-2.

For more than four decades, various editions of the *Directory of American Firms Operating in Foreign Countries* have been an indispensable reference guide for businesses, researchers, libraries, students, and others who have found the need for information about foreign subsidiaries of U.S. corporations. The 14th edition of this important resource is much enlarged; more comprehensive and updated; and comes in 3 volumes covering companies, large and small, from 3Comm Corp to Zycard Corp. This edition of the directory lists a total of 2,500 U.S. corporations with 18,500 subsidiaries or affiliates operating in 132 countries.

Volume 1 contains a summary listing of all U.S. corporations with foreign subsidiaries or affiliates in alphabetic order. Each entry in volume 1 includes the name of the corporation, U.S. address, telephone and fax numbers, principal line of business, number of employees, names of key executives, and countries in which it has subsidiaries or affiliates. Volumes 2 and 3 contain detailed listings, in alphabetic order by country, of U.S. firms' foreign subsidiaries or affiliates. Each entry in volumes 2 and 3 gives the name of the U.S. company, its U.S. address, the principal line of business in the foreign country, and the name and address of its subsidiary/affiliate in the foreign country. Because the foreign subsidiary may not have the same name as its U.S. parent company, this arrangement makes it easy for cross-references of the names and addresses of the foreign subsidiary with that of the parent company. The directory is extremely useful for businesses, researchers, and policy-makers alike and should be an indispensable reference in any library, business, university, or other organization. —**Kwabena Gyimah-Brempong**

252. **Directory of Multinationals: The World's Top 500 Companies.** 5th ed. Martin C. Timbrell and Diana L. Tweedie, eds. London, Waterlow Specialist Information; distr., Detroit, Gale, 1998. 2v. $595.00/set. ISBN 0-333-674642.

The 5th edition of this book is the only published work on the world's largest (sales in excess of U.S. $1 billion and overseas sales in excess of $500 million) international firms. The manuscript now includes for the first time service, retail, and construction companies to reflect the nature of today's high technology and service-oriented companies. The 500 profiles combine 5-year financial results and detailed analysis. Each company's entry provides contact details, including address, telephone and fax numbers, and Website information; name of directors and principal shareholders; products; structural organization; background discussion; commentary on the company's current situation; a list of subsidiary and affiliates broken down by countries; principal brand names; sales figures; geographic analysis; and product analysis. The five-year financial summary includes debt, capital expenditures, research and development and engineering expenses, earnings per share, total employees, and financial information on the current year. This two-volume set would be of interest to people who want to interact with multinational companies and organizations. The paper, printing, and binding are above average quality. This book should be in all major libraries.—**Herbert W. Ockerman**

253. **Galante's Venture Capital & Private Equity Directory.** 1998 ed. Steven P. Galante, ed. Wellesley, Mass., Asset Alternatives, 1998. 1142p. index. $395.00pa. ISBN 0-9652137-5-7.

254. **Galante's Venture Capital & Private Equity Directory.** 1997 ed. [CD-ROM]. Wellesley, Mass., Asset Alternatives, 1997. Minimum system requirements: IBM or compatible 486/66MHz. CD-ROM drive. Windows 3.1. 8MB RAM. 20MB hard disk space. SVGA monitor capable of supporting 800 x 600 resolution. Mouse. $395.00. ISBN 0-9652137-2-2.

This annual, international directory, first published in 1996, contains profiles of approximately 1,800 companies supplying venture capital. The publisher focuses on the venture capital industry, and produces four newsletters and organizes conferences.

The print directory has an introductory section containing brief essays on venture capital, a glossary of terms used in the directory, and ranked lists of the largest companies. The company profiles are the core of the directory. All sizes of companies are represented, with a range from $1.5 million to $7.5 billion in capital managed. Nearly four-fifths of the total are U.S.-based, with more than one-half concentrated in four states: New York, California, Massachusetts, and Texas. The foreign-based companies, almost one-half of which are British or Canadian, represent 34 countries. The U.S. section is arranged alphabetically by company name; the foreign section by country, and then alphabetically.

To determine which types of information were typically provided, 100 entries were randomly sampled. Beyond the standard contact information, more than one-half of the entries contained background (e.g., chief personnel, founding date, capital under management, number of staff); investment pace and policies (e.g., average new investments, current activity level, compensation method, syndication policies); investment criteria (e.g., minimum/maximum/preferred size, type of capital provided, funding stage/industry/geographical preferences); and description of the company's focus.

There are 6 indexes: company name; location (state/city, country/city); contact personnel; 18 funding stage preferences (e.g., seed, startup, acquisition); 31 industry preferences; and 23 geographic preferences. The latter three are set up as matrices, with company names listed on the left of the page and the preference at the top, with bullets in the cells indicating the companies with those preferences.

The print directory was compared with two other substantial directories: the 1997 edition of the annually published *Pratt's Guide to Venture Capital Sources* (21st ed.; see ARBA 93, entry 197); and the 1996 edition of the biennially published *Fitzroy Dearborn International Directory of Venture Capital Funds* (see entry 188). *Galante* has almost 50 percent more entries than *Pratt* and more than 75 percent more than *Fitzroy*. There are 50 entries common to the three that were analyzed for variations in the types of information supplied. Although the three contain many of the same types of information, there are variations in the frequency with which they appear. *Galante* and *Pratt* more routinely than *Fitzroy* supplied the type of organization, date of founding, capital under management, current activity, and geographic preferences. Quite often the two supplied compensation methods and syndication policies, entirely lacking in *Fitzroy*. *Galante* significantly surpassed *Pratt* in frequency of reporting data on the number and dollar amounts of investments. *Galante* uniquely contains the following: type of capital provided, number of staff worldwide, description of company focus, and brief data on venture funds managed. *Galante* should consider adding some of the unique types of information in *Pratt* (e.g., minimum operating data required from applicants, portfolio composition by industry) and *Fitzroy* (names of portfolio companies and officer background). All three have an industry preference index. *Galante*'s is the most useful because of its matrix arrangement. *Galante* and *Pratt* have funding stage indexes, with *Galante*'s the more useful, again because of its matrix arrangement. Neither has *Galante*'s geographic preference index. *Pratt* and *Fitzroy* have more extensive introductory essays about venture capital.

The electronic version comes in 2 formats, on 1 CD-ROM and 10 diskettes. The reviewer examined the CD-ROM only. In terms of content, the CD-ROM is almost a mirror of the print. However, it allows quick construction of lists of companies that meet specific criteria. Searching is performed from the initial screen, by clicking one of four tabs: Firm (by company name, state, country, city); Background (by type of organization, capital managed, number of staff); Investments (by funding stage preference, investment size); and Geography and Industry (by preferences). Searching by multiple criteria from more than one tab is possible (e.g., searching for companies providing start-up funds for biotechnology companies in the Midwest or Southeast and managing more than $100 million in capital).—**John Lewis Campbell**

255.   **Hoover's Masterlist of Major International Companies 1998-1999.** Gordon T. Anderson and others, eds. Austin, Tex., Hoover's, 1998. 313p. index. $89.95. ISBN 1-57311-043-4.

This new directory and handbook in Hoover's series of corporate information tools builds on and expands earlier Hoover titles, including *Hoover's MasterList of Major Latin American Companies* (see entry 358) and *Hoover's MasterList of Major European Companies* (Hoovers, 1996). It will interest business selectors looking at print reference tools on major non-U.S. companies.

The directory lists and profiles 1,658 corporations. The editors try to include all non-U.S. companies with sales above $5 billion and all companies making up major foreign stock indexes (e.g., FTSE, DAX, MIB, Hang Seng, Strait Times, Nikkei, SBF, TSE, Swiss Market, Amsterdam Exchange, Mexican Bolsa IPC). This is supplemented with the highest-ranking companies by sales in 22 smaller but significant economies on 5 continents ranging from Australia and Austria to Israel, China, and South Africa. All foreign corporations trading on major U.S. exchanges and having sales over $120 million are also included. There are two rankings: a top 500 list by sales and a top 500 companies by employee totals. Access features include indexes by industry, headquarters location, and short names. The last index is inaccurately labeled as one by "Stock Exchange Symbol" in the contents.

The lists themselves are arranged alphabetically by formal corporate name, although some words like *Grupo* seem to be ignored in ordering. Listings include headquarters address, telephone and fax numbers, and Website address, if available; chief executive and financial officers; ownership type; stock exchange listings; sales, net income, and employment for 1993 to 1997; and annual growth if available. Entries also include a narrative paragraph characterizing business activities. This is a handy, well-produced reference. It will be useful in business print collections with the appropriate client interests.—**Nigel Tappin**

256.　**Information Sources 1998.** Lewon, Paul, ed. Detroit, Gale, 1998. 266p. index. $125.00pa. ISBN 0-7876-1959-0. ISSN 0734-9637.

Information Sources 1998 lists information about those companies who are members of the Information Industry Association (IIA). More than 550 companies are members, including AT&T, Dow Jones & Co., The Dun & Bradstreet Corporation, several divisions of McGraw-Hill, and the Washington Post Company. The Information Industry Association represents companies that are involved in creating, distributing, and facilitating the use of information in print and digital formats. Entries for each company vary. In addition to a company address, telephone number, fax number, e-mail and Website address, most include the name of the IIA representative, key personnel, company description, key products or services, foreign operations, Internet site profile (if applicable), and how their products or services fit into the consumer market.

An index of key executives lists in alphabetic order by surname both the IIA representative and a key executive for each member company. The key executive's name in this index does not necessarily correspond to the key personnel listed for each company's main entry. This makes locating the name, title, and contact information of key executives by company name extremely difficult. One would have to know the name of the key executive, or scan through all the names, searching for the name of a specific company. Two geographic indexes categorize member companies by state in the United States and by country outside the United States. A foreign operations index lists by country all IIA companies that have international business operations. A product and service index is useful to find lists of IIA companies grouped by categories as to primary functions or types of services rendered. Additional information is provided about IIA, the 1998 IIA board of directors, past chairs, and award programs.

This directory will be most useful to those who are members of the Information Industry Association, and those who need to find more information about its 1998 membership.—**Elizabeth B. Miller**

257.　**The International Directory of Business Information Sources and Services 1996.** 2d ed. London, Europa; distr., Detroit, Gale, 1996. 550p. index. $185.00. ISBN 1-85743-007-7.

This 2d edition (see ARBA 88, entry 173, for a review of the 1st edition) has been revised to include information on 23 additional countries from Latin America, the Middle East, the Far East, the Russian Federation, and central Europe. Forty-six countries are covered, and the directory is divided into that number of chapters, one for each country. Chapters are organized into sections listing chambers of commerce, foreign trade-promoting organizations, government organizations, independent organizations, research organizations, sources of statistical information, and business libraries. Each entry lists the organization's address, telephone and fax numbers, and generally provides a description of varying detail. International organizations are listed in a separate chapter, and an index is included.

While separate directories exist for many of the sections covered by this title, and therefore exceed the amount of information presented here, this is an impressive compilation overall. However, shortcomings can be found; for example, in the chapter on the United States, under the sources of statistical information, only the Bureau of the Census and its regional offices are listed. Nonetheless, the directory is recommended for comprehensive collections. [R: Choice, July/Aug 96, p. 1774]—**Barbara E. Clotfelter**

258.   **International Directory of Company Histories. Volume 16.** Tina Grant, ed. Detroit, St. James Press, 1997. 705p. index. $161.00. ISBN 1-55862-219-5.

259.   **International Directory of Company Histories. Volume 17.** Tina Grant, ed. Detroit, St. James Press, 1997. 713p. index. $161.00. ISBN 1-55862-351-5.

260.   **International Directory of Company Histories. Volume 18.** Jay P. Pederson, ed. Detroit, St. James Press, 1997. 723p. index. $161.00. ISBN 1-55862-352-3.

261.   **International Directory of Company Histories. Volume 19.** Tina Grant, ed. Detroit, St. James Press, 1998. 673p. index. $161.00. ISBN 1-55862-353-1.

262.   **International Directory of Company Histories. Volume 20.** Jay P. Pederson, ed. Detroit, St. James Press, 1998. 695p. index. $161.00. ISBN 1-55862-361-2.

263.   **International Directory of Company Histories. Volume 21.** Tina Grant and Jay P. Pederson, eds. Detroit, St. James Press, 1998. 709p. index. $161.00. ISBN 1-55862-362-0.

Since the first volumes of *International Directory of Company Histories* (IDCH) were published in 1988, librarians, students, and business researchers have found the set to be an invaluable tool for quick reference on company backgrounds. The addition of volumes 16 through 21 brings the total number of companies covered in IDCH to more than 3,000 and includes some significant enhancements.

To be included in the directory, a company must have annual sales greater than 100 million U.S. dollars and be regarded by the editors as "influential" in its geographic region or industry. Although most are public companies, nonprofit organizations and private firms account for about 10 percent of the entries. Subsidiaries and divisions may also be included if they meet the general inclusion criteria. The companies covered are mostly from the United States. A quick tally of the non-U.S. firms in these six volumes indicates that approximately 15 percent are international in origin.

As with the earlier volumes, each company entry is two to four pages in length and has a standard format. The authors of the essays are primarily freelance journalists. The reader first finds a box with basic directory information, including address, year incorporated, number of employees, annual sales, stock exchange, and SIC code. The following narrative history is based on publicly available sources, such as articles, books, corporate annual reports, and company press releases. These short essays are informative and can include a wide range of information. Typically one can expect to find a description of the business, how the company started, growth strategies over time, acquisition information, impact of new technologies, labor conflicts (if applicable), and important personnel changes. Each entry also includes lists of principal subsidiaries or divisions and a reading list of sources for further reference.

Each volume of IDCH contains cumulative company and industry indexes for the entire set. So, one need only consult the latest volume to locate company information appearing anywhere in the set. Index entries for companies with full histories are indicated in bold typeface. Companies mentioned but not specifically covered are indicated by light typeface. Company entries that are updated from previous volumes are indicated by the letters "upd" in bold typeface. Approximately 35 of the entries in each volume are updates of earlier entries. This means that roughly 20 percent of the total number of entries are updates of earlier histories.

Several additional pieces of useful information were added to these latest IDCH volumes. Beginning with volume 16, one usually finds a "company perspective" box that includes a short summary of the company's mission, goals, and ideals. Because so many students and other business researchers are interested in company mission statements, the addition of "company perspective" information is welcome as well. However, because many researchers—especially students—need to cite specific sources, it would be more useful if this information were documented so one could tell if it came from the annual report, a press release, or a company's Website. Also, beginning with volume 17, one may find a company's URL (if available) and, according to the preface, "citations to on-line research." A significant number of the entries examined included a company URL, but there were very few citations to "on-line research" in the reading lists at the end of each entry unless one includes citations to newswire services.

Despite these minor annoyances, the *International Directory of Company Histories* remains a vital reference tool for any business collection and is highly recommended for all academic and public libraries serving business information needs.—**Gordon J. Aamot**

264. International Directory of Consumer Brands and Their Owners. London, Euromonitor; distr., Detroit, Gale, 1996. 553p. index. $450.00. ISBN 0-86338-694-6.

Business researchers and students will quickly and easily find comprehensive information about consumer brands and their owners worldwide, except for Europe, in this new directory. With its sister publication, *Directory of Consumer Brands and Their Owners: Europe* (see entry 335), this complete reference source provides comprehensive information on brands, their owners, countries where they are marketed, and competing brands in their specific product sectors. Both directories are included on the CD-ROM titled *World Database of Consumer Brands and Their Owners* (Gale, 1997). More than 16,000 brands and about 3,000 companies in approximately 60 countries are covered in the international directory.

This directory is divided into two sections with section 1 focusing on brands and their owners by product sector and subsector. The brands are classified alphabetically, including the owner's name and country, main product sector, product type, and a further product categorization such as the specific variety. Section 2 profiles the brand-owning companies, listed alphabetically by country, with a complete index of brand names and companies at the end of the volume.

Each company's entry includes contact data along with the names of key personnel, number of employees for recent years, details of sales geography, and manufacturing capacity. The table of contents and introduction also provide useful information to users. This information is a wonderful product but very expensive.—**Susan C. Awe**

265. Lanza, Sheri R. **International Business Information on the Web:** *Searcher* Magazine's Guide to Sites and Strategies for Global Business Research. Medford, N.J., Information Today, 2001. 396p. index. $29.95pa. ISBN 0-910965-46-3.

This book grew out of a series of articles in *Searcher* magazine called "Around the World in 80 Sites." It concentrates on open or public Websites that anyone can reach and includes more than 1,000 site addresses. Its purpose is to help individuals do international business research on the

Web. It has a U.S. perspective, but should be useful to people all over the world. It starts with general business sites in the United States, like the official site of the Securities and Exchange Commission and the U.S. Census Bureau. It continues with worldwide sites that include basic information such as country facts, industrial production, infrastructure, embassies, and chambers of commerce. The latter two can be very useful for businesses. The book then presents regional information starting with Western Europe, Central and Eastern Europe, Latin America and the Caribbean, the Middle East and North Africa, Sub-Saharan Africa, Mexico and Canada, and Asia and the Pacific. All countries are not included.

In addition to providing Web addresses, the reader will be given some direction on what can be found on the different sites as well as which sites are best for different types of information. In some cases, how to work through a specific site is provided. Since working on international business research can present language difficulties, some information on that situation is given with Websites that can translate text. Appendix A gives the URLs of the Websites mentioned in the book by chapter. Appendix B lists country code top level domains. Accepted country abbreviations are in appendix C. There is an index.

The book is a convenient source of many useful Websites. It will be a good introduction for those starting to do Web searches and can be used as a reference for the future. Web addresses can change over time so the book will not stay accurate. [R: Choice, Nov 01, p. 491]—**J. E. Weaver**

266.   Liu, Lewis-Guodo. **Internet Resources and Services for International Business: A Global Guide.** Phoenix, Ariz., Oryx Press, 1998. 389p. index. $49.95pa. ISBN 1-57356-119-3.

This is a well-organized guide to international information on the Internet. There are 2,500 entries for Internet sites covering 175 countries. Each entry includes a title, Website address, and an annotation. International business is the stated focus of this reference work; however, the economy, culture, religion, language and social, political, and legal systems are covered as well. The included sites were developed, organized, and maintained by government agencies, businesses, or higher education.

An introductory chapter on global economics and the impact of the Internet on international business is followed by a chapter on resources such as the International Chamber of Commerce, Organization for Economic Cooperation and Development, and the World Trade Organization, among others. The following 6 chapters are sites by countries listed alphabetically within continent groupings.

Following the site listings are generous indexes. There is a 24-page Website title index, a 25-page country index, and a 103-page subject index. *Internet Resources and Services for International Business* provides an excellent shortcut to international information. [R: BL, 15 Oct 98, p. 442; LJ, 15 Nov 98, p. 61]—**Sue Brown**

267.   **Profiles in Business and Management: An International Directory of Scholars and Their Research.** [CD-ROM]. Boston, Harvard Business School Publishing; distr., New York, McGraw-Hill, 1996. Minimum system requirements (Windows version): IBM or compatible 386 CPU. CD-ROM drive. DOS 5.0. Windows 3.1. 4MB RAM. VGA monitor and graphics card with 125K memory. Mouse. Minimum system requirements (Macintosh version): CD-ROM drive. System 7. 4MB RAM. Color or monochrome monitor. Mouse. $495.00. ISBN 0-87584-681-5.

Profiles in Business and Management provides background, publications, and current research for more than "5,600 international scholars, researchers, and practitioners engaged in business and management research." Operational with Windows, DOS, or Macintosh, the CD-ROM's instructions for installation are straightforward and easily accomplished. The program allows the user to search a single index or perform a customized search by searching up to seven indexes at one time. The options include a name index (scholars alphabetized by last name), institution (current position), main disciplines, current research, address (geographic location), publications, languages (language fluency), professional organizations, education (earned and honorary degrees), and research region. Searching just a single index, the user activates the Index Selection window, chooses "New" from the Search menu, or double-clicks on the Index Selection icon. Next, the user double-clicks on the index name or moves the highlight bar with the cursor keys and then presses Enter. In most indexes, the user can scroll through a Word List or use an Alphabetic Browser. If the user has searched by keyword or phrase, occurrences of that word or phrase are highlighted on the screen. The User Guide provides specific instructions for the Custom Searching option.

Profiles in Business and Management has value to private industry, research organizations, and the academic community, making the CD-ROM a useful purchase for large corporate libraries, research entities, and university libraries supporting graduate business programs at the doctorate level. Students contemplating graduate education in business/management fields would find the information about faculty publications and research interests a useful guide in selecting a particular institution.—**Dene L. Clark**

268. **The Thunderbird Guide to International Business Resources on the World Wide Web.** By Candace Deans and Shaun Dakin. New York, John Wiley, 1997. 142p. maps. $21.95pa. ISBN 0-471-16016-4.

Although print publications of World Wide Web-accessible materials are often quickly out of date, this book provides organized and annotated information about many international business resources on the World Wide Web that are stable as well as valuable. It is organized by major geographical region, making it easy to find resources that are specific to a region or country. The table format for each entry is particularly clear and readable. This guide is recommended for use at a reference desk because the format will make it simple to make single copies or to add URLs to a local WWW electronic library collection. The coverage is restricted to WWW sites and does not include discussion lists, newsgroups, or other Internet-accessible resources. This outstanding book is strongly recommended for anyone using the Web for business research. [R: Choice, Jan 97, p. 766]—**Diane Kovacs**

269. **The Top 5,000 Global Companies 2002.** D. Shave and J. Thomas, eds. London, Graham & Whiteside; distr., Farmington Hills, Mich., Gale, 2001. 1298p. index. $730.00. ISBN 1-86099-258-7.

This hardbound book covers the top 5,000 global companies for the time period of 2002 in the area of manufacturing and service companies—by size of sales revenue, the largest 500 banks by total assets, and the top 100 insurance companies by premium income. This information is provided in separate divisions covering these various disciplines. Where available, each company entry includes the name of the company with address, telephone, fax, e-mail, and Website information; the names of the chairperson, the president, and board members; data on principal activities of the company, brand names and trademarks, and parent companies; financial information for the past two years; public or private status; names of principal shareholders; and the number of employees. All company listings are alphabetically listed within each country and two indexes are included. One index includes alphabetic listings of all the companies listed irrespective of their main country of origin and the other is a Standard Industrial Classification (SIC) index that lists companies by their various business activities within the main country of operation. This publication has above average binding and paper printing quality. Font size is small, but adequate for this type of publication. This volume will be of interest for anyone concerned with global companies or global trade. It should be in all major libraries as a reference source for international business. —**Herbert Ockerman**

270.   **Trade Shows Worldwide 2002: An International Directory of Events, Facilities, and Suppliers.** 18th ed. Tyra Y. Phillips, ed. Farmington Hills, Mich., Gale, 2002. 1803p. index. $335.00pa. ISBN 0-7876-5904-5. ISSN 1046-4395.

Trade Shows Worldwide is an excellent international directory for business and public libraries. But the $335 price tag may be a little much for some budgets, especially for a paperback. Nevertheless, the 18th edition of this directory (the user's guide erroneously identifies it as the 17th edition) provides pertinent information for more than 10,000 domestic and international tradeshows. In all, this edition has been updated to include 243 new tradeshows, 232 new sponsoring organizations, and many new e-mail and URL addresses. Following an introduction, a user's guide, and a geographic list of organizations, the directory is divided into three parts. Part 1 lists tradeshows and exhibitions with varying degrees of information that has been accumulated from questionnaire responses from sponsors and other Gale Group publications. Typically, the numbered entries contain data such as event name, exhibition management company, worldwide agent, U.S. contact sponsor, frequency, audience, number of visitors, space rental price, number of exhibits, registrations fees, e-mail and URL addresses, dates and locations, and more.

Part 2 lists tradeshow sponsors and organizations with contact information and cross-references to the shows they are involved with. Part 3 contains five sections that list conference and convention centers, visitor and convention bureaus, world trade centers, trade show services (e.g., audio/video equipment, exhibit designs and systems, installers and dismantlers, promotional goods, signs), and tradeshow information sources (e.g., professional and trade associations, consultants, publications). After these listings, the directory contains a "Rankings" section that enables users to look up entries by size. Finally, the directory concludes with a chronological index, a geographic index, a subject index, and a master index.—**Cari Ringelheim**

271.   **World Retail Directory and Sourcebook.** 2d ed. London, Euromonitor; distr., Detroit, Gale, 1995. 886p. index. $510.00. ISBN 0-86338-549-4.

In its 2d edition, this directory remains a useful but expensive guide to the global retail sector (see ARBA 93, entry 262, for a review of a previous edition). Tailored for academic, special, and large public libraries, this edition incorporates a fifth section, retail legislation to categories (e.g., a market overview, company profiles, sources) in the earlier edition. The market overview explores trends, such as niche retailing and home shopping, with 30 informative statistical tables.

The directory's core consists of brief geographically arranged profiles for 1,700 retailers in 90 countries. This section has top 10 rankings, basic location, and financial data; however, the personnel listings are limited and new technologies (e.g., listservs, World Wide Web homepages) have been excluded. The in-depth profiles for 70 leading retailers offer excellent evaluations of corporate operations, financial results, strengths, weaknesses, strategies, trading details, and products. A fourth section identifies important associations, publishers, research firms, and a selection of print and nonprint sources, although the appearance of some data (e.g., language, price) is inconsistent.

Three indexes list retailers by name, type of outlet, and country, while the fourth tabulates information sources. A key to outlet types would assist less knowledgeable patrons. While the usefulness of this edition has been enhanced by the new indexes, the format is confusing, creates difficulties in identifying entry headings, and hinders efforts to meet access requirements under the Americans with Disabilities Act. These problems might be eased with a CD-ROM version or a searchable World Wide Web site.—**Sandra E. Belanger**

Handbooks and Yearbooks

272. Burgess, Philip M., and Michael Kelly. **Profile of Western North America: Indicators of an Emerging Continental Market.** Golden, Colo., North American Press/Fulcrum Publishing, 1995. 419p. maps. index. $39.95pa. ISBN 1-55591-907-3.

While the book is obscurely titled *Profile of Western North America*, more specifically it contains statistical information on 23 states of the United States west of the Mississippi River (omitting Louisiana but including Alaska and Hawaii), all the provinces of Canada along with its two territories, and all the states of Mexico plus its Federal District. The division of the United States seems arbitrary but may be appropriate for some purposes. In the 16 chapters, there are data on basic resources, farms and fisheries, population, health, housing, transportation, energy, communication, education, public safety, environment, economics, finance and trade, business and employment, government finance, financial institutions, and international trade. The data include such items as beef production, urbanization, national park acreage, patents issued, labor force participation, and life expectancy. They are most often presented in bar graphs and charts, usually given by state or province. Most of the data are for 1990 or 1991, with some comparisons to the recent past. There is a directory of western states' government and private organizations for business, development, commerce, and trade; Canadian government and private organizations; Mexican government offices; and selected United States, Canadian, and Mexican corporations. —**J. E. Weaver**

273. **Business Monitor International Guide to the World's Major Emerging Economies: Country Analysis and Forecast Reports 2000-2001.** Chicago, Fitzroy Dearborn, 2000. 2v. $250.00/set. ISBN 1-57958-283-4.

This 8½-x-12-inch, 2-volume set is a country analysis and forecast report for various emerging economies. Volume 1 includes Asia, which provides information on China, Indonesia, Malaysia, Thailand, Philippines, and Vietnam. The "Emerging Europe" section includes Hungary, Poland, and Russia. Volume 2 includes Latin American countries (i.e., Chile, Argentina, Brazil, Colombia, Mexico, and Venezuela). The Middle East includes Africa, Egypt, Iran, Saudi Arabia, South Africa, Turkey, and United Arab Emirates. Under each country are five sections: political outlook, economic outlook, key economic sectors, business environment, and capital markets. Each section provides profile information and recent developments. Most of the data are from 1993 and are forecast in some cases up to 2002. There are adequate graphs to visually display the data but few references. The book is well written, easy to read, and the font size and binding are good. The information, in most cases, is almost unavailable from other sources except for some FAO data. This type of information is valuable to people involved in international trade and international peace and understanding. It should be in all major libraries. [R: BL, June 01, pp. 1930-1932; RUSQ, Summer 01, pp. 378-379]—**Herbert W. Ockerman**

274. **Cases in Corporate Acquisitions, Buyouts, Mergers, & Takeovers.** Kelly Hill, ed. Farmington Hills, Mich., Gale, 2000. 1507p. index. $295.00. ISBN 0-7876-3894-3. ISSN 1526-5927.

Gale has accurately aimed this worthwhile compilation of almost 300 essays on well-known or important acquisitions, buyouts, mergers, and takeovers at the undergraduate academic user. Each case, approximately six pages long, lists the name, address, telephone and fax numbers, and Web address of the affected company along with the date of the transaction. This is followed by the meat of the essay, an overview of the company, market forces driving the transaction, how they attempted to come together, products and services, changes to the industry, a review of the outcome, and the principal sources used in the report. Sidebars give nominal financials, officer names, names of major players in the transaction such as individual stockholders, and SIC/NAICS. The book includes both successful and unsuccessful transactions, starting with the New York Central Railroad's attempted takeover of the Erie Railroad in 1868. The majority of cases, however, are from the last 15 years. One of the two participants is supposed to be U.S. based but there are many exceptions, such as the Renault-Volvo or Volkswagen–Rolls Royce.

The 11 contributors are mostly freelance writers. The sources used consist mostly of articles from the business press. Although other publications will have more articles on most cases, undergraduates will appreciate the breadth, depth, and clarity of the 2,500-word essays. There is an adequate general index, an SIC industry index (although not an NAICS index), a chronology of actions, and a list of contributors. The general index focuses on major companies, whereas many smaller companies mentioned in the essays are not found in the index. Gale succeeds in its goal of making this source undergraduate friendly. It is attractively laid out, well written, and well indexed, with enough detail and sources for undergraduates to make their reports or speeches. The title fits a unique niche, yet much more information can be found in the business periodical literature. Large public or corporate libraries that have active business departments and historical interest in the transactions may find this a good purchase. It is a worthy acquisition for those libraries seeking information on the topic. [R: BL, 1 May 2000, p. 1686]—**Patrick J. Brunet**

275.   **Consumer International 2000/2001.** 7th ed. Chicago, Euromonitor International, 2000. 551p. index. $1,190.00. ISBN 0-86338-964-3.

The latest in a series whose 1st edition was published in 1994, *Consumer International* is a compendium of consumer market information in all the major non-European countries. It is a companion volume to *Consumer Europe*, which provides coverage for 16 European markets; *Consumer Europe*'s 16th edition was recently published (see entry 351). *Consumer International*, in addition to its print edition, is available in CD-ROM through Euromonitor's annual *World Consumer Markets* (see entry 293). Euromonitor also provides an online integrated business reference system titled *Global Market Information Database*; *World Consumer Markets* is part of this database.

Consumer International's aim is to draw together, in one volume, all market information on consumer trends in all major non-European countries. The 28 countries are major non-European countries, including the United States, Japan, Canada, Saudi Arabia, India, and China. The emphasis is on consumer goods, instead of industrial goods. The consumer goods covered are foods, drinks, tobacco, household cleaning products, over-the-counter healthcare products, disposable paper products, cosmetics and toiletries, housewares, home furnishings, clothing and footwear, domestic electrical appliances, consumer electronics, personal goods, leisure goods, and automotive goods. Each of these categories is further subdivided (e.g., food is broken down into meat, fish, fresh produce, hot beverages, and so on). Market data presented for each product is in both volumes and value sales for a six-year period, from 1994 to 1999. However, some product sectors have ranges from 1994 to 1998. Value figures are provided in million units of national currency at current prices. There is also a section on socioeconomic parameters that presents statistics for population trends and forecasts, economic indicators, consumer expenditure, retailing trends, advertising trends, and tourism data.

Consumer International includes a section on "Key Information Sources," a directory of international organizations (including the World Trade Administration), and trade associations such as the American Electronics' Association—these organizations were contacted by the publishers for the gathering of data for *Consumer International*. It is helpful for further research and includes addresses, telephone numbers, and e-mail addresses (when available). A helpful index of products covered is also included.

Consumer International is an invaluable research source providing thorough statistical coverage of major markets and is recommended to both academic and research collections. Libraries purchasing this volume may also want to consider *Consumer Europe.*—**Lucy Heckman**

276. **Exchange Arrangements and Exchange Restrictions 1998: Annual Report.** Washington, D.C., International Monetary Fund; distr., Lanham, Md., Bernan Associates, 1998. 1008p. $95.00pa. ISBN 1-55775-744-5. ISSN 0250-7366.

This specialized resource does just as its title states. It is a directory of 115 standardized data elements on how funds can be exchanged, held, transferred, or paid by individuals or institutions covering 183 nations. For example, it states whether a nonresident may hold a bank account in Namibia, whether Moldava has controls on gold trade, or how long an export payment collection in Slovenia can be held up before it must be registered as credit payment with the Bank of Slovenia. The 115 elements are divided into 8 categories: exchange arrangements, resident and nonresident accounts, arrangements for payment and receipts, import and import payments, export and export payments, payments and proceeds for invisible transactions and current transfers, capital transactions, and changes during the last year. The title under review is the 1998 edition, therefore most data are from 1997. The 1999 edition has already been published. Only a small portion of the data is available on the IMF Website at http://www.imf.org as of October 1999. The report has been published since 1950, and for a reference work of more than 1,000 pages the price is reasonable. Faculty can purchase the title at half price. This volume is suitable for large public, academic, and business libraries serving an international banking or business clientele or where import and export clients are served.—**Patrick J. Brunet**

277. **Historical Statistics 1960-1994. Statistiques Rétrospectives.** 1996 ed. Washington, D.C., OECD Publications and Information Center, 1996. 180p. $39.00pa. ISBN 92-64-04850-2.

In 180 pages of tables and graphs, *Historical Statistics 1960-1994* provides an overview of the economic development of the member countries of the Organization for Economic Cooperation and Development (OECD) since 1960. There are two main types of statistics given: percentage rates of change and percentage ratios. For the most part, data have been drawn from other OECD statistical publications, including the annual and quarterly issues of *Labour Force Statistics, National Accounts*, and *Main Economic Indicators*, among others.

The work is organized in three parts. The first provides 1994 benchmark data for national accounts and domestic finance (e.g., gross domestic product), labor force participation rates and age and gender distribution, foreign trade, and exchange rates. The second contains analytic statistics intended to chart the movements of major economic variables or the structure or composition of specific economic aggregates, such as foreign trade by partner country group. The analytic tables in this second section show developments from 1960 to 1994. The last section comprises a series of graphs that illustrate some of the important changes that have been taking place in the economies of the OECD member countries. The work is also available on disk.—**G. Kim Dority**

278. **Hoover's Global 250: The Stories Behind the Most Powerful Companies on the Planet.** Austin, Tex., Hoover's, 1997. 612p. index. $29.95pa. ISBN 1-57311-008-6.

This fine Hoover product gives two pages of useful data for 250 of the most influential, global business giants outside of the United States, with one giant flaw. The volume follows Hoover's standard format. One page is text, containing an overview of the company and the company's history. The second page gives officers (sometimes with compensation); location, telephone, and fax numbers; 1995 sales; key competitors; major products or services; a chart of 12 financials for 1986-95; a stock price history chart; and nine financials for the company's last fiscal year (either

FY95 or FY96). The data is prefaced by 60 pages of lists, such as top 100 European stock companies or non-U.S. company stocks available through U.S. markets.

This title, like so many of the Hoover publications fills a need for low cost, reliable business data. Normally it can be stated that there is nothing comparable in quality and price and Hoover publications are a great value. However, Hoover has published the exact same material in hardback form under the title *Hoover's Handbook of World Business, 1996-1997* (Hoover's, 1996). The text and data are exactly the same except for the title, introduction, and the price ($44.95). This reviewer could not find any statement that tells the user that the material is a duplicate of the other title in either work, the Hoover Website, or in the publisher catalogs. Obviously the paperback is a better value. For content and utility, the *Global 250* is highly recommended for academic and public libraries.—**Patrick J. Brunet**

279. **Hoover's Handbook of World Business 2001.** Austin, Tex., Hoover's, 2001. 720p. index. $114.95. ISBN 1-57311-066-3. ISSN 1055-7199.

Published by Hoover's, the esteemed publisher of directory-type information and historical and detailed financial data on large corporations, this directory features 300 influential non-U.S.-based firms (the Big Five accounting firms being an exception). Informative data are provided for publicly held firms as well as private businesses and a selection of government-owned entities. *Hoover's* provides only two pages per business enterprise, but those two pages contain a wallop of material. Following a brief overview, there is a concise, but richly detailed, history for each firm. The second page is devoted to a listing of officers (sometimes including their age and salary), addresses, telephone and fax numbers, Websites, sales figures for the most recent calendar or fiscal year, sales by product/operation, and historical financials and employee data for a 10 year period. *Hoover's* also lists the firm's competition by name.

The two-page company profiles described in the preceding paragraph constitute the bulk of the handbook, but the diligent researcher will find even more golden nuggets. "A List Lover's Compendium" extols the world's top and largest achievers in every possible industry and category. There is also a long list of non-U.S. company stocks available in the United States. Two indexes at the back of the handbook wrap up a very compact, but information laden, source. The first index profiles the listed firms by industry. The second is an index of brands, companies, and people named in the profiles. This handbook is highly recommended for all business collections in public, academic, and special libraries that serve clients dealing with international business.—**Dene L. Clark**

280. **International Financial Statistics Yearbook 1998.** Washington, D.C., International Monetary Fund; distr., Lanham, Md., Bernan Associates, 1998. 961p. $65.00pa. ISBN 155775-749-6. ISSN 0250-7463.

This yearbook contains both worldwide and country-specific financial data for the years 1968 through 1997. The available data from 1948 through 1967 are maintained in the International Monetary Fund's Economic Information System. The yearbook is arranged in four sections, preceded by a detailed introduction that explains the arrangement and compilation of the tables. Section 1 consists of time-series charts on international reserves, interest rates, exchange rates, prices, unit values and commodity prices, and trade and national accounts. Section 2 presents world financial statistical tables on exchange rates, fund accounts, international reserves, measures of money, interest rates, real effective exchange rate indexes, prices, wages, production and employment, international trade, balance of payments, national accounts, and commodity prices. Section 3, the largest part of the volume, has individual country tables and section 4 contains country notes. The publisher indicates that additional country notes are contained in the monthly issues of *International Financial Statistics*.

This is an essential economics and business reference work for any library that serves a clientele interested in international affairs and world trade. Although the presentation of data is clear and readable, some novices may be put off by the seemingly arcane annotation system that the IMF uses throughout the volume. In addition, the country notes provide essential, useful information about the history of international liquidity, interest rates, government finance, monetary authorities, and banking institutions that gives context to the data presented.—**Robert H. Burger**

281. **International Marketing Data and Statistics 2001.** 25th ed. Chicago, Euromonitor International, 2001. 753p. index. $395.00. ISBN 0-86338-979-1. ISSN 0308-2938.

This 2-inch thick, oversized, well-organized tome provides approximately 246 tables on 25 data categories for 160 non-European countries. Tables detail demographics, economic trends, banking and finance, external trade, labor, industrial and energy resources and output, consumer expenditure, defense, retailing, advertising, consumer market size and prices, housing and household expenditures, health and living standards, communication, automobiles, transports, travel and tourism, and cultural indicators. Data are presented in easy-to-understand spreadsheet format covering 1977 to 1999, which requires three pages per table, although not all years are included for each table. The first 120 pages are split between a selective directory of major business information centers for each country and a 3 to 5 page overview of the national economy with a brief description of the political structure.

The directory, selective as it may be, is quite useful for developing countries. A seven-page index gives better than average access to the often hard to find data. Sources are listed for each table, but, because of the multiyear nature of the tables, only the general title of the source is given. European data are not found in this volume, but it is in the complementary title, *European Marketing Data and Statistics* (see entry 353). Both the European and international marketing titles are available individually on CD-ROM and collectively on the Web in the product, Global Marketing Information Database.

The *Europa World Year Book* (39th ed.; see ARBA 99, entry 66) and the *Statesman's Yearbook* (137th ed.; see ARBA 2002, entry 77) contain some of this data as well as national political and economic reviews, but provide it for each individual country, not in tables comparing the 160 potential reporting countries. This comparison of countries for a specific data element is a particular strength. Some of the reported data are also available in the National Trade Data Bank (available on CD-ROM and on LEXIS-NEXIS) and on RDS/TableBase on the Web, but this book makes it easier and quicker to retrieve data. This work is a very useful and strongly recommended tool for graduate and undergraduate libraries as well as those public libraries serving international business and marketing clientele.—**Patrick J. Brunet**

282. **International Marketing Forecasts 2001.** 3d ed. Chicago, Euromonitor International, 2001. 527p. $1,000.00pa. ISBN 1-84264-115-8.

International Marketing Forecasts is Euromonitor's opinion of how markets will develop in the future. Forecasts based on familiar economic concepts, such as price and income elastics, are modified by specific characteristics of individual countries and product markets, a country's expected policy of orientation, and the degree of interdependence between various countries and particular markets. The subjective nature of the final forecasts is acknowledged. The 1st section of the book gives socioeconomic forecasts on demography, the economy (GDP, labor force, inflation, income, and so on), consumer expenditures, retail distribution, and housing and households. The section includes a forecast of household durables, media, and communication usage. Most figures are given in 1999 U.S. dollars. For the tables relating to the economy and expenditures, data are annual for 1999-2004, 2008, and 2013. For the other tables, including those for specific markets, the data are annual for 1999-2005. The general markets found here are food, drink, tobacco, household cleaning products, over-the-counter health care, disposable paper products, cosmetics and toiletries, housewares, home furnishings, clothing and footwear, domestic electrical appliances, consumer electronics, personal goods, leisure goods, and automotive.

The purpose of the book is to provide guidance to businesses as they plan for the future. How accurate the forecasts are will only be known in time. Users of the book should supplement the data given here with information from other sources. The databases for this book are available on CD-ROM to allow users to take their own parameters and calculate forecasts from baseline figures. [R: Choice, May 02, p. 1568]—**J. E. Weaver**

283. **International Yearbook of Industrial Statistics 2001.** By the United Nations Industrial Development Organization. Northhampton, Mass., Edward Elgar, 2001. 718p. $210.00. ISBN 1-84064-619-5.

This 718-page book is written by the United Nations Industrial Development Organization, which makes it one of the few books where this type of information can be obtained. It starts with an introduction followed by appendixes that list the countries and areas and their selected groupings, a detailed description of international standard industrial classifications of all economic activities, and data and summary tables. The first major section includes manufacturing value added for the years 1980 through 1999. It breaks this information down into populations among selected groups of developing countries; annual growth in manufactured value added and per capita information equivalent are in this breakdown. It also lists shares of manufactured value added in gross domestic products for selected years.

The next section looks at distribution of world value added for selected branches along the developing regions. The next area evaluates leading products in selected branches, which includes most manufactured items. The following section evaluates structure of manufactured value added in selected country groups and in selected years. Annual growth of value added for branches of selected countries or groups is also included. The next major section looks at manufacturing products and breaks them down according to countries and selected years. Eighty-nine countries are listed and the countries not listed are covered in previous editions, including the United States, which was listed in 1998. This text would be indispensable in any libraries that have a focus on international industrial statistics. The binding is excellent, the paper is average, and the printing is below average but adequate for its purpose. [R: AG, Nov 01, p. 68]—**Herbert W. Ockerman**

284. **National Accounts Statistics: Main Aggregates and Detailed Tables, 1996–1997.** By the Department of Economic and Social Affairs Statistics Division. New York, United Nations, 2000. 2v. $135.00/set. ISBN 92-1-161425-2. S/N E.00.XVII.11.

Adopted by the United Nation's Statistical Commission, the System of National Accounts (SNA) consists of a coherent, consistent, and integrated set of macroeconomic accounts, balance sheets, and tables based on a set of internationally agreed concepts, definitions, classifications, and accounting rules. The SNA provides a comprehensive accounting framework within which economic data can be gathered and presented for purposes of economic analysis, decision-making, and policy-making. Organized by country, this work includes production, goods and services, outlay, and capital finance accounts data for institutional sectors and subsectors.

Part 1 of the country tables includes information on the basic gross domestic product (GDP), government receipts and disbursements, enterprise and household income and outlay, and external transactions. A summary capital transactions account, information on gross product by institutional sector of origin and kind of activity, plus a table showing the relation among the aggregate concepts used in the revised SNA and also commonly in national statistical systems are also included. Part 2 shows detailed breakdowns of the final expenditure components on GDP (consumption, capital formation, and imports and exports) in current and constant prices. Part 3 details institutional sector accounts. For each sector and subsector, five accounts are provided: production, income and outlay, capital formation, capital finance, and balance sheet. Part 4 contains kind-of-activity breakdowns at the major division, one-digit, and level of the International Standard Industrial Classification (ISIC) of all economic activities. All of these data are arranged alphabetically by country and then, in parts 1-4, by smaller divisions depending on statistics available. The introduction provides a description of each table as well as information on the methodology that was used for the collection of the data and an explanation of nomenclature and symbols used. Economists, students, faculty, and researchers will find this collection of data invaluable in today's global economy. This 40th issue of the *National Accounts Statistics* for 165 countries and areas will be well used in academic and special collections.—**Susan C. Awe**

285.   Pagell, Ruth A., and Michael Halperin. **International Business Information: How to Find It, How to Use It.** 2d ed. Phoenix, Ariz., Oryx Press, 1997. 445p. index. $84.50. ISBN 1-57356-050-2.

As any experienced researcher will say, locating international business information is often a difficult and frustrating job. This volume makes the job much easier. It contains excellent information resources, thoughtful analysis, and expert advice. The selection criteria for the 2d edition are the same as for the 1st edition (see ARBA 95, entry 255). The focus is on core materials that are authoritative, available, and affordable. Occasionally some works are mentioned with the recommendation not to buy them. Each chapter covers a different subtopic of international business. The book contains exhibits, tables, appendixes, citations to significant texts on the subject, and a selected bibliography with each chapter. Websites are also included where relevant.

Librarians will find this resource useful for collection development and research assistance. It is an excellent resource for academic, corporate, and public libraries.—**Deborah Sharp**

286.   **Retail Trade International.** 1998 ed. Chicago, Ill., Euromonitor International; distr., Detroit, Gale, 1998. 5v. $1,950.00/set. ISBN 0-86338-747-0.

Retail Trade International, now in its 9th edition, is published every 3 years. Euromonitor's newest edition reviews and analyzes retail trade globally and for each of 50 countries around the world in 3,070 pages of text and more than 2,500 statistical tables. An 88-page overview summarizes the data from the 50 country profiles and examines it at the regional and national level. A glossary of terms, methodology, sources, and exchange rates are included in the introduction. The glossary does not include all terms. The word "turnover" (meaning sales), which is used in many tables, is the most glaring omission. There is no index, but a detailed table of contents and list of the hundreds of tables are included.

An in-depth portrait of the retail conditions existing in the market is provided for each county. These country chapters begin with a bulleted section of key findings, followed by an analysis of the general economy and retail business, infrastructure, issues, and sales. Also covered are food and nonfood distribution. There is a section that details the major retailers, along with rankings and market shares and a description of each of these companies. In some cases, a financial, business, and competitive analysis is given. The final part presents the retail outlook, which forecasts until the year 2005. Each country chapter is structured so that narratives precede the data and place it in context. Historical data in these tables cover the years 1992 to 1997.

The amount of information presented is quite extensive. The chapter on Belgium is 60 pages long; the one on France 114 pages. Food and nonfood retailing is further broken down into 25 smaller categories, such as supermarkets, discounters, bakers, variety stores, mail order firms, footwear stores, and other. Figures are given in the national currency.

Once again Euromonitor has provided an excellent source for international business by providing information not available elsewhere or available only with great expense and difficulty.

This set is simply a gold mine of data and perspectives. It would be improved by the addition of an index, especially for the retail companies covered. It is an invaluable tool for business students and researchers interested in global retail markets. Because of its cost, this source will most likely find its way into large academic libraries and corporate information centers.—**Gerald L. Gill**

287.   Savitt, William, and Paula Bottorf. **Global Development: A Reference Handbook.** Santa Barbara, Calif., ABC-CLIO, 1995. 369p. index. $39.50. ISBN 0-87436-774-3.

This is a fascinating book. It has definitions, a survey with statistics, and a discussion of approaches, problems, and results; it is as up-to-date as can be for a printed book. Yet, the handbook is too cursory for academicians, too brief for policy-makers, and too expensive for the "just interested" reader. Luckily, it will be available (one hopes) in libraries.

The overview covers development economics, international debt, food production and shortage, the role of women in development, population, refugees, and the environment. Most interesting is the chronology of development since the 1940s. Less interesting are the biographical sketches of a few selected people considered as history makers in development. The judgment is subjective and not very complimentary, as the process of development has not been a great success. The statistical survey, based on World Bank publications, is useful but brief, as is the list of references. The list of institutions and government agencies involved in development serves as a useful reference source.

An innovative contribution is the reference list of nonprofit sources, such as audiovisuals and computer resources, that give the reader Internet homepages and e-mail addresses when available. The glossary and index add to the usefulness of this volume. The identity of the collaborating agencies and individuals reveals the humanistic objectives of the authors. How much more accessible would the message have been had this been published in paperback, with a more attractive title, and at a lower price! [R: Choice, June 96, p. 1623; LJ, Mar 96, p. 74-76; SLJ, June 96, p. 164]—**Elias H. Tuma**

288.   Seyoum, Belay. **The State of the Global Economy 2001: Trends, Data, Rankings, Charts.** Baldwin Place, N.Y., Encyclopedia Society, 2001. 394p. index. $60.00pa. ISBN 0-914746-57-X.

The author of this work teaches courses in international business at Nova Southeastern University in Fort Lauderdale, Florida, and publishes articles and books on aspects of international business and economics. The book is organized into 22 sections. It opens with a survey of recent developments, including trends in the world economy, the Asian Financial Crisis, mergers and acquisitions, the introduction of the Euro, the stock market, the influence of the Internet on the economy, the globalization of economic activity, and other developments. The succeeding sections cover a wide range of subjects, including money and investing, population, cross-country comparisons, national output and income, productivity, labor force, government expenditures, currencies and exchange rates, international trade, external debt, country risk ratings, education levels, research and development, energy production and consumption, and brief profiles of selected international economic institutions.

Each section is provided with a brief introduction followed by pages of reprinted charts and tables. The work concludes with "Country Profiles" of some countries for which the source of the data is not disclosed, although it appears to be taken largely from the CIA's *World Factbook* (http://www.cia.gov/cia/publications/factbook/). An appendix contains balance of payments data. Selected references are identified and an index is provided. Among the sources of data are the World Bank, the Organization for Economic Cooperation and Development, the International Monetary Fund, the United Nations, and the U.S. government.

In an effort to reduce the size of the volume, the textual material is printed in miniscule type, making it difficult to read. An obvious weakness of this kind of compilation is that the reprinted data tables are seriously outdated. *The State of the Global Economy 2001* does not do a good job of portraying its subject. The world has changed substantially. What is the point of a lengthy list of the top performing mutual funds in March of 1999 long after the stock market bubble has burst? What is the value of country risk ratings that are more than two years old? The world economy is such a vast subject that any selection of material is likely to be idiosyncratic. Although many of the points made in the overviews are valid and insightful, the work as a whole lacks coherence. In many instances, the source of the chart or table is not identified. The overall quality of the work is poor—difficult to read, outdated with an arbitrary selection of data, pages of reprinted data, and data that are not properly identified. The book is expensive considering that the majority of the work simply republishes data from other reference works.—**Peter Zachary McKay**

289. **Structural and Ownership Changes in the Chemical Industry of Countries in Transition.** New York, United Nations, 1997. 164p. $75.00pa. ISBN 92-1-116675-6. S/N E.97.II.E.17.

Designed for private sector investors, this report presents the status of the chemical industry in 17 Central and Eastern European countries. Based on questionnaires completed by the government and information published in the technical press, the economic and industrial development in the region is compared through primarily statistical data. The volume consists of an introduction and 17 chapters, one for each country, with the introduction assessing conversions, privatization, restructuring, and other developments in the industry during a five-year period ending in 1996. With eight tables on gross domestic product, or GDP (e.g., share of the industry GDP) and other comparative data (e.g., growth of output), this introduction emphasizes the chemical industry's importance as a backbone of all industry, illustrates beginning opportunities for foreign investment, and assesses progress in privatization efforts.

The individual country chapters, which vary in content and length depending on the extent of information received, follow a similar format in reporting production data, recent laws and regulations, ownership changes, structural changes (e.g., infrastructure, outlook), and statistical data. Private ownership information ranges from the number of companies in the industry to detailed descriptions of products and company partnerships. This work is recommended for libraries serving the chemical industry and an international business clientele.—**Sandra E. Belanger**

290. **Trade and Development Report, 2001.** By the Secretariat of the United Nations Conference on Trade and Development. By the Secretariat of the United Nations Conference on Trade and Development.

The *Trade and Development Report* has been published by UNCTAD for the past 20 years and is a report and in-depth analysis of the international economy. The 2001 edition "offers an assessment of recent trends and prospects in the world economy, with particular focus on the impact that developments and policies in the industrial economies are likely to have on prospects in the developing world." Included in this study is an analysis of the implications of the economic slowdown in the United States. It is essentially a narrative analysis, with charts and tables providing statistical summaries.

The *Report* is divided into two parts: "Global Trends and Prospects" and "Reform of the International Financial Architecture." Part 1, "Global Trends and Prospects," looks at the current global outlook and analyzes the economy in developed economies (i.e., United States, European Union, and Japan), developing countries (e.g., Latin America, Asia, Africa), and transition economies. Additionally, it studies recent developments in international trade, recent developments and emerging trends in oil markets and non-oil commodity markets, currency markets and selected financial indicators in emerging markets, private capital flows to emerging-market economies, and external financing and debt of the least developed countries. Part 2 analyzes possible reform measures for international financial architecture, including studies of how to reform the International Monetary Fund. Studied also in part 2 are weaknesses and possible reforms of standards and regulations, including accounting and auditing and securities regulation. Analyzed also are exchange rate regimes and crisis management and burden sharing. Bibliographic references are provided, including monographs, UN documents, journal articles, speeches, and working papers. Sources for statistical charts and tables provided are not from UNCTAD, but from the U.S. Department of Commerce, OECD Economic Outlook, and OPEC Monthly Oil Market Report, among other resources. The *Trade and Development Report* continues to be an outstanding source for research of the international economy and analyzes current issues, notably the implications for the slowdown in the United States economy. It is recommended for academic library collections as well as corporate and research libraries.—**Lucy Heckman**

291.   **The Washington Almanac of International Trade and Business, 1998.** Gary P. Osifchin and William O. Scouton, eds. Washington, D.C., Almanac; distr., Lanham, Md., Bernan Associates, 1998. 840p. illus. $225.00pa. ISBN 1-886222-10-X.

The almanac, primarily a directory of information on international trade and foreign policy, is sponsored by the Greater Washington Board of Trade, and includes a brief introductory section describing that organization and extolling the virtues of the Washington, D.C., area as a place to do business. This is the 4th edition of a work originally published in 1994 as *The International Washington Almanac* (see ARBA 95, entry 760). It was issued for the first time under the current title in 1995 (see ARBA 97, entry 230).

It consists of 3 main parts: Foreign Diplomatic Corps in the United States, The U.S. Government: Who Does What?, and Other Entities Dealing with Foreign Trade. In addition there is an index and a five-page section on advertisements. The 1st part is divided into 4 sections: a directory of foreign ambassadors and staff arranged in alphabetic order by country, a directory of commercial contacts at foreign embassies in Washington, a list of foreign consular offices in the U.S., and a list of local holidays (i.e., the national holidays of other countries) alphabetically by country with a two-page world timetable, listing the time in each country when it is noon in Washington, D.C.

Part 2 is divided into 3 sections. The 1st section on general export information includes 4 nondirectory subsections: export services, export regulations, customs benefits and tax incentives, U.S. export and the economy, and also an export glossary. The 2d section covers the federal legislature, and it is essentially a series of directories of U.S. congressional contacts. The 3d section is a series of directories for the Executive Branch.

Part 3 has 13 sections, including directories of multinational banks, the International Monetary Fund, international interest groups, foreign agents, Washington's international press, world trade centers, international business learning opportunities in the Greater Washington area, and chambers of commerce.

In the foreword the editors say, "Somewhere in this book every user can find an idea, a name, a telephone or fax number that will be useful." This is undoubtedly true; the almanac contains an enormous amount of information, but it is presented in the complex organization described above. There is an index, but it lists only organizations, countries, and general topics. The index does not list states, cities, products, or people. This means it is relatively easy to find information for general topics. However, it requires intimate familiarity with the complex arrangement of the sections, parts, and subsections to find information related to a particular product or to find agencies, organizations, and contacts relevant to international business interests in any specialized area of complex situation.

This work consolidates information found in a wide variety of other sources. However, nothing contains all the information gathered here. The almanac should provide practically all the information needed by anyone interested in international business. An electronic version would be superb, but even in its current less-than-user-friendly print version, it is recommended to any library with an interest in international business. —**Richard H. Swain**

292. **World Commodity Survey 2000-2001: Markets, Trends and the World Economic Environment.** Philippe Chalmin and Charles Prager, eds., with the UNCTAD Secretariat Coordination New York, United Nations, 2001. 348p. index. $85.00pa. ISBN 92-1-101030-6. ISSN 1020-7813. S/N GV.E.00.0.16.

Produced by the United Nations Conference on Trade and Development in conjunction with CyclOpe (an informal amalgam of academics, industry representatives, and other international commodities experts from France), this fine work provides a short, three-to four-page essay reviewing the current situation and recent world trends for approximately 70 commodities. Tables detailing production and prices supplement each essay. Coverage includes commodities in the fields of agriculture and fisheries, metals and diamonds, fertilizers, forestry products, and textiles. The first 90 pages of the annual offer short essays on globalization, world economic environment by continent, financial and commodities markets, a review of the commodity market for the past few years, and the future of commodities. The text is clearly written and would be understandable to undergraduates. Some data are as recent as March 2001, which is good for any annual, but unusually current for a United Nations sponsored publication. Furthermore, the $85 price is also quite reasonable for a UN statistical volume.

The CRB Commodity Yearbook (see entry 136) offers more U.S. based tabular data for more commodities but far less textual description of the current economic condition of each commodity. The U.S. government publications, *Agricultural Statistics* (1999 ed.; see ARBA 2000, entry 1298) and *Minerals Yearbook* (United States Government Printing Office, annual), report U.S. and world production and consumption for more commodities among its extensive coverage but are also more tabular in nature. The *World Commodity Survey* is more analytical on the state of the commodity and provides a better understanding of market conditions than the other titles listed above. Taken together, they are more complementary than competitive. Published since the mid-1980s, it is very strongly recommended for business schools and large public and other libraries interested in commodities and international business and is a good choice for libraries wanting only one title on world commodities.—**Patrick J. Brunet**

293. **World Consumer Markets 1999/2000 on CD-ROM.** 5th ed. [CD-ROM]. Chicago, Euromonitor International, 2000. Minimum system requirements: IBM or compatible 486 DX2 66. Double-speed CD-ROM drive. Windows 3.1 or Windows 95. 8MB RAM. 10MB hard disk space. $2,390.00. ISBN 0-86338-891-4.

Euromonitor is a respected international market research firm based in London. This database is the source for three of its print publications: *Consumer Europe*, *Consumer Eastern Europe*, and *Consumer International*. It covers 330 consumer product sectors across 52 countries for the years 1993–1998. All of the major industrialized counties are included as well as many emerging markets, such as Mexico, China, India, Indonesia, Russia, Saudi Arabia, and South Africa. For each product it reports market size by value in the national currency and market size by volume. Socioeconomic and demographic parameters are included in order to make relevant calculated comparisons. Exchange rate data are provided to facilitate cross-country comparisons. The full gamut of consumer products are covered, from automobiles, clothing, and consumer electronics to beverages, bakery products, canned and frozen food, home furnishings, cleaning products, leisure products, books, newspaper and magazine subscriptions, personal care, and over-the-counter health care products. The data are compiled from official sources published around the world and from thousands of telephone and personal interviews.

The software is extremely well designed, flexible, and easy to use. After selecting the countries, products, and years of interest a worksheet with the selected data is opened. The software enables users to build sophisticated analyses of a market within a country or across countries. Preset macros calculate per capita sales and quantity consumed, index data to base periods the user selects, insert key indicators selected from the menus, and convert exchange rates. Data may be exported to spreadsheets.

This database is useful to students studying international markets, business people interested in exporting, and any researcher analyzing international consumer markets. Comparable data sources are difficult to identify and find in most libraries. The price, at more than $2,000, makes this product most attractive to international marketers in corporations and less likely to be found in most public and academic library collections—**Peter Zachary McKay**

294. **World Country Analyst.** [CD-ROM]. Detroit, Gale, 1997. Minimum system requirements: IBM or compatible 386 (486 or higher recommended). CD-ROM drive. DOS 5.0. Windows 3.1. 8MB RAM. SVGA 256-color monitor. Mouse. $425.00/stand-alone; $475.00/2-8 users. ISBN 0-7876-1638-9.

The *World Country Analyst* states that it provides businesspeople with economic and business information on foreign countries—drawing heavily from government sources—which is true. What is not stated is that this information is almost all available, and more, in *Department of Commerce's National Trade Data Bank* (NTDB), available on CD-ROM and in an online version through STAT-USA.

The *World Country Analyst* software proved difficult to install under Windows 95 until everything from the Windows startup menu was removed. There is a brief, yet reasonable, manual provided. Online help is meager, but the software is fairly easy to use and intuitive. The software is probably easier to use than that of the NTDB but is less sophisticated. A search can be done by country, topic, clickable map, full text, and custom search, including phrase and word searches using the functions AND and NOT. A full-text search on Mexico resulted in a screen showing a colored flag, a list of 429 topics, and the beginning of the text of the first topic. If Mexico is searched under country, however, only 132 hits are made. Clicking on one of the list of topics will display a single map in the right window. Unfortunately, the screen appears to use frames, so the text cannot be expanded to fill the whole screen. It is possible to print or download all or part of the document text, map, or flag, but not the list of topics. There is information on particular industries and the country in general, including topics such as human rights practices. Almost all of this information can be found on the NTDB, and although no credit or date is given for the individual source, it is obviously from the Department of Commerce's Market Research Reports and Country Commercial Guides, as well as from other departments such as State and Labor. Formatting of documents is sloppy at times, with stray lines at the beginning or end. This is most likely the result of poor division of longer documents. A few tables appear in a scrambled display. Aside from ethical problems of sources not being credited or dated, it is difficult for the user to know how current the information is, except for dates in the text itself. Most of the information appears to be relatively recent, although not as current as the NTDB. However, the labor trends document contains 1990-1991 data, whereby most libraries government publications depository collections have 1995-1996 foreign labor trends. Also, the original source's references to other sources for the user to consult are omitted.

Aside from the above issues, this is a source of considerable useful information for businesspeople, providing easy-to-use software. Anyone considering its purchase, however, should consider the other alternatives—the National Trade Data Bank on CD-ROM or a subscription to STAT-USA. Both contain significant information not present in the *World Country*

Analyst, including references to other electronic sources. The NTDB CD-ROM may cost less for a single copy, and both NTDB and STAT-USA will provide more current information.—**Marit S. Taylor**

295. **World Development Indicators 2002**. Herndon, Va., World Bank, 2002. 405p. index. $550.00pa. ISBN 0-8213-5088-9.

World Development Indicators (WDI), an annual review published by the World Bank that provides a comprehensive overview of the world economy, contains 800 indicators and 87 tables representing 152 economies. Its underlying philosophy is that "reliable quantitative evidence is essential for understanding economic and social development" (p. vii). Data are presented in six sections. "World View" provides indicators that measure each nation's progress toward international development goals. "People" includes indicators that measure each nation's population, employment, education, and health. "Environment" contains data that measure land use, energy use, and urbanization. "Economy" includes measurements of a nation's economic indicators, such as national accounts, external debt, and trade. "States and Markets" contains indicators that measure the size and nature of financial markets, such as exchange rates, tax policies, and defense expenditures. "Global Links" provides measurements of global financial flows including aid and merchandise trade.

An overview consisting of figures and charts and an essay precedes the data in each section. Each table of indicators is accompanied by a one-page introduction that describes the data sources and provides definitions of all survey categories. This feature makes the resource especially valuable for novice as well as advanced researchers. While the heavy use of slick graphics can be distracting, this design is a minor complaint in relation to the convenience of having such ready access to explanatory information.

New features in the 2002 edition include a report on United Nations development goals for the twenty-first century, increased data on gender and development, and new data on the impact of information technology and the digital divide. WDI contains a bibliography of sources and research as well as an index of indicators. Researchers needing access to time-series indicators or charting and data-export capabilities should look to the *World Development Indicators* CD-ROM. WDI is a comprehensive and well-organized source for comparative international data. It does a superb job of presenting data in a variety of formats and is a particularly valuable source for researchers interested in exploring the ambiguous and problematic relationship between economics, social policy, and international development. It is a resource that belongs in all social science, international business, and economics collections.—**Scott Johnston**

296. **World Economic and Social Survey 2001: Trends and Policies in the World Economy.** By the Department of Economic and Social Affairs. New York, United Nations, 2001. 283p. $55.00pa. ISBN 92-1-109137-3. S/N E.01.II.C.1.

The world economic situation is the subject of the United Nations' *World Economic and Social Survey*, which offers detailed statistics and commentary on economic events and indicators. The work is divided into two major parts: "State of the World Economy," which includes statistics and analysis, and "A Globalizing World: Risks, Vulnerability, and Opportunities." Statistical charts and graphs are provided, along with extensive commentary and analysis of the data.

"State of the World Economy" describes global trends, including aggregate Gross Domestic Product (GDP), exchange rates, international trade, and commodity prices. Quarterly indicators are provided for specific countries, including Canada, the United States, the United Kingdom, Germany, France, Japan, Italy, and Poland (from 1999–2000). Quarterly statistics for each country include unemployment rate, growth of consumer prices, and growth of GDP. Monetary and fiscal policies of various countries are also discussed.

"A Globalizing World" focuses on vulnerability at the level of the country. Vulnerability is defined as the risk of being negatively affected by shocks. These shocks may include natural disasters, including cyclones and earthquakes, as well as economic shocks that are outside the specific country's control. Analyzed in this section are the impact of financial crises and possible prevention methods, the interrelationship between trade and vulnerability, external assistance programs, and population and economic effects of natural disasters. Specific cases of shocks hitting Armenia, Kyrgyzstan, and Mongolia are studied at length.

There is also an "Annex" to this volume that contains the main sets of data on which the survey is based. The "Annex" was prepared by the Development Policy Analysis Division of the Department of Economic and Social Affairs of the United Nations Secretariat. In addition to the statistical tables, explanations concerning data quality and data definitions and conventions are provided. The statistical tables are arranged within three categories: "Global Output and Macroeconomic Indicators," "International Trade," and "International Finance and Financial Markets." The *World Economic and Social Survey* is valuable in that it brings together unique data and provides analysis of these data, focusing on various issues in the world economy. It is recommended to academic and research library collections.—**Lucy Heckman**

297. **World Economic Factbook 1998/99.** 6th ed. Chicago, Euromonitor International; distr., Farmington Hills, Mich., Gale, 1998. 457p. $420.00. ISBN 0-86338-817-5.

This source provides the user with economic and political data on 207 countries in a well-organized, easy-to-use format. After an introduction explaining the various features and data elements, the *Factbook* proceeds to maps of the major regions of the world followed by country rankings in 15 demographic and economic areas. These include population, birth rate, household size, GDP, GDP growth, inflation, imports and exports, and tourism receipts.

The main body of the reference is devoted to a country-by-country analysis and statistical presentation. Each country occupies two facing pages. The 1st page is a narrative section of 13 paragraphs, including political structure, political risk, last election, international disputes, economy, main industries, and energy. The second page is a statistical portrait of the country. This includes most of the same measures found in the country rankings located at the beginning of the volume with the added benefit of a three-year retrospective. To those are added more GDP figures such as consumption, death rate, and tourist spending. A demographic table follows with such characteristics as urban population, age breakdown, life expectancy, and adult literacy. The analysis ends with a table of export and import trading partners.

Because of the differing state of statistical data gathering in individual countries, not every country has a complete set of data. Many of the same statistics may be found in other sources, such as *Europa World Year Book* (39th ed.; see ARBA 99, entry 66), the CIA's *World Factbook* (see ARBA 2002, entry 91), and Euromonitor's own duo, *International Marketing Data and Statistics* (see entry 281) and *European Marketing Data and Statistics* (see entry 353). The distinguishing features of the *World Economic Factbook* are that it is easier to find the information—it is all in one place and it includes narratives on such things as political risk that are hard to find elsewhere. Libraries that cannot afford many of Euromonitor's other more expensive sources will find this one well worth acquiring. It is recommended for undergraduate and more advanced collections. —**Gerald L. Gill**

298. **World Investment Report 1998: Trends and Determinants.** New York, United Nations, 1998. 428p. $45.00 pa. ISBN 92-1-112426-3. S/N E.98.II.D.5.

The 8th annual *World Investment Report* indicates that countries are continuing to forge stronger economic links with each other. This report looks at the implications of the Asian financial crises, analyzes current trends in foreign direct investment and international production, and examines the key aspects of the world's largest transnational corporations, noting major regulatory changes at the national and international levels. This report tends to improve the understanding of the role of foreign direct investment (FDI) in the world economy. The book is divided into chapters that look at global trends, including international production; mergers and acquisitions; the world's largest transnational corporations; the largest transnational corporations from developing countries; investment policy issues, such as trends and double taxation treaties; host country determinants of foreign direct investment; developed country's, such as the United States, western Europe, and Japan's, role in foreign investment; Africa's trends and recent country successes; Asian Pacific trends and the financial crisis in Asia; Latin American and Caribbean areas trends and FDI exports and the balance of payments; and Central and Eastern Europe trends. This is followed by a rather extensive reference section and annexes.

The printing, paper, and binding are average for the softcover publication, and the print is large enough for its intended use. The book is liberally sprinkled with boxes, tables, and figures to make the information easier to visualize and understand. Like all United Nations books, the information is of excellent quality and the only place this type of information is available. It should be in all major research libraries.—**Herbert W. Ockerman**

299. **World Investment Report 1999: Foreign Direct Investment and the Challenge of Development.** New York, United Nations, 1999. 541p. $45.00pa. ISBN 92-1-112440-9. S/N E.99.II.D.3.

This series from the United Nations Conference on Trade and Development (UNCTAD) provides an annual overview of foreign direct investment emphasizing the relationship between transnational corporations (TNCs) and economic development. The series will interest selectors for larger business or government document collections.

This 1999 report has a foreword from UN Secretary General Kofi Annan dated July 1999. He indicates this issue focuses on investment's impact on key aspects of development, including availability of capital, employment prospects, technical and skill levels, competitiveness, and environmental protection. It has 2 sections, each with multiple chapters. The 1st provides an overview of global and regional trends in investment; listings and statistics on the largest TNCs from the developed and developing countries and from the Central European transition economies; discussions of mergers, acquisitions, and strategic partnership trends; and policy changes, both international and national. The 2d presents background and analysis on the roles of TNCs in economic and social development processes and ways to maximize positive, and minimize the negative, impacts on host societies. Topics include discussions of environmental, technological, skills, competitiveness, and employment issues. The report combines extensive text with approximately 75 topical boxes of text, 76 figures, and 63 statistical tables. No index is provided, but there are detailed contents with lists of boxes, figures, and tables.

For suitable collections, this series and volume add valuable overviews of often ambiguous relationships between economic development, foreign investment, and TNCs in various regions of the world. This work belongs in larger economics research, academic, and general collections, as well as appropriate special ones, funding permitting.—**Nigel Tappin**

300. **World Investment Report 2001: Promoting Linkages.** New York, United Nations, 2001. 354p. maps. $49.00pa. ISBN 92-1-112523-5. S/N E.01.II.D.12.

With the assistance of many colorful bar graphs, pie charts, and world maps, this volume from the United Nations Conference on Trade and Development discusses foreign direct investment (FDI). Having grown by 18 percent in 2000 to $1.3 trillion, it is expected to decline in 2001. The 1st part of the book focuses on the geography of international production, separating the world into developed countries, the United States, the European Union, Japan, and others; developing countries, Africa, developing Asia, Latin America and the Caribbean, and the least developed countries; and Central and Eastern Europe. Subnational, industrial, and functional patterns are all considered. Outward and inward FDI are included in the discussion as well as the largest transnational corporations. Promoting linkages between foreign affiliates and domestic firms is the subject of the 2d part of the book. While linkages can be backward, forward, or horizontal, backward linkages are emphasized here. There is a discussion of what companies can do, such as finding local suppliers and extending financial support, and what government policies strengthen linkages, recognizing that the World Trade Organization rules and the TRIMs agreement (trade related investment measures) define what is permitted by its signatory countries. After the references, there are many annex tables and figures. The volume includes much detailed country-and region-specific information to explore the world of FDI. This book is an excellent source of information and data on FDI. It will be a basic reference on those working in the area.—**J. E. Weaver**

301.   **World Retail Data and Statistics 1999.** Chicago, Euromonitor International; distr., Farmington Hills, Mich., Gale, 1999. 277p. $590.00pa. ISBN 0-86338-830-2.

This is a new handbook of statistical information on retail trade worldwide for 1992 to 1997. There is a companion volume, *Retail Trade International* (see entry 286). In the first two sections summary data on socioeconomic parameters and on world retailing trends are given. Data are not included for all 50 countries in all of the tables. The third section has specific country information on such categories as population, average size of household, retail sales, number of retail outlets, retail sales by form of organization and type of outlet, retail prices, number of grocery retailers and their turnover number, and number of EPOS and EFTPOS installations (EPOS is electronic point of sales systems, EFTPOS is electronic funds transfer at point of sales). The last section has world retail rankings. A variety of types of stores have been included, such as chain store, discount superstore, home shopping, and cooperatives. The data come from government and nongovernment sources. Currency values are given in U.S. dollars. While the publisher has tried to check accuracy and standardize the date, care is urged when using the information. Cross-country comparisons can be difficult. For those interested in retailing, this could be a convenient source of data. It could be a main source or supplement what is known from other sources. [R: Choice, Sept 99, p. 124]—**J. E. Weaver**

302.   **World Trade Organization Dispute Settlement Decisions: Bernan's Annotated Reporter. Volume 1.** Lanham, Md., Bernan Associates, 1998. 535p. index. $75.00. ISBN 0-89059-105-9.

This book is an important reference source for a fairly small set of the population. It is produced by the exclusive publisher of the World Trade Organization (WTO). The book includes all WTO panel reports and appellate decisions for cases from January 29, 1996, through February 25, 1997. Other volumes will cover later cases. Most of the book gives detailed information on nine cases. After a two-page summary of the complainant, respondent, third parties, decision date, procedural history, conclusion, and annotations, the report of the panel is given. The specific reports vary but generally include factual aspects of the case, the main arguments, submissions by interested parties, interim review findings, conclusions, issues raised in appeal, treaty interpretation, and article interpretation, among other items. The language is very technical and detailed. There are four tables that contain an overview of dispute settlement activity, countries involved in disputes, treaty provisions interpreted, and Basic Instruments and Selected Documents (BISD) and dispute references (by case). An index is provided. The resolution of disputes by the WTO has far-reaching implications, both political and economic. Numerous businesses and industries will be affected by the outcomes. It is also important information for scholars. Although the work of the

WTO will affect everyone, this level of detail on the work of the organization will not be desired by many.—**J. E. Weaver**

303. Zuckerman, Amy. **International Standards Desk Reference: Your Passport to World Markets....** New York, AMACOM, 1997. 324p. index. $35.00. ISBN 0-8144-0316-6.

This is an excellent book on an important but often little noticed or understood subject of international standards. Standards can lead to better goods and services, help suppliers enter markets, and increase customer satisfaction. They can also be a major barrier to international trade, with their use in this regard growing as tariff levels are reduced. The primary audience for this well-written book is the people who run the companies affected by the standards.

Standards can cover many areas, such as product, quality assurance, health and safety, and environmental concerns. They can vary by industry and by country. The book explains how the standards are set and how businesses can comply with them. In the United States, compliance is largely through nongovernmental organizations, but in the countries of the European Union, governments are usually actively involved in their establishment and enforcement. The major players in international standards are groups in the United States and the European Union, but the book includes what is happening in Asia, South America, and many developing countries. Advice is given on what businesses need to know and how they should act to meet the standards for their industries. Numerous addresses are given to aid that effort. Even though the author makes an arcane subject filled with acronyms clearer, it will be necessary to supplement this text with more recent information, as this is a continuously changing field. [R: LJ, 1 Mar 97, p. 70]—**J. E. Weaver**

AFRICA

304. **Economic and Social Survey of Africa, 1994-1995.** By the Economic Commission for Africa. New York, United Nations, 1995. 224p. $46.00pa. ISBN 92-1-125070-6. S/N E.95.II.K.8.

This volume, published annually by the United Nations Economic Commission for Africa, is a basic source of information and data for recent conditions in Africa. It begins with a review of the continent's economic performance for 1994 and 1995, with some specific data by region and country. Africa's place in the world economy comes next, followed by a discussion of its major challenges in the near future. The next chapter focuses on fiscal and monetary developments and exchange rate policy. The second part of the book emphasizes main economic sectors, agriculture, forestry, and fisheries; mining; energy; manufacturing; transport; and communication. There are data on production over some years and information on privatization efforts. Part 3 discusses external trade, external debt, and regional cooperation and integration. Trade price indexes are given, along with diversification and debt service trends. In parts 2 and 3, there are many tables to supplement the text, which often describes the situation by individual country. The last part is a special study of gender disparities in formal education in Africa. The statistical annexes contain eight tables of economic and social indicators.—**J. E. Weaver**

305. **Major Companies of Africa South of the Sahara 1999.** 4th ed. D. Butler and V. Bentley, eds. London, Graham & Whiteside; distr., Farmington Hills, Mich., Gale, 1999. 1075p. index. $530.00. ISBN 1-86099-141-6. ISSN 1365-4845.

This latest entry in the Major Companies series from Graham & Whiteside covers 44 countries in Africa except the primarily Arab countries on the Mediterranean and Atlantic, plus Mauritania and Sudan. The clear, easy-to-understand format is consistent with other titles in the series. A

1-page introduction is followed by an alphabetic-by-country list of approximately 6,000 businesses (about one-third more than the last edition) and indexes. The introduction does not detail inclusion criteria more specifically than "the most important." Data for companies may include name; address; telephone; fax; telex; e-mail or Web address; chairman, major officers, and board members; principal activities, brands, trademarks, and trade names; parent companies and subsidiaries; percentage of ownership of the subsidiaries; major auditors and legal firms; brief financials for two years; principal shareholders; public, private, or state-owned status; year established; and number of employees.

Company names and official titles appear in their native language. Not every company has each of these data elements, but business data for companies in the Third World is very hard to find and there is no other print source that can compare. Companies from the Republic of South Africa comprise one-third of the company-by-country pages. The three indexes are alphabetic by company name, alphabetical by country and then by company name, and by business activity (i.e., by SIC). Although NAICS has been available for two years, it is not used. Particular strengths of the guide are the large number of individual names (estimated at 22,000), the extensive list of subsidiaries and branch offices, and the strong indexing. Users desiring economic or political coverage might find Europa's *Africa South of the Sahara* (28th ed.; see ARBA 2000, entry 81) helpful. At $530, it is a pricey item that will limit the number of libraries that can afford it. Highly recommended for graduate school, public, corporate, and academic libraries with a sub-Saharan interest.
—**Patrick J. Brunet**

ASIA

Dictionaries and Encyclopedias

306.   De Mente, Boyé Lafayette. **NTC's Dictionary of Korea's Business and Cultural Code Words.** Lincolnwood, Ill., National Textbook, 1998. 462p. (NTC's Dictionaries of Cultural Code Words). $22.95. ISBN 0-8442-8362-2.

De Mente, who compiled Chinese and Japanese code words, also wrote Korean code words. With this book, De Mente completes dictionaries of code words for three Far East countries. China, Japan, and Korea share many cultural characteristics because of neighboring geographic locations and long historical relations. Despite the close cultural contact, Korean people retained a unique character and personality that is different from Chinese and Japanese cultures. This book is designed to help foreigners understand the uniqueness of Korean culture and national characteristics. De Mente's insights make this book valuable.

In this book, De Mente explores the historical and cultural background of 231 most important "code words" of Korean language. Each entry is numbered and has a Korean character with its pronunciation. The meaning of each entry is given in the form of explanatory phrases in English. The length of definition of each word ranges from one to two pages, while more important words that convey the uniqueness of Korea take up to 15 pages. In this way, De Mente provides readers with sharper understanding of the customs of Korean people.

To make this book more valuable, there are a few things that could be improved. It would be very useful if the book included a subject guide index in English. The book has a subject guide that is indexed to the numbers of words, but it does not help foreigners to find specific words. The publisher may also want to print an errata slip to fix typos. There are typos in both Korean characters (numbers 14, 21, 36, 41, 69, 100, 161, 164, and 179) and Romanized words (107, 143, 147, 159 and

164). The Romanization system is also inconsistent: some words are Romanized according to the McCune-Reischauer Romanization System, while some are not.—**Sung Ok Kim**

307. **NTC's Dictionary of Japan's Business Code Words.** By Boye Lafayette De Mente. Lincolnwood, Ill., National Textbook, 1997. 425p. $25.95. ISBN 0-8442-8344-4.

This book will be an aid to businesspeople and others who are conducting business with the Japanese. This is not a standard dictionary of terms and brief definitions but rather a dictionary of 229 terms or keywords in which the author attempts to provide a cultural frame of reference for the term. These explanations are from one and a half to two pages in length. This contextual way of defining business practices will lead one to a great understanding on how business is to be conducted with the Japanese. This text will prove to be useful for those collections where the clientele is focused on trade with Japan. The author has published extensively in this area, including similar books for China and Mexico.—**Judith J. Field**

308. **Philippines Business: The Portable Encyclopedia for Doing Business with the Philippines.** Edward G. Hinkelman and others, eds. San Rafael, Calif., World Trade Press, 1996. 342p. illus. maps. index. (World Trade Press Country Business Guides). $24.95pa. ISBN 1-885073-08-9.

Recent years of political and economic stability in the Philippines point to a bright future for this island nation of Southeast Asia. The rapid economic growth within all of Southeast Asia has created a demand for information on the economies and opportunities for foreign investment. *Philippines Business*, part of World Trade Press's Country Business Guides series, seeks to meet the demand for business information crucial to the foreign entrepreneur wishing to establish business connections in the Philippines. As with the other volumes in this series, the 25 chapters cover the current political economy; establishing a business, including chapters on legal aspects, demographics, and marketing; foreign investment and trade, with individual chapters on trade agreements, trade zones, and import and export policies; labor; finance and financial institutions; taxation; business travel; and transportation and communications. Geared to the individual entrepreneur or small-to medium-sized business, the editors provide a wide range of practical information, from lists of trade shows in the Philippines to data on the current status and business climate of Subic Freeport Zone and other export processing zones to social skills and elementary vocabulary.

The substantial information given by the editors is both accurate and current. Equally important, *Philippines Business* is easy to use with helpful graphics, maps, and contents guides. The extensive lists of addresses expedite the search for additional contacts and sources of information from government agencies, trade organizations, and services within the Philippines. In addition, the editors suggest readings that are important Filipino trade publications. This is a useful addition to library collections attempting to meet the demand for "how-to" business and investment information for the region. As the Philippines's economy continues to attract foreign investors, there will be a need for such guides that provide an initial step for the novice to the region.—**Carol L. Mitchell**

Directories

309. **Asia: A Directory and Sourcebook.** 2d ed. Chicago, Euromonitor International; distr., Detroit, Gale, 1997. 394p. index. $430.00. ISBN 0-86338-696-2.

Asia: A Directory and Sourcebook, published by Euromonitor, is a good example of the risk business publishers take when creating expensive reference works. The spectacular decline of emerging Asian markets during 1998 renders the introductory statement, "Asia's position as the fastest-growing region in the world economy will not be challenged in the foreseeable future," somewhat regrettable. The concentration of capital in a few, powerful oligarchies and the hidden costs of garnering government support for business ventures are not mentioned. However, these problems, although perhaps a bit embarrassing to the publisher, do not make the volume useless. On the contrary, the vicissitudes of the Asian economies make this reference resource valuable to those who wish to do business while the dollar is strong and costs have dropped for Asian produced goods. Directory information includes major employers in Asian countries, contact information, product line information, and data through 1995 on employment and productivity. The section listing trade associations and publications, and information resources in Asian countries is a godsend to those who must do even more homework to make the most of Asia's economic conditions. This text is especially useful for specialized libraries emphasizing Asian business development in their collections. Its cost may deter some libraries with less interest in the region.—**Lynne M. Fox**

310.   **Asian Markets: A Guide to Company and Industry Information Sources.** 4th ed. By Washington Researchers. Washington, D.C., Washington Researchers, 1996. 487p. index. $335.00pa. ISBN 1-56365-043-6. ISSN 1044-8713.

This volume is a guide to company and industry information sources for 13 countries in Asia on such topics as the economic and political situation, business regulations, business practices, potential markets, analyses of the industries, and names of individual companies. The compilers have organized the book into three sections. The first section, which encompasses more than a third of the book, is devoted to identifying U.S. government departments and agencies that work in the area of international commerce, providing names, addresses, and titles of relevant publications. The remaining part of this section has been allocated to noting individual state offices that deal in international trade, a skimpy section listing some of the primary international organizations, and an incomplete section on private sector organizations such as banks or accounting firms that can also provide a potential importer or exporter with information for doing business in Asia.

The 2d section of 65 pages is devoted to highlighting mostly standard directories, indexes, periodicals, databases, and CD-ROM products that could also be used to find information on Asia. This section is not very helpful except for the newest of researchers. No insight is provided into how items were selected. Also, as in the first section, there have been title changes, publications have ceased, and there is no consistency in referring the reader to nonprint sources such as World Wide Web sites and electronic bulletin boards. No references to CD-ROM products are provided.

The 3d section supplies specific information on 13 Asian countries (e.g., India, China, Japan, the Philippines, and Thailand), starting with a 4-to 6-page overview of the economic and business realities of each country. This is followed by a list of sources for acquiring additional information, such as U.S. government offices and experts in that country, business associations, research organizations, financial institutions in that country, relevant publications, and information sources on the Internet. The individual country profiles average 16 pages, although Japan's coverage is 29 pages and China's is 24 pages. The most useful part of this section is the inclusion of Internet resources; much of the other material can be found in other sources, such as government documents and such standard reference tools as *The Europa World Year Book* (see ARBA 94, entry 82, and ARBA 90, entry 91). There are too many omissions and errors to make this a reliable reference resource, especially at the price being charged.—**Judith J. Field**

311.   **Directory of Consumer Brands and Their Owners 1998: Asia Pacific.** Chicago, Euromonitor International; distr., Farmington Hills, Mich., Gale, 1998. 527p. index. $990.00. ISBN 0-86338-785-3.

This title is new to Euromonitor's collection of business directories and replaces in part the previous title, *International Directory of Consumer Brands and Their Owners* (see entry 264).

This regional directory focuses on brand names and the Asian or Pacific companies that own them. Euromonitor also produces a CD-ROM that includes all of the regional brand name directories. The Asia Pacific directory lists more than 15,000 brand names and more than 2,500 companies that control those brands. There is a definite emphasis on manufacturing and retailing consumer products throughout the Asian market. The directory itself is divided into two main sections. One section lists individual brands under broader product categories and subcategories. The second section serves as a directory listing for the companies and is arranged alphabetically by country. Information such as mailing address, Website location, e-mail, parent or holding companies, key personnel, and brand name portfolios are all given. Hong Kong is treated as a separate political entity from China for this edition only. Several Asian countries such as Laos and Sri Lanka are not covered. Some of the information may also be found in Gale's *Brands and Their Companies* (see entry 199) and *Companies and Their Brands* (see entry 200), but neither is as broad nor as deep as Euromonitor's publication. Also a plus for Euromonitor is the market share data they provide for the brand names. Because of its relatively high price tag, however, this resource is recommended only for major business collections in academic and public libraries. It is essential for special libraries involved in Pacific Rim or Asian business or marketing activities. [R: Choice, June 99, p. 1762]—**Stephen W. Green**

312.   **Directory of Japanese-Affiliated Companies in the EU: 1996-97.** Tokyo, Japan External Trade Organization; distr., Bristol, Pa., Taylor & Francis, 1996. 471p. index. $240.00pa. ISBN 4-8224-0733-0.

Published by the Japan External Trade Organization (JETRO), this directory lists almost 3,000 companies operating in 15 European countries in mid-1995. The countries are Austria, Belgium, Denmark, Finland, France, Germany, Greece, Ireland, Italy, Luxembourg, the Netherlands, Portugal, Spain, Sweden, and the United Kingdom. *Japanese-affiliated* is defined as "any firm owned in whole or in part by a Japanese entity . . . subsidiaries of Japanese affiliated firms, as well as subsidiaries of subsidiaries." Religious organizations and personal service firms are not included. The companies are arranged by country and listed alphabetically. Each entry includes the company name; type of establishment (e.g., subsidiary, branch, representative/liaison office, affiliate); address; telephone and fax numbers; year established; executive officers; annual sales; number of employees; and type of business. Businesses are categorized as manufacturing, distribution/wholesale, import, export, retailing, service provider, and other.

Three indexes provide additional access. In the first index, the companies are arranged by type of product or service (e.g., accounting, construction, industrial machinery and equipment, toys, and transportation services). The second index lists the companies by type of business. The third index lists the companies alphabetically. Two appendixes focus on country information. The first appendix covers Japanese information sources in the European Union (EU) and lists, by country, government offices and trade associations. The second appendix lists EU information sources in Japan and includes embassies, consulates general, and chambers of commerce. The directory is recommended for libraries needing such specialized information.—**Barbara E. Clotfelter**

313.   **Directory of Trade and Investment Related Organizations of Developing Countries and Areas in Asia and the Pacific.** 7th ed. By Economic and Social Commission for Asia and the Pacific. New York, United Nations, 1995. 196p. index. $40.00pa. ISBN 92-1-119716-3. S/N E.96.II.F.8.

This is a networking tool for business and economic associations and institutions in Asia and the Pacific, and those dealing with them. The prefatory materials indicate that approximately 300 organizations are included. There has been a title change since the 6th edition, from *The Directory of Trade Promotion/Development Organizations of Developing Countries and Areas in*

Asia and the Pacific. The work is issued about every second year. It will be of interest to larger business collections with client interest in this high-growth region.

The directory is divided into two parts. The first part lists national organizations by country, from Afghanistan to Vanuatu and Vietnam. The second part lists regional organizations. The detailed table of contents lists all the groups by name. In addition, there are name and classified indexes. The entries themselves include sections for directory information (including address, cable, and telephone, telex, and fax numbers); principal function; services/activities; local branches; membership structure; offices abroad; regional offices; publications; and training. Headings are omitted where not relevant or information is not available. Most entries seem to take at least an entire double-columned, 11-by-8½-inch page, with some being longer. The typeface is quite small. The information was assembled largely from questionnaires sent to the groups, as well as through regional organizations and other sources. The classified index groups organizations under 13 headings, from "Chambers of Commerce/Trade Associations" through "Trade Facilitation Bodies" to "Others."

This work seems a competently produced directory on business organizations in a high-interest part of the world. As such, it should be considered by larger business collections with the relevant mandate.—**Nigel Tappin**

314.   **Japan Trade Directory 1997-98.** Tokyo, Japan, Japanese External Trade Organization; distr., Detroit, Gale, 1997. 1v. (various paging). illus. maps. index. $335.00. ISBN 4-8224-0779-9.

An importer or exporter will find a wide variety of materials available in this comprehensive reference source on more than 22,000 Japanese products and services and 2,800 companies. Part 1 includes an alphabetic list of products and services for import and export. Part 2 lists, in separate alphabets, company information, trade and industrial associations, and trade names. The prefectural guide is found in part 3 with tourist attractions; business and tourist information; and their main products, crafts, and industries. Part 4 contains advertising of products and services, including numerous illustrations. The detailed alphabetic list of companies in part 2, B provides the English and Japanese names of companies, address, telephone number, telex and fax numbers, e-mail address, name of president, type of business, year established, capital available, annual sales, number of employees, bank references, office hours, major overseas offices, trade name, and availability of a catalog.

Compared with the 1993-1994 edition that was last reviewed (see ARBA 94, entry 244) this 1997-1998 edition lists approximately 1,500 fewer products and services and some 200 fewer companies. A CD-ROM version of the directory also is enclosed in the book with accompanying operating instructions. This updated, specialized directory is quite useful and will fill a gap in business collections that need information on Japanese companies engaging in import and export activities.—**O. Gene Norman**

315.   **Major Companies of South West Asia 1999.** 3d ed. Sandra James and Y. McLelland, eds. London, Graham & Whiteside; distr., Farmington Hills, Mich., Gale, 1999. 841p. index. $530.00. ISBN 1-86099-140-8.

This directory is part of a series of publications covering businesses in all parts of the globe and is updated annually. Information is provided on more than 5,000 companies in Bangladesh, Bhutan, India, Iran, Nepal, Pakistan, Sri Lanka, and Turkey. Data listed include company name, street address, telephone and fax numbers, e-mail and Web addresses, names of key contacts from the board and senior management, principal activities of the company, branch offices, any subsidiaries, trademarks held, private versus public status, associated bankers, auditors and legal counsel, date the entity was established, the number of employees, and financial indicators for the 2 most recently available years (1996 and 1997). Firms are listed alphabetically for each country. Entries are selected on the basis of sales volume, premium income, or total assets.

The volume is indexed alphabetically by company name regardless of the country of origin, alphabetically by nation, and by Standard Industrial Classification. This reference is useful to identify potential customers, joint venture partners, and possible acquisitions.—**Adrienne Antink Bien**

316. **Major Companies of the Far East and Australasia 1998.** J. L. Murphy and D. Walsh, eds. London, Graham and Whiteside; distr., Detroit, Gale, 1997. 3v. index. $1,395.00/set. ISBN 1-86099-072-X.

This 3-volume set is the 14th edition of this annual publication. The 1st volume covers Brunei, Cambodia, Indonesia, Malaysia, the Philippines, Singapore, Laos, and Thailand. China, Hong Kong, Japan, North Korea, South Korea, Mongolia, Myanmar, Taiwan, and Vietnam are featured in the 2d volume. The 3d volume includes Australia, New Zealand, and Papua New Guinea. Data on about 12,000 of the largest companies in the region, selected on the basis of the size of their sales volume, premium income, or total assets as appropriate, are given. As available, the set includes name of the company, address, telephone number, telex number, fax number, e-mail address, and Website; names of the chairman, president, board members, and senior management; principal activities of the company; principal brand names and trademarks; principal agencies and branch offices; parent company; principal subsidiaries and associates, bankers; auditors; principal law firm; financial information for the past two years; public/private status; principal shareholders; date of establishment; and number of employees.

Company entries are arranged alphabetically within each country section. There are 3 indexes. The 1st is an alphabetic index of all companies in each volume irrespective of their main country of operation; the 2d is an alphabetic index to companies within each country; and the 3d starts with the Standard Industrial Classification (SIC) index categories and then lists the companies by their various business activities within their main country of operation within the SIC code. —**J. E. Weaver**

317. **World Investment Directory: Foreign Direct Investment, and Corporate Data. Volume VII, Asia and the Pacific.** By the United Nations Conference on Trade and Development. New York, United Nations, 2000. 2v. $80.00pa./set. ISBN 92-1-112481-6. S/N E.00.II.D.11.

This two-volume book covers trends in foreign direct investments both inward and outward. It covers data, in most cases, through January 1999 for 41 countries in the Asia and Pacific Rim areas, including summary tables on foreign direct investments and production. More detailed tables look at types of investment, foreign direct investment in the host economy, foreign direct investment abroad, foreign direct investment stocks, foreign direct investment in stocks abroad, and distribution of foreign affiliation and foreign direct investment by percent of ownership. There are also tables for the number of transnational corporations, assets of transnational corporations, employment of transnational corporations, sales of transnational corporations, value added by transnational corporations, profiles of transnational corporations, exports and imports of transnational corporations, research and development expenditures of transnational corporations, royalty receipts of transnational corporations, royalty payment of transnational corporations, and the largest transnational corporations. The books also contain numerous tables covering the period in general from 1987 through the late 1990s.

The paperback binding, printing, and paper are of average quality and of adequate size for the intent. The books should be useful for anyone interested in investments in Asia and the Pacific Rim area. Like most United Nations books, this work is the only source of this kind of information and is as good as can be obtained in the current worldwide situation. It should be in all business-oriented libraries since this area of the world is becoming a major business player.—**Herbert W. Ockerman**

Handbooks and Yearbooks

318.   **The China Handbook.** Christopher Hudson, ed. Chicago, Fitzroy Dearborn, 1997. 334p. index. (Regional Handbooks of Economic Development: Prospects onto the 21st Century). $55.00. ISBN 1-884964-88-5.

This is the 1st volume in a series of development handbooks intended for college-level students. It could be used as a text or readings in courses in comparative economics, development studies, political economy, or area studies as well as a basic reference book.

The text aims to place Chinese economic development in broad political, sociological, and post-1949 historical contexts. It is a series of essays by academics from North America, Hong Kong, and Europe. Each chapter includes further readings and full bibliographic citations. Chapters end with paragraph-length characterizations of contributor's qualifications and affiliations. Extensive charts and tables with statistical information accompany the many essays. Two advisers from Oberlin College and the University of Illinois assisted the editor in selecting topics.

The 21 chapters are divided among 4 subject sections. History leads off with chapters on Maoist and Deng periods. Regional context offers scholarly essays on relations with Taiwan, Hong Kong, Japan and Korea, and Southeast Asia. There are 10 chapters that deal with various aspects of the economy, including industry, agriculture, finance, and private enterprise. The 5 chapters on social issues include information on population, minorities, and education. The essays average about 13 pages in double-columned format. The academic style is accessible to both scholars and laypeople.

A number of attractive features are in appendixes—a chronology from 1949 through July 1997, a glossary of political and economic terms, a list of holders of the highest offices with thumbnail biographies, and an annotated bibliography of major reference and specialist works. The index is short but adequate.

This quality reference will be useful to academic and large public libraries with the relevant subject mandates. It would make a useful course reading or text for college courses as well.—**Nigel Tappin**

319.   **China Marketing Data and Statistics.** By the China State Statistical Bureau. Chicago, Ill., Euromonitor International; distr., Detroit, Gale, 1997. 643p. maps. $390.00. ISBN 0-86338-780-2.

Chinese economic policies have evolved from the closed door policy of the Cultural Revolution to the reign of Deng Xiaoping's policy of economic reconstruction. A highlight of the economic reconstruction was the return of Hong Kong to China in 1997. This event helped to focus the world's attention on China and its evolving economic policies. This directory is the result of China's government departments cooperating with the publisher, Euromonitor, to compile a thorough survey about China's economic resources and its physical characteristics for the information needs of individuals and businesses wanting to do business in China.

The 1st chapter is an overview of China's geographic and natural resources and China's place in the world today. Following are individual chapters on each of the major cities, provinces, and regions. Each of these chapters describes the location within China; the geography; natural resources; population; administrative areas; the economy; industry, markets, and retail sales; infrastructure, foreign trade, and economic cooperation; education, science, and culture; scenic spots and historical sites; and the standard of living. The latter section of the book is a section of statistical tables covering industry, education, the economy, employment, and family income. The text and the labels for the maps and tables are in English and Chinese.

It is a thorough collection of information about China substantiated by marketing data and statistics. This directory is recommended to large academic and special business libraries who require information about doing business in China. [R: BL, 15 Oct 98, p. 437; Choice, Nov 98, p. 500]—**Kay M. Stebbins**

320.   **China Markets Yearbook 1999.** Shaomin Li and David K. Tse, eds. Hong Kong, City University of Hong Kong; distr., Armonk, N.Y., M. E. Sharpe, 1999. 1148p. index. $350.00. ISBN 0-7656-0638-0. ISSN 1527-1587.

This volume is the sequel to *China's Industrial Markets Yearbook 1997.* It is the joint effort of three organizations—one in Beijing and two in Hong Kong. Although the original data are from the State Statistical Bureau of China, the editors write that this work goes beyond a simple compilation of census data in that it includes their knowledge of key factors that influence profitability and productivity of an industry in China. It covers 563 industries (the entire industrial and consumer goods sector) on the 4-digit level of the Chinese industrial classification code. For each industry, the number of firms, the number of employees, revenue, profit, return on assets, return on equity, labor productivity, debt-to-assets ratio, and total assets is given for the industry overall and as averages for the subcategories by ownership, by size, and by regional distribution. For each industry major products, the top 10 firms by revenue, the top 10 cities by production output, and the top 10 wholesalers are given, with selected information for each. Data on the number of firms, the number of employees, total revenue, and total profit are given annually for years 1993 through 1996 along with rates of change. The position of each industry in the country's industrial sector is provided, along with information on percentages within the industry of those firms making a profit and those with negative returns. Although an explanation of terms is included, it is not clear that all of the terms, such as profits and assets, conform to the usage commonly found in the United States. This book, with its detailed data on the Chinese industrial sector, will be useful to those interested in working in and studying about the sector. Combined with other sources it provides additional understanding of the change occurring in the entire Chinese economy.—**J. E. Weaver**

321.   **Consumer Asia 2000.** 7th ed. Chicago, Euromonitor International, 1999. 652p. maps. $950.00pa. ISBN 0-86338-874-4.

This book begins with a textual overview of recent trends in the region and then addresses each country individually. The 11 countries covered are China, Hong Kong (China), India, Indonesia, Malaysia, Philippines, Singapore, South Korea, Taiwan, Thailand, and Vietnam. Japan is not included. The majority of the book is comprised of tables. The first two tabular sections provide side-by-side country comparisons for regional marketing parameters and consumer markets. The remainder of the book profiles each country separately.

Here one will find a statistical gold mine of Asian demographics, economic indicators, media access, and consumer market information for agricultural goods, personal hygiene products, and durable goods. Data coverage is usually from 1993 to 1998. Tables list their sources and the table of contents and list of tables is extensive.

Consumer Asia 2000 is a great resource for anyone investing, manufacturing, marketing, or creating subsidiaries in Asian countries. International business students will profit from access to this resource. The textual part needs better editing as there are rather frequent typographical errors and omissions that sometimes alter the meaning of the sentence.—**Holly Dunn Coats**

322. **Consumer China 2001.** 7th ed. Chicago, Euromonitor International, 2000. 567p. $970.00pa. ISBN 0-86338-974-0.

This is the 7th edition of *Consumer China*. Each edition provides in-depth and accurate information as the Chinese government allows its markets greater accessibility to world markets. Information is provided for both China and the Special Administrative Region of Hong Kong. Section 1 provides a brief overview of the market trends in China, focusing on such aspects as the merging role of China in the world market place, economic growth prospects, demographic trends, and marketing opportunities. The remainder of the book is devoted to statistical tables. This layout is the same format the publisher uses for other books in this series.

Sections 2 and 3 provide general statistical information on such topics as standard of living, consumer expenditures, cultural indicators, economic indicators, and household characteristics. Sections 4 and 5 constitute more than 80 percent of the book and provide a comprehensive consumer market database of almost 300 tables. The format for these tables covering the period of 1994-1999 have been standardized to provide information on total volume/unit sales, value of retail sales, per capita sales, and retail sales in constant 1994 RMB or HK$. The last item in each table calculates retail sales in U.S. dollars. This information is currently hard to obtain for many of the individual product categories, as many researchers will attest. If libraries have a clientele who are regularly asking for this information, then this book is a title they should place a standing order for.—**Judith J. Field**

323. Dori, John T., and Richard D. Fisher Jr., comps. **U.S. and Asia Statistical Handbook.** 1997-98 ed. Washington, D.C., Heritage Foundation, 1997. 95p. maps. $9.50pa. ISBN 0-89195-243-8.

Although this handy statistical reference is intended as a convenient aid to U.S. legislators, congressional staff, and other influential people, it is of potential use to a broader audience. The main text is a collection of economic, political, and social information (mainly statistics) on about 35 countries, including the United States. The title is a bit of a misnomer in that a number of Pacific countries outside Asia, including Australia, New Zealand, and some larger island states, are included. Material is drawn from major statistical handbooks. The information for each nation is arranged under 5 headings—land, population, politics, economy, and military. Included are statistics such as literacy rates, gross domestic product (GDP), imports and exports, and trade and investment balances with the United States. Under the "Politics" heading such items as indexes of "economic freedom," political and civil liberties, and how often the country voted with the United States at the United Nations are included. Statistics mainly date from 1995 and 1996.

Many other features are of potential interest, especially to those favoring deregulation, economic liberalization, free trade, and minimal government. There are 9 charts covering topics such as U.S. bilateral trade deficits, foreign direct investment, and defense spending for selected countries or regions. There are political maps to locate the countries. Notes on "Barriers to U.S. Asian Trade" highlight issues under 15 countries, including the United States, from the foundation's pro-globalization perspective.

This is an inexpensive, user-friendly publication with an avowedly right-of-center perspective. Large libraries with many statistical yearbooks will own many of the sources from which it is drawn. Smaller collections with the relevant clientele may find it worth considering.—**Nigel Tappin**

324. **Economic and Social Survey of Asia and the Pacific 2001.** By the Economic and Social Commission for Asia and the Pacific. New York, United Nations, 2001. 262p. $65.00pa. ISBN 92-1-120031-8. ISSN 0252-5704. S/N E.01.II.F.18.

In narrative form, with statistical tables and charts, the *Economic and Social Survey of Asia and the Pacific 2001* presents an analysis of several countries, including China, Japan, India, New Zealand, Australia, the Republic of Korea, India, Afghanistan, Iran, Indonesia, Pakistan, and the Philippines. The term "ESCAP region" is used to represent these countries. The "Central Asian republics" refers to Armenia, Azerbaijan, Kazakhstan, Kyrgyzstan, Tajikistan, Turkmenistan, and Uzbekistan.

Each annual issue studies a specific issue, in addition to reviewing population, economic situations, and related policy concerns. Previous years' topics have included "International Trade in Primary Commodities," "Policies and Planning for Export," and "Education and Employment." The 2001 issue, "Financing for Development," will also be studied at the High-Level Event on Financing for Development "to be held under the aegis of the United Nations in 2002" (p. iii).

Part 1, "Recent Economic and Social Developments," presents and analyzes macroeconomic performance and trends on a global basis and for regions and countries, policy issues, trade and exchange rates, inflation rates, index of stock markets, and fiscal developments. "Socio-Economic Implications of Demographic Dynamics" analyzes the population of countries and regions, trends in poverty in selected countries, education, health services, and urbanization. Part 2, "Financing for Development," focuses on various aspects of the mobilization of resources for development (domestic, foreign private, and foreign official) and reviews current trends and experiences and recommends areas where further progress is needed. Topics analyzed in part 2 include official development assistance, bank lending for financing countries' economic development, taxation, capital markets, and suggestions for reform of the international financial architecture. The survey is an important research tool for academic and research libraries' collections on international economics and finance. The data are enhanced by descriptive analysis, recommendations for policy changes, and the outlining areas for reform.—**Lucy Heckman**

325. **Economics Blue Book of the People's Republic of China, 1999: Analysis and Forecast.** Liu Guoguang and others, eds. Hong Kong, University of Hong Kong; distr., Armonk, N.Y., M. E. Sharpe, 1999. 533p. index. $95.95. ISBN 0-7656-0562-7. ISSN 1527-1595.

This is one of the most important annual reports and forecasts for China's economy. This annual report has been prepared by two groups of economists, one from the Chinese Academy of Social Sciences and the other from the Centre of Asian Studies of the University of Hong Kong. China's economy is one of the three largest in the world today and one of the most evolutionary. This is the second economic report written by this quasi-official of Chinese government.

The coverage includes general forecasts and policy analyses on the Chinese economy, reports on specific regions within China (including Hong Kong), reviews of the global economic situation, and prospects for China's future. There is an excellent appendix of statistics covering world economic indicators and a subject index to help researchers find information easily.

Information about the Chinese economy has not been readily available in the past but with the publication of this volume Chinese economic annual reports researchers will be able to find information about the economics of China and how it compares to the world economy. Academic and special libraries with business collections should purchase this book as a standard reference for their Pacific Rim economics coverage.—**Kay M. Stebbins**

326. **Guidebook to Trading with China 1999.** 5th ed. New York, United Nations, 1999. 334p. $75.00pa. ISBN 92-1-119827-5.

This guidebook was written by the International Trade and Economic Cooperation Division of the United Nations (ESCAP), which received cooperation and financial support from the government of China for printing this edition of the guidebook. The current revised edition is largely a result of feedback received through readers' surveys of previous editions. The volume was updated to the first half of 1997 and forecasts were made to the end of the century. The book describes the transformation of an economy from a central controlled to a socialistic market system. It is intended to allow new business opportunities and better understanding of China's economic policies, rules, and regulations. The book is divided into sections that cover economic geography and administration, economy, foreign trade, foreign trade organizations and their functions, foreign trade operations and procedures, banking systems and foreign exchange management, customs administration, commodity inspection, insurance, China's foreign trade transportation, promotion of foreign direct investment, protection of intellectual property rights, general information on travel, basic information on various provinces, autonomous regions, and municipalities directly under the central government, and a section on acronyms that are used. The book is interesting and easy to read and is printed on average paper with average fonts and paper quality and binding. The book would be useful to anyone interested in China as well as those anticipating doing business there and also for anyone interested in foreign travel. It should be in any library that has an international dimension.—**Herbert W. Ockerman**

327.   **The India Handbook.** C. Steven LaRue, Lloyd I. Rudolph, Susanne Hoeber Rudolph, and Philip Oldenburg, eds. Chicago, Fitzroy Dearborn, 1997. 335p. index. (Regional Handbooks of Economic Development: Prospects onto the 21st Century). $55.00. ISBN 1-884964-89-3.

This volume is the 2d in a series of economic development handbooks intended for an audience of college-level students. It is designed to be used as a text or book of readings in courses on comparative economics, development, political economy, or area studies, as well as a basic reference book. It covers the Indian Union, but not the entire subcontinent.

The editor was assisted in selecting topics by a panel of three advisers affiliated with Columbia University. Chapters are contributed by academics with affiliations in North America, Europe, and India. Each ends with a list of further readings and a paragraph-length author note, and many have statistical charts and graphs.

The work is divided into 5 sections that deal with historical context since independence (1947), economic policy, social and cultural aspects of growth, the international context, and outlook for the future. These are similar, but not identical, to those in *The China Handbook* (see entry 318), suggesting suitable tailoring of the standard format to the scholarship on each country or region. The 19 chapters cover a diverse range of issues, including agriculture, planning globalization, regional organizations, population, and multiculturalism. The work has a number of features that make it useful as a ready-reference work, including a detailed chronology from 1947 through April 1997, a glossary of relevant terms, notes on several major political and economic figures, and a 10-page bibliography with paragraph-length annotations. The index is a bit short, but adequate.

This reference book will be useful for academic and large public libraries with the relevant subject mandates. It would make a useful course reading or text for a college course.—**Nigel Tappin**

328.   **Statistical Yearbook for Asia and the Pacific 2000.** By the Economic and Social Commission for Asia and the Pacific. New York, United Nations, 2001. 644p. $90.00pa. ISBN 92-1-019109-9. ISSN 0252-3655. S/N E/F.01.II.F.1.

This volume represents the 32d issue of the *Statistical Yearbook for Asia and the Pacific* prepared by the Statistics Division of the Economic and Social Commission for Asia and the Pacific. Data presented were compiled from national sources and national statistical publications, supplemented by data compiled or published by the United Nations' Statistics Division and other specialized agencies of the United Nations. Statistics included cover all 57 regional members of the Economic and Social Commission for Asia and the Pacific (ESCAP). Countries studied include China, Australia, India, Indonesia, Iran, Afghanistan, Cambodia, the Republic of Korea, the Russian Federation, and the Philippines. Subjects covered for each of these countries include population, national accounts, wages, prices and consumption, finance, and social statistics. In addition to country statistics, regional statistical indicators are provided for the world, the ESCAP region, and the developing ESCAP region (which excludes Australia, Japan, New Zealand, and the Russian Federation).

For each country, statistical data cover 1990-1999 and data are presented for external trade; wages, prices, and consumption; finance; social statistics (including number of medical facilities and schools); population; manpower; national accounts; and data by industry. The annex section lists principal sources of the data presented, including publications and their issuing authorities as well as conversion coefficients and factors. The text of the *Statistical Yearbook* is in English and French. It presents unique and specialized statistical data involving ESCAP. The series should be considered for purchase by academic and research libraries.—**Lucy Heckman**

AUSTRALIA

329. **Australia Business: The Portable Encyclopedia for Doing Business with Australia.** By James L. Nolan and others. San Rafael, Calif., World Trade Press, 1996. 328p. maps. index. (World Trade Press Country Business Guides). $24.95pa. ISBN 1-885073-03-8.

World Trade Press specializes in authoritative but inexpensive country business guides. They have a series of import-export manuals, almanacs, CD-ROMs, and guides, principally to profitable countries around the Pacific Rim, such as Canada, China, Hong Kong, Japan, the Philippines, and Australia. This book on Australian business covers economic and commercial policy, as well as foreign investments and government. For its sources, it relies on the Australian Trade Commission for statistics, reference librarians in California for some "steps and tips," specialized researchers and writers, and some reprints from both the International Monetary Fund and Ernst & Young.

Standard formats for the series ensure that everything is covered. There are 25 broad topics, including labor, marketing, law, demographics, etiquette and culture, foreign exchange, trade fairs, and taxes. There is a 450 word/phrase business dictionary, as well as 1,000 addresses, some small maps, and even some advertisements. Some obvious defects here include nary a word about the wine industry (one of Australia's greatest exports and potential for foreign investments), few e-mail addresses, and only a handful of Websites. The book has a 1996 copyright date, so the editors surely had some time to track down more Internet connections. It is a shame, considering how far away Australia is and how many international businesses have e-mail access; it would seem realistic for this book to include more of these cost-saving devices.—**Dean Tudor**

CANADA

330. **Canadian Company Histories, Volume 1.** Tina Grant, ed. Toronto, Gale Canada, 1996. 293p. index. $170.00; $125.00 (U.S.). ISBN 1-896413-06-4.

Gale Canada is a division of the same company (ITP Thomson) that owns *The Globe and Mail* in Toronto. This book details in 4 double-column pages the basic history of 80 Canadian companies that did $1 billion (Canadian) in annual revenues in their most recent reporting year.

For some reason, ITP Thomson is not among these companies, even though competing media giants such as Southam and Rogers Communications are.

Arrangement is alphabetic by corporate name, and corporate logos are included in most cases. After basic directory data (names, addresses, Standard Industrial Classifications, incorporation date, stock exchanges traded on), there is a narrative profile written mostly on a freelance basis by one of 24 authors (usually from the United States). This profile is based on annual reports, newspapers, business news sources, magazines, and material from the companies themselves. Each profile concludes with a brief bibliography of recent books and articles and an author's name. At the back of the volume, there are indexes to companies, people, and industries. Overall, the book is fair, with balance in the profiles. However, the title is grossly overpriced for the announced audience (librarians, researchers, and students). Also, there is no indication of when volume 2 will appear.—**Dean Tudor**

331. **Canadian Insurance Claims Directory 1997.** 65th ed. Gwen Peroni, ed. Buffalo, N.Y., University of Toronto Press, 1997. 404p. index. $40.00pa. ISBN 0-8020-4901-X. ISSN 0318-0352.

This standard directory provides insurance professionals with addresses, telephone numbers, and fax information on claims adjusters and related services in Canada and the United States. It also provides material on insurance organizations and companies.

The main part of this work is organized geographically by country, followed by province, territory, or state, and then by locality. Under each locality, entries are subdivided by service type. Most of the entries are adjusters and to a lesser extent counsel, with other categories occurring principally in the sections for larger communities. Canadian listings occupy 212 pages, and U.S. entries cover 152 pages. U.S. communities have fewer numbers of listings, even for large centers. There are no significant prefatory materials, leaving no indication of selection criteria or of whether the list is comprehensive for Canada. The one-page section titled "International" contains a boxed advertisement for a service network covering South and Central America and the Caribbean.

There are maps for 10 Canadian provinces and 4 U.S. states (Florida, New York, Pennsylvania, and Washington) with major communities marked. There are few listings for the Canadian territories, probably explaining the absence of maps for them. At the back, Canadian directory information is provided for four national and regional adjusters and claims managers associations, insurance crime prevention bureau offices, fire marshals and commissioners, superintendents of insurance, five insurance associations, and insurance companies (a 15-page list). Access features include a general index (mainly consisting of organization names), an index of advertisers by class of insurance-related services, very brief indexes of insurance-related services (other than the main categories of "adjusters" and "counsel") and associations, and a contents. This established work belongs in large business reference collections and special libraries with the relevant client interests. —**Nigel Tappin**

332. **Researching Canadian Markets, Industries, & Business Opportunities.** Rockville, Md., Washington Researchers, 1997. 263p. index. $275.00pa. ISBN 1-56365-085-1.

Canada is the world's seventh largest economy and the United States' primary trade partner. Washington Researchers' purpose for this guide is to provide the researcher with current and accurate information about the Canadian markets and industries, and spotlight and identify other Canadian business opportunities.

The 1st chapter begins the research with a guide titled "How to Research the Directory." The editors believed that it is important to aid the researcher in retrieving information quickly and easily. This chapter helps to simplify one's research strategy. The guide is divided into 4 parts. The 1st addresses U.S government sources that would be helpful in tracking Canadian business interests. It is a complete list of federal and state agencies and departments that have information about

Canada. Each entry has an explanation of the benefits of requesting information (e.g., newsletters, key people, statistics) from the particular government office agency or department. The 2d part lists Canadian government sources, both federal and provincial. The 3d section presents publications, databases, CD-ROMs, and Internet sources for researching Canadian markets, and the 4th part describes international and private sector organizations, security analysts, and banks of Canada.

This guide to Canadian business and investments will be helpful for the researcher in special libraries concerned with banking and investments. It would also be helpful in academic libraries with international business programs as well as large public libraries with business information sections.—**Kay M. Stebbins**

333.   **Scott's Directories 1999: Greater Toronto Business Directory, Volume 1.** 6th ed. Don Mills, Ont., Southam Information Products, 1999. 1v. (various paging). index. $199.00. ISBN 1-55257-029-0.

This annually revised tool meets the demand for sales leads—it is a directory to manufacturing, wholesale, distribution, medical, government, and educational markets in the Greater Toronto area. The first volume covers the base city of Toronto and the second volume covers the dozen or so other municipalities that encircle Toronto. Between them, both volumes have references to 31,800 businesses. Half of the companies have undergone some kind of change since the previous edition in 1998.

The first section is an alphabetic listing with street addresses and a reference to the main entry. The second section is a geographic listing. This is the main section where (under street) users can find the full name of the company, phone and fax numbers (but no e-mail), names of the major executives, products produced and Standard Industrial Classification code numbers, number of employees, sales generated, size of the headquarters, and year established. The last section is an SIC listing, in numerical order, with page references to the main entry. Scott's has a whole line of directories as well as CD-ROM products; it is a reliable company with a century or more of service providing leads. A useful acquisition if you need this type of data.—**Dean Tudor**

EUROPE

Directories

334.   **Directory of Consumer Brands and Their Owners 1998: Eastern Europe.** Chicago, Euromonitor International; distr., Farmington Hills, Mich., Gale, 1998. 310p. index. $990.00. ISBN 0-86338-784-5.

This volume in the Euromonitor series aims to be the most comprehensive guide to Eastern European product brands, owners, marketing areas, and competitors in that region. Companion volumes in this series cover Asia Pacific, Europe, and Latin America, and are available in a CD-ROM version entitled *The World Database of Consumer Brands & Their Owners* (see entry 348), which also covers North America.

An introduction explains the scope, organization, definitions, criteria, and research methods used to compile a vast amount of information. A table of contents breaks down the level of categories so the reader can go directly to the product area of interest. The data are presented in two sections: the first lists brands by product sector, together with the owner's name and the country where it is headquartered; and the second section profiles brand-owning companies, sorted by country and arranged alphabetically by the brand-owner's name within each country. Profiles consist of the owner's name, corporate affiliations, Eastern European headquarters address and contact information (including Internet addresses where available), main activities, shareholding information, number of employees, and a brief financial snapshot. Some entries include notes that give additional information such as plans for expansion, mergers, trade and market share disputes, and exports. Euromonitor has tried to include not only all of the major companies, including multinationals with headquarters in the region, but also the smaller companies that own well-known or established brands.

Brands are classified into three levels of categories. Nineteen broad categories are broken down into smaller sections, some of which are further refined. The "Food" category, for example, has 34 subcategories into which are sorted 136 types of foodstuffs—making the "Food" category the largest section of the volume, followed by "Cosmetics and Toiletries" with 13 subcategories, and "Drinks" with 5 subcategories and 49 third-level categories. A sample search through the "Food" category led to some surprising classifications. "Hot Beverages" is included with "Food" and not with "Drinks," and pasta has become a "Bakery Product." "Delicatessen Foods" becomes its own subcategory, without an explanation of the types of foods that it covers. Unless the reader is already familiar with the brands, the information will not be helpful. Two indexes, one of consumer brands and one of brand-owning companies, allow the reader to look up proprietary names quickly, and also to see where U.S. parent companies are headquartered in Eastern Europe.

This volume in the Euromonitor series will be invaluable to businesspersons who are considering expansion into Eastern European markets and thinking of identifying possible partnerships as well as monitoring competition. This work is recommended for business and corporate libraries as well as large reference collections.—**Kerie L. Nickel**

335.   **Directory of Consumer Brands and Their Owners 1998: Europe.** 3d ed. Chicago, Ill., Euromonitor International; distr., Detroit, Gale, 1998. 2v. index. $1,190.00/set. ISBN 0-86338-750-0.

This 2-volume directory is part of a larger series that also includes volumes on Eastern Europe, Asia Pacific, and Latin America as well as Western Europe and Turkey. The 1st volume deals with brands by 20 broad product categories, divided into subcategories and within those into finer classifications. It provides brand names, their corporate owners, and the country of the owner. More than 54,000 brands are included, owned by almost 6,000 companies. An index of consumer brands, not shown in the table of contents but occupying 114 triple-column pages, closes that volume.

The 2d volume shows the brand-owning companies by country—18 Western European countries in all. The information on companies provides address, telephone and fax numbers, e-mail address, main activities, parent company, name(s) of key personnel, number of employees, a list of brands owned, and financial information for one to four years. The volume is completed with an index of brand-owning companies, taking up 29 pages with triple columns. The two volumes together make for easy study of individual brands, of competing brands internationally or within national markets, and for the basic assessment of the firms in question. The information provided is voluminous but compact, and it is impeccably presented.—**Bogdan Mieczkowski**

336.   **Eastern Europe: A Directory and Sourcebook.** 2d ed. Chicago, Euromonitor International; distr., Farmington Hills, Mich., Gale, 1998. 252p. index. $590.00. ISBN 0-86338-804-3.

This pricey directory lists major companies in the old Warsaw Pact countries of Bulgaria, the Czech Republic, Estonia, Latvia, Lithuania, Poland, Romania, Russia, Slovakia, and the Ukraine. It is divided into 4 sections: 1-page textual overviews of the socioeconomic environment of each country; an alphabetical list of major companies by country; an information directory listing trade development bodies, trade and business associations, market research companies, major business libraries, major business and trade journals, business directories, online resources, and databases; and a 13-page datafile of statistics. There are two broad indexes: a product and service index and an alphabetic list of companies by company name. In section 2 the type of data that may be provided for each company include name; address; telephone, fax, and telex numbers; e-mail and Website addresses; year established; main activity; major subsidiaries; chief executives; number of employees; details of products, operations, and brands (such as market share); and notes and limited financials. Data are mostly from 1996 and 1997, although textual remarks describe changes as recent as September 1998.

The book is substantially changed from its 1st edition. No comparable title is published in the United States, but Gale distributes *Major Companies of Central & Eastern Europe and the Commonwealth of Independent States 1998* (see entry 345), which is jointly published by Dun & Bradstreet and Graham & Whiteside. Data elements are essentially the same for both titles, although *Major Companies* has an extensive list of directors and managers and some financials as recent as mid-1998. Both have alphabetic indexes by company name and product and subject or SIC. *Major Companies* includes approximately 9,000 companies from 27 countries (from Albania to Kazakhstan), whereas *Eastern Europe* lists approximately 1,500 companies from the 10 countries noted above. A comparison of the number of entries found only 8 of Euromonitor's 34 Bulgarian companies duplicated in the Dun & Bradstreet title. A second comparison found 62 of Euromonitor's 133 Polish companies duplicated in the Dun & Bradstreet title. About 40 percent of the addresses of the duplicated titles were different. They complement, not compete with each other. Both are expensive, but Eastern European data is hard to come by. Both can be recommended for academic, large public, and corporate libraries serving clients with a strong interest in Eastern European business. Libraries that can afford only one East European business directory will find Euromonitor's *Eastern Europe: A Directory and Sourcebook* a more useful tool and the first choice for purchase for its relative affordability, geographic focus, and the many leads it can provide in the highly volatile Eastern European business environment.—**Patrick J. Brunet**

337. **European Directory of Retailers and Wholesalers.** 2d ed. Chicago, Euromonitor International; distr., Detroit, Gale, 1997. 618p. index. $990.00. ISBN 0-86338-577-X.

This title is more than just a directory of more than 4,800 Western European retailers and wholesalers of consumer goods, it also ranks the largest retailers of these items on the basis of product turnover. The work begins with a list of the top 100 retailers in Europe, ranked by their turnover computed in U.S. dollars. Each of the following 17 chapters addresses the retailers and wholesalers of an individual Western European nation, and each chapter starts with a ranking of the top 25 to 50 retailers in the country. Subsequent chapter entries are arranged in alphabetic order by company name, and provide additional data such as contact information, retail or wholesale sector (e.g., consumer electronics, food), type of retailer (e.g., mail order company, supermarket operator), number of outlets, number of employees, private labels, and brief financial information. Four indexes follow—a company name index, an index of retailers by sector, an index of wholesalers by sector, and an index of both retailers and wholesalers by type. Each index entry includes the country in which the business is based. The additional information allows an individual to easily determine which companies located in a particular country transact in a given retail or wholesale sector, or to recognize retailers with a particular type of business operation. This expensive work will find use in libraries whose patrons demand ready-reference information on the Western European retail and wholesale industry.—**Mark A. Allan**

338. **European Drinks Marketing Directory.** 4th ed. London, Euromonitor; distr., Detroit, Gale, 1996. 438p. index. $425.00pa. ISBN 0-86338-626-1.

The *European Drinks Marketing Directory* is the premier beverage marketing directory for Western Europe. It profiles more than 1,600 leading drinks companies in 17 major Western European countries. The directory is divided into three main sections. Section 1, which constitutes the core of the directory, arranges the companies in an alphabetic sequence by country and includes "every type of company involved in the drinks sector, such as manufacturers and product marketing companies, retailers, wholesalers, distributors, importers and exporters."

The drink products run the gamut from milk, fruit juices, mineral water, and soft drinks to beers, wines, and spirits. The directory lists companies dealing with beverages exclusively as well as companies carrying drink products only as incidental items. Section 1 provides standard directory information but, more importantly, it contains in-depth company information regarding manufacturers' products and brands and up-to-date financials. Information in the profiles comes from the companies' annual returns, supplemented by desk research from Euromonitor.

Section 2 profiles key information sources for drinks marketing in Western Europe, including official organizations and publications, trade and business associations, trade and business journals, market research companies, and online databases. Section 3 consists of 5 indexes. *Beverage World Databank* (Keller International, annual) is a competing directory only in a limited sense. *European Drinks Marketing Directory* is a necessary purchase for corporate libraries that support firms carrying beverage items. It is highly recommended for large public libraries and academic libraries that support international marketing clientele.—**Dene L. Clark**

339.   **European Private Label Directory.** London, Euromonitor; distr., Detroit, Gale, 1996. 257p. index. $450.00pa. ISBN 0-86338-519-2.

A private label is a brand owned by a retailer. There are four types, with changing price and advertising spending attached to the four "generations." The retailer owns the brand exclusively all the way through the process of development and sale, from conception through putting it on the shelf. This directory, on European firms, provides information on 500 retailers who sell private label products and 500 manufacturers who make them. The information given includes address; key personnel or chief executive officers; parent company and major subsidiaries; contract details; size of the company (such as number of employees, manufacturing capacity, financial information on profits and turnover); and what is being produced or sold. While most of the book consists of the listing of retailers and manufacturers in 17 major European countries (the member states of the European Union and all major European Free Trade Association countries), the first 2 sections provide an overview of the concept of the private label in Europe and statistics showing relevant trends and data for Europe and individual countries. This book provides specific company information on a small (approximately 12.5 percent of total retail sales), but growing, part of the market. —**J. E. Weaver**

340.   **Europe's Medium-Sized Companies Directory.** 2d ed. Chicago, Ill., Euromonitor International; distr., Detroit, Gale, 1997. 661p. index. $590.00. ISBN 0-86338-724-1.

The 2d edition of this directory (see ARBA 97, entry 242, for a review of the 1st edition) profiles 6,500 companies that represent main sectors of the western European economy, including manufacturing, mining, trading, banks and insurance companies, service companies, and utilities. Other criteria involve ranking by turnover, which varies from between $100 million and $10 million for smaller countries and between $299 million and $50 million for larger countries. Entries are alphabetic first by country and then by company and typically provide address, telephone, fax, and telex numbers; year established; business activity; ownership; major subsidiaries; key personnel; main products or brands; number of employees; turnover for three years; profit figures that are somewhat dated; analysis of turnover; financial year-end date; and occasional notes about business developments. There is a general index of company names, but no index for the user who wants to search by industry type.—**Jean Engler**

341. **Europe's Top Quoted Companies: A Comparative Directory from Seventeen European Stock Exchanges.** London, Kogan Page; distr., Chicago, LPC Group, 2001. 889p. index. $150.00pa. ISBN 0-7494-3513-5.

This paperback, nearly 900-page volume allows comparing profiles of different companies across national borders. Information is given on a five-year historical period. The most recent information is from January 1, 1992 to August 31, 2000. It covers 850 of the largest European companies quoted on 17 stock exchanges, which include the United Kingdom, France, Germany, Italy, Spain, The Netherlands, Finland, Sweden, Greece, Norway, Portugal, Switzerland, Denmark, Belgium, Austria, Ireland, and Luxembourg. All companies are standardized in a common format and financial information is converted to Euros at a standard conversion rate. Companies are indexed by country, name, and sector, making it easy to locate an individual company. Information on each company includes company name alphabetized in order within country, business sector, corporate address or headquarters, contacts, chairperson or CEO, shareholders, corporate profile, codes corresponding to principal stock exchange market listing, stock market data, highlights, frequency of income and balance sheet over a five-year period, ratios over a five-year period, and a stock market chart for each of the companies. Binding, paper, and font size are adequate for the purpose and the companies are indexed in such a manner that it is easy to find individual profiles. This information will be extremely useful for people doing business or people investing in European companies and wanting a way to compare companies across national boundaries. —**Herbert W. Ockerman**

342. Konn, Tania. **Guide to Business Information on Central and Eastern Europe.** Chicago, Fitzroy Dearborn, 2000. 235p. index. $60.00. ISBN 1-57958-263-X.

Until recently, business information on Central and Eastern Europe appeared largely in languages that were not widely spoken outside of those nations. Translation into English, the most widely used language of business, was frequently not utilized. In order to reach the majority of potential investors and marketers, information sources in the Central and Eastern European countries began to provide English versions. *Guide to Business Information on Central and Eastern Europe* provides a comprehensive description of information on Central and Eastern Europe available in English and, consequently, brings sources of printed and electronic data on these countries together in one convenient, accessible location.

After a brief general introduction, business information on Central and Eastern Europe, as a region, is given. Information specific to each of the 12 countries is then presented. The regional and country profiles are provided in similar format: overview, current developments, companies and contacts, industries and services, legislation, and organizations. Some of the sources provide information at no cost, but most require payment, ranging from very little to larger amounts.

The guide is an excellent introduction to the growing wealth of business information on Central and Eastern Europe and should do much to satisfy the increasing demand for information on that region. Readers who are seriously interested may wish to search further for information in local languages that may not have been translated into English, since translation is relatively new to some of the countries. Access to specific sections of the guide is greatly facilitated by an extensive index. [R: Choice, Mar 01, pp. 1249-1250]—**William C. Struning**

343. Konn, Tania. **Guide to Business Information on Russia, the NIS, and the Baltic States.** Chicago, Fitzroy Dearborn, 2000. 310p. index. $60.00. ISBN 1-57958-322-9.

The purpose of this directory is to serve as an introduction to English-language sources, in electronic and conventional print forms, dealing with business issues in Russia, the NIS, and the Baltic States—in short, the countries constituting the Former Soviet Union. In addition to the general section covering multi-country sources, 15 individual countries are covered, with varied degrees of completeness. The best coverage is for the Russian Federation, followed by such countries as Ukraine or Kazakhstan.

There is a brief overview for each country, with entries arranged under five general categories: current developments, companies and contacts, industries and services, legislation, and organizations. The information is in general current, the majority of the sites were last checked during the period April-May 2000. Obviously, in a publication of this type the information will occasionally be obsolete—some organizations come and go and change their addresses and names. —**Bohdan S. Wynar**

344. **Major Business Organisations of Eastern Europe and the Commonwealth of Independent States 1995/96.** 5th ed. Diane Butler, ed. London, Graham & Whiteside; distr., Detroit, Gale, 1995. 809p. index. $720.00. ISBN 1-86099-000-2. ISSN 0966-0372.

The newest edition of this reference source has grown to list more than 4,200 organizations with a broad territorial coverage of all countries created from the former Soviet Union and the former communist countries of Eastern Europe (with the exception of Yugoslavia, of which only Slovenia is included here). The main part of the book, running almost 700 pages, consists of an alphabetically arranged list of business organizations by country. Each entry includes the address, the telephone number with a separate international telephone number, telex and fax numbers, a list of principal officers, a description of main activities, names of the principal banks, the date of establishment, and the number of employees.

Three indexes add to the accessibility of the basic information: an alphabetic index of all firms; an index of firms by country; and an index of business organizations by their four-digit Standard Industrial Classification (SIC) code, again in each of those classifications divided by country (SIC codes are listed in the introduction). Diplomatic representatives are listed separately. Carefully prepared with a view to encouraging contacts, this source testifies to the impressive growth of commercial links between the former communist countries and the noncommunist, more industrialized countries, and, consequently, to increasing business opportunities in the trade between those areas.—**Bogdan Mieczkowski**

345. **Major Companies of Central & Eastern Europe and the Commonwealth of Independent States 1998.** 7th ed. C. Tapster and A. Ford, eds. London, Graham & Whiteside and Bucks, UK, D&B Europe; distr., Detroit, Gale, 1997. 1323p. index. $935.00. ISBN 1-86099-076-2.

The 7th edition of this publication has been completely revised by a joint publishing venture of Graham & Whiteside and Dun & Bradstreet. It includes 8,000 of the most prominent businesses in the central, the eastern, and the former Soviet republics. The kinds of businesses include trade organizations, privatized companies, manufacturers, financial institutions, and key government organizations relating to business.

The most helpful section of the directory is the "Country Summaries." It contains overviews of individual countries and an assessment of their business environment. Dun & Bradstreet has assigned an indicator number of the risk of doing business with these countries. The information provided gives insight into the demographic, political, and economic factors of the countries.

Each country's entry lists the capital city, major cities, land area, population, languages and dialects, heads of state, gross national product, currency and exchange rates, and membership in political and economic groups. The key information in this section is economic indicators for the years 1992 to 1996. The business environment includes the investment policy, banking system, company framework, and import and exchange controls. The "Country Particularities" is a helpful section because it provides information to alert one to the cultural and practical variations that will facilitate successful business in the particular country. A list of 108 companies that were founded from 1397 to 1846 are listed. It is an interesting list because the year 1848 is "Europe's Year of Revolutions," and these companies have survived for more than 150 years of political struggle.

The index is printed on blue pages for easy access. There are three indexes: alphabetic company index, alphabetic country with companies index, and a U.S. SIC number and business activities index. This 7th edition is recommended to the large academic and public library that requires international business information.—**Kay M. Stebbins**

346. **Major Companies of Europe 1998.** J. Bradley and others, eds. Detroit, Gale, 1997. 4v. index. $1,645.00/set; $515.00/vol. ISBN 1-86099-067-3.

This is an extensive 4-volume series providing current and comprehensive information concerning approximately 22,000 of Europe's largest public and private companies in more than 20 Western European countries. Volume 1 includes Austria, Belgium, Denmark, Ireland, Finland, and France, for a total of 1,265 pages. Volume 2 covers Germany, Greece, Italy, Liechtenstein, and Luxembourg and contains 1,118 pages. Volume 3 includes the Netherlands, Norway, Portugal, Spain, Sweden, and Switzerland and consists of 1,087 pages. And volume 4 covers the United Kingdom and requires 778 pages, for a total of 4,248 pages. Each entry contains the company name, contact information, senior executives (more than 164,000 total), principal activities, subsidiary companies or parent companies, banking information, law firm utilized, financial information, shareholders, and number of employees. Each volume includes an alphabetic index, index by country, SIC code listing, and business activities index. This is an extensive library resource and would be valuable to anyone doing business in the European area. The fact that the information is current makes it even more valuable. If only a portion is needed, individual volumes are available. The printing, paper, and binding are acceptable for library use.—**Herbert W. Ockerman**

347. **The Top 5,000 European Companies 2002.** R. Crawford and others, eds. London, Graham & Whiteside; distr., Farmington Hills, Mich., Gale, 2001. 1215p. index. $645.00. ISBN 1-86099-257-9.

The 3d edition of this straightforward business directory offers up to 27 data elements for the 5,000 largest manufacturing and services companies in Austria, Belgium, Cyprus, Denmark, Eire, Finland, France, Germany, Greece, Israel, Italy, Liechtenstein, Luxembourg, the Netherlands, Norway, Portugal, Spain, Sweden, Switzerland, and the United Kingdom. Inclusion is determined by sales volume. No Eastern European countries are included and no reason is given as to why Israel is listed. Each company entry has the following information listed when available: name of company; address; telephone, telex, and fax numbers; e-mail and Web addresses; names of chairperson, president, board members, and senior management; principal activities, brand names, and trademarks; parent company; public or private status; principal shareholders; and number of employees. Nine financials for the 1999 and 2000 fiscal year may be also offered: sales, profit before tax, retained profit, dividends, dividends per share, earning per share, share capital, and shareholder funds. Two additional rankings report the largest 500 banks by total assets and the largest 100 insurance companies by premium. There is both an alphabetic index of companies by name and a 150-page SIC (Standard Industry Code) index, although it uses the 1987 edition of the SIC index. The directory is also available on a CD-ROM that can be very useful for personnel searching since the very large number of individuals named is a strong point of the volume.

Hoover's Handbook of World Business (see entry 279) lists much of the same data with a full page of text on company history and products, but only for 300 companies. *Hoover's MasterList of Major European Companies* (annual), or its companion volume on international companies (see entry 255), each cover about 2,500 companies with about one-third of the data of the title under review. The Hoover's products would be good choices for smaller libraries only needing limited coverage of major companies since they cost around $135. Dun & Bradstreet appears to have restricted its European information to electronic format and Euromonitor's *Global Market Share Planner: Europe* is more complementary than similar. The International Public and Private Companies volume of the multivolume *Directory of Corporate Affiliations* (National Register Publishing, 2002) covers much of the same data for approximately 3,500 mostly European companies. It has far more personal names due to coverage of subsidiaries, but fewer financials. There is significant overlap between this title and the 2002 edition of the *Top 5,000 European Companies*. Libraries that only want a list of names of larger European companies and their addresses will find that *Europages* (www.europages.com) and *Marconi's International Register* (Marconi International Register, annual) list far more companies (more than 100,000 and 40,000 respectively) and both are under $200. Still, the *Top 5,000 European Companies 2002* is a good title that has found a niche in the middle range of scope and price in the competitive directory business and is recommended for any library needing a one-volume directory with personnel of major European businesses.—**Patrick Brunet**

348.   **The World Database of Consumer Brands and Their Owners 1998 on CD-ROM.** 2d Issue I ed. [CD-ROM] Chicago, Ill., Euromonitor International; distr., Detroit, Gale, 1998. Minimum system requirements: IBM or compatible 486 DX2 66. Double-speed CD-ROM drive. Windows 3.1 or Windows 95. 8MB RAM (16MB RAM for Windows 95). 10MB hard disk space (10MB for Windows 95). $1,990.00. ISBN 0-86338-748-9.

Aimed at the market researcher or businessperson, this database offers online access to information drawn from the print version of *Directory of Consumer Brands and Their Owners 1998: Europe* (see entry 335). Coverage includes extensive information on more than 6,200 consumer good manufacturers and the 55,600 brands they market across 815 consumer product sectors in 12 Western European countries. The product sectors cover the gamut, from adhesives to home furnishings, from pipe tobacco to writing instruments. A typical company record includes contact information, subsidiaries, key personnel, an employee census, financial information, market share data, major products and brands, and general notes. The publisher emphasizes that every effort was made to include accurate and current information.

It is unfortunate that the user interface of this product somewhat hinders access to the remarkable amount of brand, company, and market information provided. This reviewer found navigating the database confusing without the aid of a user guide, and even with instructions, found searching initially cumbersome. Users are presented with a main screen sectioned into quadrants of region/country, market sector, brand name, and company name information, and may combine those elements in searches. However, one may find the search and viewing options outlined in the user guide complicated and must also become familiar with 15 tiny search tool icons. The nature of the information contained in this database clearly calls for flexibility of access points in searching, but the particular search design presented here might be refined to make it more intuitive. A positive feature to note includes the ability to print mailing labels of company addresses.

Despite the patience required to become adept at using this comprehensive database, this CD-ROM product is a rich source of consumer brand information. It is recommended for corporate or academic business libraries.—**Judith A. Matthews**

Handbooks and Yearbooks

349. **The Book of European Forecasts.** 2d ed. London, Euromonitor; distr., Detroit, Gale, 1996. 441p. $320.00. ISBN 0-86338-557-5.

Today's world economy presents challenges as well as opportunities to investors and traders. Before a firm commits to investing in or trading with entities within a foreign country, however, it first engages in an extensive market research program. Along with other concerns, it studies the economic, social, and demographic profiles of the nation, considering the present situation and projections for the foreseeable future. *The Book of European Forecasts* was created to answer just such market research questions on Europe. The volume begins with background information on broad topics, such as macroeconomic prospects, employment trends, demographic changes, and policy shifts. This is followed by forecasts for specific sectors and services ranging from automobiles and transport to chemicals and pharmaceuticals, cosmetics, and toiletries.

The forecasts were developed by pan-European and international sources, pan-European trade associations, private consumer research publishers, and national statistical offices. Financial data in tables appear in U.S. dollars, making this source particularly useful for U.S. audiences. The searcher will discover that some tables cover both western and eastern European nations, while other tables understandably give forecasts only for European Union countries. Similar data may be available in *Worldcasts*, published by Predicasts. The Economist Intelligence Unit (EIU) publishes journals and country forecasts, which also provide comparable information. Predicasts and EIU titles are expensive, however, making *The Book of European Forecasts* a bargain by comparison.

The title under review is highly recommended for special libraries where budgetary concerns are not paramount. It would also be valuable in large public libraries and academic libraries with strong international marketing collections.—**Dene L. Clark**

350. **Consumer Eastern Europe 2000/2001.** 8th ed. Chicago, Euromonitor International, 2001. 680p. maps. $1,090.00pa. ISBN 0-86338-965-1.

This work is the 8th edition of *Consumer Eastern Europe* and provides the reader with a vast array of statistical information regarding the various consumer markets. The countries included in this volume are Bulgaria, Czech Republic, Hungary, Poland, Romania, Russia, Slovakia, and the Ukraine. Regular users of these volumes will find the same standardized format as has been used for this title and other titles in this series. Some of the consumer markets that the reader can find information on are consumer electronics, leisure goods, automotives, housewares, clothing, and electrical appliances. The section on consumer markets is approximately 180 pages long and has been gathered from a variety of official sources—although consistency in definitions is still a problem for this region.

The information provided for individual countries, which comprises the bulk of the publication, includes demographics, economic indicators, standard of living, household characteristics, advertising and media access, retail distribution, consumer expenditure, consumption rates, and service industries. While primarily a statistical handbook, the reader will find a 24-page regional overview that summarizes the current outlook for this region. This feature is particularly useful as this region is still undergoing some serious adjustments as they adapt to a free market economy. With this factor in mind, libraries that have clients doing business in this area will want to acquire the latest volume.—**Judith J. Field**

351. **Consumer Europe 2000/2001.** 16th ed. Chicago, Euromonitor International, 2000. 606p. index. $1,190.00. ISBN 0-86338-932-5.

Now in its 16th edition, this well-known compendium of pan-European market information presents 1994 to 1999 market data for 16 countries, along with comprehensive revisions of a number of existing data sets. *Consumer Europe* is one of seven country and regional market reference books published by Euromonitor.

Presented in easy-to-read tables, over 330 consumer product sectors and synopses of all the major retail items purchased in a European household, are collated into 1 volume. Some of the 16 major segments covered include foods, drinks, tobacco, household cleaning products, over-the-counter healthcare products, disposable paper products, consumer electronics, leisure goods, and automotive goods. Socioeconomic parameters, such as demographics, income, consumer lifestyles, advertising and retailing trends, and tourism trends, are also provided. The final section, "Key Information Sources," lists international, pan-regional, and specific country organizations as well as major trade associations for key consumer products. Searching the comprehensive index accesses relevant tables quickly and efficiently.

An important factor for U.S. researchers is that although the market value for 1994 through 1999 is reported in national currencies, the percent of change for 1994 to 1999 is volume and value is represented in U.S. dollars as is the total for 1999. Per capita value for 1999 is also in U.S. dollars, while per capita volume for 1999 is in relevant units.

Consumer Europe allows students, faculty, and market researchers to delve into the preferences and habits of pan-European consumers as well as reveals important facets of foreign economic systems. Academic and corporate business libraries will want to purchase it.—**Susan C. Awe**

352.   **Economic Survey of Europe 2001, Number 1.** By the Secretariat of the Economic Commission for Europe. New York, United Nations, 2001. 270p. $70.00pa. ISBN 92-1-116780-9. ISSN 0070-8712. S/N E.01.II.E.14.

This United Nations (UN) publication begins with explanatory notes, abbreviations, and a preface. It is then divided into chapters that cover the Economic Commission for Europe situation in the Spring of 2001, an overview of current situations, and selective policy issues. Chapter 2 looks into the global context and Western Europe, including a section on the United States. Chapter 3 covers the transition in economies and the factors that influence them. Chapter 4 outlines domestic savings in the economy. Chapter 5 covers the growth of foreign direct investment in the transition economies. Chapter 6 describes the economic transformation and real exchange rate in the 2000s—the Balassa-Samuelson connection. This information is then followed by a statistical appendix containing 28 tables. This paperback is printed on average paper, with adequate font size and three-color printing that makes is easier to read. It has many tables and graphs that make the commentary more understandable. Like all UN publications, this work is one of the few sources where this information is available and consequently should be in all major libraries that are concerned about economic survey, particularly of the European Continent.—**Herbert W. Ockerman**

353.   **European Marketing Data and Statistics 2001.** 36th ed. Chicago, Euromonitor International, 2001. 505p. index. $395.00. ISBN 0-86338-978-3. ISSN 0071-2930.

This work is a comprehensive, oversized book covering European marketing data and statistics. It is broken into chapters entitled: "Key European Marketing Information Sources," "Marketing Geography," "Demographic Trends and Forecasts," "Economic Indicators," "Banking and Finance," "External Trade," "Labor Force Indicators," "Industrial Resources and Output," "Energy Resources and Output," "Defense," "Environmental Data," "Consumer Expenditure Patterns," "Retailing and Retail Distribution," "Advertising and Media Patterns," "Consumer Market Sizes," "Consumer Price and Cost," "Housing and Household Facilities," "Health and Living Standards," "Literacy Education," "Agriculture Resources," "Communications," "Automobiles,"

"Transport and Tourism," "Cultural Indicators," and "Incomes and Earnings." Many of these sections are broken down into various countries, giving detailed information on those areas. A sizable portion of the manuscript is in table format giving information, usually up to 1999, on various areas of Europe. The book is above average in binding, paper quality, and font size. It should be useful for anyone interacting, or who anticipates interacting, with the European marketing system and should be in all comprehensive libraries.—**Herbert W. Ockerman**

354. **European Marketing Forecasts 2001.** 3d ed. Chicago, Euromonitor International, 2001. 570p. $1,000.00. ISBN 1-84264-113-1.

This is the 3d edition of Euromonitor's coverage of the European market forecasts, a companion to the *International Marketing Forecasts* (see entry 282). The researchers gather the forecast data from all of the national economic sources, the International Monetary Fund (IMF), the United Nations, the Office of Economic Cooperation and Development (OECD), the European Union, and the World Bank.

The base year of 1999 is used for the economic experts to predict the socio-economic forecasts for the next 14 years and to supply "backcasting" for 20 years past, retrospectively. There are 52 countries and more than 320 markets from around the world covered. The selection of the countries is based on the local economy and its growth. This 3d edition should be purchased for all academic business collections and business libraries, especially the ones with international interests.—**Kay M. Stebbins**

355. Yuill, Douglas, John Bachtler, and Fiona Wishlade. **European Regional Incentives, 1999.** 18th ed. New Providence, N.J., Bowker-Saur/Reed Reference Publishing, 1999. 480p. maps. $130.00pa. ISBN 1-85739-272-8.

This annual review and analysis of regional aid policies in the EU15 (and Norway) is an easy-to-use guide to all the grants and other aid available to industry within the designated "problem regions" of the European Union. Supported by funding from 10 European governments, this edition has been expanded and enhanced to provide examination of regional disparities and give a full discussion of Agenda 2000 and the March 1998 Guidelines on National Regional Aid as well as detailed comparative analysis of regional incentive spending over the past 10 years. Also included is an in-depth study of the impact of competition policy on national regional aid policies as well as an overview of the operation of the structural funds, focusing on the current position. This definitive guide on European regional aid is invaluable to understanding European funding. Its analysis includes practical information on application procedures as well as detailed statistics, charts, and maps. Used by regional policy makers and development organizations, companies considering investing in these European countries will want to consult this reference. This work is recommended for large international business collections.—**Susan C. Awe**

LATIN AMERICA AND THE CARIBBEAN

Dictionaries and Encyclopedias

356. **Argentina Business: The Portable Encyclopedia for Doing Business with Argentina.** Edward G. Hinkelman and others, eds. San Rafael, Calif., World Trade Press, 1996. 372p. illus. maps. index. (World Trade Press Country Business Guides). $24.95pa. ISBN 1-885073-04-6.

Argentina Business provides a broad range of information of value to any organization or individual contemplating doing business in this important South American country. The encyclopedia's 25 chapters include survey information (economy, current issues, industry reviews, and the like) plus specific, practical coverage of such high-interest topics as export and import policies and procedures, trade fairs, business law, and international payments. These materials are supplemented by a 450-entry dictionary of terms (and their pronunciations) appropriate for conducting business in Argentina; a directory of 750 business contacts; cross-references; chapter lists for further reading; numerous tables; and occasional listings of electronic resources where appropriate. A thorough index concludes the handbook.

The value of *Argentina Business*, part of this publisher's Country Business Guide series, is its clear focus on practical information for the business reader. For example, one table details the average lease prices for types of commercial real estate in Buenos Aires. In another chapter, one finds three pages of tips for attending trade fairs. Although much of this information will become dated fairly quickly and will need updating on a regular basis, this moderately priced work is nevertheless a solid resource for anyone contemplating business in Argentina.—**G. Kim Dority**

Directories

357. **Directory of Consumer Brands and Their Owners 1998: Latin America.** Chicago, Euromonitor International; distr., Farmington Hills, Mich., Gale, 1998. 282p. index. $990.00. ISBN 0-86338-786-1.

The aim of this directory is to provide a complete list of Latin American consumer brands and their owners in South America. The editors of the directory have listed 7,000 leading brand products and more than 1,000 major companies.

The directory is easy to read. The first half of the book is a classified list of the products. Each entry is arranged in broad categories ranging from "automobiles" to "writing instruments." Each product entry names the product by brandname and the company that owns the brand. The second half of the book describes the companies that own the products. The company entry contains the name of the company, address, e-mail address, telephone number, corporate information, subsidiaries, number of employees, and a summary of financial information and notes of interest about the company. An index of consumer brands and an index of brand-owning companies are available at the back of the volume.

Euromonitor has attempted to provide a complete guide to worldwide consumer brands and the companies that own them. This Latin American directory joins the other three publications: *Directory of Consumer Brands and Their Owners: Europe* (see entry 335), *Directory of Consumer Brands and Their Owners: Eastern Europe* (see entry 334), and *Directory of Consumer Brands and Their Owners: Asia Pacific* (see entry 311).

This reviewer recommends this volume for large public, academic, and special libraries' business collections. Many of the brands are familiar to the American public and it is interesting to see the Spanish brand names in the same U.S. products.—**Kay M. Stebbins**

358. **Hoover's Masterlist of Major Latin American Companies 1996-1997.** Austin, Tex., Reference Press, 1996. 149p. index. $79.95. ISBN 1-878753-69-X.

In a sense, this book may be looked upon as an inexpensive version or abridgment of D. Shave's monumental and expensive *Major Companies of Latin America & the Caribbean* (see entry 360). The entries here are concise, with the barest minimum of information regarding the companies listed, a sort of "yellow-pages" telephone book. Nevertheless, for the price, *Hoover's Masterlist* is well worth the money if all one requires are addresses, telephone numbers, type of industry or commercial enterprise, and names of managers or officers.—**S. D. Markman**

359.   Latin America: A Directory and Sourcebook. 2d ed. Chicago, Euromonitor International; distr., Farmington Hills, Mich., Gale, 1998. 272p. index. $590.00. ISBN 0-86338-805-1.

The publisher's intention in this 2d edition of *Latin America: A Directory and Sourcebook* is not to provide exhaustive coverage of the Latin American market, its leading companies, and principal business information resources. Rather, the goal is to provide, in a single volume, a balanced mix of these three categories that researchers will find useful and valuable. The volume covers the major economies of Latin America. The countries included are Argentina, Brazil, Chile, Colombia, Ecuador, Mexico, Peru, and Venezuela.

The work begins with an 18-page "Overview of the Socio-Economic Environment." This relatively brief market overview provides background information on key issues that affect foreign businesses operating in the Latin American environment. These include macroeconomic information as well as demographic and consumer trends. Nearly half of the volume is devoted to the 2d section, "Major Companies." This listing provides basic directory information for almost 1,000 companies. The arrangement is by country and then by company. Entries are brief, but can include e-mail and Website addresses, brand names, and market share information. Turnover information (sales) is provided for the latest three or four years available. A few companies have 1997 sales data listed, but the most recent information for the majority of entries is 1996 or 1995. An especially nice addition to the 2d edition is the list of companies ranked by sales that appears at the beginning of each country section.

Approximately one-quarter of the work is devoted to the 3d section, "Key Sources of Information." This section lists more than 1,000 sources a researcher might consult for further information on the Latin American markets. Arranged by category, it includes "Official Organizations and Publications," "Trade Development Bodies," "Major Trade and Business Associations," "Leading Research Companies," "Major Business Information Libraries," "Major Trade and Business Journals," "Business Directories," and "Major Business Information Web Sites." Each entry provides a short description of the resource and contact information. The last section consists of 36 tables that provide comparative market information for the 8 countries covered in the volume. The data are derived from national statistical office sources, inter-governmental agencies, and Euromonitor reports. The volume concludes with 2 indexes—a general index and one arranged by industry sector.

This work is well organized and as current as most print sources can be, and it contains a lot of information. The publisher has achieved its goal of packaging a wide range of information useful for researching the Latin American market into one volume. At $590, however, it is not inexpensive, and prospective purchasers will want to consider whether or not this source might duplicate some of the information they already have in their collections. For example, one might find some overlap between the contents found here and that found in other directories, bibliographies, international business services, and government publications that cover Latin American markets and companies. However, the real value of *Latin America: A Directory and Sourcebook* is not so much in the extent of the information provided in each category as in the convenience of having it all pulled together in one easy-to-use volume. With that in mind, it is recommended for reference collections supporting international or Latin American business programs.—**Gordon J. Aamot**

360.   Major Companies of Latin America and the Caribbean 1998. David Shave, ed. London, Graham & Whiteside; distr., Detroit, Gale, 1998. 1330p. index. $730.00. ISBN 1-86099-103-3. ISSN 1369-5428.

The 3d edition of this directory has been expanded to cover 9,000 companies. Data provided include the director and senior executives, description of business activities, brand names and trademarks, branches and subsidiaries, number of employees, financial information for the past two years, principal shareholders, and date of the company's establishment. The 8½-by-12-inch format is composed of 1,330 pages. Companies are organized under countries, and this is followed by an index that alphabetically lists all companies, an alphabetic index to companies within each country, and business activity index, including CIS code listing. The paper and binding are above average, and the print size is adequate for a directory. The book will be useful for anyone doing business in this part of the world and should be an excellent reference for most major libraries.—**Herbert W. Ockerman**

Handbooks and Yearbooks

361.   **Argentina Company Handbook: Data on Major Listed Companies.** 1995/96 ed. Rio de Janeiro, IMF Editoria; distr., Austin, Tex., Reference Press, 1995. 86p. index. $34.95pa. ISBN 1-57311-006-X.

The handbook gives concise factual coverage on each of 32 major companies in the Balsa de Comercio de Buenos Aires (BCBA, Buenos Aires Stock Exchange). The small-sized format is packed with general information on Argentina: basic information, a computer-produced map, the political background, an economic overview, and an analysis of the Argentine economy from January 1994 to June 1995. The text reviews Argentina's securities market and the stock market performance in 1994.

The data of the stock market are in a table format that lists the 32 companies and what sector each belongs to with market capitalization, net income, EDS and price/book ratios, and index participation. In addition, the Merval Index, Burcap Index, and Value Index are explained. Most comprehensive information and data on public companies come from reports of Standard & Poor's Corporation records, stock reports, stock guide, and market scope. A comprehensive review of the Argentine stock market is provided, which is needed if the user wants to participate in the BCBA.

Each company's data are organized in a large table in alphabetic order by sector: banking, beverages, carports, cement, electric power, food, gas distribution, holding, iron and steel, paper and pulp, petroleum and petrochemical, telecommunications, textiles, and tobacco. A company index follows. The company table gives background, officers, number of shares, affiliations of market and competition, major stockholders, per share data, a balance sheet, income statement data, and ratios for the three years from June 1992 to June 1994.

A handy little guide for the international business investor, the handbook provides analysis for those who do not have *Moody's International Manual*. It is affordable and should be in Latin American business collections.—**Gerald D. Moran**

362.   **Consumer Latin America 2001.** 8th ed. Chicago, Euromonitor International, 2001. 499p. $970.00pa. ISBN 0-86338-984-8.

Latin America is a very important emerging market and this Euromonitor guide covers the consumer and socioeconomic world of Argentina, Brazil, Chile, Colombia, Mexico, and Venezuela. It does not cover the entire Central and South American region. This lack of coverage is a decided failure for such a statistical handbook. Also, the data would be much more effectively used if it were in a digital format. Nevertheless, the print guide format gives regional commentary with statistics derived from national, international, and Euromonitor sources. The written commentary provides important factors driving the six countries' economies.

Businesses, investors, and students of international business will find this expensive handbook useful, but not essential. It has tables on consumer products (e.g., food, drinks, domestic electrical appliances) and it covers demographics, economic indicators, standards of living, household characteristics, advertising and media access, retail distribution, consumer expenditures, and service industries of the six countries listed above. This edition is not an essential purchase if a recent edition is at hand. Truly there is nothing new in this 8th edition, although the Euromonitor series provides the best available analysis of the trading environment and statistical tables.—**Gerald D. Moran**

363. **Economic Survey of Latin America and the Caribbean, 1999-2000.** By the UCLAC Economic Development Division. New York, United Nations, 2000. 330p. $50.00pa. (w/CD-ROM). ISBN 92-1-121278-2. ISSN 0257-2184. S/N E.00.II.G.2.

This annual survey (see ARBA 2000, entry 191 and ARBA 98, entry 210, for previous reviews) that reviews regional economic conditions and reports the economic performance of 20 Latin American countries for 1999 and early 2000 remains an essential reference work for those analyzing regional economies. The 8 chapters of part 1 provide an overview of the region (e.g., macroeconomic policy, employment and wages), with chapter 8 analyzing the impact of economic reforms on the region. Figures in these chapters are expressed in U.S. dollars, with 1995 as the base year.

Part 2 consists of individual country reports arranged in alphabetic order. Each report covers general trends, economic policies (e.g., fiscal, monetary, exchange), structural reforms, and external factors (e.g., trade balances). There are numerous tables and figures to help the reader understand the significance of events and reforms. For this section, the methodology is based on national accounts statistics expressed in the local currency rather than U.S. dollars.

Using an organizational structure similar to that of previous editions, the movement from printed tables to diskettes to a CD-ROM demonstrates that the publishers are concerned about providing usable data that will assist research efforts. The report text, graphics, and extensive statistical tables on the accompanying CD-ROM can be used to create Excel spreadsheets and other analyses. While there is no index, the table of contents and list of illustrations is detailed enough for anyone. As an essential tool for achieving a broad understanding of the regional and global economies, this annual is recommended for academic libraries, particularly those serving scholars in regional studies and international business programs.—**Sandra E. Belanger**

364. **Foreign Investment in Latin America and the Caribbean, 2000.** New York, United Nations, 2001. 240p. $20.00pa. ISBN 92-1-121301-0. ISSN 0257-2184. S/N E.01.II.G.12.

This United Nations' publication covers Latin America and the Caribbean. It concentrates on regional outlook, Chili, Japan, and telecommunications. It is broken down into sections covering recent trends in foreign direct investment, strategies, agents and modalities of foreign direct investment, and national strategy on foreign direct investments. The second chapter concentrates on Chili's foreign direct investments and cooperative strategies. Chapter 3 investigates Japan's investment and cooperative strategies in Latin America and the Caribbean. Chapter 4 evaluates telecommunication, investment, and cooperative strategies. This is followed by information in boxes, tables, and figures. The book has adequate tabular material and figures to condense information presentation and to make reading easier to understand. The manuscript is adequately referenced and the writing style is easy to read and comprehend. This paperback has average paper quality and font size is adequate, with printing in a column format. Information presented is widely distributed in various publications and this is a good source for concentration of these data in the arena of Latin America and Caribbean studies. It should be in all libraries where foreign investment, international trade, and international understanding are a focus.—**Herbert W. Ockerman**

365. **Latin America and the Caribbean in the World Economy 1999-2000.** New York, United Nations, 2001. 333p. $25.00pa. ISBN 92-1-121261-8. S/N E.00.II.G.17.

The ever dramatic swings in expectations regarding the behavior of the international economy makes this analysis of the Latin American economy an informative guide. This edition is divided into four sections: "International Situation and Trends," "Trade and Trade Policy in Latin America and the Caribbean," "Regional Integration in Latin America and the Caribbean," and "World Trade Organization Imbalances and the WTO General Agreement on Trade in Services."

The international economy section covers world economy in 1999-2000, growth and structural change, the performance in 1999-2000, and world trade in 1998–1999. Part 2 covers the trade, trade policy, and market in Latin America and the Caribbean. It includes performance structure, trade in goods and services in 1998-1999, long-term trends in the 1990s, trade policy in the countries, the tariff structure, and U.S. barriers applied to trade with Latin America and the Caribbean.

Part 3 on regional integration in Latin America and the Caribbean provides recent trends, intra-regional economic relations in the 1990s, and a review of open regionalism in light of experiences in Latin America and the Asia-Pacific region. Part 4 reviews trade policy issues, including persistent asymmetries in the multilateral trade system, market access and tariff policy in the industrialized countries, and the commitments of Latin America and the Caribbean under the general agreement on trade in services. This guide is an effective annual summary of the economic trade situation for all collections dealing with Latin America and Latin American business and the price is right.—**Gerald D. Moran**

MIDDLE EAST

366.   **Consumer Middle East 2001.** Chicago, Euromonitor International, 2001. 556p. maps. $970.00pa. ISBN 0-86338-931-7.

This 556-page paperback is primarily composed of tables concerning information on the Middle East. The 1st section is an overview of the Middle East, section 2 is on regional marketing perimeters, and section 3 in on consumer markets. Section 4 covers demographics, economic indicators, standards of living, household characteristics, consumer expenditures, and service industries—including consumer markets broken down into 20 to 30 categories. The following sections cover each individual country and their consumer markets, again broken down into numerous categories. The countries covered include Egypt, Israel, Jordan, Morocco, Saudi Arabia, Tunisia, Turkey, and United Arab Emeritus.

Tables include economic growth and prospects and regional marketing perimeters, including demographics, economic indicators, standard of living, household characteristics, advertising and media access, retail distribution, consumer expenditures, and service industries. Information on consumer markets is broken down by several categories, such as food, pet food and pet care products, drinks, tobacco, household cleaning products, health care, disposable paper products, cosmetics and toiletries, leisure goods, and automobiles. The binding, paper, and print quality are average and the font size is small but adequate for its purpose. This manuscript contains a massive quantity of information on an area where sources are limited. It should be in all libraries that are considered experts in international perspective, and particularly the Middle East.—**Herbert W. Ockerman**

367.   Khan, Javed Ahmad, comp. **Islamic Economics and Finance: A Bibliography.** New York, Mansell/Cassell, 1995. 157p. index. $80.00. ISBN 0-7201-2219-8.

This bibliography covers sources in English on the disciplines of Islamic economics and finance, which are emerging as an alternative to and critique of Western practices primarily in the Arab and Islamic worlds. As such, the volume will be welcome to researchers in Middle Eastern and Islamic studies, as well as to those interested in alternative economic theories and practices. It is not annotated.

The bibliography itself is arranged into 2 main sections ("Islamic Economic Systems" and "Money, Banking and Finance") , which are in turn divided into 16 subject chapters ranging from Islamic economic alternatives and economic history of the Muslim people in the first part, through Islamic financial institutions and commercial laws in the second. Most of the material is drawn from a wide variety of specialty journals published both in the Islamic countries and in the West. An appendix contains annotations on 12 journals on Islamic economics. In addition to a detailed table of contents, there are author and subject indexes.

The work was based upon research projects undertaken by the author starting in 1990 at the Centre for West Asian Studies, Aligarh Muslim University, Aligarh, India, apparently as part of a doctoral program. This book should be strongly considered for academic research collections covering Middle Eastern and Islamic studies and alternative economics.—**Nigel Tappin**

368. **Major Companies of the Arab World 1998.** 21st ed. J. Wassall and Y. McLelland, eds. London, Graham and Whiteside; distr., Detroit, Gale, 1997. 1221p. index. $830.00. ISBN 1-86099-074-6.

This unique, well-produced, and very expensive directory lists an estimated 7,500 companies from 20 Arab countries or areas: Algeria, Bahrain, Egypt, Gaza/West Bank, Iraq, Jordan, Kuwait, Lebanon, Libya, Mauritania, Morocco, Oman, Qatar, Saudi Arabia, Somalia, Sudan, Syria, Tunisia, United Arab Emirates, and Yemen. Non-Arab Muslim countries such as Pakistan are excluded, as are non-Arab Middle Eastern countries like Israel. Data for each entry can include company name; address; local and international telephone, telex, and fax numbers; e-mail address; board of directors; management; principal business activities; trade names; major branch offices; principal banks and auditors; limited financials, such as sales, profits before and after taxes, returned profit, and earnings per share; shareholder capital; principal shareholders; date of establishment; private or public status; and number of employees.

Data are submitted without charge by companies who meet one of seven criteria, which include sales, national importance, prominence of directors or shareholders, new market players, major importers and exporters, or large branches of multinational corporations. There is a blue section in which SIC/activity and alphabetic-by-country indexes are provided. These are in a more easy-to-read format than indexes in most business directories of this size. No print equivalent exists. A CD-ROM version is available, which costs £690, or about $1,100. There are many valuable data here, although one wonders how this would compare to some of the online services available from Dun & Bradstreet or Kompass. Gale is selling this English product for $830, whereas Graham and Whiteside advertise the price as 460 pounds (about $750). This work is highly recommended for the quality of the data for all libraries serving business interests in Arab countries. Libraries with DIALOG or other computerized services and limited interest may find that on-demand searching will be more cost effective than purchasing the directory, no matter what the quality of the contents.—**Patrick J. Brunet**

10 Labor

GENERAL WORKS

Bibliography

369. Ross, John M. **Employment/Unemployment and Earnings Statistics: A Guide to Locating Data in U.S. Documents.** Lanham, Md., Scarecrow, 1996. 244p. index. $45.00. ISBN 0-8108-3099-X.

This bibliographic guide brings together references to publications issued by the U.S. government on the subjects of employment, unemployment, and earnings. It lists only documents that are issued serially or that are revised periodically. All relevant publications from the Census Bureau and the Bureau of Labor Statistics are included, but only representative samples of industry and occupation reports are cited. No single-issue reports are covered.

The three bibliographic sections (one or more chapters each) cover comprehensive reports on employment/unemployment and income/earnings data, other reports on employment or unemployment, and other reports on income/earnings. Each section is organized by frequency of publication, then lists titles alphabetically, concluding with irregularly published documents. A complete citation is given for each publication, and the highly compact annotation details the relevant labor force characteristics. Notations for title changes are given.

A three-page ready-reference guide lists publication titles, with a checklist showing coverage of geographic, ethnic, congressional district, zip code, industry, occupation, and foreign country information for employment, unemployment, and income/earnings. An entry number for each title refers the user to the bibliographic guide. The appendixes include abbreviations, a glossary, a title index, and two subject indexes. Entries in each of the subject indexes encompass occupational, industry, and geographic terms.

This guide is highly recommended for any library providing information on employment and earnings from U.S. government publications. This valuable resource will provide a useful entrée into the extensive data published by the U.S. government, and even those familiar with the structure of government publications will find it to be a time-saver.—**Joan B. Fiscella**

370. Stern, Robert N., and Daniel B. Cornfield, with Theresa I. Liska and Dee Anne Warmath. **The U.S. Labor Movement: References and Resources.** New York, G. K. Hall/Simon & Schuster Macmillan, 1996. 356p. index. (Reference Publications on American Social Movements). $40.00. ISBN 0-8161-7277-3.

The U.S. Labor Movement is a useful annotated bibliography of literature published on the U.S. labor movement since World War II. This reference work reflects the multiple disciplines that have an interest in this subject, including economics, political science, and psychology. There is, however, a distinctly sociological bent to the volume, reflecting the background of its authors.

The book lists more than 1,200 entries in 9 chapters. The first chapter provides an overview of the work, and the remaining eight chapters divide the literature reviewed into topical areas. These areas include social movement theory, the organizational structure of the labor movement, movement mobilization, labor and politics, the impact of the labor movement on social inequality, antilabor countermovements, the labor movement in relation to other social movements, and data sources and reference works. The chapters are divided into subtopics, with each section of a chapter beginning with a brief essay. The entries are arranged alphabetically, and each entry includes a synopsis of the source. Author and subject indexes are included. This work is highly recommended for academic libraries and for scholars interested in the U.S. labor movement.—**Paul F. Clark**

371. Switzer, Teri R. **Telecommuters, The Workforce of the Twenty-First Century: An Annotated Bibliography.** Lanham, Md., Scarecrow, 1997. 176p. index. $34.00. ISBN 0-8108-3210-0.

This book is an annotated bibliography on telecommuting, with its primary focus on telecommuting as an alternative to working in the traditional office. Some citations are to articles about home business. There are 649 entries organized into 7 chapters from a variety of sources, mostly magazines. The first 3 chapters on monographs, general issues, and management and human resource issues have 337 entries. Then come chapters on environmental, legal, and tax concerns; telecommuting programs (articles that discuss different real-life applications of working away from the traditional office); and hardware and software issues. The last chapter, on telecommuting resources, is broken down into sections on magazines, tapes, videos, and newsletters; directories; Internet resources; selected World Wide Web engines; selected Websites; reports, policies, and procedures; consultants; associations; and companies with telecommuters. The entries are largely dated in the late 1980s and early 1990s; the most recent were published in 1995. This book is likely to become dated quickly because the subject matter is rapidly changing, with relevant articles being published frequently. Libraries that allow patrons to use indexes and Internet access may not find this bibliography especially valuable.—**J. E. Weaver**

Dictionaries and Encyclopedias

372. Docherty, James C. **Historical Dictionary of Organized Labor.** Lanham, Md., Scarecrow, 1996. 357p. (Historical Dictionaries of Religions, Philosophies, and Movements, no.10). $54.00. ISBN 0-8108-3181-3.

The intent of this volume is to allow readers "to know what has been achieved by organized labor in the advanced countries" (p. vii). It is not meant to be encyclopedic in coverage. The author's objectives are threefold: to make the subject accessible, to show the variety of labor studies, and to encourage a greater international outlook on the topic. His efforts are successful in all three areas.

The book includes the editor's foreword, a preface, a list of acronyms, an introduction to organized labor, 277 entries, a glossary, a chronology, union membership statistics, and a bibliography. The author has somewhat subjectively, and (admittedly) with bias toward his native Australia, selected 277 entries covering countries, labor organizations, major labor unions, leaders, ideas, political parties, and changes in composition of union membership. The scope is international and historic. Entries range from one paragraph to three or four pages in length—succinct but informative. Each entry is supported by the extensive bibliography. Most of the bibliographic entries are annotated.

Docherty has incorporated a vast amount of information into a small volume. This dictionary will be valuable to the beginner and useful to almost anyone, including specialists in the field. It is recommended for academic libraries.—**Joanna M. Burkhardt**

373.   **JIST's Electronic Enhanced Dictionary of Occupational Titles.** 2d ed. [CD-ROM]. Indianapolis, Ind., JIST Works, 1997. Minimum system requirements: IBM or compatible 386SX with Intel or Pentium processor (486DX recommended). CD-ROM drive. Windows 3.0. 4MB RAM. VGA monitor (SVGA preferred). Mouse. Windows-compatible printer. $295.00.

JIST's Electronic Enhanced Dictionary of Occupational Titles combines the information of four familiar occupational resources—*Dictionary of Occupational Titles* (DOT; see ARBA 79, entry 855), *Guide for Occupational Exploration* (see entry 449), *Occupational Outlook Handbook* (OOH; see entry 402), and the *Worker Traits Data Book* (WTDB; JIST Works, 1994)—on one CD-ROM. The DOT covers 12,741 jobs, whereas the OOH information encompasses 250 occupations from the 1996-1997 edition and includes a color photograph of a worker performing a task from that job. Military jobs are divided by branch of service and are listed with the civilian equivalent. Clicking on one of the jobs takes the user to the DOT information with links to the OOH and the WTDB. The user may look up information in this resource through five choices: DOT numbering system, GOE interest groups, OOH clusters, military occupations, and the general search function. The search function allows for multiple criteria and the use of operators to narrow the search; it also provides a list of available words and allows searches to be saved.

Cross-references are extensive. With any occupation, the researcher may click at the top of the entry for related information within the other resources. Related jobs listed at the end of the article may also be clicked for a direct link to information on that job. With the Back, Home, Print, and Exit buttons, it is easy to flip back and forth between the entries. The print function gives the user the ability to print any of the occupational reports. Program information from the main menu provides sources used, ways to use the program, and information about the program plus additional content from the DOT, the OOH, and the WTDB. This electronic resource will be useful for students researching occupations or the job market, as well as for counselors and employment professionals.—**Elaine Ezell**

374.   Kushner, Michael G., Virginia L. Briggs, and Michael J. Schinabeck. **Employee Benefits Desk Encyclopedia: An Annotated Compendium of Frequently Used Terms.** Washington, D.C., BNA Books, 1996. 245p. $95.00pa. ISBN 0-57018-005-9.

This reference provides in-depth explanations of more than 500 key terms in the area of employee benefits. It includes citations to statutory and regulatory references to both the Employee Retirement Income Security Act (ERISA) and the Internal Revenue code, as well as citations to rulings, case law, and treatises. The entries also use minimal legalese jargon; they are written in layperson's English, easily understood even by the novice. Common acronyms (such as ADA, COLA, FICA, FMLA, HMO, IRA, and RIF) are listed, along with many unfamiliar ones used in this specialized area of the law (such as ADEA, GULP, and ISO). Some of the general topics of employee benefits covered are insurance, securities, compensation, retirement, and health care. All three authors are lawyers who have written or edited books and articles on federal taxation. This reference work would be especially useful as a learning tool to people new to this area of the law, as well as a ready-reference to those who work in this area. It is recommended for large public and academic libraries.—**George A. Meyers**

375.   Murray, R. Emmett. **Lexicon of Labor: More Than 500 Key Terms, Biographical Sketches, and Historical Insights Concerning Labor in America.** New York, New Press, 1998. 207p. $13.95pa. ISBN 1-56584-456-4.

The *Lexicon of Labor* is basically a short, 1-volume encyclopedia of the American labor movement. It has more than 500 entries and provides concise definitions of commonly used labor terms, sketches of important labor figures, descriptions of labor organizations, and information about key events in labor history. Although not comprehensive, this volume's listings are representative and, taken together, they provide a reasonable introduction to American labor. Its value would appear, however, to be greatest to those with little knowledge or background in the subject. In this sense the book would seem to be most useful as a reference work for high school and college students, news reporters, and members of the general public, as opposed to scholars and professionals involved in labor-related work.—**Paul F. Clark**

Directories

376.   Betrus, Michael. **The Guide to Executive Recruiters.** new ed. New York, McGraw-Hill, 1997. 874p. index. $25.95pa. ISBN 0-07-006280-3.

More than 6,000 recruiting firms in the United States are listed in this geographically arranged work. Each entry gives contact information, minimum salary placed, and recruiting specialty. Useful indexes follow the main body of the work: by industry (64 classifications) and by company name. Short chapters at the beginning of the book outline the process of working with recruiters and suggest that the job-hunter will have more success using a contingency firm (rather than a retained firm); however, in the entries that follow, there is no indication of the firm's status. Furthermore, no information as to how and when this information was gathered is described.

This book may be compared to *The Directory of Executive Recruiters* (10th ed.; BNA Books, 2002), which gives information on 4,400 firms. These entries include more information and are listed alphabetically by company under two main headings: retainer firms and contingency firms. Five indexes assist users to further narrow their search: industry, functions, geography, key principal, and company name.

For an executive job-hunter, the directory is preferable, but with a few improvements, the guide could be just as helpful. An exhaustive collection will want both titles.—**Juleigh Muirhead Clark**

377.   **Directory of U.S. Labor Organizations.** 2001 ed. Court Gifford, ed. Washington, D.C., BNA Books, 2001. 290p. index. $95.00pa. ISBN 1-57018-280-9.

Well conceived and thoughtfully executed, this volume is the premier sourcebook for directory information on U.S. labor organizations. The work is organized into four parts. The introduction consists of statistics and background information on U.S. labor organizations. Part 2 contains directory information on the AFL-CIO and its departments, affiliate organizations, regions offices, state federations, and central labor councils. Part 3 is an alphabetic list of international, national, and state trade unions found in the United States. In addition to standard directory-type information, this part includes membership data for each organization, the year of their foundation, the name of their newsletter, and the date and city of their next convention. Part 4, containing slightly more than half of the directory, is an alphabetic listing by state of local, intermediate, and independent unions. The balance of this reference work contains appendixes with statistics and statements on reporting requirements of unions as mandated by the U.S. government. An index of all the labor organizations included, an index of officers and key staff personnel mentioned within, and a Website index bring the work to a conclusion.

The audience for this directory includes U.S. labor unions, corporations and entities with a heavy concentration of unionized workers, and labor-management think tanks. All large and mid-sized public libraries will need this directory, as will large and mid-sized academic libraries with business collections.—**Dene Clark**

378.   Gove, Thomas P. **The Best Directory of Recruiters.** 4th ed. Dracut, Mass., Gove Publishing, 1996. 814p. index. $39.99pa. ISBN 0-9636121-2-3.

379.   Gove, Thomas P. **The Best Directory of Recruiters On-Line.** Dracut, Mass., Gove Publishing, 1996. 228p. $34.99pa. ISBN 0-9636121-6-6.

Two sections, by industry and by geography, form the major portion of these directories of recruiters. Recruiters pay fees to be listed. Entries include e-mail and homepage addresses, contact and company names, addresses, telephone numbers, and recruitment specialties; however, not all information is provided for each entry. A firm's full listing is available in each of its specialty areas and its geographic section. Directory introductory material contains information about recruiters' roles and how to interact with recruiters, both as a potential candidate and as a recruiting company, as well as a brief guide to using each resource. The concluding eight career resource appendixes are advertisements, four of which are for companies affiliated with Gove.

The Best Directory of Recruiters (BDR), with more than 5,500 recruiting companies listed, is organized alphabetically by company name within each category. *The Best Directory of Recruiters On-Line* (RON), with more than 1,100 recruiters listed, is organized similarly, but each entry begins with an e-mail address; this arrangement does not promote easy lookup. The single index of BDR is a list of recruiter names referring to the state location of the full entry. RON has e-mail and homepage address indexes; the former has no apparent use, as it does not refer to a full listing or even a recruiter name.

BDR is a potentially useful resource for libraries that support job seeking or personnel recruitment activities, the lack of company names and addresses in a small percentage of cases notwithstanding. RON, a subset of BDR, is not recommended as a print work, due to its lack of effectiveness as a reference or a lookup tool. A check of selected homepage addresses indicated numerous missing files or incorrect server addresses, not unexpectedly given the rate of change in electronic communications. This same volatility raises the question of the worth of a directory organized around such information.

Both directories indicate that a computer disk is available, but it was not provided for review. BDR would be more useful on disk, particularly with an interface that allows searching by any of the fields within the individual entry, and with the possibility of changing information as necessary.—**Joan B. Fiscella**

380.   **Hoover's Directory of Human Resources Executives 1996.** Austin, Tex., Reference Press, 1995. 421p. index. $39.95pa. ISBN 1-878753-97-5.

Another in the series of Hoover's business directories, this employment-oriented book includes entries for 5,000-plus public companies with annual sales of more than $500 million or at least 5,000 employees. The directory is organized by state, then by company, in alphabetic order. Each company entry lists the highest-ranking officer of human resources, the number of employees, and the number of jobs added or eliminated the previous year, as well as basic directory information. An icon indicates the availability, by fax, of an in-depth profile of the company; there is a charge for the company profile.

The directory also provides two rankings of companies: the largest companies, by state, and the biggest job creators. Indexes by company name, by industry, by human resource executive names, and by metropolitan area increase the usefulness of the directory. An introduction explains how the information was gathered and suggests how to make effective use of the directory.

The names of human resources executives and the jobs census make this directory particularly valuable for those interested in charting directions for career planning. The numbers of new jobs are suggestive rather than solid, however, because it is not clear whether the numbers indicate new jobs or new hires for open positions. The book is easily readable thanks to significant white space and the judicious use of bold typeface. Reasonably priced, *Hoover's* will be useful in public, academic, and corporate libraries. Its one drawback is that some pages began to tear out during the review; if this is typical, the binding will not stand up to heavy use. [R: Choice, May 96, p. 1450; RBB, 1 April 96, pp. 1388-1389]—**Joan B. Fiscella**

381.   **Internships 2002.** Lawrenceville, N.J., Peterson's Guides, 2001. 719p. index. $26.95pa. ISBN 0-7689-0697-0. ISSN 1082-2577.

This directory, an annual volume, updates the information on thousands of short-term, learning-oriented positions in many career fields. The fields are broad and include arts; health care/social assistance; manufacturing; and information, professional/scientific, and technical services. For each entry, the sponsor is fully identified with a brief description of the nature of the organization, followed by the internships available and the benefits anticipated for the intern. Generally, the listing identifies the number of positions, the nature of the work, and skills required.

Introductory material includes extensive information describing the internship experience in general, how to apply for an internship, and what sponsors are seeking from interns. The Smithsonian, the computer industry, and international internships are singled out for in-depth chapters, focusing on their unique possibilities. Indexes, invaluable in a source like this, include geographic, field of interest, and academic level. Lists of paid internships and those that have the possibility of permanent employment are also included.

The extensive material included is very compacted and requires the ability to cross-reference to the various sections to find what is needed. Yet it is not the kind of tool that career and guidance counselors would peruse. Rather, it is intended for the strongly motivated internship-seeker who is willing to expend some time to glean the most salient information needed. The long history of this volume has given a base of experience and interest, particularly in academe, to perpetuate its use.—**Barbara Conroy**

382.   **The JobBank Guide to Employment Services 1998-1999.** Steven Graber and others, eds. Holbrook, Mass., Adams Publishing, 1997. 429p. index. $200.00. ISBN 1-55850-826-0.

This employment guide is published every other year by Adams Publishing, known for its annual "companion directory" to this guide, *The National JobBank* (see entry 400), and dozens of geographic-specific JobBank series titles, as well as other job-related titles. This is the 6th edition of *The JobBank Guide to Employment Services*, and it provides information on more than 5,000 employment service firms. The employment services are listed alphabetically by state and then by agency type within each state in the 1st section and listed by more than 70 specializations in the 2d section. The work distinguishes agencies that offer services under one or more categories of these five types of employment services: temporary employment agencies, permanent employment agencies, executive search firms, contract services firms, and career/outplacement counseling firms.

Each listing contains some or all of the following information: name of employment service; mailing address; telephone, toll-free telephone, and fax numbers; recorded job line; contact person and title or department; e-mail address; World Wide Web address; employment service profile; area of specialization; positions commonly filled; benefits available; corporate headquarters location; other area, national, and international locations; average salary range of placement; and number of placements per year. The index is arranged by specialization and by state within the specialization for optimal use. Adams Media's CareerCity Website, an electronic career center at www.careercity.com, now houses the missing résumé and cover letter advice section found in the previous edition of this guide.

Given today's increased employee mobility and the changing job market, this reference makes a welcome source for job-seekers thinking of moving or getting employment assistance in a job search just about anywhere in the country. The tool is highly recommended.—**Edward Erazo**

383. Oldman, Mark, and Samer Hamadeh. **America's Top Internships.** 1998 ed. New York, Princeton Review/Random House, 1997. 408p. $21.00pa. ISBN 0-679-78394-6.

Engagingly written by two recent college graduates who, together, have completed a total of eight internships as each acquired a bachelor and master's degree from Stanford University, this directory profiles 107 of the firms offering the best internships in the United States. To illustrate the diversity of the internships profiled, the entities range from giants in the computer field to organizations in arts management. In fact, every conceivable facet of corporate society, both for profit and nonprofit, is included. The entries range from the environmental field to fashion model management, and from public policy think tanks to television production.

The companies offering internships appear in alphabetic order by firm name. Each entry consists of three to four concisely edited pages, all in a common format. A table on the first page of each entry denotes selectivity, compensation, quality of life, location(s), fields (of endeavor), duration, prerequisites, and deadlines. A "busyword meter" for each entry appears on the same page as the table. The authors have done their homework. In most cases, a history of each firm is provided as well as a history of the firm's internship program. Past interns who have completed the programs are extensively quoted and frankly describe pluses and minuses of their experiences. A number of useful tables in the appendix categorize the 107 firms. Categories included range from "highest compensation" to "most selective," and from "internships open to graduate students" to "free housing." Other tables in the appendix list "internships of interest" and "internships by location." This work is highly recommend for all academic libraries, most secondary school libraries, and all mid-size and large public libraries.—**Dene L. Clark**

384. Oldman, Mark, and Samer Hamadeh. **The Internship Bible 2001.** New York, Princeton Review/Random House, 2001. 621p. illus. $25.00pa. ISBN 0-375-75638-8. ISSN 1073-5801.

Internships are a popular way for students to either experience or try out a field while earning college credit. This directory pulls together 850 such programs in a wide variety of companies and other organizations. Actually, as the authors admit, not all of these programs are actually internships since some, like the Peace Corps, are only available to college graduates.

Designed to appeal to young adults, the listings are interspersed with interviews with famous people about their internship experiences, profiles of other well-known former interns, lists of information, and trivia with titles such as "How to Marry a Senator" and "Caddy Shack Internship." The entries provide basic information, including the selectivity of the applicant pool, compensation, location, fields of employment, duration of internship, deadlines to apply and how to do it, a description of the organization, and perks of the job. Comparable to Petersons' *Internships* (see entry 381) and *America's Top Internships* (see entry 383), this work is another place for students to look for that perfect internship.—**Christine E. King**

385. **Plunkett's Companion to the Almanac of American Employers: Mid-Size Firms 2000-2001.** Jack W. Plunkett, ed. Houston, Tex., Plunkett Research, 2000. 639p. index. $149.99pa. (w/CD-ROM). ISBN 1-891775-13-8.

This volume contains profiles of 500 midsize American employers (defined as those with 200 to 2,300 employees). A companion volume to the *Almanac of American Employers* (see entry 419), which covers firms with 2,300 or more employees, this resource work includes information on the types of business companies are involved in, top management officials, basic financial information (e.g., sales and profits), and the firms' potential for growth. It also includes data on executive salaries, benefits, pension plans, profit-sharing programs, and other employment practices, as well as contact information (telephone numbers, addresses, and Websites). The one-page synopses should be of particular use as a starting point for job seekers. It also could be potentially helpful as a quick reference for investors.

The 500 profiles are accompanied by 3 brief introductory chapters that focus on major trends in the American and global economies, advice to job seekers on researching companies, and important Websites for prospective employees.

A number of indexes make the volume particularly user friendly. The companies are indexed alphabetically; geographically; and by industrial sector as well as by sales volume; number of employees; and subsidiaries, brand names, and selected affiliations. Finally, the volume includes an index that classifies companies by the type of backgrounds they seek in employees. This is particularly helpful for job seekers. The volume should prove useful to most general and business libraries.—**Paul F. Clark**

386. **Plunkett's Employers' Internet Sites with Careers Information 1999-2000.** Jack W. Plunkett and others, eds. Galveston, Tex., Plunkett Research, 1998. 701p. index. $149.99pa. ISBN 1-891775-01-4.

This book is intended to facilitate online job searches by identifying which companies are posting the most useful career information on the Internet. The primary audience is the job seeker with little or no Internet experience. There are 517 companies covered. To be included, a company must have user-friendly, useful career information on its company site, must be a public U.S. company, and must be a mid-to large-size employer.

The introductory matter includes basic advice on applying for a job online and a directory of important World Wide Web job sites. Most of the work is devoted to company-specific information. Each entry is one page and companies are arranged alphabetically. A typical entry includes basic directory information, a brief description of the business, and the company's URL. A table at the top of each page tells readers if the site contains job opening data, company data, college internship or recruiting data, benefits information, and if the site is searchable. Another section provides information on how to most effectively navigate through the Website. The entry also provides information on the types of career opportunities the company generally offers. For example, under "Management" it indicates whether or not the company typically looks for "management trainees," "experienced management," "international business," or "MBA graduates."

The volume also contains some useful indexes, including industry, geographical (by state and region), and a listing of firms with international operations. Purchasers may also write to the publisher for a free diskette version of the database. As with any print directory that accepts the challenge of documenting Web resources, a reader should be concerned about the currency and accuracy of the information. This is especially true for a work whose primary intent is to provide guidance to novice Internet users about company Websites. However, the information contained in this work is useful and well organized and, with the caveat mentioned above, is recommended for libraries serving job seekers. [R: Choice, Sept 99, p. 122]—**Gordon J. Aamot**

387. **Profiles of American Labor Unions.** Donna Craft and Terrance W. Peck, eds. Farmington Hills, Mich., Gale, 1998. 1700p. index. $275.00. ISBN 0-8103-9059-0. ISSN 1099-5358.

Formerly titled the *American Directory of Organized Labor*, this new edition is reorganized and updated to include information on more than 280 parent unions, 33,000 locals, and 1,200 independent unions. Also included are nearly 800 current bargaining agreements and biographical profiles of more than 170 U.S. labor leaders from past and present.

Information about each parent union includes contact information, organizational data, key officials' names, union finances, a general description, a brief history, and present activities. A list of local, state, and regional branches linked to the parent union follows. The "Independent Unions" section includes contact and financial information and, when available, selected bargaining contracts linked to the union. There are 4 indexes: industry, geographic, key officials, and the master index. The foreword is written by United Auto Workers (UAW) president Stephen P. Yokich, who addresses the topic of labor unions at the dawn of the new millennium. This is followed by the preface, which discusses the developments in organized labor in the late 1990s, the decline in union membership, notable mergers and absorptions, a few labor disputes, and the future of labor unions. This easy-to-use source will be valuable to labor researchers, labor-law attorneys, sociologists, historians, and union personnel, and belongs in reference collections of most public and academic libraries. [R: BL, 15 Dec 98, p. 765]—**Michele Russo**

Handbooks and Yearbooks

388. **American Salaries and Wages Survey.** 5th ed. Helen S. Fisher, ed. Farmington Hills, Mich., Gale, 1999. 770p. $120.00pa. ISBN 0-7876-2428-4. ISSN 1055-7628.

This work is a compilation of 2,660 occupations and their corresponding salaries. Job titles and wage information were obtained from more than 190 federal and state government sources, trade associations, and journals. This book will be useful to those seeking jobs, employment counselors, economic planners, industry, and sociologists. It includes 48,000 entries. It covers the U.S., individual states, 113 cities, and 14 regions.

The book contains an introduction explaining its use and purpose. This is followed by an outline of contents—an alphabetic list of job titles. Next comes a geographical outline—job titles in specific geographic locations. The following section comprises the bulk of the volume. An eight-column chart lists job title, secondary occupation or industry designation, geographical locations for this title, intervals at which a wage is paid, low-mid-high wages for that job title, the source of the information, and the date the data were collected. The abbreviations key appears at the bottom of each page. There are four appendixes: organizations that contributed information, wage conversion table, abbreviations, and employment by occupation from 1996 projected to 2006. In general, job titles follow federal naming conventions. No fringe benefits are included in salaries listed. The editor provided the caveat that the data are compiled from a large number of sources. No attempt was made to standardize the data. Fisher warns readers to use care in making data interpretations. Information is clearly presented and easy to use. Having all these data compiled in one place is very convenient. Geographical listings and projections into the future make this an excellent planning tool.—**Joanna M. Burkhardt**

389. Buckley, John F. **Multistate Payroll Guide.** New York, Panel, 1996. 1v. (various paging). $145.00pa. ISBN 1-56706-309-8.

Over time, public policy concerning the employment relationship has expanded significantly. This is particularly the case in the payroll and tax area, where state laws have become increasingly complex. The *Multistate Payroll Guide* was compiled to guide practitioners through the tangled web of legislation addressing this issue. Information in this comprehensive volume is organized in a concise and user-friendly format that allows the reader to find how each state treats several different payroll issues. The issues include wages and hours, employee benefit requirements, unemployment compensation, benefits and unemployment compensation taxation, payroll administration, calculation of income, state withholding and reporting requirements, and workers' compensation laws. The guide is a valuable reference work that brings together widely dispersed information. It is recommended for business, law, and professional libraries.—**Paul F. Clark**

390.   Derks, Scott. **Working Americans 1880-1999, Volume 1: The Working Class.** Lakeville, Conn., Grey House Publishing, 2000. 558p. illus. maps. $125.00. ISBN 1-891482-81-5.

This volume is the first of a series that looks at the lifestyles, work experiences, and economic conditions of different strata of American society during the period 1880 to 1999. This volume focuses on the working class; a future volume will explore the middle class.

Using government surveys, social worker histories, economic data, family diaries, and newspaper and magazine accounts, this volume provides a fascinating look at the experiences of the American working class. Each chapter examines one decade (except for the first, which covers 1880 to 1899). The chapters contain detailed accounts of the lives of three to five families. Altogether the volume looks at 72 families, 34 occupations, and more than 25 ethnic groups. These accounts are drawn from all geographic regions of the United States.

The accounts of the families make compelling reading. The overview of the decade that begins each chapter and the economic profile provided for each decade are useful for setting the context of the lives of the families examined. But it is the accounts of each family's experiences that make for the most compelling reading. Although existing sources contain the economic data and major events of the decades covered, this volume is unique in that it puts a human face on the statistics. Among the issues addressed for the families are diet, clothing, entertainment, social customs, religious practices, pay, and working conditions. Each family profile also provides great insight into the manner in which the challenges and struggles of working-class families has changed across the decades.

The volume "promises to enhance our understanding of the growth and development of the working class over more than a century." It capably fulfills this promise. This work will be a valuable tool for both researchers and educators. It is recommended for all types of libraries. [R: LJ, July 2000, p. 76; Choice, Nov 2000, p. 511; BL, Aug 01, p. 2174]—**Paul F. Clark**

391.   Derks, Scott. **Working Americans 1880-1999, Volume 2: The Middle Class.** Lakeville, Conn., Grey House Publishing, 2001. 591p. illus. index. $125.00. ISBN 1-891482-72-6.

In *Working Americans* Derks tells the story of American workers decade by decade from 1880 until the end of the twentieth century. This volume focuses on middle class professionals and small businessmen. Each section covers a decade and is comprised of a brief introduction; profiles of three middle class families including life at home, at work, and in the community; data on family budgets (per capita expenditures); and excerpts from contemporary periodicals and advertisements from the period. "Historical Snapshots" highlight important contemporary events and an "Economic Profile" lists wages for selected occupations and prices for an assortment of goods. The occupations of the families chosen for profile are a very eclectic mixture: a Texas cattle rancher, the manager of an Alaskan salmon cannery, the owner of a small dress manufacturing company that sells to Sears Roebuck, an Air Force captain from Kansas, an African American reporter from Pennsylvania, and a female automotive engineer from New Jersey. Altogether, 76 families are profiled covering 32 occupations, including a variety of ethnic groups from urban and rural locations across the United States.

Rather than being a comprehensive survey of middle class American workers, this work is primarily an impressionistic account of each decade as seen through details of the lives of a few families supplemented with some period background material, news accounts, photographs, and advertisements. As such, it is revealing and brings to light the family life and working experience of some middle class families and professionals. [R: LJ, 15 June 01, p. 62; BL, Aug 01, p. 2174]—**Peter Zachary McKay**

392.   **Enhanced Occupational Outlook Handbook.** 3d ed. J. Michael Farr and LaVerne L. Ludden, comps. Indianapolis, Ind., JIST Works, 2000. 849p. index. $37.95pa. ISBN 1-56370-802-7; 1-56370-801-9pa.

This complex, but useful, handbook combines information from the *Occupational Outlook Handbook* (see entry 402), the *Dictionary of Occupational Titles* (4th ed.; see ARBA 93, entry 301), and the latest Occupational Information Network (O*NET) information. The introduction explains the content and use of the book in fine detail. An essay on jobs of the future, with data taken from the *Occupational Outlook Handbook, 2000-2001*, follows the introduction. The essay covers population, the labor force, education and training, employment, fast growing jobs, and total job openings. The bulk of the volume contains job descriptions for 253 jobs.

Listings include the job title or name, the O*NET number(s), the nature of the work, working conditions, employment opportunities, training, other qualifications and advancement, job outlook, earnings, related occupations, and sources of additional information. These data are followed by a list of related O*NET occupations and descriptions and a list of related *Dictionary of Occupational Titles* jobs and descriptions. Jobs with common tasks, such as "Manager" or "Supervisor" are grouped together, regardless of the specific job area, as many of the qualifications are repetitive.

Appendix A includes a list of the *Dictionary of Occupational Titles* positions not described, giving the title of the job and the numeric listing for the job in the *Dictionary of Occupational Titles*. Appendix B provides information for occupations not studied in detail in this work. There is an index of jobs in alphabetic order. Overall, there are descriptions of 2,700 jobs. While this volume is complex and it will take a few minutes to learn how to use it, it will be useful for employers writing job descriptions and for job-seekers wanting to write résumés, prepare for interviews, and make career plans. It is recommended for reference collections with career related materials.
—**Joanna M. Burkhardt**

393.   Exter, Thomas G. **The Official Guide to American Incomes.** 2d ed. Ithaca, N.Y., New Strategist, 1996. 364p. index. $89.95. ISBN 1-885070-00-4.

This 2d edition, a useful, reasonably priced statistical compendium, contains current and historical statistics from U.S. government and private sources. The 300 clear, concise tables represent unpublished (50 percent), census Website (27 percent), and author-calculated (5 percent) 1994 data, with some tables reflecting trends since the late 1960s or mid-1970s. The introductory material focuses on major demographic trends and data importance but fails, like the 1st edition (see ARBA 94, entry 283), to explain how the data have been analyzed. Following the structure adopted previously, each chapter offers a brief introduction, highlights several results, and presents tables in nine topical areas (e.g., consumer spending, poverty results) for the United States, with some regional data. A detailed list of tables, a brief glossary, and a topical index complete the volume.

Some of the problems noted with the 1st edition have been addressed; for example, some tables now include Asians/Pacific Islanders. Although patrons will be delighted with access to hard-to-find numbers, the presentation relies too heavily on demographic jargon and poor indexing. The list of tables more clearly defines the content than the index, which fails to incorporate more general terminology and to refer users from those terms to demographic jargon that has not been defined in the glossary. [R: Choice, Mar 97, p. 1146]—**Sandra E. Belanger**

394.   **Grievance Guide.** 10th ed. Washington, D.C., BNA Books, 2000. 464p. $55.00pa. ISBN 1-57018-217-5.

The goal of this book, which was first published in 1959, is to help both management and labor advocates understand and anticipate possible rulings in labor arbitration. While arbitration awards do not set binding precedent, most arbitrators take them into consideration. Rulings tend to follow a general pattern. In this volume, BNA tracks those general patterns in several categories: discharge and discipline (both general and specific); safety and health; seniority and its application; leaves of absence; promotions; vacations; holidays; health and welfare benefits; management rights; union rights, strikes, and lockouts; union security; checkoff; and wages and hours. The 10th edition includes rulings in new areas such as sexual harassment, drug testing, AIDS, off-duty misconduct, and job evaluation.

In each of these categories key materials have been compiled from BNA's Labor Relations Reference File. Each category includes an overview, summaries of cases with issues and distinctions noted, a policy guide summary, and an application of policy summary with examples and guidelines.

This book is an invaluable guide for both labor and management. It provides a wide range of examples in the most common areas of grievance, giving both sides a quick reference to rulings and the rationale behind those rulings.—**Joanna M. Burkhardt**

395. **Handbook of U.S. Labor Statistics 1999: Employment, Earnings, Prices, Productivity, and Other Labor Data.** 3d ed. Eva E. Jacobs and Kendall J. Golladay, eds. Lanham, Md., Bernan Associates, 1999. 380p. index. $65.00pa. ISBN 0-89059-182-2. ISSN 1526-2553.

In its 3d edition, the *Handbook of U.S. Labor Statistics* provides a lot of information on population; employment and unemployment by industry; hourly and weekly earnings; consumer and producer prices; export and import prices; consumer expenditures by household type; employment costs; productivity; employment benefits; and other labor data that will be useful to those in business, labor, health care, or the social sciences. Besides current data, the handbook contains both historical data (some back to 1913) on labor market trends and projections of future employment by industry and occupation to 2006. Among the new features in this edition are annual data on employment and unemployment in families, data on employee tenure with current employer, wages and employment by detailed occupation, and union affiliation by industry.

The introductory articles summarize the new Standard Occupational Classification and the revision of the standards for the classification of federal data by race and ethnicity. The tables are organized by subject matter, with each section preceded by descriptions of data sources, definitions, and methodology. The primary focus is on national data, but some of the statistics are by state and city. There are also some international comparisons. The scope and depth of information provided make this an indispensable volume for any library.—**Michele Russo**

396. **JIST's Multimedia Occupational Outlook Handbook.** 2d ed. [CD-ROM]. Indianapolis, Ind., JIST Works, 1997. Minimum system requirements: IBM or compatible 386. CD-ROM drive. Windows 3.1. 8MB RAM. SVGA 640 x 480 pixels, 256-color monitor. Mouse. Printer (for printing). $295.00.

Based on the *Occupational Outlook Handbook* (see entry 402) published every two years by the U.S. Department of Labor, this CD-ROM program is a user-friendly alternative for students who like to use computers rather than books to find information. The Main Menu presents three options: Search by Occupational Cluster, Search Alphabetically, and Search by Custom Criteria. When one chooses Search by Occupational Cluster, a screen then presents a number of clusters, such as "Administrative Support, Including Clerical," "Construction Trades," or "Service Occupations." If one clicks on "Professional Specialty Occupations," the next screen offers "Teachers, Librarians, Counselors, etc." After selecting that, the next screen offers "Adult Education Teachers," "Archivists and Curators," "College and University Faculty," "Counselors," "Librarians," and "Special Education Teachers." Thus, each broad cluster has been subdivided into individual professions.

Information offered for each profession chosen includes nature of the work, working conditions, employment, education/training, job outlook, earnings, related occupations, and more information sources. There are buttons for Back, Print, Help, and To Menu at each step. When Print is selected, all of the above information is printed rather than only the most recent, a sad lesson learned after getting 35 pages of print-out.

When the user selects Search Alphabetically, a screen appears that has a large button for every letter in the alphabet. If one is interested in finding information about veterinarians, one can click on the V button and the list of all occupations beginning with the letter "V" appears. Clicking on the desired profession will then lead to the information described in the above paragraph. When one selects Search by Custom Criteria, there are three lists from which choices must be made: "Minimum Earning Requirements," "Job Growth Outlook," and "Education/Training Requirements." Based upon the choices made, a list of professions meeting all three combined criteria appears. From there, one may click on any one of those to go to the primary information for that profession. If no profession meets all three criteria, such a message is given and one must adjust choices.

Other content of the program includes "Tomorrow's Jobs," which presents highlights of the Bureau of Labor Statistics projections of industry and occupational employment and the labor force; "Sources of Career Information," which identifies selected sources of information about occupations and career planning, counseling, training and education, and financial aid; "Finding a Job and Evaluating a Job Offer," which includes a list of where to learn about job openings; "Occupational Information Included in the Handbook," which is an overview of how the occupational descriptions are organized; "Data for Occupations," which presents summary data on 79 additional occupations for which employment projections are prepared, but for which detailed occupational information is not developed; and "Assumptions and Methods," which describes the steps by which the Bureau arrives at employment projections. Although this version claims to be multimedia, it is modest in such features as color and a voice speaking information when a new screen is first encountered. This lack of graphics is somewhat disappointing, as the earlier edition showed video clips of workers engaged in various occupations.

Although the same basic information can be obtained in the print version, it is important to provide students with electronic research tools. Because the information is authoritative and thorough, is presented in an easy-to-use format, and covers a subject widely studied across the curriculum, this disc is a good reference program that belongs in any library serving youth or job-seeking adults.—**Dana McDougald**

397.   Jupina, Andrea A. **The Recruiter's Research Blue Book.** 2d ed. Fitzwilliam, N.H., Kennedy Information, 2000. 422p. $179.00pa. ISBN 1-885922-61-2.

The cover of this resource states this book is "a how-to guide for researchers, search consultants, corporate recruiters, small business owners, venture capitalists and line executives." That pretty much covers the landscape, although the focus of the first section of 167 pages (in 26 short chapters) is on the process of researching and recruiting executives by professional recruiting consultants or company human resources departments. These chapters cover the executive search process, such as creating a working library, identifying plant locations, finding information on privately held companies, prospecting calls and telephone interviews, and checking references.

The second section is an annotated bibliography of print and Web resources for over 220 categories such as apparel, Canada, fax numbers, marketing, publishers' Websites, and video. Some categories have only one listing while others go on for several pages. Sources may be repeated in certain sections, such as the *Encyclopedia of Association*'s appearance under both "Conferences" and "Associations." The annotations are generally kept to paragraph length, with some descriptions being direct quotes from publisher information. Detailed ordering information is also included. In some instances this attention to ordering information resulted in that being the only annotation given, such as for each of the *Marquis Who's Who* biographies.

Overall this would be an excellent source for its intended audience of recruiting professionals. Academic and public libraries may not find it as necessary a purchase since the sources listed are covered in standard bibliographies. Recommended for special libraries and large research collections. [R: Choice, Oct 2000, pp. 310-312]—**Gerald L. Gill**

398.   **Key Indicators of the Labour Market 1999.** Washington, D.C., International Labour Office, 1999. 600p. illus. maps. $99.95pa. ISBN 92-2-110833-3.

This is a new volume of statistics from the International Labor Organization (ILO). The ILO considers this a "living data set" that will be refined and expanded over time. There are 17 key indicators of the labor market (KILM) now: labor force participation rate, employment-to-population ratio, status in employment, employment by sector, part-time workers, hours of work, urban informational sector employment, unemployment, long-term unemployment, unemployment by educational attainment, time-related underemployment, inactivity rate, educational attainment and illiteracy, real manufacturing wage indexes, hourly compensation costs, labor productivity and unit labor costs, and poverty and income distribution. The countries are put into six groups based on development and geography. As many countries as possible are included, from 29 to more than 200, depending upon the indicator. Years covered varies with KILM and country. There is a discussion on how to use the specific indicator, highlights of the data presented, definitions and sources of data, and limitation to comparability across countries. The tables have detailed notes. There are appendixes that provide background indicators and availability of KILM data. It is likely to become an important, basic source on the world's labor markets.—**J. E. Weaver**

399.   Lencsis, Peter M. **Workers Compensation: Reference and Guide.** Westport, Conn., Greenwood Press, 1998. 173p. index. $59.95. ISBN 1-56720-174-1.

Workers compensation in the United States is a simple concept in theory, but complex in practice. State, territorial, and federal laws are not uniform and questions frequently arise as to whether "payments are due from workers compensation as opposed to general liability insurance, health insurance, disability insurance, automobile no-fault, Social Security, Medicare, and other sources." In this guide to workers compensation, the author does a superb job of sorting out these distinctions. He writes in a simple, direct manner that is comprehensible to the layperson yet respectful of the legal principles and their ramifications.

Lencsis begins his work by tracing the history of workers compensation in Europe, England, and the United States and follows this with forerunner legislation on the federal level in the United States. From here he goes on to discuss current coverage in state and federal workers compensation laws as well as benefits and claims. He then covers related topics, such as the actual insurance policy, endorsements, rates, and experience and retrospective rating. Besides discussing rating and advisory organizations, he devotes a full chapter to special funds and residual markets. The final chapter covers current trends and issues.

Jack B. Hood, Benjamin A Hardy Jr., and Harold S. Lewis Jr. authored the 2d edition of *Workers Compensation and Employee Protection Laws in a Nutshell* in West Publishing's esteemed Nutshell series in 1989. Recent developments in the field suggest that many libraries need an updated source, and Lencsis' book fills this need very well. This work is highly recommended for all law libraries, large public libraries, academic libraries with business programs, mid-size and large business firms, and students and practitioners in the workers compensation field.—**Dene L. Clark**

400. **The National JobBank 1998.** 14th ed. Michelle Roy and others, eds. Holbrook, Mass., Adams Publishing, 1997. 1099p. index. $320.00. ISBN 1-55850-825-2.

This is the 14th edition of a compendium containing more than 20,000 profiles of potential employers. The entries provide key employment information on typical job positions, principal education background required, and contact information to inquire about employment. The text is arranged alphabetically first by state and then by employer. An effort has been made to include e-mail addresses and World Wide Web site information when known. There is a modest index by major industry grouping and a list of companies arranged by states. At the back of the book is a brief, 18-page guide on how to do a job search, which should prove useful when others books on résumés and cover letters are missing from the collection. This title has proven to be useful to libraries that maintain a career guidance collection, and this new edition should be acquired because of the volatility of this type of information.—**Judith J. Field**

401. **North American Labor Markets: A Comparative Profile.** Lanham, Md., Bernan Associates and Dallas, Tex., Commission for Labor Cooperation, 1997. 137p. $35.00pa. ISBN 0-89059-070-2.

This comparative profile of labor markets in North America is the first report issued by the Secretariat of the Commission for Labor Cooperation, a body established through a supplementary accord to the North American Free Trade Agreement (NAFTA). Spanning the 11-year period from 1984 to 1995, the report presents charts and graphs comparing labor market trends in Canada, Mexico, and the United States. The charts and graphs portray similarities and differences in such basic concepts as employment, unemployment, earnings, labor productivity, income distribution, and employment benefits. The charts and graphs covering employment issues go into extensive detail by industry, occupation, gender, firm size, hours of work, nonstandard employment, part-time employment, occupational skill level, and unionization. The charts and graphs are naturally based on data furnished by agencies within the three countries that are signatories of NAFTA. Two outstanding features of the work are discussions of the data and their sources and the interpretation of the data.

Many of the data on the U.S. workforce are readily available to libraries within the United States. Aside from selected large research and academic libraries, this fact is not true for comparable data from Canada or Mexico. *North American Labor Markets* is therefore a particularly valuable tool to libraries within the United States. It should be equally valuable in Canadian and Mexican libraries. At the low retail price, all but the smallest public libraries should acquire this work as well as all academic libraries with business or social science collections.—**Dene L. Clark**

402. **Occupational Outlook Handbook.** 2000-01 ed. Lanham, Md., Bernan Associates, 2000. 554p. illus. index. $49.00pa. ISBN 0-16-050250-0.

This government document, published by the Bureau of Labor Statistics, has been published on an annual basis for the last 50 years. The *Occupational Outlook Handbook* is arranged in related occupational clusters: executive, administrative, and managerial occupations; professional and technical occupations; marketing and sales; administrative support, including clerical occupations; services, mechanics, installers, and material-moving occupations; and handlers, equipment cleaners, helpers, and laborers. Each entry describes the occupation, training, and education required; advancement possibilities; earnings; job outlook; and sources of additional information from professional organizations and associations.

Career and job search information is provided through the chapters entitled "Tomorrow's Jobs." This chapter outlines projections of the labor force, economic growth, and industry and occupational employment from 1998 to 2008. The chapter titled "Sources of Career Information" lists national, state, and local information for careers, education and training programs, and financial aid information.

The *Occupational Outlook Handbook* remains the best source for up-to-date and reliable career information. This source should be a standard for schools, college and university, and public and special libraries.—**Kay M. Stebbins**

403. **Specialty Occupational Outlook: Trade & Technical.** Joyce Jakubiak, ed. Detroit, Gale, 1996. 252p. index. $49.95. ISBN 0-8103-9645-9. ISSN 1083-4680.

This is another Gale career reference, a companion volume to *Specialty Occupational Outlook: Professions* (SOOP; see ARBA 96, entry 274). These resources are creative enhancements of career information found in the U.S. Department of Labor's *Occupational Outlook Handbook* (OOH; see entry 402), with 150 additional occupations including ultrasound technicians, bodyguards, gambling dealers, locksmiths, and nuclear reactor operators. Ten occupation areas are covered: technicians and related support; marketing and sales; administrative support; service; agriculture, forest, and related; mechanics, installers, and repairers; construction trades and extractive; production; transportation and material moving; and handlers, equipment cleaners, helpers, and laborers.

These 10 trade and technical areas contrast very much with the 3 areas used in SOOP. Each job description reviews the nature of work, the working conditions, employment, availability, training, other qualifications, advancements, job outlook, earnings, and related occupations. Each occupation has a fact box that gives the *Dictionary of Occupational Titles* reference number; preferred level of completed education; average salary; and useful information about the occupation, such as employment trends, training requirements, and industry outlook.

Although similar to the OOH, *Trade & Technical* is an essential reference for vocational/technical schools, community college libraries, and all school career centers. The price is expensive for the school market, but it is still a reasonable cost for grades 9 and up. The OOH is still the essential first purchase. [R: Choice, May 96, p. 1458]—**Gerald D. Moran**

404. **State Occupational Outlook Handbook.** David Bianco, ed. Detroit, Gale, 1998. 759p. index. $95.00. ISBN 0-7876-1705-9. ISSN 1096-2859.

This reference work is a useful compilation of state-level market information. It includes information on an average of 600 occupations for each state. Entries provide data on three important aspects of the labor market—outlook, wages, and employment. The outlook section for each occupation includes projected employment through the year 2005, the wages section lists the most recent wage and salary levels, and the employment section provides the number of individuals currently employed in that occupation. A useful index of occupations by states makes the handbook easy to use. This handbook will be a valuable resource for virtually any library. It is highly recommended. [R: Choice, Sept 98, p. 102]—**Paul F. Clark**

405. **Statistics on Occupational Wages and Hours of Work and on Food Prices 1997. Statistiques des Salaires et de la Durée du Travail par Profession et des Prix de Produits Alimentaires. Estadisticas Sobre Salarios y Horas de Trabajo por Ocupacion y Precios.** Washington, D.C., International Labour Office, 1997. 309p. $31.50pa. ISBN 92-2-007353-6. ISSN 1020-0134.

Statistics on Occupational Wages and Hours of Work and on Food Prices, published in English, French, and Spanish, is a compilation of a worldwide study made each October by the International Labour Organization (ILO) on the subjects indicated in the title. This latest issue covers the years 1995 and 1996.

The 159 occupations and 49 industry groups covered are selected for their importance in relation to the number of workers employed, those that fall within the scope of the ILO Industrial Committees, and those seen as important in relation to certain terms of employment of workers, such as women and salaried employees, among others. The 93 food items covered represent, as much as possible, the dietary habits in countries throughout the world. This detailed study, produced by the ILO's Bureau of Labor Statistics, also carries a list of articles published by the bureau between 1990 and 1993.

Although the ILO advises care in the use of this publication, in view of the rapid expansion of globalization in manufacturing, finances, and communications, this publication is an invaluable reference source for industry, statisticians, researchers, and others interested in changing developments both at home and abroad. —**George A. Meyers**

406. **U.S. Employment Opportunities.** Denver, Colo., Washington Research Associates, 1997. 1v. (various paging). $184.00.yr. looseleaf w/binder. ISBN 0-937801-11-9. ISSN 1076-4798.

This looseleaf service attempts to provide career information for white-collar job-seekers. The information is categorized into 14 major U.S. industry groupings. The publisher supplies a year of supplements as part of the subscription price. Each industry section gives a summary of what is happening in the industry, including background information on the industry and what the employment outlook is. Most of these sections are approximately eight pages in length, except for the sections dealing with employment in the federal government and teaching, which are longer. In many of the sections, quotations from publications such as *Fortune* are furnished, but not the citation. There is nothing unique about the material provided. Part 2 of each section lists companies with a brief general description of their business and the address of their human resources office. A list of relevant periodicals and other job information services are also found here. Some of the sections are fairly comprehensive, and others are not. The reader will also note that these sections are not in alphabetical order, nor do they include World Wide Web addresses.

The introductory material includes a two-page article entitled "On-line Jobmarket Research—A Primer." Considering that the issue this reviewer evaluated was published in February 1997, this was a scanty article dealing with online employment opportunities. Since then, more sites have been developed, and many can be located by consulting the homepages of various libraries with large career centers. In contrast, librarians will find the article in the June 1997 issue of *Searcher* entitled "Job Search Sites on the Web" by Aggi Raeder very comprehensive.

Public libraries, placement services, and career counselors are always seeking new creditable career information resources; unfortunately, this is not such a resource. Only the largest career information centers should consider this item for purchase.—**Judith J. Field**

407. **Workplace Health and Safety Sourcebook.** Chad T. Kimball, ed. Detroit, Omnigraphics, 2000. 625p. index. (Health Reference Series). $78.00. ISBN 0-7808-0231-4.

Workplace health and safety are concerns of every worker and this book was written to provide information about specific topics ranging from asbestos and carbon monoxide poisoning to carpal tunnel syndrome and back injuries. The book has 53 chapters, arranged into 11 parts, including lung issues; skin and eye issues; reproductive and pregnancy issues; and child labor, workplace violence, and job stress issues. The information provided is from documents and excerpts of publications issued by several federal and state agencies and other associations (e.g., the American Medical Association and the American Cancer Society).

However, a major criticism of this title is that it is often unclear whether a chapter is a complete reprint, an excerpt, or a combination of excerpt and editorial remarks. Sometimes a footnote appears at the bottom of the first page of a chapter indicating that it is excerpted from one or more sources (but the reader never knows what information is from which source); other times, a note is under the chapter title.

The stated goal of the book is to provide information to help the layperson identify workplace hazards and ways that they can be avoided. However, the periodic change of the intended audience is problematic. For example, the intended audience at the beginning of the first chapter appears to be the worker, but later changes to physicians as it directs the reader to what should be considered when examining a patient. Other chapters seem to be directed to supervisors. Another major concern is the currency of the information collected here. Workplace safety is also a legal issue and readers must be assured of having the most up-to-date information whether they are physicians, workers, or supervisors.

The validity of some of the statements made in this title is also a concern. For example, in discussing asbestos-related lung diseases, readers are told that "there is no treatment" and "they are invariably fatal" (p. 57). A search in any medical database indicates that there are many treatments for these diseases, some of which are quite promising.

The introduction also states that this book will provide information on prevention and treatment of workplace-related disorders. Unfortunately, this is only true of some topics. While it is perhaps difficult to provide consistent types of information when compiling a sourcebook from so many different references, the editor might have done a better job of selecting sources than was done.

While certainly much of the information in this book is useful, there are too many concerns to recommend it. Most of these problems could have been prevented with more careful editing. Someone needing information on any of the topics covered in this book would be better advised to search an appropriate database.—**Michele Russo**

408.   **World Employment Report 2001: Life at Work in the Information Economy.** Washington, D.C., International Labour Office, 2001. 371p. $34.95pa. ISBN 92-2111630-1.

The *World Employment Report* explores the effects of the information and communications technologies (ICT) "revolution" on productivity, growth, employment, and disparities in income. Among mainstream government and business economists, the report is relatively critical and does not assume that these effects will automatically be positive. It does assume technological change means productivity growth with more benefit for the extreme poor (defined as those with an income less than $1 per day). Oddly, this absolute poverty definition is never adjusted for inflation, perhaps because measures of international inflation are even more problematic than those within currency blocks.

Three main issues are covered, starting with ICT changes' effects on work quality, quantity, and location. Second, whether economic development can be enhanced and poverty alleviated, or will the digital divide and the trend over recent decades of deregulation toward increased disparities in income and wealth be increased is discussed. Finally, the report examines if the dialogue amongst workers, employers, nongovernmental groups, and state representatives can steer economic change toward reducing disparities. Conclusions include an increased need for life-long learning, the likelihood of disadvantages for developing country economies and entrepreneurs, the fact that job growth will be net positive, and the fact that the ICT "revolution" can be "steered."

There is a detailed contents listing of the 10 chapters and their subsections, followed by lists of statistical annexes, 49 tables, 31 figures, and 98 issue-specific text boxes. The report is a work for academic and research libraries collecting materials on global economic and labor trends. It is well executed and is recommended.—**Nigel Tappin**

409. **World Labour Report 2000: Income Security and Social Protection in a Changing World.** Washington, D.C., International Labour Office, 2000. 321p. $34.95pa. ISBN 92-2-110831-7.

Published by the International Labour Organization, whose purpose is to promote social justice, and prepared by the Social Security Department, this report indicates where nations stand globally on income security and social protection. It also discusses the instruments that have been used for successes and failures. It looks at the challenges for the future and has demographics on social patterns that are changing the needs for social security. This volume examines trends in social security expenditures and looks at specific problems such as pensions, health care, disability, unemployment, and other benefits. It also discusses how protection might be extended to reach the population as a whole and describes restructuring to meet new needs. Gender equality is also discussed. The chapters include information on income security and social protection; demographics within family and labor markets structures; social security expenditures in the economy; existing mechanisms for social protection, such as health care, social protection during incapacity, old, age, and survivors' pension; social protection against unemployment; social benefits for parents and children; and social assistance. Future needs and prospects, including extending personal coverage, restructuring social protection systems, and the main policy conclusions, are examined. Statistical indexes include tables looking at dependency ratio, aging, fertility, child and mental immortality, life expectancy at birth, economically active population, economic development, unemployment rates, informal sector employment, poverty, income distribution, access to health services, social protection coverage, coverage of pension schemes, benefit levels, pensions, and public social security expenditure.

The volume is scattered with graphs and tables to illustrate the various points, and the reference area is adequate. This increasing globalization and trade liberalization have created greater insecurities for many individuals. This book should be of interest to people who have administrative responsibilities for these areas and also for the general public who has to live under their decisions. The report should be in all general-purpose libraries and also libraries that concentrate on labor and social security problems.—**Herbert W. Ockerman**

410. **Yearbook of Labour Statistics 1999. Anuaire des Statistiques du Travail.** 58th ed. By the International Labour Office. Washington, D.C., International Labour Office, 1999. 1353p. index. $184.00. ISBN 92-2-011651-0.

This is an annual publication of the International Labor Office (ILO). It covers more than 190 countries, areas, or territories for 10 years, although data are not available for all countries for all of the years. The data come from information sent to the ILO by national statistical services or are taken from official publications. There are nine chapters covering economically active population, employment, unemployment, hours of work, wages, labor costs, consumer prices, occupational injuries, and strikes and lockouts. Each chapter has detailed explanatory notes. All material is given in English, French, and Spanish. The appendixes provide information on the international classifications used in the volume. There is an index that shows which countries are included in each table. This yearbook is a basic reference work on labor statistics. It can be used, for example, to see unemployment data by age, economic activity, level of education, and occupation in different countries or under occupational injuries, persons injured, and rates of fatal injuries and workdays lost. While not likely sought by the average library user, it is a valuable reference volume.—**J. E. Weaver**

411. **Young Person's Occupational Outlook Handbook: Descriptions for America's Top 250 Jobs.** Indianapolis, Ind., JIST Works, 1996. 262p. illus. $19.95pa. ISBN 1-56370-201-0.

With the publication of the 22d edition (1996-97) of the *Occupational Outlook Handbook* (OOH), the U.S. Department of Labor, Bureau of Labor Statistics celebrates the 50th year in print of occupational outlook information. During those 50 years, schools, colleges, veterans' offices, guidance counselors, employment agencies, and community organizations have used this information to educate individuals about the world of work. The demand for such information has been so great that this government publication has been widely reprinted by private publishers. Some have published the identical source under the same title (Bernan Press and VGM Career Horizons, to name a couple). Others have reorganized the information and retitled their editions, such as *The Big Book of Jobs* from VGM Career Horizons (1996) and *America's Top 300 Jobs* from JIST Works (see ARBA 2003, entry 227). More recently, publishers have repackaged the handbook in a variety of formats (a slide series, a video, microcomputer versions, multimedia editions on CD-ROM, and hypertext translations available on the Internet).

Occasionally, the repackaging is designed to target a specific audience. The *Young Person's Occupational Outlook Handbook* is one such republication. While not so stated, its content, format, and length appear to be crafted for young adolescents. Cartoon-like illustrations on the cover and first page of each section will appeal to preteens, but the vocabulary, differing little from the government source, rules out a younger audience. Each one-page entry includes a clarified version of the Department of Labor's job description, working conditions, and list of related occupations, but for only 250 jobs. While the title implies that these are the top jobs, there is no rating of the occupations or substantiation for this claim. Simple black-and-white graphics for the categories of earnings, education and training, and outlook add little to the information. The user must turn to the inside back cover for an explanation of the ratings.

Other attempts to add value are interesting, but not always informative. A large portion of each page is made up of a box labeled "Something Extra," which provides interesting facts, occasionally vaguely related to the job. For instance, a discussion of the discovery of gold is added to the entry for mining engineers. An account of early attempts at flight seems better suited to pilots than flight attendants. The "Subjects to Study" is a nice link from school to work, but inconsistencies in subjects abound. What is listed as "social sciences" on one page, is "social science" on the opposing page. Both "physics" and "physical science" appear in the same list. This lack of attention to detail carries over into the text as well. Several job descriptions lack uniform style, and "complishments" rather than "accomplishments" appears on page 89. The paper cover and glued binding will not hold up to frequent copying any better than the original OOH.

While young people may appreciate the abbreviated format of the *Young Person's Occupational Outlook Handbook*, it refers readers to OOH for more information. Parents, teachers, and counselors dedicated to helping adolescents explore career possibilities may prefer the original. Middle school libraries may want to offer both to their students. [R: BR, Nov/Dec 96, p. 47]—**Debra S. Van Tassel**

CAREER GUIDES

Bibliography

412. **Vocational Careers Sourcebook: Where to Find Help Planning Careers....** 3d ed. Maki, Kathleen E. and Kathleen M. Savage, eds. Detroit, Gale, 1997. 701p. index. $79.00. ISBN 0-8103-6470-0. ISSN 1060-5630.

This publication continues to provide crucial information to individuals seeking employment or a career change (see ARBA 93, entry 412, for a review of the 1st edition). It complements the federal government's *Occupational Outlook Handbook* (see entry 402) by providing citations to numerous career and test guides, periodicals, associations, and other resources that supply additional data about the 134 vocational occupations listed in the *Occupational Outlook Handbook*.

Bibliographic information for the print titles is supplied and, in most cases, a brief description of the work is included. The publisher's or association's address, telephone, and fax numbers are provided, as well as the organization's e-mail address and Website address when available. Three appendixes round out the *Vocational Careers Sourcebook*, including a listing of resources about careers and job-hunting on the Internet; a directory of state occupational licensing agencies; and a Bureau of Labor Statistics ranking of occupational growth. This work is highly recommended for all libraries, although some academic institutions may chose to forgo the title due to its focus on careers that do not require higher education.—**Mark A. Allan**

Dictionaries and Encyclopedias

413.   **Career Discovery Encyclopedia.** [CD-ROM]. Chicago, Ferguson, 2000. Minimum system requirements: Pentium 90, Four-speed CD-ROM drive. Windows 95, Windows 98, or Windows NT. 24MB RAM. 20MB hard disk space. 640x480 (16-bit color). Windows-compatible sound card. Internet Explorer 4.0. $139.95.

As a basic introduction to careers and career planning, this product will be enthusiastically received by students and high school counselors. Information is accessed using a variety of methods: a general alphabetic index, a customized career search, or through the dictionary of occupational titles. Entries for each occupation follow the same format with an indication of school subjects and personal skills needed, minimum education level required, and a general job outlook. This is followed by a section of two to three pages that explains in greater depth what people in that occupation do, exactly what education and training are needed, examples of typical earnings and outlook, organizations to contact for further information, and related articles to look at within this career encyclopedia. Some entries include videos showing people at work in various settings.

The customized search allows users to locate pertinent occupations once they have created a personal profile regarding interests, education level achieved, and type of job outlook they prefer. Included in a separate section are graphs that provide comparative data relating to job outlook, growth and decline of various occupations, and so on. Also included is a form letter to be used to obtain more information regarding a particular career. Once addressed, the letter can be mailed to an identified organization. Full print options are available from any of the sub-menus of this product.

Although this product aims to be comprehensive, the entry for librarianship curiously omits academic librarians. However, for the general scope of information presented, this product can prove valuable to teenagers and those who are contemplating a change of careers or career reentry. [R: BR, Nov/Dec 2000, p. 68]—**Edmund F. SantaVicca**

414.   **Career Guidance. http://www.fofweb.com/subscription.** [Website]. New York, Facts on File. Prices start at $299.00 (school libraries) and $450.00 (public libraries). Date reviewed: Oct 2001.

Profiling more than 1,200 career positions in 49 industries, this Web source is ideal for high school and college students trying to decide on a career, general readers planning a career path, professionals looking for a career change, and career counselors. Navigating the database is basic and easy. Users can begin their searches by scrolling the list of industries (e.g., architecture, education, health care, Internet/Multimedia, publishing, travel) or by doing a customized or keyword search. They can also use an "A to Z Career Index" that lists the various job titles featured within the site. In the industry list, when users click on an industry they are interested in they are taken to an additional list of sub-industries. From there, users are presented with a list of career titles.

Under the career titles, links to related industries and sub-industries are provided. The job title pages contain information on duties; salary range; employment and advancement prospects; required education, training, experience, skills, and traits; and unions and associations. At the top of the pages, users can link to a lengthy job description and additional details on the aspects listed above—they can also access this information by scrolling to the bottom of the page. The data on these pages are general and will not always be fully accurate. Actual job duties and salaries will vary depending on the size of the company and their geographic location. This aspect is noted on the career pages.

From the main page, users can also access several career resources and a contributor list. The resources include information on educational institutions and programs; associations and unions; periodicals, Websites, and books; and scholarships. Advice on career opportunities without a four-year degree and an employability checklist are also provided. This online resource is recommended for all high school, college, and larger public libraries.—**Cari Ringelheim**

415. **Encyclopedia of Careers and Vocational Guidance.** 3d ed. [CD-ROM]. Chicago, Ferguson, 2000. Minimum system requirements: IBM or compatible 486. CD-ROM drive. Windows 3.1x, Windows 95, or Windows 98. 16MB RAM. 12MB hard disk space (single user). 620MB hard disk space (network installation). VGA video adapter (256 colors). $159.95. ISBN 0-89434-290-8 (single user); 0-89434-291-6 (network).

The stated goal for this product is to bring together the greatest possible amount of accurate information about occupations. This CD-ROM goes a long way toward reaching this goal. This encyclopedia contains seven sections: an introduction/tutorial, "Career Guidance," "Career Fields A-Z," "Careers A-Z," "Government Indexes," "Military Occupational Database," and "Custom Search." The introductory section includes a description of what is new in this version, general information about the database, and tutorials for each section of the CD-ROM. Tutorials are easy to use and provide quick answers about various sections of the database. "Career Guidance" is divided into four sections: preparing for a career, finding a job, applying for a job, and hiring procedures (e.g., salaries, benefits, personnel management, employment laws, employee rights). Each section includes lists of Websites to which the user may refer for further information.

"Career Fields A-Z" gives specific elements of 91 general employment fields. For each field the database supplies background and current status of the field or industry. It then gives an overview of the structure of the field or industry. Outlook for the field in terms of growth or decline is taken from the *Occupational Outlook Handbook* (see entry 402), the *U.S. Industry and Trade Outlook* (see entry 229), and statistics from various associations and agencies. Each entry lists organizations that supply information on training, education, internships, scholarships, and job placement. Each entry has an attached glossary of terms relating to the field. This section also includes a personal search feature and a letter-writing feature, which provides form letters that request additional information about a field. "Careers A-Z" supplies job-specific articles on 1,500 occupations. Each article includes a short job description, definition and history of the job, primary and secondary duties, requirements (e.g., training, education, licensing), exploration of the job, typical places of employment, getting the job, career path, typical salary ranges and fringe benefits, typical surroundings and conditions, general economy and industry projections, Web links for additional information and related articles.

The "Military Occupational Database" is prepared by the Department of Defense and covers career options and descriptions for jobs in all of the U.S. armed forces. The "Custom Search" section allows searching using multiple variables, including school subjects, personal skills, outlook, certification and licensing, minimum education, work environment, salary range, and full-text work search. The user can enter personal skills, education, and salary range, for example, and find out what jobs match the information provided. Typing "information" into the free text search returned a list of jobs that deal with information. The Help function includes contents, how to perform options, an overview, how to use custom search tools, information on types of links, and technical support. The program allows entries to be viewed at different magnifications, up to 200 percent. Printing and exporting options are included. Navigation tools are located at the top of each page or with a tool bar above the written pages. Pictures and video clips have been attached to some career descriptions.

This CD-ROM is easy to use and the information in it is accessible in a variety of ways. It can be used for exploring career options as well as to locate specific jobs. Web links, lists of relevant organizations, and additional information provide easy ways to extend a job search and gain more detailed job descriptions. Cross-references allow easy movement from one section of the database to the next. This resource is recommended for libraries collecting career resource materials.—**Joanna M. Burkhardt**

416.　**VGM's Careers Encyclopedia: A Concise, Up-to-Date Reference for Students, Parents, & Guidance Counselors.** 4th ed. By the Editors of VGM Career Horizons. Lincolnwood, Ill., VGM Career Horizons/National Textbook, 1997. 456p. index. $39.95. ISBN 0-8442-4525-9.

This career encyclopedia provides detailed information on approximately 200 of the most popular jobs in the United States today. The jobs, ranging from blue collar to professional, appear in alphabetic order. The table of contents is an alphabetic list as well. The index consists of a keyword list, and it includes association names as well as numerous cross-references and *see also* references. Each occupational entry follows a uniform pattern, describing "The Job"; "Places of Employment and Working Conditions"; "Qualifications, Education, and Training"; "Potential and Advancement"; "Income"; and "Additional Sources of Information." The entries for many occupations list related jobs. The editors use such phrases as "strong demand," "average growth," or "little growth" to describe the job outlook for each occupation through the year 2005.

Public and academic libraries of all sizes require current information about occupations and the educational requirements for those occupations. Guidance counselors in secondary and academic institutions likewise need such basic material. *VGM's Careers Encyclopedia* is a basic, one-volume source eminently suitable for high school and junior college students seeking career advice. Libraries and schools with limited budgets will find this title to be current and authoritative. Academic libraries and public libraries serving a medium-sized or larger clientele should consider the four-volume *Encyclopedia of Careers and Vocational Guidance* (see entry 415), a much more comprehensive source. Libraries that can afford to duplicate holdings should also consider the *Occupational Outlook Handbook* (see entry 402).—**Dene L. Clark**

Directories

417.　**Adams Internet Job Search Almanac 2001-2002.** Michelle Roy Kelly, Michael Paydos, and Jennifer M. Wood, eds. Holbrook, Mass., Adams Publishing, 2001. 274p. illus. index. $10.95pa. ISBN 1-58062-426-X.

This thorough, up-to-date guide helps job hunters tap into the electronic job market. Adams Media Corporation has been publishing career books since 1980. This updated, expanded guide will help readers find job listings using the Internet, Usenet newsgroups, and commercial online services. And readers will learn how to research the hidden job market, targeting potential employers with electronic or multimedia résumés. The alphabetically arranged Web listings are grouped into large subject areas, such as "Nationwide Sites," "International Sites," "Arts and Entertainment," "Computers," "Health Care," "Legal," "Retail," and so on. Users should be aware that numerous similar publications exist, and, because of the dynamics of the Internet, the Websites listed have sometimes merged or disappeared. This fact is also true for the Usenet newsgroups listings. However, these listings give readers solid information on places to begin their online job search.

The chapter on "Computerized Interviews and Assessment Tests" explains what to expect and provides sound advice on preparing and answering sample questions. A short glossary and index complete the work. Finding a job can be a frustrating, stressful event and any help in making it quicker and easier will be appreciated by all.—**Susan C. Awe**

418.   **Adams Jobs Almanac.** 8th ed. Michelle Roy Kelly, Heather L. Vinhateiro, and Anne M. Grignon, eds. Holbrook, Mass., Adams Publishing, 2001. 946p. index. $16.95pa. ISBN 1-58062-443-X.

The 8th edition of *Adams Jobs Almanac* provides detailed information about 7,000 company employers in the fastest growing industries in the United States. Each employer profiled has a business description, hiring managers, street address, telephone and fax numbers, and job line number. Many of the entries have e-mail and Web addresses, common positions hired, educational requirements, internships, and benefits.

An overview of the latest developments in the U.S. job market and working for the federal government is provided. A concise guide for writing résumés and cover letters, lining up interviews, and negotiating salaries is available. A listing of professional organizations and online resources for all industries is listed in the back of the volume. A helpful index of potential employers is provided as well. Public libraries and academic libraries need to have this excellent job guide for their business and career collections. It is highly recommended.—**Kay M. Stebbins**

419.   **The Almanac of American Employers 2002-2003.** Jack W. Plunkett, ed. Houston, Tex., Plunkett Research, 2001. 718p. index. $179.99pa. (w/CD-ROM). ISBN 1-891775-25-1.

The Almanac of American Employers 2002-2003 is a directory of successful corporate businesses focused on the job-seeker, whether they are a new college graduate or an employee considering a change in employment. The main section of the directory describes 501 companies with name, address, voice and fax number, and industry group code information. Details on professional degrees they hire, salary and benefit rankings, and the company's ranking within its industry group are also included. Descriptions continue with the company's plans for expansion and special features, such as new plant locales, special benefits for employees and their families, the corporate financials, a list of officers, and a statement of the company's competitive advantage. An indication of whether the company complies as a "Hot Spot for Advancement for Women/Minorities" and data on the "Number of Women Officers and Directors" are also provided.

The "Seven Keys for Job Seekers" guides readers in locating information about a company. The "Important Contacts" chapter provides names of organizations and associations that will provide job-seekers with a network of professionals. The 501 companies listed in the almanac are not the same list as the Fortune 500. The companies were chosen because they offered more job openings or long-lived jobs to the greatest number of employees. This guide is a must-purchase for career collections.—**Kay M. Stebbins**

420.   **Career Exploration on the Internet: A Student's Guide to More Than 300 Web Sites!** Elizabeth H. Oakes, ed. Chicago, Ferguson, 1998. 208p. index. $15.95pa. ISBN 0-89434-240-1.

The Internet is transforming many facets of life. Its impact on the job search is dramatic for those in business, technical, and professional fields. This volume is a comprehensive narrative directory opening abundant information resources for anyone with access to the World Wide Web.

Throughout the book, sites are listed and given helpful annotations that include scope, approach, and deficiencies where they exist.

Aimed primarily at the student or newly graduated job-seeker, these resources are most helpful for the job search, with chapters on how to find out about companies, nonprofit and public organizations, and international careers. Volunteer, internship, and summer job information and listings are covered also. Employment agencies, professional recruiting firms, and professional associations, as well as Websites of individual companies, are listed.

The opening chapters focus on sites for career exploration—sources of information on various fields and occupations. Some sites, frequently academic, offer self-assessment tools as well as occupational information. Clearinghouse sites are offered as "headquarters" for searching for career information. An individual's decision-making process may be made more difficult by such an abundance of information.

This guide assumes the reader is computer-proficient, particularly with the Internet. The style is lively and fast-paced, muck like where the listings lead. The only problem is that this means of job searching takes time and effort and diligence is clearly provided. This volume and others like it are essential tools for libraries and career centers. Anything in this venue will be outdated the minute after it is written, much less published, but the key resources and links will most likely linger even after newer and better sites come online. Thus, it provides an excellent base. [R: BR, Nov/Dec 98, p. 66]—**Barbara Conroy**

421.   **CareerExplorer.** [CD-ROM]. Indianapolis, Ind., JIST Works, 1999. Minimum system requirements: IBM or compatible PC. CD-ROM drive. Windows 3.1 or Windows 95 (or later). 16MB RAM. SVGA graphics card and compatible monitor with 512 video memory. $295.00 (single user); $600.00 (lab pack). ISBN 1-56370-477-3.

This CD-ROM is easy to install on a PC with Windows 95 software. The opening menu is also straight-forward and offers three choices: "Introduction," "Start," and "Quit." Users expect clarity in an introduction, but this one fails—the text even concludes with a sentence fragment. There is no scroll bar and pressing "page down" or the "down arrow" key does not bring any more text to the screen.

The "Start" option leads the user into an aptitude test with questions such as "In your work would you like to work outdoors as in gardening or farming?" If the answer is yes, the user is given several more choices, such as "Managing farming, breeding, forestry, or logging operations?" and "Supervising farming, forestry, and logging, or nursery or ground keeping?" To the general public, managing and supervising are similar, so a link to a precise definition of these terms would be helpful. When in doubt, however, it is best to choose both options. People who do not follow this advice may find themselves with puzzling choices. Free Internet sites will provide better career assistance instead of purchasing this expensive CD-ROM.—**Juleigh Muirhead Clark**

422.   **Certification and Accreditation Programs Directory: A Descriptive Guide to National Voluntary Certification and Accreditation Programs for Professionals and Institutions.** 2d ed. Michael A. Paré, ed. Farmington Hills, Mich., Gale, 1999. 626p. index. $99.00pa. ISBN 0-7876-2843-3. ISSN 1084-2128.

Certifications, required for many professions and occupations, are designed to regulate individuals. Requirements and procedures that certify individuals are developed by professional, trade and specialty fields, and sometimes the law. These standards become the basis for accrediting organizations that are then established and charged with the task of ensuring the practitioner's competency, training, and credibility. This process has expanded greatly in recent years to embrace new fields, technologies, and practices that require regulation or standardization.

This volume brings together 1,700 current and voluntary certification programs listed in occupational chapters similar to the *Occupational Outlook Handbook* (see entry 402). Each program details the title awarded, requirements, exam information, fees, number of individuals certified, and accreditation information, along with contact information for the certification granting organization.

Some 250 accrediting organizations at the national, regional, or state level are listed. These organizations must be for individuals and must be current, voluntary, and available throughout the U.S. No state licensing agencies are included. Of the many continuing education programs available, only medical programs are included. Information for each listing includes full contact information (including Website), membership, application procedures and accreditation requirements, renewal, state requirements (i.e., licensure), and fees.

This volume can be of value to consumers, individuals seeking professional advancement or development, and parent and students identifying educational institutions. Businesses can review the benefits of certification for the organization and its employees. Access is relatively direct, with one index profiling certifying bodies with a list of the positions certified, another giving acronyms, and a third listing positions and accrediting organizations.—**Barbara Conroy**

423.   Crispin, Gerry, and Mark Mehler. **CareerXRoads 2001: The Directory to Job, Résumé, and Career Management Sites on the Web.** Kendall Park, N.Y., MMC Group, 2001. 437p. index. $26.95pa. ISBN 0-9652239-1-4.

This work is the 6th edition of a directory of Websites for job-seekers and recruiters. The sites have been selected by the authors based on viewing the sites, comparing those sites with others in the field, and using their opinions and observations about the future direction of online recruiting. This book is available in a Web version as well.

The bulk of the book consists of the alphabetic listing and rating of the 504 Websites rated "best" by the authors. Each listing contains the Website name, the URL, contact information, an indication of how many jobs or résumés are posted, the cost (if any) for posting or seeing job listings and résumés, the skills emphasis, disciplines covered, geographic location, and special features. This is followed by a description of the site, its ease of use, and any other special considerations. Listings are indexed and cross-referenced by categories: "Best of the Best"; "Career Management"; "College"; "Diversity"; "Jobs"; "Location"; "Newspapers"; "Résumés"; and "Skills." URLs for sites that were not among the top 500 are listed in the index as are URLs for Fortune 500 companies.

The remainder of the book includes a disclosure statement, author information, predictions (i.e., how they did last year and what they predict for this year), suggested resources for their audience (employment agency Websites, books, and odd sites), and a dozen three-to seven-page articles written by experts in their fields covering topics of interest to job-seekers and recruiters.

The authors have extensive backgrounds in human resources and seem to know what resources recruiters and job-seekers are looking for in a Web environment. For those individuals, this is a most helpful tool. *CareerXroads 2001* is recommended for career office libraries, corporate offices of recruitment, and libraries with collections in this area.—**Joanna M. Burkhardt**

424.   Cubbage, Sue, and Marcia Williams. **National Job Hotline Directory: The Job-Finder's Hot List.** River Forest, Ill., Planning/Communications, 1999. 376p. illus. $16.95pa. ISBN 1-884587-12-7.

Intended for job hunters and based on the authors' queries, this directory identifies 6,500 job hotlines operated by employers in the United States and Canada. An introduction discusses the search process, use of the telephone as part of a strategy, and its relationship to Internet and more traditional employment resources (e.g., newspapers).

Arranged alphabetically by state, chapters provide key state contacts and information. They are divided into as many as 10 topical categories, with alphabetic entries consisting of name (e.g., companies, agencies), city, and telephone number. Additional sections offer national and toll-free number hotlines, Canadian listings, free World Wide Web updates (http://www.jobfindersonline.com), and discount coupons. The separate resource lists refer job seekers only to other publications available from the publisher rather than important works available elsewhere.

This volume contains a lot of valuable information and deserves the attention of the serious job seeker. It has the makings of an excellent reference tool; however, several flaws should be noted. The lack of descriptive abstracts identifying types of jobs used by an employer and more specific topical divisions increases both time and monetary costs. An alphabetic list of all companies and agencies would improve access and assist those who have identified an employer but not a location. These limitations make it less useful for basic reference collections. [R: LJ, 15 Mar 99, pp. 66-68]—**Sandra E. Belanger**

425.   Dikel, Margaret Riley, Frances Roehm, and Steve Oserman. **The Guide to Internet Job Searching.** 1998-99 ed. Lincolnwood, Ill., VGM Career Horizons/National Textbook, 1998. 278p. index. $14.95pa. ISBN 0-8442-8199-9.

This guide is issued under Public Library Association auspices. It is well designed, user-friendly, and compares well with similar guides. The authors, lead by Dikel, formerly of Worcester Polytechnic Library, are experts in their fields.

Chapters conceptually divide into 2 main parts. The first 3 chapters cover the main issues in using the Internet as an aid to job searching. This 33-page section serves as a concise, accessible overview from which to access the Internet free or for low cost, to e-mail résumés, to do employer research, and to network. It is amazing how much is packed into relatively little space. The format of these chapters, with headings, subheadings, and tips in bold typeface, makes it easy to skim for what the reader may want. Six related titles are recommended for further reading. The book is an ideal starting point for reference librarians as well as users.

The remaining 11 chapters provide annotated listings of Internet job search sites by field of employment. In addition to various business categories these include health care, sciences, humanities and social sciences, government, and general resources. Readers outside the United States will note a 22-page international resources chapter. It includes eight pages on Canada subdivided by province, as well as sections for Latin America, Europe, New Zealand and Australia, and elsewhere. Listings include site titles, Internet address, and a sentence-or paragraph-length description. These chapters are subdivided by industry or relevant topical divisions.

Appendixes cover job search services and online networking. Access points include contents, general index, and index of cited resources. The absence of any reference to remote employment and contract opportunities is notably missing from this work. All public, research, and specialty libraries with the relevant mandates should buy this key reference tool.—**Nigel Tappin**

426.   **Employment Opportunities, USA—A Career News Service and Internet Guide.** Denver, Colo., Washington Research Associates, 1998. 1v. (various paging). $184.00 spiralbound. ISBN 0-937801-10-0. ISSN 1076-4798.

Employment Opportunities, USA is a looseleaf service with quarterly updates, which covers 14 industries, including telecommunications, teaching, banking, health care, computers, law, art, music, dance, and social work. There is no prefatory section that might explain the rationale for selecting some industries and not others.

The section for each industry begins with an overview describing the general opportunities and major issues. These overviews are well researched, often quoting from leading publications in the field. Information in these sections includes the general work environment; career trends in the industry; potential problems, such as the high rate of burnout in the teaching field; the effects of technology within a field; and average salaries. The 2d section for each industry is a listing and brief description of print and Internet sources to locate potential jobs in the industry. For some industries there is also a listing of job information services with their addresses and telephone numbers. There is no index. Although it is virtually impossible to have a comprehensive listing of available jobs, *Employment Opportunities, USA* is an excellent source for learning about the primary resources for the industries covered.—**Michele Russo**

427.   **Job Hunter's Sourcebook: Where to Find Employment Leads and Other Job Search Resources.** 4th ed. Kathleen E. Maki Potts, ed. Farmington Hills, Mich., Gale, 1999. 1079p. index. $90.00. ISBN 0-7876-2645-7. ISSN 1053-1874.

This valuable, comprehensive presentation identifies employment leads and key resources for job-seekers, students, and career counselors. The resources address all levels of employment (executive, technical, professional, and support), enabling individuals to pinpoint essential sources for 193 broadly representative jobs. Organized by occupation, entries include publications, organizations, audiovisual and electronic resources, and other tools to use in designing an effective job-search strategy. These resources provide full citations for print sources, directories, job banks, clearinghouses, employment agencies, and executive search firms and organizations that lead to employment opportunities. Handbooks relevant to a particular occupational field are offered as guides to the job-hunting process particular to those fields. An extensive index offers broad access.

In addition, a 2d section (about 15 percent of the volume) gives citations and brief, informative descriptions of those resources focused on special job-hunting considerations for specific situations. For example, sections cover interviewing skills; government employment; international opportunities; résumés; relocation; and address special populations, such as the disabled, ex-offenders, independent contractors, and minorities.

All aspects of this guide have tapped useful, current, and reliable resources for the ever-challenging and competitive job search. Some of these will be available in local libraries and guidance centers; some might be feasible to purchase. As with any such compilation, it will be outdated quickly with more recent Internet and print resources, but it provides an excellent starting point for anyone exploring employment possibilities, motivating and guiding the pursuit of work.—**Barbara Conroy**

428.   Krannich, Ronald L., and Caryl Rae Krannich. **The Directory of Federal Jobs and Employers.** Manassas Park, Va., Impact Publications, 1996. 278p. index. $25.95pa. ISBN 1-57023-033-1.

The federal government, with nearly three million employees, is the largest single employer in the United States. It offers the most diverse opportunities of any employer in terms of types of jobs, ranging from such trades as plumbing and carpentry to medicine, science, and law. It also offers diverse opportunities in terms of geographic location, with job sites across the nation and the world. These jobs, however, are difficult to identify and the application process is somewhat complex.

The Directory of Federal Jobs and Employers is a useful resource for those interested in exploring the arcane world of government employment. The book provides a clear and complete guide to federal departments and agencies in all three branches of government. It furnishes a road map for applying for jobs and discusses strategies that can benefit jobseekers. Finally, the directory gives a useful discussion of employment trends in federal government, looking specifically at recent employment trends in various departments and agencies. This is a reference work whose benefits clearly outweigh its reasonable cost.—**Paul F. Clark**

429. **Major Employers of Europe 1999/2000: The Jobfinder's Directory.** Ann Wilson and Susan Hoernig, eds. London, Graham & Whiteside; distr., Farmington Hills, Mich., Gale, 1999. 1369p. index. $270.00. ISBN 1-86099-155-6.

This directory gives information on the 10,000 largest companies by number of employees in 20 western European countries. The brief introduction does not state how the information was gathered; nor does it inform readers of how this title would be particularly useful to a job-seeker, other than knowing that these companies employ many people. Some companies list number of employees worldwide; others, it is presumed, list the number at one European site. All of the information in this directory can easily be found in a number of other sources on European companies, such as Dun & Bradstreet's *Europa*.

The arrangement is alphabetical by country and then by company. Each entry includes address, telephone and fax numbers, name of the CEO, principal activities, trade names, parent companies, financial information for the past two years, private or public status, principal shareholders, and the number of employees. An index lists all of the companies in alphabetical order. A second index is by SIC code, although the individual entries do not list the SIC. Because this directory is expensive and gives information that can be easily found elsewhere, it is not recommended.—**Michele Russo**

430. **Pathways to Career Success for Minorities: A Resource Guide to Colleges, Financial Aid, and Work.** Tim Schaffert, ed. Kansas City, Mo., CRC Publishing, 2000. 378p. index. $29.95pa. ISBN 0-89434-303-3.

Following the brief introduction, this work is divided into two major parts. The first part consists of nine essays on minority issues: minorities in media, minorities in the arts, mentors, workplace diversity, technology, affirmative action, legal rights, and starting a business. These essays are intended to provide insights into the issues affecting today's minorities.

The second part is a directory that is subdivided into three sections: "Financial Aid," "Organizations," and "Additional Information." The subsection on financial aid lists fellowships, grants, loans, awards, scholarships, and internships and career guidance opportunities for minorities. The subsection on organizations lists professional organizations, minority colleges, fraternities and sororities, and groups that are known to assist individuals in pursuit of careers and education. The last subsection includes listings of magazines, journals, newspapers, and Websites of relevance to minorities.

Each directory entry includes name, mailing address, and telephone number. Many entries also include Internet addresses. This information is followed by a brief description of the organization or opportunity. Many of the listed Websites include application guidelines, deadlines, and links to related material.

The work includes several indexes by institution and financial aid name, state, academic subject, and opportunities by minority group. This work provides only the basic information needed to determine who offers what kind of assistance to minorities. Undoubtedly, Websites listed will supplement this information considerably.—**Joanna M. Burkhardt**

431. Weddle, Peter D. **Weddle's Job-seeker's Guide to Employment Web Sites 2001.** New York, AMACOM/American Management Association, 2001. 184p. index. $12.95pa. ISBN 0-8144-7097-1.

Online employment-related sites now total 40,000. This makes the task of locating and selecting the most productive sites very challenging. This directory highlights 350 of the most helpful sites available. Some sites listed are the characteristic general ones, such as hotjobs.com or monster.com, but the main use of this guide is in the lesser-known specialty sites for professions, industries, or functions.

Each site profile indicates a self-described and sometimes promotional sketch of the occupations and industries represented. In addition, the profile specifies whether full, part-time, or contract jobs are posted; top salary ranges; regional territory; links to other relevant sites; and where the postings originate. Profiles also indicate whether résumés can be stored onsite and what restrictions and terms are required to do so.

In this field that changes daily, this volume even at its moment of publication was somewhat out of date. However, the compilation is written by the author and publishers of the leading print newsletter devoted exclusively to online recruiting and the author is also a national columnist.
—**Barbara Conroy**

432. Weddle, Peter D. **Weddle's Recruiter's Guide to Employment Web Sites 2001.** New York, AMACOM/American Management Association, 2001. 374p. index. $27.95pa. ISBN 0-8144-7096-3.

Weddle is a prolific writer in the employment field and writes about Internet job hunting from both the employer and employee viewpoint. The present paperbound volume is the first of a projected annual publication for corporate and third party recruiters, employment managers, and human resource practitioners. This guide is not a textbook of strategies for using Internet resources and forums. Instead, 350 Websites have been selected from the many employment Websites available. Each site has completed an extensive questionnaire, and the results are listed in the page-long profile for each Website. General site statistics, job posting services, résumé sourcing services, other recruiting services offered, and contact information are described for each organization.

The sites are alphabetically listed by name of the site. Some of the sites are geographical in orientation, such as Seattle Careers, and many are focused on a particular field, such as JobsInLogistics.com. However, most of the sites profiled are classified as business/management or information technology. There is little offered for academic, museum, or art fields according to the cross-reference index that follows the main entries, although some listings for these fields can be found in general Websites, such as Monster.com. Furthermore, the index is not as helpful as it could be—the Website ArtJob Online is profiled in the main entries, but it is not found under the most likely subject, "Specialty Sites," in the index.

This book would be of interest to special libraries serving a human resources audience. But it is more likely to be used as a desk book for recruiters, along with books that describe Internet recruiting strategies and techniques, such as *Poor Richard's Internet Recruiting* (Top Floor Publishing, 2000) or *Internet Recruiting: A Human Resource Guide to Global Sourcing* (Ginn Press, 2000). For job hunters and most libraries, Weddle has started another annual publication, *Weddle's Job-Seekers Guide to Employment Web Sites* (see entry 431), which is similarly formatted, but focused to that audience.—**Juleigh Muirhead Clark**

433. Wolfinger, Anne. **The Quick Internet Guide to Career and Education Information.** 2000 ed. Indianapolis, Ind., JIST Works, 2000. 154p. illus. index. $16.95pa. ISBN 1-56370-622-9.

The Quick Internet Guide to Career and Education Information is an easy-to-use directory and sourcebook of career and college Internet Websites. After reading the introduction one gets the feeling this book is intended for Internet users new to the information highway. It begins with simple instructions on how to use the Internet, along with tips on which search engines to use, how to send e-mail, and e-mail etiquette. The bulk of the work is divided into nine chapters on using the Web to find information on college and financial aid, distance learning, career exploration, job openings, career clearinghouses, labor market resources, military careers, self-employment, and contract and freelance work. After a short introduction the book lists Website URLs that are intended to be useful to students or job-seekers. Each Website is given a one-paragraph summary. A seven-page glossary at the end of the book covers Internet terms such as Boolean logic, FTP, and modem. The book concludes with an index.

This Internet directory bypasses the problem of out-of-date Web addresses by supplying readers with a Website to register with for free address updates, new listings, and a newsletter from the author. At such a reasonable price, this directory will be a worthwhile purchase for both public and academic libraries.—**Shannon Graff Hysell**

Handbooks and Yearbooks

434. Bolles, Richard Nelson. **Job-Hunting on the Internet.** Berkeley, Calif., Ten Speed Press, 1997. 110p. illus. (The Parachute Library). $4.95pa. ISBN 0-89815-909-1.

Excerpted and expanded from the author's well-known publication, *What Color Is Your Parachute?*, this book has added Internet job-hunting to its repertoire. First, nine large, gateway locations, comprising university-sponsored, commercial, and favorite sites, are identified. This list is followed by a discussion of the benefits and limitations in using the Internet for job listings, résumés, career counseling, contacts, and research. Obviously based on extensive research, the World Wide Web sites, evaluated and annotated, offers discussion of guidelines, exercises, techniques, opportunities, specialized resources, and other forms of assistance. A symbol, the parachute, connotes the best within each category. Advice for the unsuccessful job search and basic search instruction complete the volume.

This handy reference guide, also available on the Internet (http://www.washingtonpost.com/parachute) offers a realistic approach to job hunting. Even though the Internet is shown as both a superlative and a limited tool, patrons will appreciate the oft-neglected security considerations covered here. The lack of a master site list and index presupposes a readership, for the printed version, limited to those moving through the entire process.—**Sandra E. Belanger**

435. Brommer, Gerald F., and Joseph A. Gatto. **Careers in Art: An Illustrated Guide.** 2d ed. Worcester, Mass., Davis Publications; distr., New York, Sterling Publishing, 1999. 256p. illus. index. $29.95. ISBN 0-87192-377-7.

The authors indicate that this guide is for anyone who is interested in an art career—students, teachers, curriculum specialists, guidance counselors, and parents. The introduction discusses the general career area, typical jobs, qualities needed for success in those jobs, alternate careers, college programs, and portfolios and résumés. Each of the first six chapters covers a specialized job area: environmental design, designing for communication, product and fashion design, entertainment, cultural growth and enrichment, and art services. Major job categories are discussed within those chapters.

Notable people from each field are profiled in each chapter, along with some noteworthy projects in that field. For example, chapter 1 covers environmental design and begins with a profile of Michelle Rickman, a designer for an architectural firm. This profile is followed by a definition and description of the field of architecture and an explanation of what architects do. A brief summary of the Denver Public Library project is presented next and a profile of architect Frank O. Gehry concludes the section. Sections on urban design, landscape architecture, and other careers in architecture round out the chapter.

The final chapter is called "Resources." It includes a bibliography of books, videos, and art magazines, along with a list of professional societies and organizations, Websites, and colleges and art schools. A chart profiles many U.S. and Canadian college art programs, indicating the art areas in which they excel. The book also includes an index. This work will be useful for general career collections and would probably be most useful in public and high school libraries. [R: LJ, 15 June 99, p. 68]—**Joanna M. Burkhardt**

436.   **Career Opportunities in Television, Cable, Video, and Multimedia.** 4th ed. New York, Checkmark Books/Facts on File, 1999. 274p. illus. index. $35.00; $18.95pa. ISBN 0-8160-3940-2; 0-8160-3941-0pa.

This book offers coverage of a wide variety of career opportunities in the popular and expanding fields of broadcasting (radio aside), video technologies, and multimedia production of entertainment and information resources. It is an update of the 3d edition published nine years ago under the title *Career Opportunities in Television, Cable, and Video*. Nine years is a long time in these fields, and an update is welcome. The industry has expanded, and job responsibilities and titles reflect this. The whole new area of multimedia, including its Web aspects, has been added.

The introductory overview that precedes each section has been significantly updated to reflect changes in the field, new terminology, and to bring the numerous and varied statistics up-to-date.

Well organized and well laid out with better typography than the 3d edition, the material is basically divided into a television broadcasting and a cable, video, and media section. Within each of these two areas, the book is arranged by job function within a few broad areas of expertise. Each includes a job description, salary range, the education and skills required or expected, and information on unions. Within each of the two areas the book offers broad coverage of job opportunities. Nontechnical jobs as they relate to the electronic media industry are covered.

The television section is divided up by function within the areas of management, programming, production, engineering, performance, advertising, and news reporting. The functions are listed alphabetically within each area and are also included in the subject index at the back. In the 2d section, the functions or areas of competency are organized more under subject areas in which cable, video, and multimedia are used. Employment in private industry, government, the health field, the education field, commercial technical products, training, and producing (e.g., managing, engineering, programming, writing) are specified, and specific areas of competency are then arranged under each.

This guide is highly recommended for both public and academic libraries. Readers should find it comprehensive, readable, and a good place to start in seeking vocational information in electronic media production.—**Florence W. Jones**

437.   **Career Perspectives Software Series.** [CD-ROM]. Moravia, N.Y., Chronicle Guidance, 1997. Minimum system requirements: IBM or compatible Pentium-grade 486. CD-ROM drive. Windows 3.1. 8MB RAM. 33MB hard disk space. VGA monitor. $250.95.

When examining electronic devices such as CD-ROMs, one notices there often is an embarras de richesses of information. Unfortunately, the emphasis is too often on the embarras, rather than the richesses. Chronicle Guidance Publications has produced a CD-ROM that brings this to mind. Clearly there is a considerable amount of material here. Often getting there, however, can be difficult. Installation is fairly easy, however, some configuration is required. Available to the user are four databases: CGP Career Perspectives Occupations Briefs for two-year, four-year, high school, and "all subjects" careers. Access to each requires a CAN code that accompanies the CD-ROM. All occupation codes come from several sources: Holland Code, Dictionary of Occupations Titles, Guide for Occupational Exploration, and SIC codes for industry careers. Thus, while viewing a brief or summary of a chosen career, users may click on related codes for information about those areas. Special counselor features provide two useful hallmarks for helping students.

Counselors may print by brief number as well as results from optional criteria searches. The optional criteria search allows for exact matching by name, data, people, reasoning skills needed, language, and specific vocational prep time. Users are reminded that choosing too many may result in a null set. Each entry provides the familiar outline of careers listed in printed sources, such as the *Dictionary of Occupational Titles*. A brief introduction about the career is followed by a description of work performed, working conditions, training required, qualifications (both personal and educational), entry methods, advancements, and more. In all, over 640 briefs covering more than 2,500 occupations are included. CGP updates the material on a four-year cycle. In the hands of a qualified user, this CD-ROM will reap its richest harvest. Even in the hands of patrons with limited knowledge of the printed tools, CGP will prove helpful. Although the information, clickable options, and search options are overwhelming at times, this CD-ROM will be put to good use almost anywhere it finds a home.—**Mark Y. Herring**

438. **Civil Service Career Starter.** New York, LearningExpress, 1997. 1v. (various paging). index. $14.00pa. ISBN 1-57685-120-6.

It is well known that the government is a big employer, so big, in fact, that it is intimidating. This publication endeavors to make information about government jobs more accessible. It does so in this attractively formatted paperback volume. The paper is bright ivory instead of grayish newsprint, and the large print and the space between the lines and in the margins invite the weary job-hunter to spend the evening at home studying.

The opening chapters describe what types of positions are typically available, the federal and state classification systems, and how to find out what jobs are available and what is needed for an application. Information on job duties, responsibilities, salaries, and application procedures for 4 of the "top 40" federal job titles—postal worker, law enforcement officer, administrative assistant, and firefighter—follows. Two practice examinations are interspersed with helpful advice for improvement, including methods of practice and useful books for more help. This guide concentrates on skills for understanding, communicating, and reasoning and has sections on reading comprehension, grammar, vocabulary, spelling, and mathematics. It provides 20 math questions and 20 vocabulary and spelling questions. The list of contributors includes adult educators and test skills specialists and their skills are evident in the arrangement and content of the test questions. Future civil servants will use this book.—**Juleigh Muirhead Clark**

439. **The Complete Guide to Environmental Careers in the 21st Century: The Environmental Careers Organization.** Kevin Doyle, ed. Washington, D.C., Island Press, 1999. 447p. illus. index. $39.95; $17.95pa. ISBN 1-55963-585-1; 1-55963-586-Xpa.

The Complete Guide to Environmental Careers in the 21st Century is a thoroughly updated, revised, and re-titled 3d edition of the *Complete Guide to Environmental Careers* (1993). This is an outstanding resource that is produced by the Environmental Careers Organization (ECO), an important nonprofit group dedicated to protecting and enhancing the environment through development of professionals, promotion of careers, and inspirational sharing. The book supports these goals very well. There is a 3-chapter overview of the environmental job field that is complete with statistics, major drivers behind trends, and useful advice. The remainder of the book provides detailed information in each chapter on where the jobs are, what is growing and what is not, earnings, education requirements, excellent resources in print and on the Web, case studies of active professionals, and profiles of people making a difference.

The "at-a-glance" section at the beginning of each detailed chapter is a valuable resource on its own. For example, in the chapter devoted to the planning segment of environmental professionals, the number of planners nationwide is given, along with the percentage of growth per year and predictions about future growth; a public, private, and nonprofit sectors breakdown; a list of 18

key job titles; a list of influential organizations; and a salary overview. Useful as an encyclopedia, dictionary, and bibliography, this is a resource highly recommended for all types of libraries.
—**Barbara Delzell**

440.   Echaore-McDavid, Susan. **Career Opportunities in Education.** New York, Facts on File, 2001. 307p. index. $45.00. ISBN 0-8160-4223-3.

This guide offers a comprehensive digest of more than 90 positions in the broad field of education. It covers a wide range, from teachers, specialists, and administrators to support staff, counselors, and librarians. In addition to traditional school settings, it also addresses employee training specialists, fitness and recreation professionals, environmental educators, and animal trainers. For each of these categories more specific positions are described in terms of responsibilities and duties, salaries, and the employment and advancement prospects viewed nationally. Indicated also are the required licensure and training, special skills and personality traits, and tips for entry into the field.

A brief profile capsules these factors and draws a career ladder of the position and places it in an upward mobility career path. This enables the tool to be helpful in career management for the individual, career counselors, academic advisors, and mentors. Its use would enhance the *Occupational Outlook Handbook* (see entry 402) and the *Encyclopedia of Careers and Vocational Guidance* (see entry 415) by making it more specific in addressing particular positions. [R: RUSQ, Summer 01, p. 379]—**Barbara Conroy**

441.   Echaore-McDavid, Susan. **Career Opportunities in Law Enforcement, Security, and Protective Services.** New York, Checkmark Books/Facts on File, 2000. 239p. index. (Career Opportunities). $35.00. ISBN 0-8160-3955-0.

This vocational guidance aid covering occupations in law enforcement and related fields will make a useful addition to career-planning collections. The main body of the work is divided into 12 sections ranging from police work, forensic investigation, private investigations, and computer security to construction inspectors and aviation security. The 70 jobs profiled range from the obvious, such as police officer or sheriff's deputy, to the more unexpected (e.g., locksmith, food inspector, plumbing inspector, lifeguard).

Individual entries provide duties, salary range, prospects, advancement, career ladder, education and training, skills, entry tips, and unions or associations. Each entry is about two 11-by-8½-pages in length, with 1 or 2 slightly longer (e.g., fire fighter, security guard). All entries start with a brief summary, with more detailed text of expanded information below. The entries give a good description and idea of what occupations are about.

The clear introductory materials outline how to use the book, give sources, and make suggestions for following up interesting prospects. In addition to contents and index, there are 10 appendixes providing a variety of useful information, including Internet resources, state and federal employers and certification agencies, occupational groups, colleges and universities, a bibliography, and a glossary. The educational institutions, however, only cover those offering programs related to fields where formal training is not widely available. This book is a thorough and useful career guide that is well worth considering for employment collections. [R: LJ, 15 Mar 2000, p. 70; RUSQ, Sept 2000, p. 402]—**Nigel Tappin**

442.   **Exploring Tech Careers: Real People Tell You What You Need to Know.** Chicago, Ferguson, 2001. 2v. index. $89.95/set. ISBN 0-89434-310-6.

The growing reliance on technology has brought about a strong demand for technicians in the workplace. Many professional fields (i.e., medicine, law, and engineering) have developed specialties at technician level. Thus, the future for such specialties is bright. Technical careers often provide an avenue to a respected, well-paying field that requires a two-year or, at most, a four-year academic degree. Technicians work in office, laboratory, business, and government venues alongside professionals, often as a member of a team.

This breadth of careers is well detailed in these volumes. Each technical occupation is described in an overview of key points that outlines requirements, job outlook, salaries, and skills required. Then, an individual already in the field is profiled to give a subjective perspective. Next, for each job there is a description of basic tasks, requirements of skills and personal qualities, and the need for lifelong learning to keep abreast of changes.

The educational section of each occupation covers important high school classes, postsecondary training options, and courses of study and certification or licensing processes. Pre-job opportunities are given in a section on internships and volunteer possibilities. Employment areas are scanned along with networking and job search strategies most relevant to that field. Related jobs, career outlook, and advancement ladders are given with sources of additional information.

This tool will be invaluable for career and guidance counselors in high schools and colleges. The writing approach presents this work as a very adult resource, yet it has great personal interest and appeal. It is useful for an individual seeking a mid-life or retirement career with a fresh approach. A wide span of fields are covered, centered around the theme of specialized and focused work that interfaces with the technology of our times.—**Barbara Conroy**

443.   Farr, J. Michael. **America's Fastest Growing Jobs: Detailed Information on the 140 Fastest Growing Jobs in Our Economy.** 6th ed. Indianapolis, Ind., JIST Works, 2001. 472p. illus. $16.95pa. ISBN 1-56370-718-7.

America's Fastest Growing Jobs is designed for those just entering the career field as well as those looking for a change of careers. It offers detailed information on 140 of the fastest growing jobs in the United States and provides an estimation of the percentage of growth in the field up to the year 2008 for most. Section 1, the largest section in the volume, describes the fastest growing jobs. Each job is described in two to three pages and addresses the nature of the work, working conditions, training and qualifications, job outlook, earnings, related occupations, and offers sources for additional information. The author is thorough in his descriptions and offers both the pluses and minuses of all positions. Section 2, "The Quick Job Search," presents activities that will help readers find the right career for themselves and then gives practical advice on interviewing and résumé writing that will help them land the job. It also includes a brief section providing advice on what to do when one has lost their job. The final section gives projection data on all of the occupations in the book up to the year 2008. It provides statistics on the number of people currently employed in the position as well as how many will be employed in the position in 2008, how many are self-employed workers, average unemployment ratings, and the average number of job openings, among other things.

The author writes in an easy-to-understand style that makes this book both informative and interesting to read. It will be a valuable addition to the career sections of public, high school, and academic libraries.—**Shannon Graff Hysell**

444.   Farr, J. Michael. **America's Top Jobs for College Graduates: Detailed Information on 114 Jobs for People with Four-Year and Higher Degrees.** 4th ed. Indianapolis, Ind., JIST Works, 2001. 430p. $16.95pa. ISBN 1-56370-720-9.

The author has written a publication that provides a handbook of various professional job descriptions, job searching checklists, sample letters and résumés, and, finally, articles on the professional and industrial job trends for the future. Section 1 lists 114 jobs that require 4-year college degrees or higher and jobs usually held by college graduates but that do not require a degree.

The job descriptions are derived from the *Occupational Outlook Handbook* (see entry 402) and provide the O*NET classification code numbers. Section 2 is entitled "Quick Job Search Advice on Planning Your Career and Getting a Good Job in Less Time." This section has excellent job-seeking tips and letters and résumés written by top graduates and designed by professional résumé writers. Section 3 provides insight into important labor trends that will be prevalent through the year 2008. The article contains excellent graphs covering the trends in population, the labor force, education, employment, and occupations. Farr illustrates the fast growing jobs compared with the total job openings. The second half of this section is devoted to trends in major goods-producing and service-producing industries.

This book has some excellent advice for job-seekers. It provides names, up-to-date addresses, and URLs for various organizations that will enable new graduates or seasoned professionals to find fulfilling jobs and careers. This book is an excellent addition to the career collections in school, academic, and public libraries.—**Kay M. Stebbins**

445.   Farr, J. Michael. **America's Top Jobs for People Without College Degrees.** 3d ed. Indianapolis, Ind., JIST Works, 1997. 361p. (Top Jobs). $14.95pa. ISBN 1-56370-282-7.

Part of JIST Work's Top Job series and a new edition of *America's Top Technical and Trade Jobs*, this reasonably priced, paperbound volume contains four parts: job descriptions, labor market trends, job-hunting advice, and articles of interest. Section 1 (the majority of the contents) reprints 100 job descriptions (50 more than the 2d edition) from the *Occupational Outlook Handbook 1996-97* (OOH; see entry 402). Section 2 also depends heavily on the OOH for charts and facts but is rearranged and expanded to improve readability. In section 3, Farr guides career-seekers with helpful charts and questionnaires to match their skills to careers. He outlines job search skills in a friendly, organized way and includes brief assistance with résumés, communication, and coping—both emotionally and financially. Suggestions for further reading lead one to many other JIST Works publications. The articles in section 4 are reprinted from various Department of Labor publications. Sections 2 and 3 are identical in the Top Job books examined, but the articles in section 4 vary. The book is well formatted—the typeface is clear, with varying fonts, boldface, and italics for emphasis. The format and the emphasis on 100 "top jobs" for people without college degrees will appeal to people who do not want to tackle the OOH or the alarming array of career advice books available.—**Juleigh Muirhead Clark**

446.   Farr, J. Michael. **America's Top Medical, Education, and Human Services Jobs: Detailed Information on 73 Major Jobs with Excellent Pay and Advancement Opportunities.** 4th ed. Indianapolis, Ind., JIST Works, 1999. 341p. $16.95pa. ISBN 1-56370-492-7.

This informal, pragmatic, and lively presentation focuses on 73 occupations and trends in rapidly growing fields. The lively introduction, "top job" lists, and sections on employment trends, earnings, and growth for the major occupations and industries offer a handy overview. An advantage to this work is the organization, the bibliography (with its limitations), and the brief overview of job searching, with tips on networking and how to track contacts.

Aside from passing mention in the introduction, no acknowledgment is offered to reveal the specific Department of Labor published sources that have been incorporated in this volume. Occupational descriptions and tables are wholly included from the *Occupational Outlook Handbook* (see entry 402) and other series, with no change or interpretation. However, no citation is offered to assist the individual who wishes to pursue a search.

The section on career planning and job search—essentially a short course on the job search—outlines essentials in a breezy fashion. This section serves as a reminder for the savvy and a hint for the naïve. Here, indeed, along with the brief introduction is the author's sole original contribution.

The 27-page selected bibliography includes key published and Internet resources grouped in useful categories to pinpoint quickly subjects like government jobs, interviewing, international jobs, and displaced workers. Unfortunately, citations are incomplete, omitting publishers other than JIST Works. This poses a barrier to easy and independent access by the reader and seems self-serving. Although useful for the individual, most libraries and career counselors would have the original sources incorporated in this volume.—**Barbara Conroy**

447.   Farr, J. Michael. **America's Top Office, Management, Sales, & Professional Jobs.** 3d ed. Indianapolis, Ind., JIST Works, 1997. 377p. (Top Jobs). $14.95pa. ISBN 1-56370-291-6.

This paperbound volume contains four parts: job descriptions, labor market trends, job-hunting advice, and "Good Articles." Section 1 (the majority of the contents) reprints 100 job descriptions (40 more than the 2d edition) from the *Occupational Outlook Handbook 1996-97* (OOH; see entry 402), the majority in business. Disturbingly, librarians will note that careers for library assistants are described, but not careers in librarianship (or even information science). Section 2 also depends heavily on the OOH for charts and facts but is rearranged and expanded. In section 3, Farr aids the undecided with helpful charts and questionnaires to match skills to careers. He outlines job search skills in a friendly, organized way and offers cursory assistance with résumés, communication, and coping. Suggestions for further reading lead one primarily to other JIST Works publications. The "Good Articles" and appendixes are reprinted from various Department of Labor publications. Sections 2 and 3 are identical in the Top Job books examined, but the articles in section 4 vary. The book is well formatted in a clear typeface with varying fonts, boldface, and italics for emphasis.

Complementary books on the job-seeking process for business to consider are *Business and Finance Career Directory* and *Marketing and Sales Career Directory* (both Visible Ink Press, 1992), which include informative job descriptions written in a conversational style by people in the field but focus more attention on likely companies to approach. Also of interest is *Peterson's Job Opportunities in Business* (see ARBA 96, entry 280), which lists companies and notes what type of people (accountants, market researchers) they hire.—**Juleigh Muirhead Clark**

448.   Farr, J. Michael. **America's Top White-Collar Jobs: Detailed Information on 110 Major Office, Management, Sales, and Professional Jobs.** 5th ed. Indianapolis, Ind., JIST Works, 2001. 402p. $16.95pa. ISBN 1-56370-719-5.

The main section of *America's Top White-Collar Jobs* consists of descriptions of 110 white-collar jobs that the author believes to be among the fastest growing. These descriptions, which include information about working conditions, skills required, growth projections, and so on, are the complete entries found in the *Occupational Outlook Handbook* (see entry 402). The third section of *America's Top White-Collar Jobs* focuses on labor market trends and includes more reprints from U.S. Department of Labor sources.

Sandwiched between these two sections is the only segment that the author can claim as his own, although this has also been published elsewhere. This section, entitled "The Quick Job Search," gives excellent advice on planning a career and finding a job. Major topics include skill identification, career planning, interview skills, résumé writing, dealing with job loss, and handling finances while out of work. There are also a number of sample résumés for some of America's top white-collar jobs that were written and designed by professional résumé writers. This section, and the introduction that also includes some job-hunting tips, would be highly valuable to job seekers and is the only reason readers should purchase the book since the remaining 350-plus pages are readily accessible online or from the Department of Labor.—**Michele Russo**

449.   Farr, J. Michael, LaVerne L. Ludden, and Laurence Shatkin. **Guide for Occupational Exploration.** 3d ed. Indianapolis, Ind., JIST Works, 2001. 532p. index. $39.95pa. ISBN 1-56370-636-9.

Long an essential tool for career counselors and individuals seeking to pursue their occupational interests and skills, this new edition contains a number of changes that significantly bring the 1984 edition up to date. As with the earlier edition produced by the U.S. Department of Labor, interest areas and work groups are displayed in a structure that groups work venues logically. Both old and new editions describe each grouping/subgrouping in terms of the nature of the work and the training required. Also, each group addresses the individual's interests and skills and how those fit into the particular occupational field. Other sections of both editions address work values and settings, skills, abilities, and knowledge of the individual in a "Crosswalks" sections.

One of the new edition's strengths is its restructuring of major groups and occupational subgroupings. Major revisions include more prominence for law, construction, and transportation fields. Management and technology are brought up to date and incorporated into the various fields rather than in separate categories. Another strength is a section that incorporates job descriptions of all the occupations included in the groups. Included throughout both sections are the code numbers that lead to additional information in the Occupations Information Network (O*NET), the Department of Labor's all-new resource for jobs. Although the new edition covers fewer named occupations, the coverage frames today's workforce and labor market more effectively.

With the dynamic nature of today's workforce, the new *Guide for Occupational Exploration* is a key reference for libraries, career counselors, academic guidance personnel, and do-it-yourself individuals seeking new or renewed careers. The volume also includes an appendix with information for developers who wish to use this occupational structure in developing products.
—**Barbara Conroy**

450.   Field, Shelly. **Career Opportunities in Advertising and Public Relations.** 3d ed. New York, Facts on File, 2002. 307p. index. $49.50. ISBN 0-8160-4490-2.

In this book 86 positions and their permutations in the areas of advertising and public relations are examined in detail. Each job listing begins with a career profile. This profile includes job duties, alternate titles, salary ranges, employment prospects, advancement possibilities, best geographic area for jobs with this title, education and training needed, experience needed, special skills needed, and personality traits that are useful on the job. This information is provided in narrative form. Each job listing also includes much of the same information in tabular form, making comparisons between and among jobs easy. A career ladder is also provided, which suggests possible avenues for promotion from this job to a higher level. Each listing includes some tips for getting a job with that title. Contact information for unions and associations associated with the job are also provided.

The book contains an introduction that describes how the job entries are organized and a preface that describes how to use the book and the organization of material in the book, as well as stating the sources of the information contained in the book. This is followed by the job entry section, nine appendixes, a glossary, and an index. Also included in the book is an organization chart for a typical advertising or public relations agency. The nine appendixes include: educational institutions with degree programs in advertising and public relations; organizations offering internships in the fields; organizations offering seminars, workshops, and training in advertising and public relations; trade associations, unions, and other relevant organizations; a bibliography; a list of advertising agencies; a list of public relations agencies; a list of advertising and public relations recruiting agencies; and a glossary.

The author owns a public relations and management firm specializing in celebrity clients in music, sports, and entertainment. She has written 25 books, including 3 others on career opportunities in other fields. She is also known for motivational speaking. The publishers indicate that 30 percent of the 3d edition is new or updated material. The majority of the appendix materials have been updated.

The book is well organized. It is clearly laid out and easy to understand. Presentation of the materials in both narrative and tabular form allows both quick reference and more in-depth use of the materials. This work is recommended for job-seekers in the fields of advertising or public relations, and for library collections that support degree programs in these areas.—**Joanna M. Burkhardt**

451. Field, Shelly. **Career Opportunities in Casinos and Casino Hotels.** New York, Checkmark Books/Facts on File, 2000. 268p. index. (Career Opportunities Series). $45.00; $18.95pa. ISBN 0-8160-4122-9; 0-8160-4123-7pa.

The growing career opportunities in the casino and casino hotels industry are illustrated in this comprehensive guide. More than 90 occupations are covered within 10 general employment sections. These sections cover not only careers on the gaming floor, but also administration and management, security and surveillance, entertainment, hotel management, and food and beverage services.

Each two-page entry begins with a career profile, including salary range, employment prospects, and prerequisites. A career ladder showing the normal progression within that career also appears at the beginning of each entry. For example, a credit manager begins as a credit clerk shift supervisor and could move up to casino credit supervisor or director of casino credit. The main text describes each position in detail covering salaries; employment prospects; advancement prospects; education and training; desired experience, skills, and personality traits; unions and associations; and tips for entry, such as taking classes, relocating, or attending job fairs.

The book concludes with a series of useful appendixes listing gaming academies and dealer schools, college programs, and trade associations and unions. There is also a directory of casinos and cruise lines, gaming conferences and expositions, seminars and workshops, and gaming industry Websites. This well-written and organized book is recommended for public libraries and academic libraries where there is particular interest in the gaming industry or hotel and restaurant management.—**Erin C. Daix**

452. Field, Shelly. **Career Opportunities in the Music Industry.** 4th ed. New York, Checkmark Books/Facts on File, 2000. 280p. index. (Career Opportunities Series). $45.00; $18.95pa. ISBN 0-8160-4083-4; 0-8160-4084-2pa.

The 4th edition of *Career Opportunities in the Music Industry* gives information about 86 jobs in all aspects of the music industry, including such diverse positions as artist relations and development representative, sound technician, piano tuner, opera singer, or nightclub manager. Each entry gives alternative titles, a career ladder that illustrates a normal job progression, a position description, salary ranges, employment and advancement prospects, and minimum education and training required. Entries also contain helpful advice on desired experience, skills, and personality traits; the best geographic location to find a job; valuable unions and associations; and tips for entry. These tips include suggestions on where to look for jobs (i.e., classified ads), if internships are available, and how and where to market businesses. These are particularly helpful, especially when considering that over 80 percent of the jobs described are listed as having either poor or fair job entry prospects.

There are 11 appendixes that include information such as the names and addresses of colleges and universities that offer degrees in related fields, relevant unions and associations, record companies and distributors, booking agencies, music publishers, and entertainment industry attorneys and law firms. There is also a bibliography that includes publications as recent as 1999. The major omission from this work is information regarding the use of the Internet for job searching. Although the appendix that lists unions and associations includes e-mail and homepage addresses, there could be more information throughout the book on how to take advantage of this medium. Overall, however, the book is informative and should be helpful for anyone exploring a career in the music industry. [R: LJ, 1 Sept 2000, pp. 192-194]—**Michele Russo**

453. Field, Shelly. **Career Opportunities in the Sports Industry.** 2d ed. New York, Checkmark Books/Facts on File, 1999. 280p. index. $18.95. ISBN 0-8160-3794-9.

Essential information on career opportunities in most aspects of sports is detailed for professional athletes, sports teams, and for individual sports such as boxing, wrestling, and horse racing. Positions in sports business and administration, coaching and education, officiating, sports journalism, recreation and fitness, sports medicine, and wholesaling and retailing are also described. Even though comprehensive, there are gaps, such as the position of team psychologist and the sport of auto racing.

Entries give a brief overview of the position and then expand that brief information into a longer narrative of two to three pages. Each entry describes the nature of the position together with its salary range and the employment and advancement prospects that can be anticipated. Strategic tips for entering the position are given. Entries also detail the characteristics, experience, and training required. Information about relevant unions and associations is included.

Helpful appendixes supplement the directory. One lists academic degree programs for sports administration and physical education. Sponsors of relevant workshops, seminars, and symposiums are cited in another. Leagues, associations, and unions offer contact points for information and a diligent job search. Listings of promoters and cable/network television sports departments will be helpful for the more specialized seeker.

This update of the 1991 edition evidences the rise in sports interest and participation. The field is, in many ways, informal and the diversity of titles and positions pronounced. This volume presents a useful framework for viewing scope and possibility. The approach is somewhat promotional, blending pragmatic information with enthusiasm for the field. The information has been gathered from interviews, questionnaires, and publications, so it is largely informal.—**Barbara Conroy**

454. Field, Shelly. **Career Opportunities in Theater and the Performing Arts.** 2d ed. New York, Checkmark Books/Facts on File, 1999. 257p. index. $35.00; $18.95pa. ISBN 0-8160-3798-1; 0-8160-3799-Xpa.

Although this book was written for "the many thousands of people who aspire to work in theater and other performing arts," it is very basic and would probably not be useful beyond the high school level. It is divided into nine sections according to type of career, such as performing artist or educator. Within each section are descriptions of individual careers (e.g., actor, playwright), which include duties, salary, employment prospects, prerequisites/preparation, advancement, unions/associations, and tips for entry into the career. Position descriptions are generally adequate, but information on education, skills, training, and experience is often vague and frequently states the obvious (e.g., dancers "need to be flexible, agile, and coordinated") .

There are several appendixes of varying usefulness. Useful are lists of educational opportunities in the performing arts and of theater and music companies that employ performing arts professionals. Less useful are a list of New York City-area theaters, a list of performing arts periodicals (not annotated), and a rather randomly selected bibliography. Although entries in the list give addresses and telephone numbers, it would have been helpful for the compiler to have included Website addresses, as many organizations and companies listed have excellent Websites that include e-mail addresses as well as information about auditions, educational programs, and job opportunities. In spite of its several flaws, this book covers an unusually wide range of careers, from secretarial to management, and may be appropriate for larger high school and public libraries or where there is particular interest in the performing arts.—**Gari-Anne Patzwald**

455.   Guiley, Rosemary Ellen, and Janet Frick. **Career Opportunities for Writers.** 4th ed. New York, Facts on File, 2000. 244p. index. (Career Opportunities Series). $45.00. ISBN 0-8160-4143-1.

The 4th edition of *Career Opportunities for Writers* continues the Facts on File series designed to provide the best single source of information about jobs for all kinds of writers. Students considering a writing career will find information about entry-level jobs, while experienced writers desiring a career change can get specific information on possible employers. The book begins with an introductory essay on the outlook for employment for writers and other communicators. Individual chapters cover the mass media: newspapers and news services, magazines, television, and radio. Other chapters discuss book publishing; arts and entertainment; business communications and public relations; advertising; federal government; scholastic, academic, and nonprofit institutions and freelance services; and self-publishing. Each job listing has a quick-look heading listing the job's duties, salary range, employment prospects, and prerequisites, followed by complete information garnered from many sources, including interviews with present holders of similar positions.

The job descriptions are followed by four appendixes that list educational institutions offering undergraduate degrees in journalism and communication; useful Websites for writers; professional, industry, and trade associations and unions; and major trade periodicals. Also provided are a bibliography and an index.

Volumes like *Career Opportunities for Writers* will be most valuable to high school students and others in search of a career or seeking to make a career change. The volume is clearly written and easy to use. As with all such books, part of the material will soon be outdated, but for the foreseeable future, this volume contains much to recommend it as part of a collection of career guidance materials.—**Kay O. Cornelius**

456.   Haubenstock, Susan H., and David Joselit. Bressler, Karen W. and Elise Rosen, eds. **Career Opportunities in Art.** 3d ed. New York, Facts on File, 2001. 196p. index. $45.00. ISBN 0-8160-4245-4.

This guide provides occupational information for those seeking employment using their studio art or art history backgrounds and interests. Eight major career categories include areas such as museums, galleries, education, and art funding agencies as well as various types of artists. Eighty-four occupational sections describe jobs with basic information about their salaries, academic requirements, typical environments, and suggestions for entry and advancement in such careers. Each has a career ladder diagram that shows typical career paths.

Since artists often prefer to be self-employed, the volume may be useful for its appendixes. One appendix lists 66 educational institutions—both graduate and undergraduate, and includes trade, industrial, and vocational schools—with contact information. There is also an appendix listing scholarships and another with a limited number of internship opportunities. Likewise, the appendix of organizations and associations is not comprehensive, even in terms of the occupations listed. The bibliography includes periodicals, books, and Websites leading to additional information in these occupations.

In spite of a two-page overview of the "Romance vs. Reality" of finding a career in art, some limitations are noted in the volume that may be interpreted by a reader as being limitations on the possibilities. Most noteworthy is the omission of accessing areas of the industry, such as ceramics, that use art and design concepts in their product manufacturing. Another lack is the larger area of the craft industry, including pottery.—**Barbara Conroy**

457.   **Job Hunter's Sourcebook: Where to Find Employment Leads and Other Job Search Resources.** 3d ed. Kathleen E. Maki, ed. Detroit, Gale, 1996. 898p. index. (A Gale Career Information Guide). $70.00. ISBN 0-8103-9075-2. ISSN 1053-1874.

In today's competitive job market, up-to-date references of this type are essential for assisting job-seekers in finding career information. This 3d edition of the *Job Hunter's Sourcebook* (JHS) provides just such information, and its coverage of occupations is impressive. This edition varies from the 2 previous editions (see ARBA 94, entry 279, and ARBA 92, entry 222) not in the number of entries of sources, 10,403 (many of which are duplicate entries listed under several occupations), but in the number of categories for specific professions and vocational occupations: 179, up from 155 in the 1st edition and 165 in the 2d. New also to this edition are e-mail addresses and Website information (URLs) for some of the entries. Additionally, the reference sources section has 26 essential topics of job-hunting information, including electronic databases, periodicals, and software; tips for finding jobs, such as interview skills; and opportunities for special populations (e.g., military, minority, and young and old workers). A thorough index assists job-seekers in finding occupations and sections of interest easily. The three-column format maximizes the amount of information on a page yet is easy to read.

This work is similar in size and scope to another Gale reference, *Professional Careers Sourcebook* (7th ed.; Gale 2002), which lists 121 occupations. JHS differs in its much wider audience and leads on all kinds of jobs, not just those that require a degree. This reference will get ample use. It is reasonably priced and highly recommended for public and academic libraries. —**Edward Erazo**

458.   Lauber, Daniel. **Government Job Finder 1997-2000.** 3d ed. River Forest, Ill., Planning/Communications, 1997. 325p. illus. index. $32.95; $16.95pa. ISBN 1-884587-08-9; 1-884587-05-4pa.

Lauber has done an excellent job of providing people who are seeking positions in the government sector with a wide array of sources that can be used to identify available jobs at local, state, regional, and federal levels. In this edition, he has included Internet addresses and Websites plus online databases, recommended professional and trade periodicals, and a comprehensive list of government agencies directories. Approximately 98 percent of the contents have been revised when compared to the 2d edition published in 1994 (see ARBA 95, entry 315), reflecting the volatile nature of this material. In addition to sources, the author has included information to help guide the job-seeker through applying for a job and interviewing, plus some salary guidelines. This book can be updated by visiting the Job Finders' Internet homepage. Libraries with extensive career collections will want to acquire multiple copies of this title. Small libraries and job placement centers will consider this title an absolute must for their collections because it is so comprehensive and inexpensive.—**Judith J. Field**

459.   Lauber, Daniel. **Non-Profits and Education Job Finder 1997-2000.** River Forest, Ill., Planning/Communications, 1997. 340p. illus. index. $32.95; $16.95pa. ISBN 1-884587-09-7; 1-884587-06-2pa.

The edition of this title that covers the years 1997 to 2000 contains 2,222 sources of job leads and job-search resources in the nonprofit and education fields. This edition is divided into 30 chapters. The core material for individual disciplines, such as the arts, housing, museums, social services, and the like, is found in chapters 4 through 29, with each chapter devoted to a different specialty, all in alphabetic order. Chapter 30 is a geographic listing of resources by state for users who wish to target a specific geographic locale. The typical user may proceed immediately to these core chapters, but the author wisely cautions the reader, again and again, to read chapters 1-3 before proceeding. Chapter 1 is an excellent overview of job-hunting tools. Chapter 2 is a detailed discussion of the online job search and includes countless sources on e-mail, the World Wide Web, Gopher servers, newsgroups, mailing lists, and bulletin board services as well as a discussion of books that will simplify online job searches. Chapter 3 reports on offline job-hunting tools that are common to all in the nonprofit sector and in education.

Until the recent past, jobs and internships in the nonprofit sector were often filled by word of mouth. Today, nonprofits use advertising in specialty and trade periodicals, job hotlines, and the Internet as well as networking. *Non-Profits and Education Job Finder* is worth its weight in gold as the only reference tool to explore all these venues. It is highly recommended for most academic libraries as well as all mid-sized and large public libraries.—**Dene L. Clark**

460.   Lauber, Daniel. **Professional's Job Finder 1997-2000.** River Forest, Ill., Planning/Communications, 1997. 518p. illus. index. $36.95; $18.95pa. ISBN 1-884587-07-0; 1-884587-04-6pa.

Beginning with the premise that only 7 percent to 20 percent of job vacancies make it into the local newspaper, Lauber lists and describes other avenues for job hunting. Instead of listing companies topically or geographically as many job-hunting books do, the author takes a different strategy. He concludes that if they are not advertising in the newspaper, organizations are likely locating their candidates in professional journals and job services.

Professional's Job Finder is arranged by topics and these include "Animals," "The Arts," "Entertainment," "Financial Industry," and "Pest Control." The coverage varies. "Education" has only two entries, and the reader is referred to another book in the series. "Theater" has 3 pages with 10 sources for job advertisements, 4 job services (3 on the Internet), and 5 theater directories. Each entry is annotated with contact information, cost, and abstracts that vary in length from one line to two paragraphs and generally describe how this source can be useful to the job hunter. For instance, after reading this section, a job seeker would far rather subscribe to *ArtSearch*, which comes out semimonthly and features 200 to 400 positions, than to *TCI*, which publishes only 10 issues per year with 4 or 5 job advertisements in each issue.

The last part of the book is a list of job sources by state. These typically list state employment agencies and regional publications by this publisher and others. The publisher also supports a Website at http://jobfindersonline.com, where updated information will be available. An index concludes the book. Job-seekers will use the information and ask librarians to supply the periodicals described.—**Juleigh Muirhead Clark**

461.   Maxwell, Bruce. **Insider's Guide to Finding a Job in Washington: Contacts and Strategies to Build Your Career in Public Policy.** Washington, D.C., Congressional Quarterly, 2000. 256p. index. $29.50. ISBN 1-56802-473-8.

This career guide to job hunting in Washington, D.C., is published by a well-respected publisher of political materials. The author clearly explains the kinds of careers available in Washington as well as the process of hiring that many of the offices use. The book is divided into eight chapters, which are further divided into shorter sections. The book begins by giving tips on how to research jobs in Washington, D.C., both before one arrives and after one is in the city. It then goes on to cover how to get a Washington, D.C., internship, a congressional job, a job with a federal agency or department, a position with an interest group, a job with a trade association or labor union, or a job working with the Washington media. The chapters cover such topics as what qualities those hiring are looking for, what kind of work will be required, and the pluses and minuses of the positions. Each chapter concludes with a directory of organizations job seekers can contact. The five appendixes provide sample résumés and cover letters, a list of what college majors are appropriate for what federal job, examples of federal government vacancy announcements, a government job application, and Internet sites for government job hunting. The book concludes with a bibliography, a subject index, and a contact index.

This book will be very useful in academic libraries with strong political science departments. It will also be well received in larger public libraries.—**Shannon Graff Hysell**

462. **Professional & Technical Careers: A Guide from World Book.** Chicago, World Book, 1998. 496p. illus. index. $35.00. ISBN 0-7166-3311-6.

Professional & Technical Careers contains more than 600 careers described in terms appropriate for an international adolescent audience. Colorful, friendly, cartoon-like pictures illustrate the introductory section on career planning. In the chapter entitled "What Is Work?" the differences between paid employment, self-employment, volunteer work, and unemployment are described, as well as practical information to help the student understand the implications for mental and physical health, gender, age, personality, and appearance.

The main body of text is an alphabetic guide to specific careers. It begins with a guide to using the book, which is followed by a general subject index. The student can review the list of careers arranged topically, with headings such as "Outdoor/Active," "Artistic/Creative," or "Service and Sales." The articles are usually one page in length, but sometimes as long as seven. The longer articles have profiles of individuals who do a particular job—for example, an Indian broadcaster, a Malaysian teacher, an Irish international aid worker, a Canadian writer. Usually, the educational requirements for the United States and the United Kingdom are listed. Highlighting the articles are color-coded boxes listing skills and personal qualities needed, school subjects a student should enjoy, and general advice to contact a relevant professional organization. To find out what this organization would be, the student must consult another source.

The final chapter of the book tells the reader where to go for further information in the reader's specific country. The U.S. section relies heavily on the *Occupational Outlook Handbook* (see entry 402), but also includes a list of state employment agencies. The most unique feature is how to get information on finding a job in a foreign country, such as the topic "Working in New Zealand for Foreign Nationals." An index concludes the book and will send the fledgling toy maker to the article on "Craftwork."

The articles are informative, and the international flavor is refreshing. Not only are adolescents learning about the world of work, they are also learning about work in the world. Pair this volume with the *Occupational Outlook Handbook* for specifics on work in the United States. [R: BL, July 98, p. 1908; SLJ, Nov 98, p. 158]—**Juleigh Muirhead Clark**

463. **The Top 100: The Fastest Growing Careers for the 21st Century.** rev. ed. Chicago, Ferguson, 1998. 415p. index. $19.95pa. ISBN 0-89434-265-7.

The information found in *The Top 100* is based on the projections of the Labor Department of the United States and its division, the Bureau of Labor Statistics. Among the top growth fields for jobs in the near future are health care, computers, and education. Health care should expand because of the increase in the number of older people. Everyone has seen the growth in the computer field, but this book provides the caveat that layoffs and downsizing are not unknown in an industry in which constant change is the order of the day. Career subfields, often mentioned in the text (in italics for easy recognition) and included in an overall index, bring the number of occupations discussed to more than 500. Not all of the 100 careers projected to be the fastest growing up to the year 2006 will require a college education. High school completion and job training are all that is required for 33 percent of these jobs. A bachelor's degree claims 28 percent, whereas 8 percent must have a master's degree or higher.

The book is arranged by career so that using it is easy and fast. Entries are roughly three pages in length and follow this sequence: definition, nature of the work, requirements, opportunities for experience and exploration, methods of entering, advancement, employment outlook, earnings, conditions of work, and sources of additional information (with particulars for relevant associations, unions, and government agencies). Shaded bars at the bottom of each page show the classification codes for the occupation, school subjects that fit in with the job, minimum education level, salary ranges, and personal interests. In the text, aspects of each career are covered practically and candidly, with little attempt to gloss over the drawbacks or unpleasant parts of a job.

The idea behind this book is almost the same as that of the competing Macmillan title, *100 Best Careers for the 21st Century* (Arco/Macmillan, 1996). Although the purposes, scope, and treatments are much alike, the arrangements differ, with the title under discussion here using an A to Z format and the other title grouping careers by nature of the work. The sound profiles offered by *The Top 100* make it a necessity for any setting that attracts young people. [R: RBB, 1 Jan 98, p. 868; VOYA, April 98, p. 77]—**Randall Rafferty**

464.   **25 Jobs That Have It All.** Chicago, Ferguson, 2001. 195p. index. $12.95pa. ISBN 0-89434-327-0.

The 25 jobs listed in this book are jobs that are unusual in 3 respects: they pay salaries higher than the 2000 national average of $29,900, they are fast growing jobs, and they offer the most new jobs in a single category. Fast growing jobs are defined as those with demand expected to grow 21-35 percent ("faster than average") or more than 35 percent ("much faster than average") through the year 2000 according to the U.S. Department of Labor.

Listings begin with an overview of duties that people in this career might expect to have. This section also lists alternative job titles for the same type of work. The 2d section provides a description (approximately 2 pages long) of the primary and secondary duties of the job; the types of tools, machinery, or equipment used; other types of workers in this environment; and growing subfields or subspecialties in this area. Requirements for the job are listed in a 3d section. These data include formal education, training, certification, licensing, and continuing education requirements for each job. This section also lists personal qualities recommended in this work environment.

The 4th section is called "Exploring," and lists resources that will help the job-seeker find out more about the job. This section lists periodicals, summer job opportunities, volunteer opportunities, clubs, associations, and so on. Section 5 lists the major employers in the job categories covered. Section 6 provides advice on how to find a job and how to conduct oneself in an interview. Section 7 describes career paths and possibilities for advancement in each job category. Section 8, entitled "Earnings," lists the salary ranges expected for people in beginning, middle, and experienced ranges for each job category. Fringe benefits that can be expected are also listed. Section 9 presents the work environment by describing a typical day on the job. Clothing, hours, overtime, and travel are some of the issues covered. The potential for long-term employment in each field is discussed in section 10. The final section lists names, addresses, telephone numbers, and e-mail and Web addresses for groups that can provide more information.

The book includes an index and an alphabetic list of the 25 job categories covered. As most of the 25 job categories listed require higher education or training, this book would be most useful for the early stages of career planning. High school students and college freshmen, sophomores, and perhaps juniors would likely benefit from the information in this book. Older job-seekers who already have professional credentials or work experience might also benefit. This guide is recommended for public and academic libraries.—**Joanna M. Burkhardt**

465.   Wischnitzer, Saul, and Edith Wischnitzer. **Health-Care Careers for the 21st Century.** Indianapolis, Ind., JIST Works, 2000. 436p. $24.95pa. ISBN 1-56370-667-9.

The growing and aging of the population is putting demands on the health care field and therefore providing a surplus of openings in the job market for qualified health professionals. This career guide helps those interested in pursuing a health-related career find out more about career opportunities and discover how to go about getting those jobs. Part 1 presents an overview of the field and discusses the education needed for health care positions. Part 2 discusses the skills needed to work in health-related fields and the importance between developing a trusting relationship between health care workers and patients. Part 3 deals with the job search processes, such as networking, finding job openings, and writing a résumé. Part 4, which constitutes more than one-half of the work, outlines the various job opportunities in the health care field. More than 80 careers, organized into 5 groups, are discussed here. These include diagnosing and treating practitioners, associated health-care personnel (e.g., nurses, pharmacists), adjunctive health care personnel (e.g., anesthesiologists, laboratory technicians), rehabilitative personnel (e.g., physical therapists), and affiliated personnel (e.g., health educators). Each of the 80 careers presented has information on education, a list of schools offering a degree or certificate in the area, rate of growth of career opportunities, salary range, work setting, and an overview of what the professional does on a daily basis. The five appendixes provide additional information on alternative health care careers, admissions tests, addresses for allied health professional organizations, job search resources, and Websites for health organizations.

This volume will serve as a good starting point for those seeking introductory information into health care careers. The information presented here is straightforward and easy to understand; however, more research may need to be done for those seriously considering a career choice in one of the 80 professions listed. This resource will be useful in high school and undergraduate academic libraries as well as many public libraries.—**Shannon Graff Hysell**

466.   **The World Almanac Job Finder's Guide 1997.** By Les Krantz. Mahwah, N.J., World Almanac Books, 1996. 672p. index. $14.95pa. ISBN 0-88687-806-3.

This book is full of useful information for anyone just entering the workforce, considering changing jobs, or working abroad, as well as those seeking summer employment, relocating, or temping. The book covers such needed information as preparing a résumé, interviewing tips, and networking. Krantz's book lists jobs by career field, then by state. Each entry lists address; telephone number; employees; revenues (when available); key personnel; and a description of the company, including background.

Interestingly, a section on job descriptions is included, in which 250 jobs are profiled. There is also an annual earnings survey, literature that is available from the government, and a listing of professional magazines/journals. An added feature is a section on job opportunities, including jobs in the federal government, job hotlines, internships for students, and summer jobs for students. There is a section on job hunting in cyberspace and a section listing temporary agencies, employment agencies, computer-search agencies, and executive/sales recruiters.

The index typeface is a little small, but the index is quite adequate for this book. All in all, this is an excellent resource for anyone job hunting in the 1990s. The book is highly recommended.
—**Pamela J. Getchell**

11 Management

BIBLIOGRAPHY

467. **A Critical Guide to Management Training Videos and Selected Multimedia, 1996.**
William Ellet and Laura Winig, eds. Boston, Harvard Business Reference/Harvard Business
School Publishing; distr., New York, McGraw-Hill, 1996. 381p. index. $49.95pa. ISBN
0-87584-680-7.

One of the most effective qualities of this guide is its user-friendly format. In a well-written
preface, the editors clearly delineate the need for a review of training media and pinpoint the audience: trainers and managers who want objective information about available management training
videos. From beginning to end, the format and layout make the content accessible and useful to its
designated audience. Each page is divided into two columns: The wider one provides the video title, producer, running time, price, release date, and an in-depth review. The narrower column rates
the video in categories such as holding viewer attention, acting or presenting, instructional value,
and production quality. Other potentially useful categories are portrayal of women and minorities
and value for the money. Reviews also include overall ratings.

Chapters are arranged by content. These cover areas from change management, communication skills, customer service, and diversity to innovation, leadership, and team building. The su-
pervisory and managerial skills topic includes the largest number of training materials. In addition
to a comprehensive index, a separate listing of videos that the reviewers rated most highly supplements this format. Another useful index lists the training materials by price range. This book is an
invaluable source of information for managers and educators who regularly rent or buy training
products. As such, it can help them to avoid expensive mistakes. [R: Choice, Sept 96, p. 94]
—**Renee B. Horowitz**

DICTIONARIES AND ENCYCLOPEDIAS

468. **Encyclopedia of Management.** 4th ed. Marilyn M. Helms, ed. Farmington Hills, Mich.,
Gale, 2000. 1020p. index. $225.00. ISBN 0-7876-3065-9.

Revised and completely rewritten by 94 business scholars from 11 countries, this is the 1st
revised edition of the *Encyclopedia of Management* since the 3d edition, edited by Carl Heyel, in
1982 (see ARBA 83, entry 802). The editor worked with a panel of two other distinguished business educators to identify important topics to include and to select qualified contributors. The volume contains 348 essays on many newer topics as well as older ones, including balance sheets,
budgeting, span of control, balanced scorecards, benchmarking, chaos theory, cultural diversity,
e-manager, ergonomics, participative management, and teams. The essays are arranged alphabetically by topic, but quicker access to specific topics may be found in the detailed index. Numerous

cross-references are scattered throughout the book in bold typeface in the text and at the end of essays. Many essays are enhanced by black-and-white illustrations in the form of graphs, charts, tables, and mathematical formulas, and most essays have bibliographies and URL citations for further reading. A more in-depth reading program is outlined in the "Guide to Functional-Area Readings" at the front of the book.

The editor, editorial advisors, and contributors succeed in providing a current, comprehensive, and authoritative reference source that covers the various aspects of management. This 4th edition will be a most welcome source in most business and large academic and public libraries, especially those that own the 3d edition.—**O. Gene Norman**

469.   **Encyclopedia of Small Business.** Kevin Hillstrom and Laurie Collier Hillstrom, eds. Farmington Hills, Mich., Gale, 1998. 2v. index. $395.00/set. ISBN 0-7876-1864-0.

The *Encyclopedia of Small Business* provides information on the various issues and topics related to entrepreneurship from franchising to tax planning to home-based businesses. This reference work includes 505 essays arranged alphabetically by topic with a master index at the end of volume 2. Entries include various small business-related topics as well as names of key organizations and agencies, among which are the Internal Revenue Service and the International Franchise Association. Cross-references are provided where applicable, and each entry includes a selection of books and articles for further reading. Each entry's essays are thorough in definitions and explanations. For example, the entry for *accounting* defines the term, describes related agencies and rulings, and discusses how to choose an accountant. The entry for the *International Franchise Association* describes the history and purpose of the organization in addition to its address. The editors started their own editorial services business, Northern Lights Writers Group.

The *Encyclopedia of Small Business* is recommended to entrepreneurs interested in starting a business, and to those studying entrepreneurship. It serves as an excellent starting point for researching various topics and issues as well as a point of reference for entrepreneurs to locate information. This reference source is recommended to both university and public library collections. [R: LJ, Dec 98, p. 88; BL, 15 Dec 98, p. 763]—**Lucy Heckman**

470.   **The IEBM Dictionary of Business and Management.** Morgen Witzel, ed. London, International Thomson Business Press; distr., Albany, N.Y., Thomson Learning, 1999. 329p. $24.95pa. ISBN 1-86152-218-5.

This new dictionary is an off shoot of the publisher's six-volume *International Encyclopedia of Business and Management* (1996). With more than 7,500 terms, this is one of the most comprehensive business dictionaries available. However, the definitions are very brief—in most cases only one or two lines of text. All major areas of business are covered: accounting, economics, finance, human resource management, industrial relations, information technology, international business, management information systems, manufacturing operations, marketing, and organizational behavior. Acronyms are included, with cross-references to the definition. In the introduction, the editor, clearly identifies the limitations of the dictionary. For example, current "jargon" terms are not included, nor are those terms that are linked to specific business sectors or countries. This will be a useful edition to most business reference collections, although libraries that own Jerry Rosenberg's *Dictionary of Business and Management* (see ARBA 95, entry 187), which also contains over 7,500 terms, might not need this one.—**Thomas A. Karel**

471.   **The IEBM Regional Encyclopedia of Business and Management.** Malcolm Warner, ed. Florence, Ky., International Thomson Publishing, 2000. 4v. index. $475.00/set. ISBN 1-86152-403-X.

The IEBM Regional Encyclopedia of Business and Management is a comprehensive, authoritative, and beautifully presented 4-volume set on the business and management practices of numerous countries and regions throughout the world. The globalization of business has brought the need for such a work, which provides a comparative, interdisciplinary, and analytical snapshot view of the current state of management throughout the globe. Considerable history is included, as are commentary about the prospects of a certain country or region and the factors that would influence this. The list of contributors for *The IEBM Regional Encyclopedia of Business and Management* is impressive and reads as a "who's who" of topic scholars from universities and scholarly organizations throughout the world.

This work is divided into 4 volumes by world region: Asia Pacific, Europe, the Americas, and emerging countries. Each volume is a stand-alone work, with its own contributors; however, there is considerable cross-referencing between volumes, particularly where countries could be both in the Asia Pacific or the Americas volume as well as in the emerging countries volume. Each volume begins with a brief introduction. The first part of each volume covers general themes, providing a concise perspective on the management of the region. Part 2 is devoted to specialization themes and presents more detailed information on accounting, banking, finance, business culture and strategies, economic cooperation, human resources, industrial relations, management education, technology management, manufacturing, and marketing. The 3d part of each volume provides information on management in most of the countries in that volume's region. For example, the section on management in Australia covers managers' characteristics and employment, women and management, recruitment and mobility, remuneration, career planning, factors influencing managerial success, unionization, and employee relations. Each individual section also includes a page or two of additional readings, *see also* references, and a list of related topics available in the encyclopedia. Each section is a stand-alone essay with the author and institutional affiliation provided.

The IEBM Regional Encyclopedia of Business and Management is an impressive set. The text is crisp and clean, with considerable use of headings and subheadings and a brief table of contents for each section. There are figures and tables throughout the set, although these are provided sparingly. At first glance, the set might appear both overwhelming and boring. However, the arrangement of the set by region, then into general and country-specific sections, lets the reader quickly find the appropriate information. Although detailed and complex, the sections read smoothly and are not overly technical. For example, country profiles of Hong Kong, New Zealand, and Argentina are enjoyable to read in spite of being comprehensive; they give the reader a good perspective on the state of business and management in these countries. Similarly, the section on banking in Asia Pacific is informative, well written, and up-to-date.

With the global marketplace becoming a reality, many publishers are rushing to offer sources that provide detailed information on countries beyond the United States and Western Europe, particularly emerging countries. *The IEBM Regional Encyclopedia of Business and Management* compares favorably with other offerings, particularly because of its comprehensive and finely written text, its beautiful presentation, and the credentials of its contributors. The set would be an excellent addition to academic and special library collections. It would also be a good choice for public libraries that serve patrons with business or investment interests in the global marketplace.—**Sara Anne Hook**

472.   Keen, Peter G. W., and Ellen M. Knapp. **Every Manager's Guide to Business Processes: A Glossary of Key Terms & Concepts for Today's Business Leader.** Boston, Mass., Harvard Business School Press; distr., New York, McGraw-Hill, 1996. 219p. index. $24.95; $14.95pa. ISBN 0-87584-627-0; 0-87584-575-4pa.

Concentrating on 100 leading business process concepts, this book is less a glossary and more of a guidebook to an area that has taken on increasing importance. The volume begins with a 36-page introduction to business processes, their history, significance, and development in terms of process movements. The terms covered range from the familiar, such as *total quality management* and *benchmarking*, to the more exotic—*informate* or *penzias axiom*. Entries vary from one paragraph to several pages. Most constitute essay-length articles going well beyond straightforward definitions. Almost every entry gives the historical, conceptual, and business context in language that is uncluttered and free of jargon. Value judgments are sometimes included, such as for the entry for *folklore processes* where the authors advise, "They can and should be abandoned."

Cross-references give links to related terms. Notes in the margin provide anecdotes, reports on major corporations' experiences, extended remarks, and other supplementary information. Tables, charts, and diagrams are supplied in many articles. Bibliographic citations are in the introduction in full form and in the entries as abbreviated references. An index at the end completes the volume.

Much more than a simple glossary, this book is a guide to the conceptual landscape of business processes, giving insight and perspective to ideas that are quickly passing into popular speech and culture. The writing is so interesting and instructive that this book could be used as a supplement to management texts. It is suitable and highly recommended for any academic or public library.—**Gerald L. Gill**

473.   Keen, Peter G. W. **Business Multimedia Explained: A Manager's Guide to Key Terms & Concepts.** Boston, Harvard Business School Press; distr., New York, McGraw-Hill, 1997. 379p. index. $39.95; $24.95pa. ISBN 0-87584-718-8; 0-87584-772-2pa.

Depending upon one's perspective, business multimedia tends to be seen as either "presentation" software (about as welcome as a vacation slide show) or an oxymoron. Keen, in the preface and introduction, does suggest some potentially useful applications in training and specialized forms of modeling. He makes a reasonable argument for further investigation of the topic, although nowhere near a compelling case for investment in the technology. His examples are isolated, and the results, although suggestive, are not backed up by any kind of analysis, let alone conclusive evidence.

The majority of the book is a glossary. A variety of terms, phrases, and concepts prompt miniessays, generally a page or two in length. Entries are numerous but by no means exhaustive. For example, compact disc technology is represented by listings for "CD-Audio," "CD-I," "CD Plus," "CD-R," "CD-ROM," "CD Technology," and "CD-XA," but not "CD-RW" (rewritable). In the introduction, Keen insists that the book is not about the Internet—but a great many of the terms are. The essays cannot really be called definitions, because many times they overlook important aspects of the technologies in question or get them wrong. For example, the entry for "CD-XA" states that it is a file format that is unique in storing both video and sound together, but the book's own coverage of the Motion Picture Expert Group standard contradicts this statement. The listing for Virtual Reality Modeling Language (VRML) makes no mention of the need for a compatible browser and states that VRML is not interactive. The book does provide a sort of "once over lightly," with a few nods to such controversial topics as censorship and pornography.—**Robert M. Slade**

DIRECTORIES

474.   Landskroner, Ronald A. **The Nonprofit Manager's Resource Directory.** New York, John Wiley, 1996. 522p. $65.00pa. ISBN 0-471-14839-3.

This directory is a compendium of more than 2,000 information sources that any not-for-profit organization needs. It brings together both reference and bibliographic citation information in an annotated guide format. The chapters cover subjects in a wide spectrum of topics, such as financial management, human resources, governance and boards, legal issues, marketing, planning, volunteerism, and 10 other areas. Within each chapter, resources are grouped into these subsections: providers of products and services (generally commercial companies); support organizations; subject-interest periodicals; publications/software/tapes; and, where relevant, Internet resources, e-mail addresses, and Websites.

With few exceptions, entries have a descriptive annotation, and many are quite extensive. Entries relevant to another chapter are repeated with cross-references to the main annotation. An unusual feature is the directory of colleges and universities offering classwork on managing nonprofit organizations, which includes a description of the programs of study. The appendix surveys general reference books serving nonprofit interests (e.g., *Encyclopedia of Associations* [Gale, 1997]) that would be found in most libraries.

Many items covered here could be found in other reference books, but not without a laborious search process. The annotations add much value, and the bibliographic sections will be highly effective as a collection development tool. The logical arrangement and up-to-date content will provide an excellent introduction for any user. It is unfortunate that there is no index, but the expanded table of contents and cross-references will provide adequate access for most users. [R: Choice, Mar 97, p. 1138]—**Gary R. Cocozzoli**

HANDBOOKS AND YEARBOOKS

475.   Avery, Christine, and Diane Zabel. **The Quality Management Sourcebook: An International Guide to Materials and Resources.** New York, Routledge, 1997. 327p. index. $125.00. ISBN 0-415-10831-4.

The purpose of this work is to provide a resource for information about quality management. It begins with an overview of the total quality management (TQM) movement, including basic TQM concepts. An annotated bibliography of some of the most important works on quality improvement follows.

The next section of this sourcebook examines applications of TQM. Writings summarized here are organized according to the U.S. government's system for classifying economic activities. Thus, the authors look at books and articles about quality in the construction industry, publishing, pharmaceuticals, hospitals, educational institutions, and other manufacturing and service areas. Most of these works are case studies that analyze TQM implementation in particular companies or institutions. Other subdivisions of this book focus on various essential aspects of quality management, such as teams, customers, analytic and statistical tools, corporate culture, leadership, training, and communication. Another section includes quality in the future and the role of ISO 9000. Also of help to researchers are the glossary of terms associated with TQM and name, title, and subject indexes.

Although new books on quality improvement will continue to appear, the authors have made their sourcebook independent of time constraints by defining strategies for ongoing research. They list presses that publish books about quality improvement, databases, training materials, executive development programs, quality management consultants, and TQM associations. Perhaps most useful is the list of periodicals and newsletters relating to quality. Such information, added to the authors' recommendation of Internet sources, ensures that Avery and Zabel's work remains an outstanding resource for up-to-date material on total quality management. [R: Choice, June 97, p. 1635]—**Renee B. Horowitz**

476.   Berryman-Fink, Cynthia, and Charles B. Fink. **The Manager's Desk Reference.** 2d ed. New York, AMACOM, 1996. 370p. index. $24.95. ISBN 0-8144-0342-5.

Updating the 1989 edition (see ARBA 90, entry 266), the authors have included new topics such as change management, diversity in organizations, and violence in the workplace among the 45 subjects covered in this alphabetically arranged source. Each chapter attempts to provide "practical, yet substantive, sources of information" for managing people—peers, subordinates, supervisors, customers, the press, and the public. Topics average from five to seven pages in length and chapters begin with a brief introduction and conclude with an unannotated bibliography of three to six current books or journal articles to provide additional sources of information. Depending upon the subject, the discussion may also include legal issues, how to overcome obstacles, and guidelines for influencing desired behaviors.

To its credit, the writing style is clear and concise. Cross-references in the text help to guide the reader to other related topics, and a 13-page index provides detailed access into the body of the work. As a general introduction to the popular management literature, patrons and library managers may find this work useful. Yet, library managers may benefit more from *The Library Manager's Deskbook* (American Library Association, 1995), which is specifically tailored to a library setting (e.g., "how can library professionals be distinguished from paraprofessionals?") , with a "library management tip" section in each chapter. Nonetheless, this modestly priced, quick-reference source provides a current overview of timely issues written in a concise fashion, suitable for both the beginner and the seasoned professional.—**Ilene F. Rockman**

477.   Bryce, Herrington J. **Financial and Strategic Management for Nonprofit Organizations: A Comprehensive Reference to Legal, Financial, Management, and Operations Rules and Guidelines for Nonprofits.** 3d ed. San Francisco, Calif., Jossey-Bass, 2000. 776p. index. (The Jossey-Bass Nonprofit & Public Management Series). $49.95. ISBN 0-7879-5026-2.

This tome is intended for use as a manual, reference, or textbook for nonprofit-sector managers. Its main focus is on the U.S. regulatory environment, but it includes two brief summary sections on charitable status in Canada and one on associations in South Australia for comparative purposes. The work's 19 chapters group into 5 sections dealing with classes of nonprofits and rules governing them, funding, risk and cost control, managing finances, and strategic planning. The chapters in each section are in turn subdivided into many parts of a few pages each on specific subtopics. The 13 appendixes relate to 11 chapters. Added features include further readings and notes. Contents provide detailed access to sections, chapters, subtopics, figures, tables, sidebars, and exhibits. A subject index presents another entry point.

In a note to management professors, the author indicates that for business schools this hefty reference is too long for use in a single course, but its modular design with relatively self-contained chapters allows it to be used flexibly as the principal text in more than one course. The writer is a business academic at the College of William and Mary, with past associations with the Brookings Institute, MIT, Harvard, NATO, and other institutions. He has also served as president or board member with a variety of nonprofit and governmental organizations.

This text will be a necessary acquisition for business schools. Larger general management collections and appropriate special collections will also be interested where funds permit.—**Nigel Tappin**

478.   Codes of Professional Responsibility: Ethics Standards in Business, Health, and Law.
4th ed. Rena A. Gorlin, ed. Washington, D.C., BNA Books, 1999. 1149p. index. $95.00. ISBN
1-57018-148-9.

This collection of 59 codes of ethics covers a variety of professions and organizations, primarily in business, health, and law. Most are full-text, but seven present only the important sections of the text with the remaining portions summarized. An information section that details the
goals and enforcement policies of the organization accompanies each code. There are also the expected address data, with e-mail and Website, and a history of the adoption of the code. While the
scope of professions is not all-encompassing, what is included covers a wide range of the most
commonly sought associations.

The appendixes are a convenient source of a variety of ethics resources. The 1st section covers organizations, but is grouped into 3 subsections (the U.S., elsewhere, and U.S. government).
This may confuse some users, as the page headers do not reflect the subdivisions. The 2d section
deals with informational resources: ethics-oriented periodicals arranged by title, reference
works arranged by publisher, and Websites. The periodical listing uses shortcuts by referring users elsewhere for information on certain publications. But these *see* references are rather unclear,
and it is inconvenient as well as confusing. The reference works section lists only title (and author
where relevant), with no further publication date or annotation. An arrangement only by publisher
(including address date) is odd, as the individual titles are not retrievable through any of the indexes. The 3d section brings together hard-to-find electronic resources. It is divided into bibliographies available online, Internet listservs, and discussion lists with information on how to
subscribe.

The index is grouped into sections. The 1st is an index of ethics issues that have appeared
within individual codes. The 2d is a listing of professions, along with an index of subjects covered
in the corresponding code. This is useful for codes with many pages and subsections, but less important for shorter ones. The final segment is an index of organizations mentioned within the text
of the codes. The multi-index format is complex, and users will need to take the time to become familiar with it.

The convenience of having in one place the actual codes of ethics for diverse organizations
and professions makes this volume worthwhile for any public, academic, or corporate library and a
recommended purchase. Having the information on organizations, the Websites, and other contact
data as a source will be much appreciated by anyone seeking updated versions, corrections, or supplements of the codes.—**Gary R. Cocozzoli**

479.   Dienhart, John W., and Jordan Curnutt. Business Ethics: A Reference Handbook. Santa
Barbara, Calif., ABC-CLIO, 1998. 444p. index. (Contemporary Ethical Issues). $39.50. ISBN
0-87436-863-4.

The goals of the authors, both members of the Philosophy Department at St. Cloud University, were "to write a comprehensive reference book for business ethics by providing brief discussions of major topics in the field and to provide a theoretical orientation to integrate these topics."
The book is organized into 5 broad thematic areas and then broken down into 18 chapters. For example, in "The Employee" section one finds chapters on "Terms and Conditions of Employment,"
"Health and Safety," "Privacy," "Discrimination and Affirmative Action," "Sexual Harassment,"
and "Whistleblowing and Loyalty." Each chapter is 15 to 25 pages long and is organized into standard subsections. These include "Ethics," "International Issues," "Economics," "Law," "Selected
Cases," and "Statutes and Regulations."

In addition to covering a wide range of business ethics topics, the authors provide supplementary reference material. These include a discussion of Codes of Ethical Conduct; brief
biographical sketches of 41 business ethics scholars; a 10-page directory of business

organizations and associations related to business ethics; a bibliography of relevant print and nonprint materials; a 27-page glossary of terms; and a list of court cases, federal statutes, and agencies. An index is included.

This work provides a valuable service by pulling together a wide range of business ethics themes and issues into a format accessible to students and laypersons. *Business Ethics* is recommended for academic business libraries and others whose patrons have an interest in business ethics.—**Gordon J. Aamot**

480.   Kemper, Robert E. **Quality, TQC, TQM: A Meta Literature Study.** Lanham, Md., Scarecrow, 1997. 559p. index. $59.50. ISBN 0-8108-3346-8.

This interesting study compiles the most influential writings of the last half-century on "quality." Using citation indexing as a meta-analysis methodology, the author attempts to identify the present state of quality knowledge. To define "quality," the author, a professor of management at Northern Arizona University, uses both a dictionary definition and a definition from an authoritative business text. For the purposes of the study, "quality" was also seen as interchangeable with the following terms found in the literature: property, attribute, character, and trait. The process of quality also includes at least six other variables: effectiveness, efficiency, leadership, management, assertiveness, and cooperation. The intended audience consists of readers with a general interest in quality—managers, supervisors, and others who practice, or (as the author says) should practice, quality routinely; researchers investigating quality; and students seeking an imaginative area for interesting study and research.

This work is arranged in 2 related parts. The 1st section is a 40-page bibliographic essay that discusses key theoretical approaches and authors. It also lists the most-cited quality literature identified in the study. These lists include key sources of quality literature; most-cited authors (cited at least five times); most-cited professional associations; most-cited publishers; most-cited periodical sources; and works about or based on the philosophy of W. Edwards Deming. The 2d section, which comprises the majority of the work, is an alphabetically arranged list of 5,839 citations covering some aspect of quality. Items from the "key sources" list are identified by bold typeface, and a number noting multiple citings is also included if appropriate. The work also includes subject and contributor indexes.

This work is significant in several ways. First, it identifies the most influential works—as determined by citation analysis—from many different areas of quality research. Second, its scope is such that it has allowed the author to assemble a broad range of quality literature. The result is a work that not only pulls together much of the literature on quality, but also identifies the elite literature for researchers and other interested persons. Flipping back and forth between the lists and citations may be tiresome for researchers and librarians, but both will find this work useful. It is highly recommended for academic and public libraries serving users with interests in quality. —**Gordon J. Aamot**

481.   **Management Consulting: Exploring the Field, Finding the Right Job, and Landing It!** [CD-ROM]. Boston, Harvard Business School Press, 1996. Minimum system requirements (Windows version): IBM or compatible 486. Double-speed CD-ROM drive. Windows 3.1. 8MB RAM. SVGA 256-color monitor. Soundblaster-compatible sound card. Minimum system requirements (Macintosh version): 68040. Double-speed CD-ROM drive. 8MB RAM. 8 bit color monitor (16 bit recommended). $39.95. ISBN 0-87584-752-8.

This well-designed, easy-to-install, smooth-running hypermedia CD-ROM teaches prospective consultants about the work, client expectations, major firms, and strategies for successfully obtaining work. Text introductions, a glossary, self-tests of management concepts,

QuickTime movie clips, and listings for 50 top firms are all integrated into a lively and colorful approach to educating the viewer. Viewers are given a rare and relatively candid peek into the world of consulting. Industry representatives with varying years of experience share their views on a variety of topics. Case interviews, standard practices, and general impressions are shared by emissaries from all segments of the business, representing a variety of ethnic and racial groups. Unfortunately, although most female informants are asked about balancing work and home responsibilities, few of the male informants give opinions on that topic. In addition to this slight evidence of sexism in the interviews, a more glaring flaw is the lack of an index or table of contents, which would allow the viewer to track completion of sections or to pick up easily where they had left off. Despite these annoyances, the disc offers libraries a rich resource of information about the work of management consulting and major firms in the area in an appealing, engaging format. —**Lynne M. Fox**

482.   **The Portable MBA Desk Reference: An Essential Business Companion.** 2d ed. Nitin Nohria, ed. New York, John Wiley, 1998. 680p. index. (The Portable MBA Series). $35.00. ISBN 0-471-24530-5.

    The 2d edition of *The Portable MBA Desk Reference* was prepared under the editorial direction of Nohria, a professor at Harvard Business School. It is one of 11 titles in the Wiley Portable MBA Series. Roughly one-half of the reference work consists of an alphabetically ordered encyclopedia of a wide spectrum of current business terms and topics. Each entry is concisely defined in nontechnical language, followed by a discussion of its application in the business world and, in many cases, one or more practical examples. Extensive cross-references to other entries enable the reader to appreciate relationships among concepts. Approximately one-third of the book is devoted to sources of business information, arranged by 48 subject areas. Much more than simply a list, each entry for a printed reference contains title, author(s), frequency of publication, publisher or source, and a brief but pertinent description of the information offered. Electronic entries are also accompanied by descriptions as well as access information. A directory of publishers, vendors, and providers gives contact information, such as addresses, telephone, and fax numbers. A 3d section of the volume contains appendixes that offer a wide variety of interesting and useful facts in list or tabular form. The table of contents, list of entries by topic, list of references, and an index enable readers to quickly locate desired information. The book provides authoritative and readable data in user-friendly format at a relatively modest cost.—**William C. Struning**

483.   Sitarz, Daniel. **The Complete Book of Small Business Legal Forms.** 3d ed. Carbondale, Ill., Nova Publishing, 2001. 255p. index. (The Small Business Library). $24.95pa. (w/CD-ROM). ISBN 0-935755-84-5.

    The Complete Book of Small Business Legal Forms, revised and updated in its 3d edition, is intended for small business owners who either cannot afford or who want to avoid the need to hire expensive attorneys. Intended to be legally valid in all 50 states, it combines text and simple forms into a comprehensive source of information on basic legal issues that a small business might encounter in its formation and daily operations. *The Complete Book of Small Business Legal Forms* is part of Nova Publishing's series for legal self help. The author is an attorney who has written several books on legal matters for the general public, including business law, family law, and estate planning.

    The Complete Book of Small Business Legal Forms is divided into 19 chapters. Chapter 1 is a brief overview of the use of legal forms in business as well as an introduction of how to use the book. The remaining 18 chapters each cover a particular aspect of small business law, including contracts, powers of attorney, real estate leases, rental and sale of personal property, financing agreements, collections, and promissory notes. Each chapter contains a short overview that sets a foundation for the topic and introduces the most common terminology. The writing style is clear and straightforward and uses language that the general public can understand. Each chapter then provides a variety of generic forms that are also available on the CD-ROM. There are 138 forms offered in *The Complete Book of Small Business Legal Forms*. These forms are quite basic in content and design. There is a three-page index as well as a detailed table of contents and list of the forms and their numbers on the CD-ROM. Instructions are provided on the use of the CD-ROM, as well as a short statement that describes the terms and conditions of use.

There are numerous form books available for attorneys and their staffs. The publication of form books for the general public is a more recent phenomenon. However, a quick search on OCLC's WorldCat revealed a considerable number of offerings, particularly for business law matters. Legal form books for the general public like *The Complete Book of Small Business Legal Forms* can be useful in providing the business person with a basic working knowledge of the kinds of legal matters he or she needs to address in setting up and operating a small business. However, they will never be a substitute for the advice of a trusted attorney who is skilled in business law and who can craft documents that meet the specific needs of the particular business and that are drafted according to applicable state and federal laws.

The Complete Book of Small Business Legal Forms is easy to read, logically organized, and attractively produced. As a basic introduction to legal issues and forms related to small business, it would be an appropriate volume for public libraries to have on hand for their local small businesses and entrepreneurs. Libraries that purchase this book will want to be mindful of the conditions of use for the CD-ROM.—**Sara Anne Hook**

484.   Sitarz, Daniel. **The Complete Book of Small Business Management Forms.** Carbondale, Ill., Nova Publishing, 2002. 255p. index. (The Small Business Library). $24.95pa. (w/CD-ROM). ISBN 0-935755-56-X.

This book will be a useful handbook for the busy small business manager needing access to the proper forms that will better organize his or her business. This work contains more than 140 forms that are photocopy-ready or can be printed through the use of a personal computer with the aid of the attached CD-ROM. The forms provided cover a variety operations, including personnel (e.g., application, job description forms, performance reviews), federal tax and workplace forms (e.g., W-2 forms, INS form 1-9), accounting forms (for bank accounts and petty cash, business assets and inventory, business expenses, among others), federal income tax forms checklists and schedules, and general management forms (e.g., telephone call records, mail sent log). Also provided are marketing forms, business credit documents, business financing documents, and collection documents. Forms for purchase of goods, sale of goods, and basic receipts round out the volume. A list of the forms on the CD-ROM follows the table of contents and will aid the user in finding which form they need. Along with the forms, the author, a professor and business attorney, also provides valuable advice on how to organize and use the forms. Tools such as this and *The Complete Book of Small Business Legal Forms* (see entry 483) will be useful in public libraries that cater to business entrepreneurs within their community.—**Shannon Graff Hysell**

12 Marketing and Trade

ATLASES

485.   **Rand McNally Commercial Atlas & Marketing Guide 2000.** 131st ed. Skokie, Ill., Rand McNally, 2000. 578p. index. $395.00. ISBN 0-528-84173-4.

The goal of this publication is to bring together the most current economic and geographic information for marketing and commercial use. The resource is arranged into six sections, each with its own introduction that includes a glossary of terms used and suggestions for how to use the data. Section 1 presents 14 detailed maps of U.S. and Canadian metropolitan areas. Each area map shows in detail the areas transportation routes, industrial areas, airports, major shopping areas, universities and colleges, military bases, parks, and selected areas of interest. The second section focuses on the transportation and communications industries within the United States. The data provided give information about highway, airline, and railroad systems, as well as telephone industries and the postal service (including zip codes). Section 3 provides data on the economy of the United States in the states and counties. Section 4 provides data on population statistics and trends. The final two sections provide state maps and an index to places in the United States. The maps provide urban areas, railroads, and rivers and lakes. A key to the symbols on the maps, population symbols, and a list of railroads serving the state are also given.

This resource is a must-have for business libraries, academic libraries featuring business graduate programs, and larger public libraries. The maps and the demographic information will be useful to many in need of up-to-date business-planning information.—**Shannon Graff Hysell**

BIBLIOGRAPHY

486.   Metz, Allan, comp. **A NAFTA Bibliography.** Westport, Conn., Greenwood Press, 1996. 491p. index. (Bibliographies and Indexes in Economics and Economic History, no.18). $89.50. ISBN 0-313-29463-1.

As stated in the introduction, this volume is the first book-length bibliography covering the development, passage, and status of the North American Free Trade Agreement (NAFTA). The bibliography covers English-language books, journal articles, and other materials from 1988 through 1995, excluding review literature, television transcripts, and letters to the editor. Works in which NAFTA is not the primary focus are also excluded unless the item is unique or covers a particular subject matter.

The book is divided into 3 format-based parts. The 1st part covers serial publications. Items indexed are arranged under broad subject headings, such as "business," and are defined as either multiple entries or single entries. Multiple entries list articles from the same magazine that have appeared over time. Most of these entries are not annotated. Single entries are annotated, for the most part, and are derived from scholarly journals. The multiple entry lists are especially useful because they identify those magazines that contain comprehensive coverage of NAFTA. The 2d part covers books, government documents, selected dissertations, and pamphlets. Entries are categorized by format and then chronologically by publication date. Of particular use in this section are references to special reports from research institutes. The final part covers nonbook materials. This section is rather lean but does introduce the reader to a variety of useful sources, although only six Internet sites are listed, and they are not accompanied by any commentary about their specific content or usefulness. Author and subject indexes complete the volume.

The book's strengths are notable. It is generally well organized, the content has been informed by a broad range of indexing services, and the inclusion of both magazines and scholarly serials adds a significant dimension to the understanding of NAFTA's development. However, aside from the choice of typeface that makes the pages difficult to read, the lack of clearly delineated criteria used for selecting or not selecting materials beyond references to language and period leaves the reader without any framework for understanding what additional resources have been excluded from the bibliography. [R: Choice, May 97, pp. 1476-1478]—**Robert V. Labaree**

DICTIONARIES AND ENCYCLOPEDIAS

487.   **The Elgar Companion to Consumer Research and Economic Psychology.** Peter E. Earl and Simon Kemp, eds. Northhampton, Mass., Edward Elgar, 1999. 649p. index. $200.00. ISBN 1-85898-554-4.

This fine scholarly reference work analyzes and surveys consumer research and economic psychology. It includes more than 100 commissioned entries, which run from "acculturation" to "work effort." The editors, both university professors in New Zealand, have assembled an impressive, international group of more than 110 scholar/researcher contributors. Each entry includes a brief overview of an area of research and interest in addition to a brief listing of some important journal articles and books in that area. Some of the especially interesting and varied topics covered in this work are brand loyalty, gambling, culture shock, shoplifting, tax evasion, children's savings, vanity, the psychology of poverty, and the history of economic psychology. All entries are signed and include bibliographies. An extensive index readily locates related topics not found in the alphabetic list of topics. Several well-done tables and figures are also provided. The editors state that the work will meet the needs of undergraduates, graduates, and researchers alike from various disciplines—business administration, economics, marketing, and psychology, to name a few. Edward Elgar Publishing has several other notable titles on economic psychology. This work is expensive, but highly recommended for large academic and public libraries.—**Edward Erazo**

488.   **The IEBM Encyclopedia of Marketing.** Michael J. Baker, ed. Florence, Ky., International Thomson Business Press/International Thomson Publishing, 1999. 865p. index. $149.95. ISBN 1-86152-304-1.

This comprehensive work is a combination textbook and reference resource. First published in 1995, most of the chapters have been significantly revised for this edition. There are 63 chapters, organized into 6 major areas: the nature and scope of marketing, theoretical foundations, marketing management, the marketing mix, marketing in practice, and special topics. The last section includes eight new chapters (e.g., "Green Marketing" and "Postmodern Marketing") . The encyclopedia is written by more than 75 contributors, most of which are American and British academics, although several other countries are also represented. Each chapter is well organized with the subsections highlighted for ease of use, and each concludes with a bibliography (ranging from two items to four pages of citations) and cross-references to other chapters. Some of the chapters contain flowcharts, diagrams, and tables (e.g., "the retail growth cycle" and "an integrated model of product promotion"). This book will fill the need for "deep background" reference information on marketing, although it is not well suited for ready-reference use. Two recent reference works that better serve that function are *The AMA Marketing Encyclopedia* (NTC Business Books, 1995) and *Marketing: The Encyclopedic Dictionary* (Blackwell, 1999).—**Thomas A. Karel**

489. **Importers Manual USA and the Dictionary of International Trade.** 1996-97 ed. [CD-ROM]. San Rafael, Calif., World Trade Press, 1996. Minimum system requirements (Windows version): IBM or compatible 386. CD-ROM drive. DOS 3.3. Windows 3.1. 8MB RAM. 10-20MB hard disk space. VGA 640 x 480 monitor (SVGA recommended). Windows-compatible mouse. PostScript or PCL printer and ATM or TrueType font manager (only for printing). Minimum system requirements (Macintosh version): 68020. CD-ROM drive. System software 6.0.7. 5MB RAM. 5MB hard disk space. 13-inch monitor or PowerBook. $149.00.

The electronic version of *Importers Manual USA* consists of a CD-ROM and an 11-page guide. The guide provides instructions for easy installation and an explanation of the nine main sections of the manual. One of these sections, the "Commodity Index," is the main feature of the reference. It is organized according to the 99 chapters of the Harmonized Tariff Schedule of the United States (HTSUS), used by the U.S. Customs Service to classify and assign duties for U.S. imports. The paper version of this title (see ARBA 96, entry 298) includes a product index. This index is not available on the CD-ROM, yet finding the appropriate chapter for a given product in the "Commodity Index" proves to be relatively easy.

The other eight sections of the manual, covering topics ranging from "International Banking" to "Container Packing," may be accessed directly from the main screen by clicking on the appropriate icon or through hot links (blue underlined items) found in tables, indexes, and text throughout the CD-ROM. When the user clicks on a hot link, it becomes highlighted and the screen shifts to that chosen topic. When initially played on a 486DX66 with 8MB RAM and CD-2X, the disc yielded disappointing results—the response time was too slow. However, when the CD-ROM was switched to a Pentium 100 MHz with 16MB RAM and CD-6X, response time evaporated and desired screens appeared in split seconds following appropriate commands. Corporate libraries, libraries that support trade promotion activities, academic libraries with major business collections, and large public libraries will all find this CD-ROM extremely useful, providing the libraries have upgraded equipment as well as the printing capabilities contained in the bibliographic description.—**Dene L. Clark**

490. **The International Dictionary of Event Management.** 2d ed. Joe Goldblatt and Kathleen S. Nelson, eds. New York, John Wiley, 2001. 279p. $25.00pa. ISBN 0-471-39453-X.

The International Dictionary of Event Management is the 2d edition of a compilation of terms, definitions, and concepts used by those who design, plan, coordinate, market, and manage large-scale meetings, exhibits, conferences, and conventions—collectively termed *events*. The editors, Joe Goldblatt (George Washington University) and Kathleen S. Nelson (University of Nevada at Las Vegas), are accredited Certified Special Event Professionals (CSEP) by the International Special Events Society. The book could be helpful for those preparing for CSEP exams, as well as to those who manage or who are associated with events.

The major portion of the book is an alphabetic listing of more than 3,500 terms and their definitions, covering a broad spectrum of terms, ranging from business to cuisine. The included terms lean toward operational and marketing aspects rather than planning. For example, PERT is classified as a "graphic tool," without reference to critical path. In future editions, it might be useful to include references to sources and provide more detailed information to specific terms, such as PERT, so that the present dictionary format is retained while serious readers are given points of departure for further study. A second section sorts terms into four functional categories pertinent to event management: administration, coordination, marketing, and risk management. All terms are given in English, suggesting that the dictionary is intended largely for English-speaking event managers or that English terms have been widely adopted as an international means of communication in the industry.

The dictionary is unique in its field. It provides a basis for meaningful and effective communication in the fastest-growing segment of the travel industry. Potential sponsors and prospective attendees of events can also find useful insights into events and their management.—**William C. Struning**

491. Koschnick, Wolfgang J. **Dictionary of Social and Market Research.** New York, John Wiley, 1996. 416p. $59.95. ISBN 0-470-23733-3.

A serious difficulty that plagues practitioners and students of social and marketing research is the vast number of terms, concepts, and techniques that are required to enable meaningful communication. Koschnick's *Dictionary of Social and Market Research* provides concise and authoritative definitions and explanations of more than 2,500 technical terms that are most likely to be encountered in the practice or study of behavioral research. More than simply a dictionary, this reference volume can be used as an overview of current research practices. Entries have been carefully cross-referenced, so that definitions used in explaining a given term are themselves defined. Most of the explanations can be understood by readers with little technical background, although some of the more quantitative entries can best be appreciated by those who have studied or practiced social or market research or who are familiar with mathematical or statistical terminology. Even students of statistics may benefit from the insightful definitions. The book is remarkable for the broad range and depth of information, understandable to a reader with only modest technical training, and compressed into a single volume.—**William C. Struning**

DIRECTORIES

492. **Business Sales Leads.** 1997 ed. [CD-ROM]. Carter Lake, Iowa, PhoneDisc, 1997. 2 discs. Minimum system requirements (Windows version): IBM or compatible 386. CD-ROM drive. Windows 3.1. 4MB RAM. Minimum system requirements (Macintosh version): Macintosh Plus/Classic. CD-ROM drive. System 6.04. $79.95.

In the past few years, many companies have developed CD-ROMs full of telephone directory information. Naturally, they have improved as technology has improved and the data have been "matched" to an electronic format. The *Business Sales Leads* product is terrific. The CD-ROM no longer has to be installed on a PC's hard drive; the software needed to run the disc is on the disc! This feature alone makes it perfect for library circulating collections.

Businesses can be searched on disc 1 by name, type, or Standard Industrial Classification, and then limited by city, state, street, zip code, county, Metropolitan Statistical Area, area code, or "within a mile circle." Disc 2 can be searched by business name, address, and telephone, with the same "limit" choices. Both discs can be limited to businesses or residences or both listings as well. Help screens are easy to locate and useful. Printing is quick and easy, and an export feature allows fast, flexible, predefined or customized formats. If a PC has a modem, an "auto dial" feature saves even more time.

Businesses can find new customers, conduct direct mail campaigns, enlarge telemarketing efforts, designate research markets, assign sales territories, and locate suppliers. Individuals will use it to find lost friends and plan trips. Reasonably priced, this or one of PhoneDisc's other business discs may be perfect for individuals or a library or business.—**Susan C. Awe**

493.   **Consumer Sales Leads.** 1997 ed. [CD-ROM]. Carter Lake, Iowa, PhoneDisc, 1997. 5 discs. Minimum system requirements (Windows version): IBM or compatible 386. CD-ROM drive. Windows 3.1. 4MB RAM. Minimum system requirements (Macintosh version): Macintosh Plus/Classic. CD-ROM drive. System 6.04. $79.95.

Identifying qualified sales leads for direct mail and telemarketing can often be difficult and expensive. One database of nationwide "white pages" that is both economical and easy to use is PhoneDisc's *Consumer Sales Leads.* The database is structured the same as another PhoneDisc product, *PowerFinder.* The search can be made by name, address, and phone number or limited by any geographic field, from zip code to metropolitan statistical area and area codes. Searching across discs is easy. By simply switching to a new disc and pressing the disc icon, the search is automatically repeated.

Consumer Sales Leads exports into formats suitable for spreadsheets, organizers, word processors, and mailing label programs and contains printing options for a wide variety of labels. It also includes some census information, including median household income and mean housing value. Unfortunately, these data are not searchable or complete in all records.

Because searching is limited to geographic fields and does not include any kind of demographic data, *Consumer Sales Leads* is a misleading name. However, for the price, it is a good start, and for libraries it is an excellent alternative to published telephone books.—**Deborah Sharp**

494.   **Directory of Business Information Resources 2002.** 10th ed. Millerton, N.Y., Grey House Publishing, 2002. 2500p. index. $275.00; $250.00pa. ISBN 1-930956-76-2; 1-930956-75-4pa.

Now in its 10th edition, this directory has proven its value as a resource to accurately identify important information sources in 98 industries and professions. Among the industries covered are accounting, advertising, banking, biotechnology, computers and data processing, food and beverage, libraries, marketing, motion pictures, printing, publishing, real estate, travel, and wholesaling. Sources covered include associations, newsletters, magazines and journals, special issues of magazines, trade shows, directories and databases, and Websites. Arranged by industry, entries include mailing address, telephone and fax numbers, Website and e-mail addresses, key contacts, and a brief description. Additional information provided includes number of members, dues, and founding year for associations; physical description, price, and frequency for publications; and date, location, and number of attendees for trade shows. The total number of listings is now almost 22,000. The introductory material has a user's guide that explains the entries and a cross-reference table correlating Standard Industrial Classification (SIC) codes with the industries covered. Indexes include an alphabetic entry index keyed to the sequentially numbered listings, a publisher index, and a magazine special issues index. Grey House Publishing also sells subscriptions to an Internet version of the directory for $495 per year. The major competing product is Gale's *Business Organizations, Agencies, and Publications Directory* (see entry 54).

In the listings for accounting, there are some troubling omissions. For instance, there is no entry under Associations for the American Institute of Certified Public Accountants (AICPA)—it is included under trade shows. There is no mention of the *CPA Journal,* published by the New York State Society of Certified Public Accountants, which is a vital source for current accounting news and analysis. There are also no listings for the Rutgers Accounting Web (RAW; http://accounting.rutgers.edu/), a leading Internet accounting directory, and CPA2Biz (http://www.cpa2biz.com/CS2000/Home/default.htm), a joint portal of the AICPA and their state CPA partners. Furthermore, while there is an entry for the Financial Accounting Foundation there is not an entry for the Financial Accounting Standards Board (FASB) Website (http://www.fasb.org), the accounting profession's standard setter where information is published about matters currently under consideration. These serious omissions raise the question of whether the compilers are knowledgeable about the industries covered.—**Peter McKay**

495.   **The Grey House Directory of Special Issues 2001/02.** Lakeville, Conn., Grey House Publishing, 2001. 624p. index. $200.00; $175.00pa. ISBN 1-930956-41-X; 1-930956-40-1pa.

Market researchers know that special issues of business magazines are a gold mine of information when researching a particular industry. These issues range from directories and buyers' guides to statistical reports and marketing studies. The desired information often exists, but the researcher may have trouble locating it unless they are intimately familiar with the magazines covering the particular industry. A new publication, *The Grey House Directory of Special Issues*, was created to assist the market researcher in finding these special issues. The directory's arrangement is immediately obvious. The staff at Grey House Publishing has organized 1,800 magazines that offer one or more special issues throughout the year into 95 industry chapters. Within each chapter, business magazines appear in alphabetical order and the listings include the title and month of each special issue. Additionally, each listing provides information on mailing addresses, telephone and fax numbers, e-mail and Website addresses, frequency, pricing and ordering information, and key contacts.

As an added feature, each chapter concludes with a list of other industry magazines that do not have special issues. Two indexes—an entry and publisher index and a subject index—round out this well-crafted directory. Users may question the exclusion of some magazines, but such quibbling aside, this directory answers a real need and is a must purchase for all market research firms, large public libraries, and large academic libraries with business collections. Midsize libraries with interested clientele should also give serious consideration to purchasing the work.—**Dene L. Clark**

496.   **Market Share and Business Rankings Worldwide.** [CD-ROM]. Detroit, Gale, 1997. Minimum system requirements: IBM or compatible 386 (486DX recommended). ISO 9660 CD-ROM drive with Microsoft CD-ROM Extensions 2.2 (double-speed or faster recommended). DOS 5.0. 4MB RAM (8MB or more recommended). 5MB hard disk space. VGA monitor and graphics card. Windows-compatible mouse. Windows-compatible printer. $1,495.00. ISBN 0-7876-0282-5.

The *Market Share and Business Rankings Worldwide* CD-ROM product includes the print contents of current and past editions of Gale products, such as the *Market Share Reporter*, *World Market Share Reporter*, *Business Rankings Annual*, and *European Business Rankings*. The information contained within this database includes corporate, industrial, and organizational rankings by a variety of criteria, such as market share, revenue, numbers of stores or outlets, research and development, opinion polls, and almost any other category imaginable. Access to these data is provided by means of several menu options. Individuals can search by company or institution (the latter including some political entities and nonprofit organizations), by type of industry, by brand, and by geographic location. Full-text (including Boolean) searching is also available, as well as Extended Searching, which allows one to limit a search to some commonly searched fields. Finally, Expert Searching, although more complicated, is useful in performing searches for specific criteria in a variety of different fields.

Although the inclusion of these data in a searchable format is useful, the database suffers from a lack of a controlled vocabulary. For example, a search for AFSCME or the Church of Jesus

Christ of Latter-day Saints will result in no hits, as compared with a search for the American Federation of State, County, and Municipal Employees or the Mormon Church. Furthermore, field-specific searching may retrieve seemingly incongruous results. An extended search for Pink Floyd requires that one must enter the name of the band in the "Person" field rather than the "Company," "Institution," or "Brand" fields in order to retrieve data, bringing to mind the eternal question of which band member is named Pink. The information contained within this product is also necessarily uneven, as it depends upon primary data collection and analysis that is not done consistently across all industrial classifications or businesses.

At approximately $1,500, many libraries may choose to buy one or more of the individual print titles that this database compiles. However, the product is recommended for libraries with a high demand for market share and business ranking data, for libraries with patrons requiring the advantages of a searchable database, or for libraries choosing to make use of networked information sources. It is also recommended for libraries with comprehensive business collections as well as pertinent special libraries.—**Mark A. Allan**

497. **Trade Data Elements Directory Volume III.** By the Economic Commission for Europe and the Working Party on Facilitation of International Trade Procedures. New York, United Nations, 1996. 33p. (Trade Facilitation Recommendations). $90.00pa. ISBN 92-1-116650-0. S/N E.96.II.E.13.

A three-volume publication, the *Trade Data Elements Directory* is intended to be used as a reference by those individuals and organizations engaged in the process of "simplifying and rationalizing" trade procedures. International trade is currently valued at an astounding $3.3 trillion; however, its continued growth will, according to the editors, depend not only "on its adherence to free trade principles, but on substantially improving the efficiency of the overall trade process." Information transfers comprise a massive part of that process, and it is the administration of these transfers that *Trade Data Elements Directory* seeks to address.

Volume 1 of the directory, *Standard Data Elements* (see ARBA 96, entry 306), constitutes International Standard ISO 7372. Volume 2 covers the User Code Lists. Volume 3 is a compendium of recommendations issued by the Working Party on Facilitation of International Trade Procedures (WP.4) of the United Nations Economic Commission for Europe (UN/ECE). These recommendations deal with such items as the organization, layout, and coding of trade documents; standardization of the two-letter alphabetic country codes; establishment of committees dedicated to facilitation of trade procedures within participating countries; and agreement upon an international standard for abbreviations for widely used and accepted trade terms. There are 26 such recommendations; for each are included the history of the issue, relevant oversight committees, the recommendation and its rationale, and occasional information about implementation. Although not a necessary purchase for most libraries, those serving clients or corporations with major interests in global commerce will want to have all three volumes on hand.—**G. Kim Dority**

498. **World Directory of Marketing Information Sources.** 2d ed. Chicago, Ill., Euromonitor International; distr., Detroit, Gale, 1998. 561p. index. $595.00. ISBN 0-86338-765-9.

The goal of this hefty 2d edition of the *World Directory of Marketing Information Sources* is to serve as a comprehensive source leading to worldwide key business research organizations and their publications and services. The introduction states that all entries have been revised, with many of the entries expanded in this edition. A new section, listing country and industry directories of companies, has been added as well as available Website and e-mail addresses throughout the volume. Focusing on consumer market information, the volume was compiled by Euromonitor's in-house team of researchers who contacted each organization.

Organized in 9 sections, the book covers official government sources and publications, trade development bodies, trade and business associations, market research publishers and companies, major business libraries, trade and business journals, company directories, and online databases. Each section subdivides into international, pan-regional, and country-by-country entities. Coverage includes 75 countries, from Afghanistan to Zimbabwe. The information varies by section but includes mailing address; telephone and fax numbers; e-mail and Website addresses; availability of the information source; frequency of updating; year established; contents; and specialties, services, and language. The top of each right-hand page indicates the section and country on that page, promoting ease of use for this massive volume.

This is a comprehensive listing of a variety of marketing sources throughout the world. It is nicely organized, although the print is small. Each country is listed in white type on a black band, and each source under that is in larger bold typeface. The information headers are in smaller bold typeface, and each publication is marked with a bullet. It is possible to find one's way once one has understood the organization. Ease of use has obviously been well considered. There are some omissions (i.e., *Fortune* is not listed in the journals); however, given the size and scope of the volume, this is to be expected. The work is an invaluable business reference source from a known quality publisher; it is recommended for all business reference collections.—**Carol Krismann**

HANDBOOKS AND YEARBOOKS

499.   **The American Marketplace: Demographics and Spending Patterns.** 5th ed. Ithaca, N.Y., New Strategist, 2001. 527p. index. $89.95. ISBN 1-885070-33-0.

In this work, the editors address market demographics in nine areas: education, health, housing, income, labor force, living arrangements, population, spending, and wealth. Data in each category are woven into customized tables and narratives that speak to how American society functions. This book is more than the usual repackaging of Census Bureau reports available on the Web and elsewhere. Each subject area begins with major recent changes followed by concise explanations of the supporting statistics for each trend. For example, the education chapter states as one of its key summary points that women earn more degrees than men. The accompanying tables show that 56 percent of bachelor's degrees and 57 percent of master's degrees were awarded to women from 1997 to 1998. In addition, the disciplines in which those degrees were earned are shown. For example, 42 percent of all master's degrees for architecture were presented to women during this period. This crafting goes beyond mere data to telling the story of life in America today—numbers are turned into usable insights. Key features include a comprehensive table of contents; a glossary; a detailed index; and a resource directory with Internet and telephone contacts for major federal agencies, subject specialists, regional Census offices, and state and industry data centers. This volume is useful for understanding how Americans live and spend their money. —**Adrienne Antink Bien**

500.   **American Women: Who They Are & How They Live.** By the Editors of New Strategist Publications. Ithaca, N.Y., New Strategist, 1997. 400p. index. $89.95. ISBN 1-885070-08-X.

New Strategist is a company that publishes statistical books aimed at the business community, particularly those in marketing who want to know as much as possible about potential consumers. Many of their books deal with a particular segment of the population (e.g., teenagers, ethnic groups, Generation Xers). This edition looks at women born in the United States since World War II and how the changes in women's lives and attitudes have altered buying habits.

The nine chapters in *American Women* suggest the broad focus of this study: There is a chapter each on attitudes, education, health, income, the labor force, living arrangements, population, spending, and wealth. The text consists of tables preceded by a few paragraphs that explain the significance of the particular table. Perhaps because this is designed for the business community, short and sweet is the rule—readers are alerted to particularly significant information by a bullet or text in bold typeface. Much of the information, which is admirably up-to-date, comes from government sources, although private and trade publications are also represented. The source of the data is clearly printed under each table. The book is easy to use and, although it lends itself to browsing, also has an index and a short glossary.

No subject is treated in depth, but the compilers have chosen a fascinating mixture of facts to illustrate women's lives today. Books of statistics are always in demand, and this one will be a good acquisition for collections in academic and public libraries.—**Hope Yelich**

501. **Americans 55 & Older: A Changing Market.** 3d ed. Sharon Yntema, ed. Ithaca, N.Y., New Strategist, 2001. 483p. index. (The American Generations Series). $69.95. ISBN 1-885070-34-9.

This excellent reference work helps to identify trends of the 55 and older demographic group. Now in its 3d edition, *Americans 55 & Older* (see ARBA 99, entry 279, for a review of the 1st edition) has kept the same format as previous editions and has added a chapter on housing. The 10 chapters are alphabetically arranged ("Attitudes and Behavior," "Education," "Health," "Housing," "Income," "Labor Force," "Living Arrangements," "Population," "Spending," and "Wealth") and are supplemented with 2 appendixes, a glossary, a bibliography, and an index. Five to seven bullet points highlight the major statistics of each chapter.

Data for this book were derived from the Census Bureau, the Bureau of Labor Statistics, the National Center for Education Statistics, the National Center for Health Statistics, and the Federal Reserve Board, with additional data from the University of Chicago's National Opinion Research Center. Statisticians who created the tables recalculated the data to reveal trends. They have found older Americans to be healthier, more educated, and more affluent than their counterparts in previous decades. The data also shows that due to their characteristics and their size, this group of older Americans is the biggest consumers of many products and services.

Appendix 1, "A Note on 2000 Census Data," explains that even though this edition was published in 2001, it does not include census data from 2000 because data from the 2000 census will not be completely processed until 2003. Instead, the data in this book are benchmarked each decade to the Census Bureau's Current Population Survey that is based on sample data collected monthly in between decennial census dates. Appendix 2, "For More Information," contains Internet addresses of agencies collecting the data analyzed in the book and contact information on subject specialists from the Census Regional Offices, State Data Centers, and Business and Industry Data Centers. This reference book continues to be a valuable tool for business researchers and others interested in demographic data and interpretation. It is highly recommended for both academic and public library collections.—**Deborah Sharp**

502. Chandler, Tomasita M., and Barbara M. Heinzerling. **Children and Adolescents in the Market Place: Twenty-Five Years of Academic Research.** Ann Arbor, Mich., Pierian Press, 1999. 669p. index. $145.00. ISBN 0-87650-383-0.

Children have been studied as potential consumers since the mid-1950s, about the same time as television increasingly became a fixture in living rooms in the United States. Television did then and continues to now greatly influence consumerism and the marketplace. Research-based studies published between 1955 and 1969 were summarized by Robert O. Herrman in *The Consumer Behavior of Children and Teenagers* (American Marketing Association, 1969).

Chandler and Heinzerling's annotated bibliography of easily accessible articles published in academic journals and proceedings covers 1970 to 1995. For inclusion articles were based on empirical research, and all are in English. The research also had to include children ages 3 to 18. The last criterion was that the marketplace had to be directly referenced. Marketing research studies were excluded as not easily accessible. The table of contents is divided into seven major subject matters: "Learning the Consumer Role," "Economic and Financial Behavior," "Expenditures," "Shopping Behavior and Brand Preferences," "Consumer Behavior Determinants," "Public Policy," and "Research." Following this is a detailed table of contents, which enumerates the topics contained in each chapter, an unusual and useful feature. The volume concludes with an author index and a title index.

This scholarly publication's intended audience is for academic researchers and students in fields such as marketing, child development, and consumer education. Practitioners developing programs for parents or children or marketing goods or services to them will also use these data. The easily usable format, over 830 entries, and many access points make this unique reference source a valuable tool to business and social science collections in academic and large public libraries. [R: Choice, April 2000, p. 1442]—**Susan C. Awe**

503.   **Consumer USA 1999.** 4th ed. London, Euromonitor; distr., Farmington Hills, Mich., Gale, 1999. 371p. $800.00pa. ISBN 0-86338-834-5.

The introduction notes the impressive strength, size, and growth of the consumer market in the United States. The purpose of *Consumer USA 1999* is to capture a wide range of data about the U.S. consumer market and to present these data in a logical fashion. In addition to past data, the volume presents trends and projects future levels of production and spending on a wide variety of goods and services. Published by Euromoniter, the data are drawn from a number of credible agencies, including the Census Bureau of Economic Analysis.

Consumer USA 1999 is divided into 3 sections. The 1st section provides a careful overview of the U.S. economy in general, along with specific commentary on consumption patterns and trends in a variety of sectors including catering, tourism and travel, retailing, and personal finance. The text is clear, easy to read, and supplemented with numerous tables of data. The 2d section, on marketing parameters, presents 223 tables covering economic indicators, gross domestic product, employment, education, demographics, and other systemic marketing data. The 3d section is the heart of the book, with 833 tables of data on specific product groups. These tables include sales of a particular product from the last 5 years, but also forecasts for these products up through 2003. For example, for oral hygiene products there are tables for sales of toothpaste and toothbrushes, forecasts for both of these items, manufacturer shares, and brand shares. Additional tables are provided for mouthwashes, mouth fresheners, and dental rinses. This is powerful information, not only for the manufacturer or marketing of these products, but also for the entrepreneurs, scientists and researchers, investors, and students. Detailed, current information for specific products is often difficult to find, particularly for some classes of consumer goods. The opportunity to have such information readily at hand makes this a particularly good reference tool. Tables are attractively presented and easy to interpret. A list of tables is provided at the beginning of the volume that will be a time-saver at the reference desk.

At a cost of $800, *Consumer USA 1999* is an expensive text. However, the detailed data contained would be useful in a variety of types of libraries, particularly those in the corporate arena, as well as public libraries that serve small businesses, entrepreneurs, and investors. It would also be a good addition to an academic library's reference collection. Although the intent of the volume seems to be to help non-U.S. companies find a niche in the U.S., it is also an excellent tool for U.S.-based patrons to find out detailed information about their country's products, services, and buying patterns.—**Sara Anne Hook**

504. **Direction of Trade Statistics Yearbook, 1998.** Washington, D.C., International Monetary Fund; distr., Lanham, Md., Bernan Associates, 1998. 477p. $32.00pa. ISBN 1-55775-748-8. ISSN 0252-3019.

This International Monetary Fund yearbook presents statistics on trade among countries and trading entities of the world on an annual basis for 1991 through 1997. Values of merchandise imports and exports are provided in tabular form for 182 states. Individual county information is broken down to show figures by major trading partners. Also included are aggregate figures for the world, major regions, and two other groupings. A quarterly version is also available. All figures are in U.S. dollars whether or not supplied in national currency by participating states and entities.

The brief introduction is repeated in English, French, and Spanish. It gives details on methodology, terminology, definitions, and other issues. There is a detailed table of contents. A table of country and area codes purports to give page references for the entries in the yearbook and the latest quarterly, but all the entries are listed as "X." The usefulness of the later is far from apparent.

The work is divided into 3 main table sets. The first covers world and regional data. The later divides into tables on industrial countries, developing countries, and those not covered elsewhere (effectively North Korea and Cuba). The developing countries section has aggregate figures and breakdowns for Africa, Asia, Europe, the Middle East, and the Western Hemisphere. Tables provide exports and imports for the world or region to or from the countries listed. The second part provides similar tables for the European Union, oil exporting countries, and non-oil developing countries. The longest section provides tables for the 182 countries or entities listed and is arranged alphabetically. Taiwan has no entry (under China, Republic of China, or Taiwan) nor is it included in the list of "not included elsewhere" entities in the introduction.

This useful source supplies detailed world, regional, national, and thematic trade statistics. It should be acquired by business or economics collections with the relevant client interests and budget.—**Nigel Tappin**

505. **Foreign Trade of the United States 1999: Including State and Metro Area Export Data.** Courtenay M. Slater and James B. Rice, eds. Lanham, Md., Bernan Associates, 1999. 444p. index. $65.00pa. ISBN 0-89059-160-1.

This comprehensive overview of the participation of the United States in the global economy provides detailed data on U.S. trade in services; time series data on U.S. exports and imports, by industry and country; state-by-state data on total good exports by industry and destination; and goods exports by major metropolitan areas. Also included is complete annual balance of payments data from 1960 to 1998, data showing U.S. exports and imports as a percentage of gross domestic product, and detailed listings of exchange rates for individual national currencies. These data were gathered from the U.S. Bureau of the Census, the International Trade Administration, and the Bureau of Economic Analysis of the Department of Commerce.

Edited by Slater, a former chief economist for the Department of Commerce, this work's introductory article analyzes trends in foreign trade, and its appendix gives detailed notes on sources, definitions, and methodology. The "Using this Book" chapter will help users understand the various charts, tables, and graphs, and the "Notes and Definitions" section provides sources, definitions, and specific notes for each section. A detailed index allows readers to access the data from many additional subject areas. This well-designed book will quickly become a standard access point to data on U.S. imports and exports of both goods and services for researchers, students, and economists.—**Susan C. Awe**

506. **Handbook of International Trade and Development Statistics 1996/1997.** New York, United Nations, 1999. 1v. (various paging). $80.00. ISBN 92-1-012042-6. ISSN 0251-9461. S/N E/F.98.IID.16.

The *Handbook of International Trade and Development Statistics 1996/1997* contains statistical data related to the analysis of world trade, investment, and development. The data are intended for use by the United Nations Conference on Trade and Development; government officials; and university researchers, faculty, and students. The data are derived from existing international and national data sources and are presented analytically, including special classifications such as growth rates, rank orderings, and shares. The text is presented in English and French.

Countries covered have been classified within three main regions: Developed Market Economy Countries (e.g., United States, Canada, Japan, Israel, Western European countries); Countries in Eastern Europe (e.g., Poland, the Czech Republic, Russian Federation); and Developing Countries and Territories (e.g., all other countries in Africa, America, Asia, Europe, Oceania). Statistics provided include annual average growth rate of exports, export structure by destination and by major commodity groups, import structure by origin and by commodity groups, balance of payments, value of exports and imports, balance of payments, and gross domestic product by type of expenditure and by kind of economic activity.

This handbook is a thorough, comprehensive source of world trade data. It belongs in the business collections of academic and research libraries.—**Lucy Heckman**

507. **International Trade Statistics Yearbook, 1998. Annuaire Statistique du Commerce International.** 47th ed. By the Department of Economic and Social Affairs Statistics Division. New York, United Nations, 1999. 2v. $135.00/set. ISBN 92-1-061181-0. S/N E/F.00.SVII.3.

This 47th edition of *International Trade Statistics Yearbook* provides information for individual countries, external trade performance, the importance of trading partners, and the significance of individual commodities imported and exported. This 2-volume edition shows annual statistics for 166 countries. Volume 1 is composed of 5 tables for each country. The first table is a history series with information from 1963 through 1998 showing merchandise quantity and value in U.S. dollars that is imported and exported, including gold. The second table indicates imports by broad economic categories and export by industrial origin for 1992 through 1998. The third table indicates trade by principal countries of origin and destination in U.S. dollars from 1994 through 1998. A subunit of this table also lists values as a percent of the world total. The data run from 1989 through 1998. The fourth table lists special imports by commodity according to Standard Industrial Table Classification (SITC) in U.S. dollars. Under each commodity is a quantity and a value. The fifth table is special exports by commodity according to SITC expressed in U.S. dollars for each commodity and running from 1995 through 1998.

Volume 2 is organized by commodity products and is subdivided into countries showing their imports and exports in U.S. dollars from 1994 through 1998. Also shown in this table is value as a percent of the total for various countries for the product in question. There are 951 commodities listed in this section. Special tables include total import and export regions and countries, listing import and export balance and figures in U.S. dollars. Special Table B lists world exports by commodity class and by regions in U.S. dollars. Table C lists U.S. growth of world exports by commodity class and region, subclassified by year. Table D indicates structure of world exports by commodity class by region and again subclassified by year. Table E indicates total imports and exports by country or area running from 1980 to 1998 for each country. Table F indicates total exports and imports by index number of quantity, unit value, and terms of trade by various regions. Table G indicates manufactured goods exported, subdivided by country and running from 1980 through 1998. Table H indicates fuel imports throughout various developed economies running from 1980 to 1998. Table I looks at some indicators of fuel imports by developing countries running from 1980 through 1998. A subportion of this table looks at the ratio of manufactured goods exported and fuel imports. Table J is a listing of export price index numbers of primary commodities and nonferrous metals subdivided by countries and running from 1985 through 1998. These two volumes are the only reliable source of international trade index in such detail. They should by in all libraries and governmental offices that are involved in international trade.—**Herbert W. Ockerman**

508.   **Major Marketing Campaigns Annual 1998.** Thomas Riggs, Elizabeth Oakes, and Patrick Hutchins, eds. Farmington Hills, Mich., Gale, 1999. 525p. illus. index. $125.00. ISBN 0-7876-3043-8. ISSN 1521-6683.

Gale's *Major Marketing Campaigns Annual 1998* (MMC) is the first of what should be a series of useful and interesting reference and research tools. MMC includes a description and analysis of 100 major marketing and advertising campaigns that appeared, at least partially, in 1997. Listed alphabetically by company, not product, the entries include an overview of the campaign, historical context, target market, competition, marketing strategy, and outcome. Short lists of further readings are found at the end of each entry and sidebars are used effectively throughout.

Gale states three criteria for selecting a campaign for inclusion: "its conceptual value or innovation (sometimes represented by the winning of awards); the importance of the company or brand for which it was run; and its effectiveness in selling the advertised product or service." For the most part, companies represented are a "who's who" of corporate America, particularly corporate America with large advertising budgets.

The depth of coverage and analysis is somewhat erratic and some of the background material is quite basic corporate information. The 100 entries take up just over 500 pages; the resulting 5-page average per entry seems inadequate to cover the intended key elements. Perhaps Gale should consider selecting a smaller number of key campaigns for more in-depth coverage, and condensing the remaining entries to a more space-saving format, including tabular or statistical material.

Illustrations depicting key graphic components of campaigns are included, although the quality of the reproduced photographs could be improved. Contact information for each company, including Website, is provided. A general index and a subject index are useful, but if the former were more detailed the book would be more useful as a reference source. As with many annuals, the dating of MMC is a bit confusing. The 1998 annual, with a 1999 copyright, covers marketing campaigns from 1997.

Overall, *Major Marketing Campaigns Annual 1998* is a good start to the series. It should be useful to business and marketing students as a starting place for research and as a basic primer, to marketing and advertising professionals doing basic competitive research and brainstorming, and to curious consumers. [R: Choice, Sept 99, p. 120; RUSQ, Fall 99, p. 97]—**Edward Kurdyla**

509.   **Markets of the U.S. for Business Planners: Historical and Current Profiles....** Thomas F. Conroy, ed. Detroit, Omnigraphics, 1996. 2v. maps. index. $240.00/set. ISBN 0-7808-0019-2.

This 2d edition updates the 1st edition of 1992 by using the most recent income and population data from the Bureau of Economic Analysis (BEA), part of the U.S. Department of Commerce. Serving the needs of business planners, marketing executives, corporate librarians, market researchers, and students, *Markets of the U.S.* presents ample statistical data, analytic commentary, graphs, charts, and maps for 183 local economies.

Examples of statistics included for rural and urban counties are personal income data, economic data on 77 major industries, population data, economic profiles for every year from 1969 to 1991 in constant 1991 dollars, and pre-calculated ratios and indexes for analysis and comparison. These data help users gauge the economic vitality of any location in terms of the personal income, and what major industry groups are responsible for that income. Volume 1 presents BEA areas 1 through 91, and volume 2 covers areas 92 through 183.

Personal income data are presented for 11 major economic sectors: farming, nonfarm resource industries, mineral industries, construction, manufacturing, transportation and utilities, wholesale trade, retail trade, financial services, services, and government. The measures presented here identify the significance of an economic activity to the local economy and its relative importance to the U.S. economy. Most business collections will want to add this outstanding resource, especially at its reasonable price. [R: Choice, Mar 96, p. 1100]—**Susan C. Awe**

510.   **The Millennials: Americans Under Age 25.** Ithaca, N.Y., New Strategist, 2001. 326p. index. (The American Generations Series). $69.95. ISBN 1-885070-40-3.

This new title follows the format used by New Strategist in other recent publications, such as *American Attitudes* (3d ed.; see ARBA 2001, entry 70) and *American Generations* (3d ed.; see ARBA 2001, entry 875). *Millennials* appears to be the designated term for the under-25 age group and this book presents data that shed light on their attitudes and characteristics. Topics covered (in charts, tables, and text) include health, income, education, employment, living arrangements, and spending habits. Some of the sections have provocative titles, such as "Asian Women Are the Best Educated Millennials" and "The Majority of 11th and 12th Graders Have Had Sex." Other findings are fairly predictable: "Household Incomes Differ Sharply by Race" and "Most Young Adults Live at Home." There is a useful glossary of terms used in the text and a selected list of federal agencies and other organizations and their major publications. Even more useful is a 10-page listing of Websites that will provide additional data.

This information will have a wide range of uses, such as for undergraduate research papers and for consumer marketing activities. While most of the data are available in a variety of government reports or on the Fedstats Website (http://www.fedstats.gov), the information is presented in a convenient and user-friendly manner that will encourage browsing as well as ready-reference use. This is a useful companion volume to *Generation X* (see entry 511) and *The Baby Boom* (see entry 513) and is recommended for academic and public libraries.—**Thomas A. Karel**

511.   Mitchell, Susan. **Generation X: Americans Aged 18 to 34.** 3d ed. Ithaca, N.Y., New Strategist, 2001. 384p. index. (The American Generations Series). $69.95. ISBN 1-885070-36-5.

Although the young Generation X and Millennial generation do not garner the attention that the Baby Boomers do, their numbers are rising and their spending, voting, and lifestyle habits are affecting the culture of America. This book takes a close look at Americans age 15 to 34 and breaks down data taken from several reliable (mainly government) sources in respect to their attitudes and behavior, education, health, income, labor force, living arrangements, population, spending, and wealth. New Strategist relies on data from the Bureau of the Census, the Bureau of Labor Statistics, the National Center for Education Statistics, the National Center for Health Statistics, and the Federal Reserve Board for the bulk of their information on this age group. The charts are not duplications of government publications but original compilations from the author for the purpose of analyzing consumer trends. The text accompanying each chart or graph will help users better understand how to use the information. At the bottom of each chart is the name of the source where the information came from, along with a Website in case further information is needed. The volume provides an appendix listing federal government agencies and their Websites, subject specialists and their telephone numbers, and telephone and Website information of state data centers and business and industry data centers. A glossary and an index conclude the volume. Most useful in academic and corporate libraries, this book will also find use in public libraries.
—**Shannon Graff Hysell**

512. **Plunkett's E-Commerce & Internet Business Almanac 2001-2002** By Jack W. Plunkett. Houston, Tex., Plunkett Research, 2001. 518p. index. $249.99pa. (w/CD-ROM). ISBN 1-891775-21-9.

This 2d edition of *Plunkett's E-Commerce & Internet Business Almanac* is similar in format and content to the 1st edition (see ARBA 2001, entry 209). However, due to the volatile nature of e-commerce, there have been significant revisions for this edition. The number of companies profiled has increased from 330 to 386 (referred to as the "E-Commerce and Internet 400") and each receives a full-page entry. Included in the company profile is a description and "growth plan," brief financial data, salaries and benefit plans, and contact information. There are several indexes; the most useful is an index of company rankings within the industry groups. The editor has also provided an introductory overview of online retailing and a discussion of business-to-business trends with some key statistical tables. Another narrative chapter explores the impact on business of recent trends in personal computers and Internet access. Finally, there is a list of Websites, organizations, and publications that are most relevant to the e-commerce arena. A CD-ROM accompanies the book, with data that can be downloaded and customized. This is a recommended purchase for most academic business collections as well as for public libraries that actively support the business community.—**Thomas Karel**

513. Russell, Cheryl. **The Baby Boom: Americans Aged 35 to 54.** 3d ed. Ithaca, N.Y., New Strategist, 2001. 402p. index. (The American Generations Series). $69.95. ISBN 1-885070-35-7.

Russell (demographer, author, and editor in chief of New Strategist) brings readers the 3d edition of this survey of the baby boomers. She has updated the data of the 1999, 2d edition (see ARBA 2001, entry 886) that was drawn from statistical information from the U.S. Census Bureau and the Bureau of Labor Statistics. The attitude and behavior surveys were developed from opinion polls taken by the General Social Survey of the University of Chicago's National Opinion Research Center.

The information is divided into eight alphabetically classified areas. The categories are: "Attitude and Behavior," "Education," "Health," "Income," "Labor Forces," "Living Arrangements," "Population," "Spending," and "Income and Wealth." Two appendixes provide additional U.S. Census information and an extensive list of telephone and Internet contact numbers and addresses.

Baby boomers account for 30 percent of the American population and continue to be the most powerful generation the United States has ever experienced. Their influence extends to the younger and the older generations. Undergraduates doing research in consumer behavior and social issues will find the data about the baby boomers in this updated edition very useful.—**Kay M. Stebbins**

514. **Services—The Export of the 21st Century: A Guidebook of US Service Exporters.** rev. ed. Joe Reif and others, comps. and eds. San Rafael, Calif., the Northern California Export Council and World Trade Press, 1997. 180p. $19.95pa. ISBN 1-885073-41-0.

This how-to manual and sourcebook runs the gamut of service export know-how and opportunities. The guide is aimed at service firms who are interested in expanding internationally and seeks to provide them with the basic strategies and tools to accomplish that objective. Although less than 200 pages, its 8 1/2-by-11-inch size allows for significant amounts of information to be presented. The first six chapters after the overview cover export basics, such as the export decision, marketing and market research, trade barriers, U.S. government regulations, and finance. These chapters include case studies, highlighted additional information emphasizing practical considerations, and occasionally lists of additional information. The case studies consist of one-page examples describing how one company has dealt with the challenges of exporting its particular service. These studies are tied into the chapter they accompany.

The 2d part, comprising all of chapter 8, is devoted to examining and analyzing 20 industries. The industries encompass banking, computer services, entertainment, franchising, insurance, retailing, and telecommunications, among others. Each industry report reviews the domestic and international markets, market barriers, market channels, opportunities in various regions, best bets for export opportunities, sources of assistance, and helpful publications. Internet sites are given where applicable. Further information is provided by the appendixes, which include data on associations, U.S. government contacts, trade statistics, and a bibliography.

On the whole, this is a well-written and -researched reference. One error, however, did surface. The authors cite the *U.S. Industrial Outlook* (see ARBA 94, entry 218) and *Worldcasts* (Information Access Company) as active sources, when both ceased publication in 1994. Despite this mistake, this excellent reference manual on marketing services overseas is appropriate for public and academic libraries.—**Gerald L. Gill**

515.   Tran, Hoai Huong. **The Official Guide to Household Spending: The Number-One Guide to Who Spends How Much on What.** 3d ed. Ithaca, N.Y., New Strategist, 1995. 492p. index. $89.95. ISBN 1-885070-01-2.

Since 1980, the Bureau of the Census has gathered ongoing, nationwide data on U.S. household expenditures, primarily for use by the Bureau of Labor Statistics (BLS) in updating the Consumer Price Index. *The Official Guide to Household Spending* provides access to an otherwise formidable accumulation of data from the Census Bureau surveys. Because there is a lag time of several years in preparing data, the 3d edition reflects data gathered in 1993.

The guide consists almost entirely of tables, the first of which shows broad spending trends, followed by more detailed information on significant products and services within major categories (e.g., apparel, health care, and so forth). The tables provide average spending, indexed average spending, total spending, and shares of total spending—each by age, income, household type, and region. In some cases, projections are made to the year 2000.

The BLS/Census Bureau surveys represent the most comprehensive source of information on U.S. consumer spending, which makes the guide an essential reference tool, especially for students of economics and marketing as well as for managers who require information on household spending for establishing plans and strategies. This is a book for serious readers, as there are no graphics and little text to illustrate points that can be drawn from the tables. Yet the well-designed tables carry a great deal of useful information for interested readers.—**William C. Struning**

516.   **U.S. Market Trends & Forecasts.** 3d ed. Amanda C. Quick, ed. Farmington Hills, Mich., Gale, 2002. 1098p. index. $315.00. ISBN 0-7876-4802-7.

U.S. Market Trends & Forecasts (USMTF) allows the user, whether a businessperson, researcher, or a student, to find the product marketing information for 400 markets. USMTF is described as a "snapshot of the U.S. markets."

The table of contents is divided into 28 industry groups (e.g., "Apparel," "Health Care") , arranged alphabetically for easy searching. The industry groups have specific markets listed (e.g., Apparel—Fur Goods, Men's Footwear, Women's and Misses' Suits and Coats). Each market entry illustrates the data with pie charts and bar graphs, with summarizations of three to four concise points that show the market value (1995-2000), market volume, competitive analysis, and the compound annual grown rate value forecasts (2000-2005). A SIC/NAICS conversion table is provided. The index provides information about companies, associations, government agencies, specific legislation, and terminology cited in the text.

This 3d edition of the USMTF still offers these data in one convenient volume. A researcher may want to check the more inclusive market references, such as *Market Share Reporter* (see entry 225) and the *U.S. Industry & Trade Outlook* (see entry 229). This is recommended for public, academic, and special business collections.—**Kay Stebbins**

517. Wholesale and Retail Trade USA: Industry Analyses, Statistics, and Leading Organizations. Arsen J. Darnay and Gary Alampi, eds. Detroit, Gale, 1995. 993p. maps. index. $195.00. ISBN 0-7876-0865-3. ISSN 1084-8622.

This book provides extensive statistics for 69 wholesale and 64 retail industries, primarily from federal government statistics. Part 1 presents national and state statistics arranged numerically by 4-digit Standard Industrial Classification (SIC) code and covering data from 1982 through 1992, with projections for later years. This section also lists the leading companies in an industry, indexes of change from one year to the next, and specific occupations employed by an industry. Small maps indicate the concentration of an industry in a particular state or region.

Part 2 of the book records tables for 591 cities and metropolitan areas arranged alphabetically. Each table lists industries, which reported the required data, numerically by SIC number. In the back of the book, five indexes provide access to the book by SIC code, subject, name of company, city or metropolitan area, and occupation. An appendix follows the indexes and briefly describes the industry represented by each 4-digit SIC number.

The purpose of this book aims toward providing accurate and current information from authoritative government sources. The book lists 20 used car dealers (SIC 2521) in the Terre Haute, Indiana, area, but the 1995-1996 Terre Haute telephone directory lists 75 used car dealers in the yellow pages, reflecting the increase since 1992. Many of the statistics in this book can be gleaned from such publications as the *1992 Economic Census* on CD-ROM (U.S. Bureau of the Census), but *Wholesale and Retail Trade USA* presents this information in a more convenient, enhanced, and expanded format. Even though the price is high, business, academic, and large public libraries will find this title especially useful for their business clientele. [R: Choice, Dec 96, pp. 596-597]—**O. Gene Norman**

518. World Consumer Income & Expenditure Patterns. Chicago, Euromonitor International; distr., Farmington Hills, Mich., Gale, 1999. 535p. $590.00. ISBN 0-86338-870-1.

The emphasis of this new handbook from Euromonitor is on providing an international database of detailed consumer expenditures. The work covers 52 countries and includes annual data from 1990 to 1998. Broad expenditure categories are broken down into 66 more detailed subcategories.

The handbook is organized into six sections. The section on socioeconomic parameters summarizes basic population, housing, and economic statistics by country. The section on personal income provides purchasing power information. The section on consumer expenditure in the domestic market by commodity breaks down spending into durable goods, nondurable goods, and services. Figures in these first three sections are derived from Eurostat, the United Nations, the International Monetary Fund, World Bank, and International Labour Organization publications. The section on consumer expenditure in the domestic market by function contains the real value-added portion of the handbook. In this section, researchers will find nine years of fairly detailed consumer spending information. Expenditure figures for the first four sections of the handbook are presented in U.S. dollars for easy comparison. The section that presents country snapshots occupies over half of the work's 535 pages and contains 5-page, country-specific summaries with information similar to that found in the first 4 sections. Users of this tool will find it important to note that the monetary figures found are no longer converted to U.S. dollars, but are presented in national currencies. Finally, a useful section on world expenditure rankings lists broad categories of consumer expenditures, from largest to smallest.

One curiosity worth mentioning is that the table of contents lists the six sections discussed above. However, the introduction lists and describes seven sections. The seventh section, on earnings of employees, is nowhere to be found in the volume as a separate section. There are 17 "earnings" tables, however, in the section on world rankings, so some earnings information is included in the volume.

Although it is quite expensive, business researchers will find this new Euromonitor offering very useful for international market information. It is recommended for all international business collections that can afford it. [R: Choice, Nov 2000, p. 516]—**Gordon J. Aamot**

519.   **World Marketing Data and Statistics on CD-ROM.** [CD-ROM]. 4th ed. Chicago, Ill., Euromonitor International; distr., Detroit, Gale, 1998. Minimum system requirements: IBM or compatible 486 DX2 66. Double-speed CD-ROM drive. Windows 3.1 or Windows 95. 8MB RAM (16MB RAM for Windows 95). 10MB hard disk space (20MB for Windows 95). $1,490.00. ISBN 0-86338-751-9.

This compact disc, originally reviewed in ARBA 97, entry 281, contains many business statistics pertaining to countries worldwide. The information included in this product is also available in two annual Euromonitor print publications, *European Marketing Data and Statistics 1998* (see ARBA 97, entry 273) and *International Marketing Data and Statistics 1998* (see ARBA 95, entry 252).

Data for 209 countries are included in the product, with information for some data types extending back to 1977. The information is divided into 23 subject categories, including advertising and media, consumer market sizes, demographic trends, economic indicators, external trade, and retailing and retail distribution. These 23 classifications are further broken down into 1,055 data types. Representative data types from the preceding categories include: "Home Ownership of TV's—Latest Year"; "Per Capita Sales of Baby Care Products 1996"; "Urban Population 1980-1996"; "GDP from Manufacturing—Latest Year"; "Imports (cif) of Basic Manufacturers, SITC Classification 6—Latest Year"; and "Retail Sales through General Food Outlets—Latest Year." As might be expected, not all data types are available for all countries, and the information reported is often dated.

A strength of this electronic product is the capability of the user to manipulate retrieved data sets, creating customized reports comparing information of different data types and countries in a variety of different formats. *World Marketing Data and Statistics on CD-ROM* is recommended for information centers requiring extensive international business data in an electronic medium. —**Mark A. Allan**

520.   **World Marketing Forecasts 1999 on CD-ROM.** 2d ed. [CD-ROM]. Chicago, Euromonitor International; distr., Farmington Hills, Mich., Gale, 1999. Minimum system requirements: IBM or compatible 486. Double-speed CD-ROM drive. Windows 3.1. Windows 95. 8MB RAM (16MB RAM for Windows 95). 10MB hard disk space (20MB hard disk space for Windows 95). $2,190.00. ISBN 0-86338-824-9.

World Marketing Forecasts is a valuable tool. Projected market data have been collected for the years 1997-2010 for 49 countries in 5 geographic regions (Asia, Australia, Latin and North America, the Middle East and Africa, and Western Europe). Coverage is slightest in the Middle East and African regions (only South Africa data are provided), but coverage for the other regions is reasonably good. There are 950 data types to choose from, including forecasting predictors (such as demographic or expenditure data) as well as market forecasts for 695 different consumer goods. Projections are created using product groups (domestic electrical appliances) or the individual products therein (microwaves).

The initial workspace screen is straightforward—users select a range of years, choose a region or country, select the data type, and push the "Find Data" button on the toolbar. Results are delivered in Excel worksheets and every executed search nets four worksheets. The default worksheet is for "selected results," displaying the data in their component parts. The more useful default would be the "all results" worksheet containing the total report, by all data sets requested. Two additional blank worksheets are created to allow users to drag data over to create tables for their own use. The resulting display could use a little redefining. The headings need to be resized in order to fit more data on the screen and the workspace windows need to be resized to view the worksheets, but the data are readily accessible by scrolling. Figures can be selected by projected sales or in volume sales. The chart icon on the toolbar allows users to create a chart to display selected data. What is not obvious is that this function is much more useful once the data are "pivoted," meaning the user will need to move the product group into another workspace on the far left of the "results" screen in order to create sensible charts.

A useful function, offered at the "results" screen, is the market driver's icon on the toolbar. By clicking on this icon, a drop-down list of drivers (gross domestic product, population, or various expenditure projections) can be toggled on or off individually for comparison to the data sets selected.

The functions that are completely unclear are the remaining icons on the toolbar. These functions are only available in the selected "results" worksheet, and while this is confusing, it explains somewhat why the default spreadsheet display is the "selected results" sheet. In a "selected results" worksheet, users can click on these icons to convert the sales figures to U.S. dollars, plot the percentage of growth, convert the data to an index, show data in per capita figures, or adjust figures for projected inflation. All information from here can be selected and charted using the chart icon.

This is clearly a tool developed for professional market researchers, but is invaluable as a one-stop shop for international market projections. It is simple enough to use for undergraduates and thorough enough for faculty. Recommended for libraries serving the intense needs of international marketing professionals and students.—**Gerald L. Gill**

13 Occupational Health & Safety

521. Encyclopaedia of Occupational Health and Safety. [CD-ROM]. 4th ed. Jeanne Mager Stellman, ed. Washington, D.C., International Labour Office, 1998. Minimum system requirements: IBM or compatible 486. CD-ROM drive. Windows 3.1 or Windows 95. 8MB RAM. 4MB hard disk space. SVGA monitor (640x480 resolution and 256 colors). $495.00.

This product contains information indispensable to those individuals interested in workplace hazards. The software encompasses the contributions of more than 2,000 specialists from more than 65 countries and is alternatively available in a print format consisting of 4 volumes. This vast quantity of information lends itself to a CD-ROM format. The electronic product utilizes the Enigma information retrieval system, Version 3.6, which the reviewer found to be an attractive and intuitive interface. Locating information in the work is made simple by allowing the user to search by either a general or an advanced query; use of an online table of contents for either tables, figures, or all material (including article text); or the use of authors, subjects, and chemical indexes. Unfortunately, the use of the electronic indexes may lead to some material with little or no relevance to the indexed entry. For example, in using the subject index to locate material on *hantavirus*, the subentry prevalence of "antibody to" was selected. A "Windows Find" command was executed to purview the located text (dealing with respiratory cancer) for variations of the terms *hantavirus* and *antibodies*. No matches for these words were located in the indexed article. Although some indexing terms did contain desired material upon searching the text via the find command, others did not. This deficiency adds to patron frustration and lessens the functionality of the product. The enclosed software license also limits the use of the software to a nonnetworked environment. Ultimately, this product is for those libraries willing to overlook the product's indexing shortcomings and that will make it available at a stand-alone workstation. [R: LJ, 1 Nov 98, p. 132]—**Mark A. Allan**

522. Stuart, Ralph B., III, and Chris Moore. **Safety & Health on the Internet.** 2d ed. Rockville, Md., Government Institutes, 1998. 351p. index. (Government Institutes Internet Series). $49.00pa. ISBN 0-86587-613-4.

This work extensively expands the 1st edition (see ARBA 98, entry 239) by providing brief descriptions of Websites and discussion groups concerning all aspects of occupational health and safety. More than a directory, however, the guide also includes chapters devoted to examining the Internet as a research tool and the different formats of information available through the Internet. Both of these chapters are sufficiently detailed to provide a basic understanding of how information is arranged and disseminated on the Internet and the ways in which the World Wide Web can serve as a resource for safety and health information. The introductory chapter is overly simplistic for even the casual user, but it gives practical information on topics such as Netiquette for new users.

The chapter devoted to searching the Internet is useful and includes a number of sample pages from the top 50 safety Websites. Other chapters also give general overviews about networking and marketing occupational health and safety information on the Internet. The list of safety and health Websites (including FTP and Gopher sites) are arranged under general categories, such as professional organizations, and by subject, such as construction safety. Entries include the site name, its URL, and a brief description of purpose. Descriptions of a site's content are rarely mentioned. The directory of discussion groups is also arranged alphabetically by subject and includes the group name, a brief discussion of its purpose, and subscription and contact e-mail addresses. The information resources listed were active as of October 1998.

An appendix of administrative notes from the SAFETY mailing list and hs-canada listserv (the purpose for inclusion is not specifically articulated) and a basic glossary of Internet terms are included with a subject index. Although this work appears to be intended for new users, its thorough coverage of the subject matter and accompanying attempt to place the Internet as a research instrument into proper context makes it a highly recommended research guide for occupational health and safety professionals and those in related disciplines.—**Robert V. Labaree**

14 Office Practices

523. **The New Office Professional's Handbook.** 4th ed. New York, Houghton Mifflin, 2001. 484p. index. $22.00. ISBN 0-618-03608-3.

As the climate of professional offices continues to change with the onset of new technologies, resources like *The New Office Professional's Handbook* will continue to be in demand—not only for professional secretaries and administrative assistants but also for busy library reference desks. This work provides many new helpful tips to succeeding in an ever-changing, ever-competitive office environment. This 4th edition updates much of the material from the 3d edition (formerly titled *The Professional Secretary's Handbook* [see ARBA 96, entry 312]) as well as provides new information on e-mail etiquette and teleconferencing, among other things.

The book gives comprehensive coverage of many topics of concern to both new and experienced office professionals. Topics are covered in 14 chapters, which include such topics as professional career development, human relations, telecommunications, document creation, arranging travel plans, and information management (e.g., filing, records management). It also focuses on the importance of communication in a professional, grammatically correct style, with chapters on business English and composition. Three of the most practical chapters that will be most helpful to those already in the business world are the chapters on how to conduct meetings and conferences, accounting basics, and the basics of business law. Interspersed throughout the volume are samples of documents, business letters and memos, and résumés.

This is a practical guide for those already in the business world and those just out of college looking for an office support position. Much of the information here is not taught in school but essential for professional success. Public and business libraries will want to keep a copy on hand as it will answer a number of business-related questions.—**Shannon Graff Hysell**

524. **The New York Public Library Business Desk Reference.** New York, John Wiley, 1998. 494p. index. $34.95. ISBN 0-471-14442-8.

Increasing complexity of the business world requires those who work in offices to have access to a rapidly growing, constantly changing body of information. Unfortunately, needed information must frequently be sought in numerous, diverse sources, many of which may well be unknown to an employee or a manager. Thus, many of those who seek information turn to libraries for help. The New York Public Library gathered often requested, essential business information in a single volume, *The New York Public Library Business Desk Reference*. The contents cover a wide range of topics, such as office design and equipment, business communications, office systems, managing people, finance, legalities, public relations, marketing, travel, and the basics of research. Wherever possible, topics are treated with respect to the interests of both employers and managers. Each chapter contains suggestions for locating further details via relevant organizations, books, and other publications as well as on-line references. Despite its broad scope, the text provides quick and ready access to many common office procedures. Moreover, it can serve as a point of departure for more detailed investigations. Clear presentation and skilled editing bring a sense of unity to diverse business activities. Cross-referencing, a table of contents, a glossary, and an index facilitate searches for specific information. [R: BL, 1 June 98, p. 1814] —**William C. Struning**

525.   **The SOHO Desk Reference.** Peter H. Engel, ed. New York, HarperCollins, 1997. 540p. $35.00. ISBN 0-06-270144-4.

The target market for this book is the business entrepreneur. Arranged in a dictionary-style, this 540-page book is actually more encyclopedic in scope and depth of topic coverage. The work ambitiously purports to be "your one-stop guide to running your small business."

This reference includes a table of contents, a section on editorial contributors, and a brief introduction stating scope and purpose. The remainder of the book is dedicated to approximately 500 alphabetically arranged entries that are more substantial than the 7,500 entries in, for example, Jerry M. Rosenberg's *Dictionary of Business and Management* (see ARBA 95, entry 187). A typical entry ends with a useful section, "Next Action Steps," that may include standard print as well as online references and addresses of potentially helpful organizations.

Engel, the author of 10 books and an associate professor in the entrepreneurial program at the University of Southern California, edited this first-of-its-kind work. He was ably assisted by an editorial board, an advisory board, seven editorial contributors, and a variety of research support associates. The expertise of these professionals is weighted toward the practical rather than the strictly theoretical, which helps to slant the book toward what entrepreneurs in the "real world" will really need to know.

The SOHO Desk Reference is seriously flawed in its lack of an index to steer readers to the correct entry. An example of how information tends to get buried in the entries without an index is the topic "organizational charts." The information, which could have been easily located with an index, may not be discovered where it appears in "Administration and Organization (A & O)." Other topics that are not evident from the table of contents and that one would expect to find in such a work include time management, records management, succession plans, business structure, systems or systems analysis, Internet, and desktop publishing and computers. If these topics are covered, an index or a more detailed table of contents would make them accessible.

Although this book, despite its flaws, can be recommended for serious business collections in public, academic, and special libraries as well as for the private collections of practicing and prospective entrepreneurs, it should not be the sole source for entrepreneurial information. A recommended supplement is William A. Cohen's *The Entrepreneur and Small Business Problem Solver: An Encyclopedia Reference and Guide* (2d ed.; see ARBA 91, entry 152), which covers the topics in a more detailed, textbook fashion and includes a back-of-the-book index.—**Linda D. Tietjen**

15 Real Estate

526. Chao, Sheau-yueh J. **Internet Resources and Services for International Real Estate Information.** Phoenix, Ariz., Oryx Press, 2001. 384p. index. (Global Guides to Internet Business Resources Series). $49.95pa. ISBN 1-57356-373-0.

Acquiring up-to-date and pertinent information is becoming increasingly important to the decision-making process in real estate. For decades, real estate business had been conducted in traditional ways—real estate agents worked with their property buyers to locate a home, investment property, or business location using their multiple listing books, referrals from other agents, or open houses—to package information needed for their clients. The need for substantial information in the real estate industry has grown exponentially now that business institutions and financial corporations are major role players, government regulations on property tax are constantly changing and increasingly complicated, and, more important, globalization of the real estate industry through the information superhighway has provided international access. Millions of investors all over the world use the Internet to locate essential financial information and to make important investment decisions. Finding relevant information in a timely manner can sometimes be quite a challenge, even for the most Internet savvy investors. *Internet Resources and Services for International Real Estate Information* analyzes and brings together the vast number of Internet sources on international finance and investment into one complete, comprehensive directory.

The guide lists and annotates Websites for 216 countries for a total of 3,085 entries. Each entry contains the name of the Web page, its URL address, and an annotation describing the site's contents. The entries represent a broad spectrum of the field of international finance and investment in three basic areas: finance, investment and related resources, and services. Contents in the book include a preface, an introduction, a list of global finance and investment resources, and an index. Africa, the Caribbean Islands, Central and South America, North America, Asia, Australia, New Zealand and the Pacific Islands, and Europe are covered. This book provides an added resource to the investment brokers and potential real estate buyers in today's global market.
—Barbara B. Goldstein

527. Shim, Jae K., Joel G. Siegel, and Stephen W. Hartman. **Dictionary of Real Estate.** New York, John Wiley, 1996. 307p. illus. (Business Dictionary Series). $19.95pa. ISBN 0-471-01335-8.

Providing succinct and precise definitions of a full spectrum of terms relating to real estate, this volume is accessible to the layperson who may be involved with a first real estate transaction and needs to define a term quickly. At the same time, the dictionary provides enough information about a term or concept to serve as an accurate introduction for the student or professional in the field. The coverage is admirably broad, including such areas as appraisal, escrow, law, agency and ethics, and even architecture and construction. Another strength is the inclusion of examples, applications, diagrams, and the like. With 3,000 terms defined in 300 pages, entries are short. Those people involved in real estate practice will obviously need to go beyond a basic definition, but for both a general and a professional audience, this volume provides an excellent place to start to understand an unfamiliar term.—**JoAnn V. Rogers**

16 Taxation

528. Collins, James T., and Robert M. Kozub. **State and Local Taxation Answer Book.** Gaithersville, Md., Aspen, 1997. 1v. (various paging). index. (The Panel Answer Book Series). $118.00. ISBN 1-56706-374-8.

This book is an attempt to provide tax practitioners with information on a wide range of state and local tax issues in a question-and-answer format. Questions are grouped in 20 chapters under broad headings, such as real property taxes, personal property taxes, corporate franchise and income taxes, and sales and use taxes. A brief table of contents and a complete list of questions begin the volume. The back of the book features a highly detailed subject index, separate indexes by court decision and Internal Revenue Code section, a glossary of tax terms, and a directory of state tax departments. The publisher indicates that the book will be updated periodically.

This is definitely a source for the professional and not the layperson. With this caveat, the book fulfills its purpose well. For tax professionals, the question-and-answer format and variety of finding aids make this an ideal quick reference or starting point for in-depth research. Answers are concise, with examples frequently provided, as well as ample references to primary sources of law. Although the book may not enable a business manager without a tax background to deal with a complex question single-handedly, it could certainly assist the manager in understanding the issues and in discussing them intelligently with a professional. The work is recommended for libraries serving tax practitioners and business managers.—**Christopher J. Hoeppner**

529. **The Encyclopedia of Taxation and Tax Policy.** [CD-ROM]. Joseph J. Cordes, Robert D. Ebel, and Jane G. Gravelle, eds. Washington, D.C., Urban Institute, 2000. $45.00. ISBN 0-87766-699-2.

The authors of this encyclopedia believe that " . . . a system of taxation is more than a compendium of dry tax law and arcane economic data. It is an expression of community relationships among individuals and between the people and their governments" (p. x). "The goal of the Encyclopedia is to provide a reference book—a complete guide—to public sector tax and tax-related issues, in a manner that makes the complex understandable" (p. x). The authors were drawn from members of the National Tax Association—nonpartisan organization of tax practitioners and administrators, policy makers, business executives, and academics whose chief concern is advancing the understanding of the theory and practice of public finance. The Urban Institute, a public policy think tank, is the publisher. The Urban Institute is concerned with public finance and good public policy.

The encyclopedia is comprised of a broad range of essays on every aspect of taxation and public policy, including both fundamental and specialized tax concepts and behavior, each type of tax levied in the United States, and forms of taxation used in foreign countries. Specific features of current taxes (e.g., charitable deductions), tax administration, tools for tax analysis, political institutions that set and interpret tax law and policy, interest groups, and related issues in public finance are also covered. There are more than 500 pages of references for further reading and study.

The quality of the work is outstanding, filling a void in the tax reference literature with clear and concisely written essays. Since taxes are at the heart of public policy, taxation is the source of endless debate over who should pay how much and for what government services. This encyclopedia serves as a valuable guide to the debate and a resource for analyzing and understanding the issues.

The format is unusual—a CD-ROM composed of Adobe Acrobat PDF files. It requires a computer to read or search the reference work. For those untutored in computers, using the book is not effortless. There is no "Back" button and the "Home" icon does not display on the Adobe Acrobat menu bar. Unlike an ordinary book, it requires time and considerable effort to find material. There is a nine-page printable "QuickHelp" guide containing shortcuts useful in searching and navigating. The format of the work suggests that it is designed for the end-user to load and use on their personal workstations.—**Peter Zachary McKay**

530. **International Tax Summaries, 1998: A Guide for Planning and Decisions.** By Coopers & Lybrand Global Tax Network. New York, John Wiley, 1998. 1v. (various paging). $135.00 (with disc). ISBN 0-471-18234-6.

Coopers & Lybrand Global Tax Network, a leading international accounting and consulting firm, has published *International Tax Summaries* annually since 1982. This edition presents an overview of the tax systems of 125 countries. Each country's entry is divided into as many as 37 topical areas, including details of income taxes on corporations and individuals, sales and value-added taxes, inheritance and gift taxes, payroll, and other types of taxes. There are several sections of particular interest to nonresidents who are contemplating living or doing business in another country, such as incentives and grants to business, exchange controls, investment restrictions, and personal income taxes on nonresidents. The book includes a CD-ROM that allows keyword searching of the complete text using the Folio Views search engine.

This volume has been a standard reference for practitioners in the international tax arena since it first appeared. However, the writing style is concise and nontechnical, making the book useful to business managers and others who are not tax specialists. Although the book, of course, should not be relied upon as a substitute for professional consultation, it will greatly assist the reader in identifying and understanding key issues and in discussing these with a practitioner. This title is highly recommended for international business collections.—**Christopher J. Hoeppner**

531. Jurinski, James John. **Tax Reform: A Reference Handbook.** Santa Barbara, Calif., ABC-CLIO, 2000. 321p. index. (Contemporary World Issues). $45.00. ISBN 1-57607-157-X.

Tax reform is the latest topic for the Contemporary World Issues series. *Tax Reform* begins with a historical overview of taxes and taxation. There is a chronology of events in this history and biographical sketches of notable people who have had an impact on the thinking of taxes and taxation. A glossary of terms and a collection of quotes about tax reform are followed by an alphabetic directory of organizations and associations affiliated with taxes and taxation. The street and Web addresses for these associations are included in each of the entries. An excellent bibliography of information sources (both print and nonprint) is published in the last section of the book. This book is recommended for business collections in academic, special, and public libraries.—**Kay M. Stebbins**

Author/Title Index

Reference is to entry number.

Subject Index

Reference is to entry number.

CATALOGS

CD-ROMS

Directory of corporate affiliations 1998, 59
Encyclopedia of global industries, 245
Hoover's billion dollar dir, 64
Hoover's co capsules on CD-ROM [CD-ROM], 93
Hoover's co profiles on CD-ROM [CD-ROM], 94
Hoover's global 250, 278
International dir of co hists, v.16, 258
International dir of co hists, v.17, 259
International dir of co hists, v.18, 260
International dir of co hists, v.19, 261
International dir of co hists, v.20, 262
International dir of co hists, v.21, 263
National dir of corporate public affairs 2001, 19th
    ed, 68
Notable corporate chronologies, 2d ed, 25
World databases in co info, 78

CORPORATIONS -ARAB COUNTRIES
Major cos of the Arab world 1998, 368

CORPORATIONS -CANADA
Canadian co hists, v.1, 330
Scott's dirs 1999, 6th ed, 333

CORPORATIONS -EAST ASIA
Major cos of the Far East & Australasia 1998, 316

CORPORATIONS -EUROPE
Directory of Japanese-affiliated cos in the EU,
    1996-97, 312
European private label dir, 339
Europe's medium-sized cos dir, 2d ed, 340
Europe's top quoted cos, 341
Major cos of Central & E Europe & the Common-
    wealth of Independent States 1998, 345
Major cos of Europe 1998, 346
Major employers of Europe 1999/2000, 429
Top 5,000 European cos 2002, 347

CORPORATIONS -LATIN AMERICA
Argentina co hndbk, 361
Hoover's masterlist of major Latin American cos
    1996-97, 358
Major cos of Latin America & the Caribbean 1998,
    360

COSMETICS
World cosmetics & toiletries dir 1999, 210

COST & STANDARD OF LIVING
Value of a dollar 1860-1999, 2d ed, 102
World cost of living survey, 89

CREDIT CARDS
Directory of MasterCard & Visa credit card
    sources, 3d ed, 160

DERIVATIVE SECURITIES
Directory of listed derivative contracts 1996/97,
    130

DEVELOPING COUNTRIES
Global dvlpmt, 287

DICTIONARIES
Dictionary of business, English-Spanish, Span-
    ish-English, repr ed, 46
Elsevier's dict of financial & economic terms, 29
Elsevier's dict of financial terms, rev ed, 180
English-Russian economics glossary, 35
English-Ukrainian dict of business, 40
Export financing & insurance vocabulary, 248
NTC's dict of Japan's business code words, 307
NTC's dict of Korea's business & cultural code
    words, 306
Routledge German dict of business, commerce, &
    finance, 43
Routledge Spanish dict of business, commerce, &
    finance, 44
Understanding American business jargon, 37
Wiley's English-Spanish, Spanish-English business
    dict, 47

DOW JONES INDUSTRIAL AVERAGE
Dow Jones averages, 1885-1995, 138

ECONOMIC DEVELOPMENT
Directory of intl economic org, 74
Global dvlpmt, 287
Global econ growth, 1950-97, 241
World economic & social survey 2001, 296

ECONOMIC INDICATORS
Guide to economic indicators, 3d ed, 90
State of the global economy 2001, 288
World consumer income & expenditure patterns,
    518
World employment report 2001, 408

ECONOMICS
Bibliographic gd to business & economics 1998, 2
Business & economic research dir, 53
Dictionary of economics, 27
Dictionary of economics, 45
Dictionary of free-market economics, 36
Economics, 85
Elgar companion to classical economics, 86
Elsevier's dict of financial & economic terms, 29
Elsevier's economics dict in English, French, Span-
    ish, Italian, Portuguese, & German, 30
Encyclopedia of Keynesian economics, 33
Encyclopedia of law & economics, 87
Encyclopedia of pol economy, 34

KEYNESIAN ECONOMICS

KNOWLEDGE MANAGEMENT

KOREAN LANGUAGE – DICTIONARIES -ENGLISH

LABOR

LABOR COSTS

LABOR DISPUTES

Elsevier's dict of financial & economic terms, 29

Routledge Spanish dict of business, commerce, & finance, 44

Wiley's English-Spanish, Spanish-English business dict, 47

SPORTS INDUSTRY -CAREERS
Career opportunities in the sports industry, 2d ed, 453

STATISTICS
Agriculture, mining, & construction USA, 215

Business stats of the US 1999, 5th ed, 84

Direction of trade stats yrbk, 1998, 504

Handbook of US labor stats 1999, 3d ed, 395

Historical stats 1960-94, 1996 ed, 277

International financial stats yrbk 1999, 280

International trade stats yrbk, 1998, 47th ed, 507

International yrbk of industrial stats 2001, 283

National accounts stats, 284

Statistics on occupational wages & hours of work & on food prices 1997, 405

Yearbook of tourism stats, 50th ed, 232

STEEL INDUSTRY & TRADE
Directory of the steel industry & the environment, 205

STOCK EXCHANGES
Handbook of N American stock exchanges, 139

Handbook of world stock indices, 140

Ranking of world stock markets, 146

Standard & Poor's smallcap 600 gd, 1996 ed, 131

World stock exchange fact bk, 155

STOCKBROKERS
Online stockbrokers dir, 132

STOCKS. *See also* INVESTMENTS
Dow Jones averages, 1885-1995, 138

100 best stocks to own in America, 133

100 best stocks you can buy 2002, 6th ed, 129

Standard & Poor's stock & bond gd, 1998 ed, 150

Topline ency of histl charts, Mar 1997 ed, 121

Walker's manual of penny stocks, 134

Walker's manual of unlisted stocks, 135

TAXATION
Encyclopedia of taxation & tax policy [CD-ROM], 529

International tax summaries, 1998, 530

State & local taxation answer bk, 528

Tax reform, 531

TECHNOLOGY -CAREERS
Exploring tech careers, 442

Professional & technical careers, 462

TELECOMMUNICATIONS
Plunkett's telecommunications industry almanac, 227

TELECOMMUTING
Telecommuters, the workforce of the 21st century, 371

TELEPHONE DIRECTORIES
Business: name & business type index [CD-ROM], 52

Business phone bk USA 2000, 22d ed, 63

Business sales leads, 1997 ed [CD-ROM], 492

Consumer sales leads, 1997 ed [CD-ROM], 493

National consumer phone bk USA 1998, 67

TELEVISION -CAREERS
Career opportunities in TV, cable, video, & multi-media, 4th ed, 436

THEATER -CAREERS
Career opportunities in theater & the performing arts, 2d ed, 454

THESAURI
Barron's business thesaurus, 26

TOTAL QUALITY MANAGEMENT
International standards desk ref, 303

Quality mgmt sourcebook, 475

Quality, TQC, TQM: a meta lit study, 480

TOURISM
Encyclopedia of tourism, 195

Yearbook of tourism stats, 50th ed, 232

TRADE. *See also* INTERNATIONAL TRADE
Foreign trade of the US 1999, 505

International business & trade dir, 2d ed, 9

US industry & trade outlook '98, 229

US market trends & forecasts, 516

Washington almanac of intl trade & business, 1998, 291

Wholesale & retail trade USA, 517

World dir of trade & business jls, 81

TRADE & PROFESSIONAL ASSOCIATIONS
Directory of trade & investment related orgs of developing countries & areas in Asia & the Pacific, 7th ed, 313

Trade shows worldwide 2002, 18th ed, 270

World dir of trade & business assns, 80

World gd to trade assns, 4th ed, 82